ANCIENT
EGYPTIAN KINGSHIP

PROBLEME DER ÄGYPTOLOGIE

HERAUSGEGEBEN VON

WOLFGANG HELCK

NEUNTER BAND

DAVID O'CONNOR and DAVID P. SILVERMAN (EDS.)

ANCIENT
EGYPTIAN KINGSHIP

ANCIENT EGYPTIAN KINGSHIP

EDITED BY

DAVID O'CONNOR

AND

DAVID P. SILVERMAN

E.J. BRILL
LEIDEN · NEW YORK · KÖLN
1995

The paper in this book meets the guidelines for permanence and durability of the Committee on Production Guidelines for Book Longevity of the Council on Library Resources.

Library of Congress Cataloging-in-Publication Data

Ancient Egyptian kingship / edited by David O'Connor and David P. Silverman.
    p.   cm. — (Probleme de Aegyptologie, 0169-9601 ; v. 9)
    Includes bibliographical references and index.
    ISBN 9004100415 (alk. paper)
    1. Pharaohs.   2. Egypt—Civilization—To 332 B.C.   I. O'Connor, David. II. Silverman, David P. III. Series: Probleme der Ägyptologie ; 9. Bd.
DT61.A624   1994
932—dc20   94-25442
                                               CIP

Die Deutsche Bibliothek - CIP-Einheitsaufnahme

Ancient Egyptian kingship / ed. by David O'Connor and David P. Silverman. - Leiden ; New York ; Köln : Brill, 1994
  (Probleme der Ägyptologie ; Bd. 9)
  ISbN 90-04-10041-5
NE: O'Connor, David; GT

ISSN 0169-9601
ISBN 90 04 10041 5

PRINTED IN THE NETHERLANDS

CONTENTS

PREFACE

This collaborative effort of several Egyptologists from the United States, Canada, Egypt, and England began, not as a publication project, but as an international symposium, sponsored by the Denver Museum of Natural History. That institution had invited several scholars to speak at the museum during the time that it was hosting the exhibition, *Ramesses II: The Great Pharaoh and His Times.* Barbara Stone, the Curator of Collections in Denver, organized the conference with a focus on kingship in ancient Egypt, since this topic was particularly relevant to the accompanying exhibition. In addition it represented an area of interest to the public and was a subject that was clearly in need of new investigation.

The symposium took place in Denver from October 30-November 1, 1987, and at its conclusion, all of those who attended the sessions agreed that the lecturers, whose areas of expertise included amongst others archaeology, language, ancient history, religion, anthropology, and art, had provided significant coverage of the fundamental aspects of kingship, within the confines of the conference. Ms. Stone, therefore, strongly urged the participants to consider the possibility of using their original oral contributions as the basis for a new publication on the subject of kingship. Each of the scholars, John Baines of Oxford University, Zahi Hawass of the Egyptian Antiquities Organization, William J. Murnane of Memphis State University, Donald B. Redford of the University of Toronto, and David O'Connor and David P. Silverman, both of the University Museum and the University of Pennsylvania, agreed to reexamine the area for which he was responsible and to write a chapter for this new study. John Baines offered to contribute an additional chapter on the origin of kingship, and David O'Connor and David Silverman accepted the position of editors of the proposed volume.

The outcome of this collaboration is a publication that has a multi-level approach to the subject of kingship, a result which may have been influenced by the wide variety of interests and disciplines of the authors involved in the project. Some of the chapters represent general surveys of broad topics interspersed with some new and innovative ideas and concepts; other chapters approach particular aspects of kingship through interpretive analyses that result in new insights and conclusions; and a few chapters concentrate on specific time periods of Egyptian history, revealing fascinating new details. The authors have examined the origin of kingship, how royal architecture relates to it, how the king and his office are referred to in the texts and art, and what the nature of the Ramesside rulers was. They have documented the changes in kingship that occurred in the volatile Eighteenth Dynasty, examined it in terms of the culture and the legitimation of rule, studied the extent of the divinity of the king, and have dealt with the pharaohs who built the pyramids in the Fourth Dynasty. The resulting study—*Ancient Egypt Kingship*—is a broad analysis of the subject that takes into consideration the nature not only of the office of kingship, but also of the individual in it and the society that created it.

The editors would like to take this opportunity to acknowledge the participation of the many individuals who contributed in some way to the publication of this volume. Barbara Stone was the organizing force behind the project and was responsible for its inception. Without her interest and support, this publication would never have come into being. Stephen Phillips, Ellen Morris, Kellee Barnard, and Melissa Robinson, all Research Assistants in the Egyptian Section of the University Museum of the University of Pennsylvania provided valuable technical assistance in the preparation of the varying stages of the manuscripts. Jennifer Houser prepared several illustrations and was in charge of the word processing of all of the manuscripts. In addition, Ms. Houser worked tirelessly on the copy editing of the final version of the text, and the editors are extremely grateful to her for the exemplary quality of her work and her dedication to the project.

The editors would also like to express their thanks to each of the contributing authors for his participation and also for his patience in seeing the project through to completion. We are fortunate to have had the benefit of critical commentary of Professor Dr. Wolfgang Schenkel on a prepublication draft, and we appreciate his efforts. Dr. F.Th. Dijkema of E.J. Brill has been extremely helpful in all of the publishing details. In the initial manuscript, we have used a special word processing font, DyPalatino, with special characters designed by Dr. Peter der Manuelian, Museum of Fine Arts, and we appreciate his generosity in granting us permission to make use of the font. The final text has been set in Baskerville.

LIST OF FIGURES

LIST OF ABBREVIATIONS

Äg Ab	Ägyptologisches Abhandlungen
AcOr	Acta Orientalia
ADAIK	Abhandlungen des Deutschen Archäologischen Intituts Kairo, Glückstadt, Hamburg, New York
ÄF	Ägyptologisches Forschungen
AHAW	Abhandlungen der Heidelberger Akademie der Wissenschaften
AHR	American Historical Review, Richmond
AJA	American Journal of Archaeology, Baltimore
AnOr	Analecta Orientalia
ARWAW	Abhandlungen der Reinisch-Westfalischen Akademie der Wissenschaften
ASAE	Annales du service des antiquités de l'Égypte, Kairo
AV	Archäologische Veroffentlichungen, Deutsches Arhäologische Institut, Abt. Kairo, Bde 1-3 Berlin, Bd 4 ff. Mainz
ÄAT	Ägypten und Altes Testament
BdE	Bibliothèque d'Étude
BES	Bulletin of Egyptological Studies
Bi Ae	Bibliotheca Aegyptiaca, Brussels
BIE	Bulletin de l'Institut d'Égypte
BIFAO	Bulletin de l'Institute française d'archéologie orientale, Kairo
BiOr	Bibliotheca Orientalis, Leiden
BMFA	Bulletin of the Museum of Fine Arts, Boston
BSEG	Bulletin de la Societé d'egyptologie de geneve
BSFE	Bulletin de la Sociéte française d'égyptologie, Paris
CAH	Cambridge Ancient History, Cambridge
CG	Catalogue Général des Antiquités Égyptiennes du Musée du Caire, Kairo
CdE	Chronique d'Égypte
CNI	Carsten Niebuhr Institute of Near Eastern Studies
CRAIBL	Comptes Rendus à l'Académie des Inscriptions et Belles-Lettres, Paris
CRIPEL	Cahier de recherches de l'Institut de papyrologie et égyptologie de Lille

CT	Adriaan de Buck, The Egyptian Coffin Texts, 7 vols, Chicago 1935-61
EEF	Egypt Exploration Fund, London
EES	Egypt Exploration Society, London
FIFAO	Fouilles de l'Institut française d'archéologie orientale, Kairo
GM	Göttinger Miszellen
GOF	Göttinger Orientforschungen, Wiesbaden
HÄB	Hildesheimer ägyptologische Beitrage
IFAO	Institute française d'archéologie orientale, Kairo
JAOS	Journal of the Americal Oriental Society
JARCE	Journal of the American Research Center in Egypt
JE	Journal d'Entrée
JEA	Journal of Egyptian Archaeology
JEOL	Jaarbericht van het Vooraziatisch-Egyptisch Genootschap "Ex Oriente Lux", Leiden
JESHO	Journal of the Economic and Social History of the Orient
JMFA	Journal of the Museum of Fine Arts
JNES	Journal of Near Eastern Studies
JSSEA	Journal of the Society for the Study of Egyptian Antiquities
LÄ	Lexikon der Ägyptologie, Wiesbaden
LÄS	Leipziger Ägyptologische Studien, Glückstadt, Hamburg, New York
LAe	Lingua Aegyptia
LD	Lepsius Denkmaler aus Aeg. und Aeth.
LRL	Late Ramesside Letters
MÄS	Münchner Ägyptologische Studien, Berlin, München
MDAIK	Mitteilungen des Deutschen Archäologischen Instituts, Abteilung Kairo, bis 1944: Mitteilungen des Deutschen Instituts für Ägyptische Altertumskunde in Kairo, Berlin, Wiesbaden, ab 1970: Mainz
MIFAO	Mémoires publiés par les membres de l'Institut français d'archéologie orientale du Caire, Cairo
MIO	Mitteilungen des Instituts für Orientforschung, Berlin
MMJ	Metropolitan Museum Journal, New York
NARCE	Newsletter of the American Research Center in Egypt
NAWG	Nachtrichten der Akademie der Wissenschaften in Göttingen, Phil. Hist. Kl.

NGWG	Nachrichten von der Gesellschaft der Wissenschaften zu Göttingen, Phil. hist. Kl., Fachgruppe I: Altertumwissenschaften ab 1941: NAWG, Göttingen
NISABA	Religious Texts Translation Series, NISABA, Leiden
OBO	Orbis biblicus et orientalis, Fribourg
OIP	Oriental Institute Publications, the University of Chicago
OLA	Orientalia Lovaniensia Analecta
OLP	Orientalia Lovaniensia Periodica
OLZ	Orientalistische Literaturzeitung, Berlin, Leipzig
OMRO	Oudheidkundige Mededeelingen uit het Rijksmuseum van Oudheden te Leiden, Leiden
PÄ	Probleme der Ägyptologie, Leiden
PM	Bertha Porter and Rosalind L. B. Moss, Topographical Bibliography of Ancient Egyptian Hieroglyphic Texts, Reliefs and Paintings, 7 Bde, Oxford 1927-52
RAPH	Recherches d'archéologie, de philologie et d'histoire, Kairo
RdA	Revue d'Assyriologie et d'Archéologie Orientale, Paris
RdÉ	Revue d'Égyptologie, Kairo
RecTrav	Receuil de Travaux Rélatifs à la Philologie et à l'Archéologie Égyptiennes et Assyriennes, Paris
SAK	Studien zur Altägyptischen Kultur, Hamburg
SAOC	Studies in Ancient Oriental Civilization, The Oriental Institute of the University of Chicago, Chicago
SOAW	Sitzungsberichte der Österreichishen Akademie der Wissenschaften; bis 1947: der Kaiserlichen Akademie der Wissenschaften in Wien, Phil.-hist. Kl., Heidelberg.
StudAeg	Studia Aegyptiaca. Rome
Urk.	Urkunden
Wb.	Worterbuch
WZKM	Wiener Zeitschrift fur die Kunde des Morgenlandes
ZÄS	Zeitschrift für Ägyptische Sprache und Altertumskunde
ZDMG	Zeitschrift der Deutschen Mörgenlandischen Gesellschaft, Leipzig, Weisbaden

INTRODUCTION

David O'Connor and David P. Silverman

This introduction consists of three distinct sections. The first two provide general background information about kingship and introduce subjects, topics, and ideas discussed in detail in the other chapters. The third part outlines areas of potential research in the field.

1. Kingship in Egypt: An Overview

Kingship is a leading preoccupation amongst Egyptologists, and it is a topic often covered in scholarly and popular literature about ancient Egypt. Extended reference seems well nigh inevitable, because the institution of kingship was such a central one, it extended over more than three thousand years of recorded history, and its individual holders—as any chronological chart reminds us—number in the hundreds.

Future research may modify our impression of kingship's centrality in Egyptian culture and society. After certain needs were met (such as revenue), it is not clear how pervasive royal governance was throughout society as a whole. Moreover, the redistributive "command economy" that typified royal government may have co-existed with a substantial private economy, the proportions of which are still a matter of lively debate. However, as things stand today, modern perceptions of Egyptian society and world view seems dominated by a concept of kingship which was uniquely Egyptian in flavor, so much so that we often refer to the Egyptian king as "pharaoh" (literally: "the great house" or "the palace," Egyptian $pr\,{}^c\!\!\textit{3}$), a term we never use for rulers elsewhere.

This concept must have had significant meaning for the whole population for otherwise, as Lanny Bell (Bell, forthcoming) has remarked, the institution of pharaonic kingship could not have survived as it did, for over three millennia. Moreover, over this long span, the institution endured many vicissitudes. Individual rulers were perceived by Egyptians as very variable in quality and ability. They might engage in religious revolution (Akhenaten), participate in immoral liaisons (Pepi II), or display extreme political weaknesses (Ramses IX). Hatshepsut crossed gender lines when she took over the throne and became pharaoh, depicting herself in male royal attire and often describing herself in texts with masculine forms of words. A particularly complex example is provided by the XXVth Dynasty ruler, Piye, himself Egypt's conqueror from the Sudan and hence of dubious authenticity from the dogmatic viewpoint. Piye would not permit some of the regional pharaohs of the time, who had submitted themselves to him, to enter his palace because they were uncircumcised and eaters of tabooed fish, hence ritually impure!

More generally, over specific spans of time—and particularly the "Intermediate Periods"—the institution of kingship itself lost much authority, prestige, and wealth. Such episodes were often treated discreetly by later scribes involved in recording the Egyptian version of history. Yet these same events also demonstrate the resilience of Egypt's kingship and its great importance to the Egyptians. For them kingship was, even with such superficially negative aspects, fundamental to both their society and the cosmos as they perceived it.

The First Intermediate Period was characterized by divided kingship, civil wars, and severe social stress. Yet subsequent generations of scribes, within the framework of the politically stable Middle Kingdom, made rich use of these experiences. Within literary works of the period, these writers not only evoked and described (in simple terms) this period of anarchy; they also explored, by reference to it, the nature of kingship itself, and the potential fragility as well as strength of the institution.

Pharaonic kingship was central to Egyptian life in two ways. First, it was fundamental to the Egyptians' own sense of themselves as a viable community, and to the survival of the cosmos of which that community was an integral part. From nothing, the creator god brought forth the cosmos in its wonderful variety; he established within it Egyptian society as the norm for all others and Egyptian kingship as the ideal form of governance. Cosmos was strong, but also vulnerable. In fact, the creator had prophesied its ultimate dissolution. In the here and now, every aspect of cosmos—divine, human, natural—had to undergo repeated rebirths or reincarnations to ensure vitality and validity. Cosmos had to be defended strenuously against the forces of chaos that surrounded it and threatened constantly to overwhelm it.

Egyptian religion was not as self-assured and free from anxiety as was once imagined. The potential for cosmos to become chaos was feared, and many incipient indications of this possibility were recognized, from the cosmological (solar and lunar eclipses) and divine (demise of deities) to the human (illness, injury, and black magic) sphere.

In these concepts, pharaoh was a key figure. As sole ritualist (all priests were merely his delegates) pharaoh maintained the essential cultic links between humankind and the gods—bonds that helped ensure the deities' own survival and inspired their benevolence towards the people of Egypt. Through governance, pharaoh brought order to Egyptian society; he ruled in conformity to Maat, the divine order of cosmos, making certain that the gods' temples and cults were maintained, that society functioned in an orderly way, and that the cults of the dead were performed. Outside of Egypt, pharaoh was understood to overthrow enemies in every direction, and to guarantee—theoretically and, in certain instances, in actuality—that Egypt's dominance was universally recognized and tribute paid.

In so doing, pharaoh was following a divine paradigm: his actions in the terrestrial realm of cosmos parallel the divine processes that were occurring simultaneously in both the celestial realm, or "heaven," and in the Duat, or "netherworld." From the sky, the sun-god ruled the universe, his agents periodically overthrowing powerful chaotic forces (akin to Egypt's earthly enemies slain by pharaoh) which would interrupt and, if possible, end his pre-ordained progress and bring cosmos to an end. In the Duat, the sun-god had to undergo a form of death and regeneration in order to be reborn the next day and to be protected from violent chaotic force while this process went on. The roles of pharaoh and sun-god were, therefore, inextricably intertwined; the sun-god was superior and pharaoh subordinate, but their dual and parallel activity was vital for the survival of the cosmos, and hence of Egyptian society.

The second central significance of pharaonic kingship was rooted in the geopolitical realm. Pharaoh was not merely a symbolic ruler and chief ritualist; he was, according to textual sources, also supreme political leader as well as warlord. In addition, the royal palace dominated much of Egypt's life: the bureaus of the central government were in its vicinity, and the faithful agents of royal power controlled Egypt's many provinces (more than forty). The administrative system, based on written records (found rarely in the early periods), was relatively sophisticated, although its primary aims were fairly narrow: defense against internal and external enemies, revenue in produce and services, building programs designed primarily to enhance elite prestige and authority, and the maintenance of a minimal level of social order to ensure that each of these ends were met. Egyptian government was not very altruistic in regard to the society at large, but it recognized that a fundamental basis of well-being had to be maintained for humankind, "the cattle of god," if social stability and elite interests were to be preserved.

Again, this description represents the ideal. In reality, even in relatively stable and prosperous periods, continuous shifts occurred in regard to the influence and power of factions within the government and the broader elite, as well as to the relationship between king and elite. Most of these processes are masked from us in the kinds of sources that have typically survived, but their presence is occasionally detectable in texts, sometimes dramatically so. The assassination of Ramses III as a result of a conspiracy involving close royal relations and members of the elite was likely not an isolated event. Amenemhat I of the Middle Kingdom, in his *Instructions to his son Senwosret I*, described his own murder, an event that may also be referred to in the *Story of Sinuhe.*

Moreover, as noted earlier, kingship in some periods was visibly weakened and diminished, for reasons both internal and external to the institution. Egypt's well-being was relatively precarious, dependent as it was on an annual inundation of adequate volume and, consequently, good harvests and sufficient food to tide the population over the fallow season of the year. Such natural phenomena as decreased inundations, for instance, were obviously beyond government's control, but they could cause problems that would lead to social stress and political instability. At other times, structural weaknesses within government itself contributed to the vicissitudes experienced by kingship. Sometimes, competition between factions, the power of the central elite vis à vis the pharaoh, or the relative independence of provincial powers became sufficiently out of balance as to diminish sharply the power and effective reach of royal government. So great could the stress become that it would permit even the rise of rival kingdoms within Egypt—theoretically, a totally unacceptable occurrence from the point of view of ideology. In fact, such a situation did happen during each of the "Intermediate Periods."

However, time and again pharaonic kingship recovered and continued; its ideology perhaps changed in nuance or emphasis, or its structure became re-organized, but it remained fundamentally the same institution as before. This resilience, this capacity to rise again, is reminiscent of the way in which Egyptians saw cosmos. Its essential nature always remained the same, pertaining to "Eternal Sameness" (*djet*), but it also experienced repeated changes, stressful but productive, that led to the regeneration of cosmos, following a cyclical process of "Eternal Recurrence" (*neheh*). So, it seemed, did Egyptian kingship until, in the early centuries A.D., the Egyptian world view and hence cosmos changed fundamentally. At that point, pharaonic kingship also ceased to be.

2. Understanding Egyptian Kingship

This generalized account of kingship in Egypt not only serves as an introduction to the essays in this book, but it also draws, like those essays, on generations of detailed research into that institution. It would surely be presumptuous to say the last word on Egyptian kingship has been said. This infinitely rich topic will continue to attract the interest of Egyptologists and other scholars, and later we shall indicate what some of the promising lines of future research (some illustrated well by the essays in this book) seem to be. However, it might reasonably be said that a great debate about Egyptian kingship that lasted for many years has reached closure and provided a fundamental baseline for future research.

The achievement of that closure, as well as some of the problems and issues future researchers must confront, are well illustrated by that standard and invaluable reference work, the *Lexikon der Ägyptologie*, a multi-volume encyclopedia that began publication in 1973. In Band III (1977-1980) of that work, clustered together, are many essays and numerous notes and references focused on kingship. This material is divisible into a few major categories: one that deals with the fundamentals of kingship (for example, the dogma of kingship and the difference between god-king and god); one with art-history, archaeology and

literature, and their relationship to kingship; and one with inci-
dental material (for example, royal letters and king lists). Each
division, however, does not receive the same attention in terms of
space allotted: the first category occupies about 24%, the second
about 60%, and the last about 16% of the total space involved.
Surprisingly then, the entries in the first section, whose material is
more interpretive than that of the others, are far outstripped by
the more descriptive entries of the second and third divisions. In
the second category, the topics receiving the longest treatment
are: royal tombs, the Valley of the Kings, and royal sculpture (this
last, 28% of the whole!). The first section contains relatively short
entries, except for that on the royal titulary.

In its allotment of space, this ratio is faithful to Egyptological
predilections; i.e., the number of fundamental and/or more
interpretive works on kingship is surprisingly small, while many
monographs and articles have been dedicated to the visual and
literary aspects of kingship. The appeal of these areas of
investigation, and the need to describe and analyze them, is very
evident. Much of the material remains of ancient Egypt's three
millennia of civilization consists of royal and elite art, architecture, and literature and the associated iconography and symbolism. To study and learn about kingship through these sources,
one must first begin with extensive description, the noting of both
large scale and subtle changes in symbols, iconography, and
reference over time and the synthesizing of these innumerable details into a comprehensive whole. Indeed, without such pain-
staking work, much of the results achieved later by more analytical
research would not have been possible.

For these reasons, full scale studies of kingship have not been
frequent, and, as a result, the picture of Egyptian kingship
achieved today, although perhaps a reasonably accurate one, took
a long time to establish and represents the accumulated analysis
and descriptions of generations of researchers. What has seemed
a particularly difficult problem has been the complex nature of
the living king: What exactly was it, and how was it to be
described? The two key words in the long debate about this issue
have been the divine and the human, the relationship between
which, so far as the ruler was concerned, was particularly difficult
to determine as a result of the unique nature of kingship in Egyptian thought.

Defining, analyzing, and expanding upon the concept of the

divine in Egyptian thought and culture is a major challenge upon
which scholars are still engaged. They do agree, however, that
while gods are divine, and humans are not, the situation with the
king is debatable. Certainly, humans can, after death and justification before the gods, be said to have achieved something
akin to divine status. Moreover, the Egyptian gods display some
startlingly human characteristics—such as aging, death, and
emotion; they appear "neither transcendent nor eternal, uncondi-
tional, absolute" (Hornung 1982,195). Yet their powers, such as
their ability to transform themselves into other entities and to
wield control over and even become the forces of nature are
evidently immeasurably superior to the attributes of humans.
Neither do humans possess the gods' special nature, their
"divinity," which is given off as radiance and aroma, by themselves,
their images, other cult objects, and sacred animals.

The king is much less easy to define, and the multiple images
presented of the ruler often seem contradictory. How do we
reconcile the picture of deteriorated mummies of aged, infirm
pharaohs with the youthful image art presents of these rulers
right up to their death? How do we move from the individual
inhabiting the private apartments of the palace, with their bed-
rooms, bathrooms, and latrines that satisfy human needs, to the
ageless, god-like figure who—according to reliefs in temples—was
the virtual equal of the gods during the performance of ritual
every day? How are we to interpret the apparent omniscience and
omnipotence of the rulers as reflected in their edifices and
inscriptions with their human weaknesses (Amenemhat I's
ignorance of the plot of assassination against him and Ramses II's
tactical errors on the battlefield at Kadesh)?

The earlier fundamental studies of kingship focused on the
divine aspects of the ruler and hence helped to create an image of
a pharaoh who was truly a god on earth, who led a highly
ritualized life, and to whom heaven and earth were responsive. In
these works, pharaoh's more human aspects are noted, but
paradoxically they are not explored in depth and are regarded as
a superficiality, an overlay upon his essentially divine nature.
Amongst the most important works in this connection were studies by Moret (1902), Baillet (1912), Jacobsohn (1939), and
Frankfort (1978). The last was perhaps the most extreme statement about the divinity of the Egyptian king. Even while noting
the fluctuations over time in pharaoh's prestige and power,

Frankfort noted: "But such observations are meaningless unless we understand the true nature of Egyptian kingship. The conception of Pharaoh as a god incarnate explains the historical phenomena even when they seem to deny it" (Frankfort 1978, 57).

That all of these works, along with many others, contributed powerfully to our understanding of Egyptian kingship is undeniable; they were all works of superb scholarship, and they often drew on comparative literature about "divine kingship" for thought provoking comments on the Egyptian case. Moret, for example, was familiar with Frazer's voluminous writings on kingship, while Frankfort invoked anthropological literature on the Shilluk and other African tribes in his analysis of Egyptian kingship. Primarily, however, the insights of these scholars came from rigorous, sometime inspired, analysis of the Egyptian data themselves, and their conclusions continue to be valued and useful.

In 1956, Georges Posener began to investigate the "other side" of pharaoh—his human aspects—in his superb study on literature. There, he studied the changing image of the king presented in the literature of the First Intermediate Period and the Middle Kingdom. His primary point was that this material, studied in an ideological and historical framework, revealed subtle variations on the themes of *both* the divinity and humanity of kingship, specifically for the purpose of rebuilding the conceptual strength and the actual political power of an institution which had diminished in prestige. Subsequently, Posener expanded this line of thinking in his ground breaking work on the divinity of pharaoh (1960). Specifically reacting to what he felt was the undue emphasis on the king's divinity that had been developed by earlier authors, some cited above, Posener, in a penetrating analysis of a wide variety of texts—religious, historical and literary—emphasized how different the king was from the gods. "Born of the gods," pharaoh was nevertheless very definitely their inferior, who kneels before them in the cult, and lacks their extraordinary powers. Again and again, pharaohs acknowledge that the successes of their reigns are gifts from the gods. To Posener, much of the divinity ascribed to kings in the texts are in reality metaphors that gloss over the king's real dependence upon the gods. In literature, grand pharaohs such as Khufu, builder of the great pyramid, can be presented as almost openly malevolent.

Posener certainly redressed the balance against an entirely divine king with a vengeance, and was, to some degree, justly criticized for it. But the essential validity of his conclusions remain.

Posener's studies, while no doubt sometimes pushing the search for the king's human side a little too far, must be seen as a major factor in shaping the concept of Egyptian kingship prevalent amongst scholars today. At its simplest, this view can be stated as follows: Kingship is a divine institution, in a way itself a god, or at least an image of the divine and capable of becoming its manifestation; each incumbent, each pharaoh, is fundamentally a human being, subject to humankind's limitations. When the king took part in the roles of his office, especially in rituals and ceremonies, his being became suffused with the same divinity manifest in his office and the gods themselves. With this capacity, the king would be empowered to carry out the actual and symbolic acts that contributed to the maintenance and rebirth of cosmos. Indeed, in these contexts, the king acted as a creator deity and *became* the sun-god. On these occasions pharaoh would be recognized by those who saw him as imbued with divinity, characteristically radiant and giving off a fragrant aroma.

How Egyptology has reached this consensus, that essentially reconciles in persuasive ways the varying viewpoints of the scholarly literature cited above, is not easy to describe in a brief introduction. No single seminal work exists yet that presents a comprehensive and deep analysis of this latest, and most convincing, theory of Egyptian kingship. Rather, change has come through a variety of specialized monographs, and focused articles and chapters in studies of Egyptian religion. For example, Hans Goedicke's monograph on the position of the king in the Old Kingdom (1960) suggested that the human, physical, person of the king was seen by the Egyptians as separate from the divine power it contained by virtue of the royal office the king held. Much more recently, Lanny Bell (1985 and 1986) has identified and explored the cult of the royal ka as practiced at Luxor temple in the New Kingdom. He suggests that the divine and the human aspects of the king fuse during the appropriate ceremonial context and then "divide," as the pharaoh returns to his more mundane activities.

Other sources, both specialized studies and comprehensive works, could be cited here which contribute to the development of the picture of Egyptian kingship current today, but since many of them are referred to in the following chapters, further citation is unnecessary. Still, the interested reader may wish to consult the recent, very competent general study on the subject by Marie-Ange Bonhême and Annie Forgeau (1988). A further book worthy of investigation is Lana Troy's penetrating and interpretive study of Egyptian queens (1986) in which the author presents the fullest analysis attempted to date of the symbolic and ritual significance of the royal women for the functioning, both political and cosmological, of Egyptian kingship.

3. Future Research into Egyptian Kingship

Given that a generally satisfactory consensus exists about, at least, the essential characteristics of Egyptian kingship, we might hazard some guesses about productive lines of future research.

Certainly, the exploration of the meaning of kingship itself has not ceased, and probably never will. Clearly, many of the existing ideas sketched out above require further exploration. It appears, however, that aspects of kingship can still be questioned. The separation of king from kingship and the recognition that each king's individual humanity is replaced with divinity only in particular, ritually charged, contexts provide useful means of analyzing the evidence, but it may be that there is yet a further mystery to be explored. Has the king's unique experiences in the cultic and ritual ceremonies left his humanity unmarked? Once his divinity is manifest, is his humanity the same as that of every one else? Does the divinity he now emanates have a special quality on account of his inherent humanity, and is it distinct from that of the gods?

The history of kingship in Egypt is another area that can be investigated further. Its origins, for example, remain in many ways mysterious. Exciting new evidence about Egypt's earliest known kings has been discovered, and this information is assessed in its broader context of previous evidence and speculation in the second of John Baines' two essays in this book. Kingship during the Intermediate Periods, specifically the First and Second, is also largely enigmatic, for royal monuments diminished in size, and inscriptional, iconographic, and archaeological evidence is correspondingly scarce. Many important and potentially illuminating sites were excavated and recorded earlier in the century, but they still remain either unpublished or poorly published. The careful analysis of their archaeological, artifactual, iconographic, and inscriptional material may help fill in the gaps in our knowledge. Henry Fischer, Edward Brovarski, and Wolfgang Schenkel have already provided much iconographic, phraseological, and lexicographical information that may aid other scholars in investigating our gaps. While not royal monuments, the elite tombs at Bersheh, Naga ed-Deir, Thebes, Beni Hasan, Meir, the Delta, and Heracleopolis, to name only a few locations, contain a wealth of information that pertains either directly or indirectly to the monarchy. Given new methodology and understanding, scholars can now reinvestigate, excavate, and record previously worked sites and excavate new ones, but the field work must now be carefully focused. In this regard, the reinvestigation by UCLA of the long-lost tombs of the XVIIth Dynasty pharaohs at Thebes, the excavations of the Middle Kingdom site at Lisht by the Metropolitan Museum, and the excavations of the Archaic period through the early Eighteenth Dynasty at Abydos by the Pennsylvania-Yale Expedition are only a very few of the examples of work now in progress.

Further research and investigation of the subject of kingship would also benefit from analytical and interpretive investigations of royal iconography and symbolism. Cycles of scenes involving the king, for example, are subtle and complex in the messages they convey, and in their interweaving of the ideal and the real and mythic and historical to a degree that we insufficiently appreciate.

Royal architecture and city planning outside the great temples are fertile areas for investigating concepts of kingship. Palaces, royal fortresses, recreational areas, ceremonial viewing grounds, and other structures remain, for the most part, largely undocumented. Ancient records indicate the presence of royal botanical gardens in the Eighteenth Dynasty, and a royal zoo has been discovered at Pi-Rameses/Qantir. Further study and excavation are required to see how these structures affect our understanding of kingship.

Some of these topics, or aspects of them, are addressed by the authors in the following chapters, but many issues remain to be identified and explored. In addition, further research, field work, analysis, and interpretation will undoubtedly result in innovative ideas and concepts, as well as more suggestions for a variety of new studies. Each investigation has the potential to provide another clue, another piece to the puzzle—to clarify yet another aspect of the many faceted subject of kingship in ancient Egypt.

Map 1. Ancient Egypt.

CHRONOLOGY OF ANCIENT EGYPT

PREDYNASTIC PERIOD (c. 5000 BC-3000 BC)
Late Predynastic
    Narmer/Menes?   c. 3000

EARLY DYNASTIC PERIOD (c. 2920 BC-2575 BC)
Dynasty I   c. 2920-2770
    Aha/Menes?
    Djer
    Wadj
    Den
    Anedjib
    Semerkhet
    Qaa
Dynasty II   c. 2770-2649
    Hotepsekhemwy
    Reneb
    Ninetjer
    Peribsen
    Khasekhemwy
Dynasty III
    Zanakht/Nebka?   2649-2630
    Djoser   2630-2611
    Sekhemkhet   2611-2603
    Khaba   2603-2599
    Huny   2599-2575

OLD KINGDOM (2575 BC-2134 BC)
Dynasty IV
    Sneferu   2575-2551
    Khufu   2551-2528
    Redjedef   2528-2520
    Khafre   2520-2494
    Menkaure   2490-2472
    Shepseskaf   2472-2467
Dynasty V
    Userkaf   2465-2458
    Sahure   2458-2446
    Neferirkare   2446-2426
    Shepseskare   2426-2419
    Raneferef   2419-2416
    Niuserre   2416-2392
    Menkauhor   2396-2388

Dynasty V (cont.)

Djedkare	2388-2356
Unis	2356-2323

Dynasty VI

Teti	2323-2291
Pepi I/Merire	2289-2255
Merenre	2255-2246
Pepi II/Neferkare	2246-2152

Dynasty VII/VIII

Numerous ephemeral kings, including Neferkare	2150-2134

FIRST INTERMEDIATE PERIOD (2134 BC-2040 BC)

Dynasty IX/X (Herakleopolitan)

Several kings called Khety; Merikare; Ity	2134-2040

Dynasty XI (Theban)

Intef I	2134-2118
Intef II/Wah'ankh	2118-2069
Intef III/Nakhtnebtepnufer	2069-2061
Nebhepetre Mentuhotep	2061-2040

MIDDLE KINGDOM (2040 BC-1640 BC)

Dynasty XI (all Egypt)

Nebhepetre Mentuhotep	2040-2010
Sankhkare Mentuhotep	2010-1998
Nebtawyre Mentuhotep	1998-1991

Dynasty XII

Amenemhat I	1991-1962
Senwosret I	1971-1926
Amenemhat II	1929-1892
Senwosret II	1897-1878
Senwosret III	1878-1841?
Amenemhat III	1844-1797
Amenemhat IV	1799-1787
Nefrusobek	1787-1783

Dynasty XIII

(About 70 kings. Better known ones are listed; their positions in the complete list are noted)

Wegaf (XIII.1)	1783-1779
Amenemhat V (XIII.5)	
Harnedjheriotef (XIII.9)	
Amenyqemau (XIII.11b)	
Sobekhotep I (XIII.12)	c. 1750
Hor (XIII.14)	
Amenemhat VII (XIII.15)	
Sobekhotep II (XIII.16)	
Khendjer (XIII.17)	
Sobekhotep III (XIII.21)	c. 1745

Dynasty XIII (cont.)

Neferhotep I (XIII.22)	c. 1741-1730
Sobekhotep IV (XIII.24)	c. 1730-1720
Sobekhotep V (XIII.25)	c. 1720-1715
Ay (XIII.27)	c. 1704-1690
Mentuemzaf (XIII.32c)	
Dedumose II (XIII.37)	
Neferhotep III (XIII.41a)	

Dynasty XIV
(A group of minor kings who were probably all contemporary with the XIIIth or XVth Dynasties)

SECOND INTERMEDIATE PERIOD (1640 BC-1550 BC)
Dynasty XV (Hyksos)

Salitis	
Sheshi	
Khian	
Apophis	c. 1585-1542
Khamudi	c. 1542-1532

Dynasty XVI
(Minor Hyksos rulers, contemporary with the XVth Dynasty)
Dynasty XVII
(Numerous Theban kings. Better known ones are listed; their positions in the complete list are noted)

Intef V (XVII.1)	c. 1640-1635
Sobekemzaf I (XVII.3)	
Nebireyeraw (XVII.6)	
Sobekemzaf II (XVII.10)	
Tao/Senakhtenre (XVII.13)	
Tao/Seqenenre (XVII.14)	
Kamose (XVII.15)	c. 1555-1550

NEW KINGDOM (1550 BC-1070 BC)
Dynasty XVIII

Ahmose	1550-1525
Amenhotep I	1525-1504
Thutmose I	1504-1492
Thutmose II	1492-1479
Thutmose III	1479-1425
Hatshepsut	1473-1458
Amenhotep II	1427-1401
Thutmose IV	1401-1391
Amenhotep III	1391-1353
Amenhotep IV/Akhenaten	1353-1335
Smenkhare	1335-1333
Tutankhamun	1333-1323
Ay	1323-1319
Horemheb	1319-1307

Dynasty XIX
Ramses I	1307-1306
Seti I	1306-1290
Ramses II	1290-1224
Merneptah	1224-1214
Seti II	1214-1204
Amenmesse	(usurper)
Siptah	1204-1198
Twosre	1198-1196

Dynasty XX
Sethnakhte	1196-1194
Ramses III	1194-1163
Ramses IV	1156-1151
Ramses VI	1151-1143
Ramses VII	1143-1136
Ramses VIII	1136-1131
Ramses IX	1131-1112
Ramses X	1112-1100
Ramses XI	1100-1070

THIRD INTERMEDIATE PERIOD (1070 BC-712 BC)

Dynasty XXI
Smendes	1070-1044
Amenemnisu	1044-1040
Psusennes I	1040-992
Amenemope	993-984
Osorkon I	984-978
Siamun	978-959
Psusennes II	959-945

Dynasty XXII
Shoshenq I	945-924
Osorkon II	924-909
Takelot I	909-
Shoshenq II	-883
Osorkon III	883-855
Takelot II	860-835
Shoshenq III	835-783
Pami	783-773
Shoshenq V	773-735
Osorkon V	735-712

Dynasty XXIII
(Various contemporary lines of kings recognized in Thebes, Hermopolis, Leontopolis and Tanis; precise arrangement and order are still disputed)
Pedubaste I	828-803
Osorkon IV	777-749
Peftjau'awybast	740-725

Dynsty XXIV (Saite)
Tefnakhte	724-717
Bocchoris	717-712

Dynasty XXV (Nubian and Theban area)
Kashta   770-750
Piye   750-712

LATE PERIOD (712 BC-332 BC)
Dynasty XXV (Nubia and all Egypt)
Shabaka   712-698
Shebitku   698-690
Taharqa   690-664
Tantamani   664-657
Dynasty XXVI
Necho I   672-664
Psammetichus I   664-610
Necho II   610-595
Psammetichus II   595-589
Apries   589-570
Amasis   570-526
Psammetichus III   526-525
Dynasty XXVII (Persian)
Cambyses   525-522
Darius I   521-486
Xerxes I   486-466
Artaxerxes I   465-424
Darius II   424-404
Dynasty XXVIII
Amyrtaios   404-399
Dynasty XXIX
Nepherites I   399-393
Psammuthis   393
Hakoris   393-380
Nepherites II   380
Dynasty XXX
Nectanebo I   380-362
Teos   365-360
Nectanebo II   360-343
Second Persian Period
Artaxerxes III Ochus   343-338
Arses   338-336
Darius III Codoman   335-332
(period interrupted by native ruler Khababash)

MACEDONIAN PERIOD (332 BC-304 BC)
Alexander III the Great   332-323

PTOLOMAIC PERIOD (304 BC-30 BC)
Ptolemy I (Soter)   304-284

ROMAN PERIOD (30 BC-AD 395)
Augustus Caesar   30 BC-AD 14

PART ONE

GENERAL CHARACTERIZATION OF KINGSHIP

CHAPTER ONE

KINGSHIP, DEFINITION OF CULTURE, AND LEGITIMATION

John Baines

Introduction: Context, Previous Studies, Strategies of Legitimation

Ancient Egypt is significant for the general phenomenon of kingship, both as an exceptionally long-lived example of the institution
and because it strongly poses the problem of the king's divinity.
Kingship is almost always associated with religious values: rulers
are very often credited with divine power and status as well as
divine sanction and support. These characteristics were present in
full measure in Egypt. The extremes of cults of living rulers found
in some societies do not seem to have occurred in Egypt, but such
monuments as the Great Pyramid, and in a broader way the
endless undertakings of Ramses II, illustrate the extent to which
the king could dominate Egyptian society and appropriate its
resources.

Although the living context of Egyptian kingship is gone, and
the understanding of much in it is uncertain or based on analogy
with more immediately accessible cases, the institution has other
paradigmatic qualities. It also fully demonstrates the capacity of
royal symbols and of discourse expressed in terms of royalty to
survive political change and the ebb and flow of power. Egypt was
the first large "nation state," with a culture virtually restricted to
that state, and thus was very self-contained. This clarity of definition seems to go with a rather low level of conflict to form a
limiting case of a stable monarchy and society, in which kingship
was an unquestioned presupposition of social order—indeed order was hardly conceivable without it. Even if the word "pharaoh"
is a distraction that should be removed from discussion as ana-
chronistic for much of Egyptian history, the king of Egypt remains
the principal symbol of his country.

Despite this centrality, the institution of kingship and individual

holders of office needed continual legitimation in order to
maintain its status in the face of developments that might devalue
it or rob it of sanctity and efficacy. In Egypt, changes analogous to
secularization took a distinctive form—a drawing-apart of religion
and kingship and a slow desacralization of the latter, rather than a
secularization in the modern sense. This pattern might be
compared with pluralizing developments in other ancient and
more recent societies. The enormous time span available for
examining social phenomena and processes in Egypt has the dis-
advantage of suppressing the actors' perspective on such changes
as this realignment of kingship and religion, but it allows one to
make correlations of developments in society and in kingship that
might be impracticable for shorter periods or between societies.

A vital aspect of the lost living context is ritual, which is central
to modern discussion of divine kingship and was as fundamental
to Egyptian kingship as it is to others (Hornung 1957, 1966; see
also Chapter 3 §3.2 of this volume). Evidence for ritual and ritual
change is insufficient to shed much light on the questions I
address in this chapter, but its presence must be borne in mind as
the living background to my mainly literary material. Ritual is
central both to the king's assumption of whatever divinity he may
have and to the negotiation of his exercise of power. It cloaks the
holder in the mantle of his office and insulates him from the
surrounding everyday world. It defines, enacts and persuades, and
in these living processes it may also soften the rigidity of written
and iconographic presentation; its performance may mobilize
both solidarity and divergences of interests to complement the
monarch's lonely supremacy. It often restricts and constrains the
ruler into accepted and acceptable patterns of behavior and so
acts as a check on power. How far ritual robs him of freedom of
action is open to dispute (here Assmann 1984b, may go too far),
but powerful Egyptian kings did so much that was autocratic and
exploitive that they must have retained considerable independence, in addition to taking advantage of the authority vested in
their office.

The problem of the king's divinity and its definition has been
the principal focus of Egyptological discussions since Alexandre
Moret's *Du caractère religieux de la royauté pharaonique* (1902). This
issue can be approached through characterizations of the king in
titularies, discursive texts and iconography, through his role and
actions, or through negative constraints—limitations on his status

and authority. Answers that have been given to how far the king
was divine have varied from its almost fervent exaltation in Henri
Frankfort's classic *Kingship and the Gods* (1948) to the deliberate
skepticism of Georges Posener's *De la divinité du pharaon* (1960,
with valuable survey of earlier discussions, viii-xv), which was
presented in large part as a corrective to views like those of Frankfort. During the generation since Posener's book, much has been
written on the detail of kingship and there have been fundamental
contributions to aspects of the problem, such as Erik Hornung's
work on the king's historical role (1957), encapsulated in his
Geschichte als Fest (1966), and Eberhard Otto's article on legitimation (1969). The only author to approach a synthesis during
that time, however, was Dietrich Wildung, in his review of stages or
levels of royal divinity (1973, reviewing Habachi 1969) principally
on the basis of iconographic evidence. Other important contributions have come from this rich field (for example, Radwan
1985). Iconography shows great subtlety and complexity in its
presentation of the king, who is the central pivot of the Egyptian
system of representational decoration, but it records official or
public, and hence mostly supportive, definitions of the king's
person and role.

In their *Pharaon. Les secrets du pouvoir* (1988), Marie-Ange Bonhême and Annie Forgeau offer a new synthesis of most aspects of
kingship, which they set in the general context of the land of Egypt
and the succession of its dynasties; their work is oriented principally to the later periods of Egyptian history. Like many Egyptologists today, they tend to restrict the scope of the king's divinity
(e.g., 1988, 319-20), and thus provide a useful corrective to images
of the institution that have been common outside Egyptology.
Their work is valuable in surveying a wide range of questions and
has important ideas about some phenomena hardly brought into
the discussion hitherto, such as the kingly child gods of the Late
Period. Some parts of their argument, however, are not abreast of
recent work; moreover, in keeping with the nature and audience
of their book, they only occasionally cite the precise evidence for
their conclusions, rendering some of the argument difficult to
evaluate.

Kingship is so central to Egyptian culture, so complex and
multi-faceted, that no single approach can exhaust its significance;
its meaning can be illuminated from many directions. The diverse
papers in the present volume demonstrate this point to the full,

and the subject continues to stimulate new studies and provide
new general insights into ancient Egypt.

Egyptian kingship originated in the Fourth millennium BC,
before or concomitantly with the state (Chapter 3), and was the
state's central institution, lasting for more than three thousand
years, into Roman times (Derchain 1962). Although its office-
holders came in the end to be absentee Roman emperors, the
kingship never itself dissolved, but was overtaken by events,
especially the rise of Christianity in the Roman Empire.

State and kingship emerged in a period from which the recov-
erable expression of ideology is restricted to wealth differentials,
some features of architecture, the distribution of sites, and
iconography. Continuous expositions of ideas of kingship were
not written until more than a millennium later. There is, however,
evidence for continuity in ideas between the earliest unified,
monarchical state and later times, and early kings will have needed
legitimation as much as later ones; in Chapter 3 of this book, I
attempt to mobilize this continuity of forms and ideas for the study
of early kingship. Here, I focus on the later discourse of continuous texts, with the intention to relate kings and kingship to
their elite social context—the only context of discourse that can be
recovered—and to long-term social change. These issues form a
foil to that of the king's divinity. The king was a human mortal
with a divine role in an "everlasting" office and institution—as the
texts constantly term it to be. Both poles of this identification were
continually renegotiated and redefined, and its formal reenactment by successive incumbents continued into the Fourth century
AD. I can only select examples from this vast range of material
here, and my presentation of the post-New Kingdom period (after
c. 1070 BC) is no more than a sketch.

Throughout Egyptian history, discourse in terms of kingship
was the essential mode of discussion about the central state and its
power, and for long periods it was vital to the presentation of
relations between humanity and the cosmos. Culture was defined
in terms of kingship; no centrally sanctioned alternative existed.
The known presentation of ideology and cosmos is an elite phenomenon, and little can be said about ideas in the rest of society.
There were, however, surely differences in belief between ruler
and ruled, and some statements of elite members imply a broader
moral context in which the definition of kingship might be sited

and human nonroyal leaders might have a significant role. Kings too utilized some of the same conceptions, but they naturally had little interest in disseminating their privileges. Developments in royal ideology that were in response to elite, and therefore in a limited sense "democratizing," pressure were probably either reactive or preemptive, in the latter case seeking to influence changes before they took root (see e.g., Fecht 1978).

The elite character of the preserved material has another important implication. Most of it is embedded in or constitutes works of art—architectural, representational, or verbal. It thus entered into specialized traditions with their own complex webs of convention and association. The interpretation of these traditions in relation to conceptions of kingship is thus doubly complex. This separate character of the material is evident enough in the case of visual art, but for texts too there is a gulf between the spoken and the slowly evolving written forms, even where the written genre is close to the spoken in its probable function and contexts. Works of art refer to the conventions and discourse of other works more readily than they refer to new outside factors. Where they incorporate new material, they may present it very strongly in terms of older practices or transform it so that it becomes hard to recognize. Kingship must be seen through these artistic and literary webs.

A very common, though seldom overt, theme in the sources is the legitimation of kings and kingship, and hence, by implication, of aspects of the institution that might be questioned. However monolithic and even indispensable a major institution is and however much it displays its self-assurance, it must continually reaffirm its right to exist. Legitimation has several basic strategies, such as ritual and persuasive discourse, to which I have already alluded. Royal display, including works of art and major monuments, forms another crucial strand. Legitimation uses a restricted range of ideological foundations, defined for ancient Egypt by Otto (1969, 385-89) as being royal action or efficacy, inheritance (not discussed in this chapter) or succession, and myth. In a different perspective, it may be explicit within a society, or the observer may consider that a feature legitimizes an institution, whether or not this is the understanding of the actors. In practice, these two cases may be impossible to distinguish, and I use the term "legitimation" indifferently for both. My focus is different from that of Otto, who was concerned chiefly to explore the implications of the three principal strategies just cited. His classification provides a valuable background against which an analysis of royal and nonroyal discourse can be set and related to a possible political setting. The modern concept of legitimation does not correspond to a single ancient term, while features of the material that can be related to it cut across other possible classifications, but these facts should not cast doubt on the reality of the phenomenon or on the validity of Otto's approach.

Because the kingship was so dominant, even dissent from official views of the institution was mostly formulated in royal terms, following a covert strategy that had advantages over a direct attack. So, in asking how kingship was legitimized and questioned, the restriction to royal and near-royal sources, which is imposed by the preservation of evidence, has positive aspects in that it creates a focus on discussion that was influential in its time and often entered into later tradition. This material allows one to study some of the shading that surrounds the stark outlines of kingship, and so provides a textual analogy for the cushioning effect of ritual. Another possible approach is to focus on what nonroyal inscriptions have to say about attitudes to the king or to kingship. Ursula Rössler-Köhler (1991) has explored these texts very fully for the first millennium BC and has demonstrated a progressive weakening of the prestige of kingship; this result is in harmony with my discussion, which is based on different sources (pp. 35-42 ahead).

In later sections, I review central definitions of the king's role before surveying material relating to change and dissent from the entire span of Egyptian history. Because I focus on these aspects, works of visual and architectural art, in which such matters can seldom be clearly identified, play only a minor part, vital though they are to legitimation in general and to the definition and projection of kingship. Changing conceptions of kingship and of its position in society and cosmos must be seen against the fact that the institution, several of whose phases are discussed in other chapters of this book, had existed for many centuries before periods from which even the most fragmentary and indirect indications of public discussion are preserved. The inextricable association of cosmos and kingship might come to seem inevitable to the actors, but in a large, complex society people's ideas could not be totally constrained. Alternative constructions of cosmos and society were probably always available. Even though evidence for them is slight to nonexistent, the possibility that they existed, together with the extremely restricted range of the social contexts from which preserved evidence is derived, should be borne in mind.

Central Definitions of Kingship and Royal Control: Early Developments

The first element in the king's titulary stated that he manifested an aspect of the principal god of early times, Horus, and that he had his chief being in the focal institutional and physical location of the royal palace. The first king of the First Dynasty was Horus Aha "The Fighter"; other Horus names emphasized the god's and the king's aggressive aspects or stated an aspect of the god's position in the pantheon, and hence of the king as a manifestation of him. Further titles identified him with the "Two Ladies," the tutelary goddesses of the two parts of Egypt, and with the "Golden Horus" (meaning obscure). The best known royal titles are *nswt-bity*, which combines two words for king and can be rendered "Dual King" (the title is also closely connected with the "Two Lands" of Egypt), and "Son of Re," which asserts that the king is the son—in mythology the bodily son—of the sun-god, the leading deity of the Old Kingdom (*c.* 2575-2134 BC). The names following these last two titles were written in cartouches, which were probably protective symbols and associated the king with the solar cycle. In the classic form, from the Middle Kingdom (*c.* 2000 BC) on, the *nswt-bity* name was a statement of the king's relation to the sun-god Re—Thutmose IV (1401-1391 BC), for example, was the "Enduring One of the Manifestations of Re" (e.g., Krauss 1978, 122-32)—and the Son of Re name was the ruler's own birth name, often with additional epithets.

The king manifested on earth aspects of the gods, but he was himself a god only insofar as there was no term for a being intermediate between human and god. He was a "perfect god." This common title was placed before a cartouche name and probably limited his divinity while stating that he had matured into a divine role in the kingship (cf. Berlev 1981, 362-65); it is almost unknown for full deities. Very occasionally the king bore the title "major god," that is, god in the full sense, but this seems to have been only in cases when he was in some sense deified (Baines 1983, 22). A being who could be deified was not a god like the other gods (see the comment of Habachi, 1969, vii).

In texts from the Middle Kingdom on, the concentrated
statements of the titulary were expanded in eulogies, often interspersed among the titles themselves or elaborated into intro-
ductions which formed the initial sections of compositions preserved on royal stelae and other monuments that continued with
narratives of the king's exploits. These texts are metrically and
thematically complex, and are probably the written counterparts
of a much older oral practice. The lack of similar early material
should be related to the slow expansion of written genres (cf.
Baines 1988) rather than to changes in practice or belief. Among
material from the Old Kingdom are brief eulogies of kings
preserved in addresses to the living by elite tomb owners (e.g.,
Roccati 1982, 96-98; Kaplony 1968); to include such a passage
would no doubt have enhanced their owners' standing with kings,
and they were probably widespread in spoken contexts. Later
"loyalist" instructions fused advice from father to son or master to
pupil with political ideas (e.g., Posener 1976).

In iconography, the king appeared either by himself or,
increasingly, on more or less equal terms in company with deities.
When he was shown with human beings, he was at a much larger
scale than they, and thus could be seen as a different order of
being from them—although the same convention applied to the
representation of tomb owners in relation to their dependents.
Until the mid-second millennium BC, human beings could not be
depicted interacting with the gods; similar restrictions operated
more weakly in later periods. The king, therefore, occupied an
intermediate and intermediary position between the gods and
humanity, but in scale and context, representations of him
connected him more obviously with the gods. This presentation is
an aspect of a system of decorum pervading pictorial representation and texts (Baines 1985a, 277-305; 1986, 44-49), but it
also demonstrates an ideological reality of exclusion: people are of
little account.

In all periods the king depended on the gods; he was not a
"god-king" who might dominate them, even if, because he was one
and they were many, and he was present on earth, he might be
more prominent than any one of them. His position is clearly
stated in a description of his role in the solar cult perhaps dating
to the Middle Kingdom (Assmann 1970), which divides the beings
of the cosmos into four categories: the gods; the king; the spirits of
the dead; and humanity. The king "propitiates" the gods, "gives

mortuary offerings" to the spirits, and "judges" humanity. These three actions convey the problematic of his position. He is marginal to the world of the gods, yet through him they rely on this world and on human efforts to sustain them and the cosmos. They must be propitiated because they are not predictable and they might at any time act capriciously or destructively. Despite his dominance of the iconographic and written record, the king is inferior to the gods: from late predynastic times he was shown receiving the gift of life from them (Kaplony 1963, vol. 3, plate 5, figure 5; Figure 3.6 here). He can be the "son" or "beloved" of any deity, both of these being positions of subordination or dependence. He relates more simply to the dead, who constitute a moral force that interacts with the living: in return for his and other people's offerings, they are benevolently disposed and will not intervene maliciously on earth. In "judging" humanity (that is, Egyptians), he should act justly toward them, but he can also condemn. Non-Egyptians are excluded from this minimal model, as are beings below humanity in the classification.

These exclusions create a dimension of the king's role in which solidarity is restricted and aggression tends to be emphasized. As in many cosmologies, country, ruler, people, and their gods and deceased are identified with the ordered cosmos (see e.g., Schele and Miller 1986). Aggression is directed outside; in its less metaphorical aspects it keeps foreign enemies at bay, or in expansionist periods it incorporates new territory. Dissent within society and in relation to the king is not a subject that is shown in public, and presentation of his role in this world focuses on foreign relations or on his constructive works. He acts aggressively and destructively toward the forces of disorder, which he casts outside the ordered realm, while his constructive actions utilize the service of humanity, but are oriented toward the gods, in whose service and dependence he stands. Gods, king, humanity, and in a sense the dead, together struggle to maintain the cosmos against a disorder that threatens all of them; the gods are mortal, but the ultimate forces of disorder stand outside space and time and might be termed immortal (Hornung 1982a, 172-85). The king's role in this fragile, threatened cosmos has a high seriousness, and is summarized in the text just cited, which states that he is there "for ever and ever, setting order ($m3^ct$) in place of disorder ($izft$)." Because of his cosmic responsibilities, his actions are not limited by conventional morality (as is true of legitimations for warlike activity in many or most societies). Although the king is shown as beneficent to humanity, his power and position outside humanity render him ambivalent. Like a god, he can be capricious and dangerous. His touch, look and anger are feared. Here, the multiple interpretations and explanations of polytheistic belief systems are visible. Misfortune may be attributed to the disordered world beyond the cosmos, to sources of disorder among the gods, to insufficiently honored reciprocities between king and gods or king and humanity, and to many other agencies.

It is possible to interpret much of the king's standing in society and cosmos in terms of the concept of the fundamental Egyptian concept of *maat* "order," which is used in the text just cited. The idea of *maat* encompasses both the harmonious cooperation which was projected as a social ideal and the constant struggle to maintain the cosmos against the forces which threatened it. This conceptual breadth contributes to the integration of notions of rule and of the proper order of society by extending the king's freedom of action and avoiding limits on its arbitrary exercise. Counter-currents to such liberty can be also found, and the embedding of the kingship in ritual and custom will have worked against it, but the king's dangerous character and potential for arbitrary action are both a legitimation of his position and an acknowledgment and incorporation of the uncertainty inherent in the unstable cosmos. Thus, I see the positive aspects of *maat* and its emphasis on social solidarity as complemented in practice by more complex notions that relativize the idealism inherent in it. In a sense, this complementarity is summarized in the scene in which the king offers *maat* to a deity, which forms a kind of culmination of offering scenes in temples. In considering how to evaluate the idealistic aspects of *maat*, it must be borne in mind that they are, in the written materials available to us, a literary construct of and for the elite whose implementation in reality remains largely unknown. (See further Assmann 1984c, 1990; Bibliographical Note and Comment at the end of this chapter.)

The king's religious role rendered his exclusive position still more crucial. A result of the convention of decorum—and perhaps of real action to the extent that human access to temples was restricted—according to which people could not interact with the gods, was that he was depicted as the only performer of the cult. The gods emerged before kingship, but this convention made the access of others to them dependent on the king. At the beginning of Egyptian history the king appears to have arrogated the gods to himself and removed them from people (this historical reading is widespread; architectural corollary: Baines 1991a; for different interpretations, see Morenz 1973b, 16-19; Hornung 1982a, 100-07). In reality, priests performed the cult, so that this presentation might be no more than a convention, but access to temples was restricted to priests, and public participation in rituals for the principal gods was largely confined to festivals. In no period was the function of temples principally to cater to the piety or concerns of the individual. The majority of royal actions recorded for the first few dynasties were directed toward the gods: construction of temples, manufacture of cult images, performance of rituals (Schäfer 1902; Redford 1986aa, 86-90)—activities that left little trace in the archaeological record. Parallel to them ran a few military campaigns abroad and a biennial progress through the country that was presented as a "following of Horus"—a service to the god as manifested in the king; the same term described both the paraphernalia of standards and emblems accompanying the progress and the personnel surrounding the king (Kaiser 1959). No doubt he acted for humanity during these progresses, for example by arbitrating in disputes, but this aspect is not visible in texts and representations. There may have existed a conception, as there certainly did later, that campaigns would be initiated or sanctioned by the gods and the fruits of success presented to them, so that historical and political actions were integrated into the meaning of the cult as actions on behalf of the gods that were performed in the outside world.

Other "records" of campaigns are iconographic motifs, which are the only widespread early representations of the king, showing him defeating his enemies and trampling or clubbing them ritually to death. These are first attested from predynastic times (Williams and Logan 1987). They sometimes appear to preserve accounts of specific events, but in all known cases the details may be conventional. Whether any particular example is the earliest of a genre and records authentic information is almost irrelevant to the meaning of the genre or of the example; because so minute a proportion of the records produced in antiquity is preserved, the chances of our having any "first" objects are very slight. For the presentation of the king's role, the use these scenes make of an ancient legitimizing form and their focus on aggression are significant, and these emphases continue in later sources. In elaborate examples (e.g., Borchardt *et al.* 1913, pls. 1-8; Jéquier 1936-40, vol. 2, pls. 8-11, 36-43; vol. 3, pls. 12-18, 30-37), this feature is part of the symbolism of temple structures, which are sanctified micro-cosms: royal aggression is a ritual action dedicated to the gods and serving to defend the microcosm against encroaching disorder.

Just as disorder and order can interpenetrate, so enemies are suppressed internally as well as externally. The possibility of rebellion is, however, hardly made public. Internal and external suppression are linked on figurines that were symbolically destroyed in a ritual of "execration" and inscribed with a formula listing all possible categories of enemy "who will rebel" against the king (Osing 1976, 153-54; Posener 1987, 42-44). Conspiracy against the king was an archetypal offense against order which those who aspired to survive in the next world had to deny having committed, and it is referred to in the same terms as blasphemy (Faulkner 1969, 156 § 892 [paradoxically a text adopted for kings]; T.G. Allen 1974, 98-99). Such things were not unthinkable, but the allusions do not make clear whether conspiracy against a king or against kingship was denied. Kings had an interest in blurring this distinction, for the kingship had little to fear from rebellions against individual kings, but individual kings might reasonably fear rebellion.

The legitimation of kingship through the gods has another aspect in myths of the rule of the gods on earth (on the dating of such myths, see Baines 1991c). Early allusions to a perfect "anti-quity" are probably connected with the rule of the gods on earth (Luft 1976; Baines 1989a, 134-35). The principal ruling god was the sun-god Re. Conflict among the gods and the disturbances people caused made him begin to destroy all of humanity and then withdraw into his domain of the sky (a conception attested in texts from the Middle Kingdom and later: Lichtheim 1976, 197-99; Hornung 1982b; Borghouts 1978, 51-55). The rule of the gods was imperfect—perfection is in a sense alien to a polytheistic system—but human imperfection led to a further distancing from the ideal. This myth has two contrasting implications: it both accounts for the imperfection of this world (compare Hornung 1982b: "an etiology of imperfection") and sets the king in an unassailable position as the heir to the sun-god—or, in versions preserved in king lists, to dynasties of gods and spirits (*ꜣḫw*—who are also the dead, the third category of being mentioned above; Redford 1986a, 11-13). The king's title as "Son of Re" therefore has a whole range of reference that could be evoked as desired.

This "royalist" and centralist view of the king cannot have been the only one that existed in the Old Kingdom. The king's relations with the gods could be problematic because of his dependence on them, and they, who created the world and partook of it, might sustain and care for it more broadly than through his sole person. This possibility is confirmed by proper names from all periods and all accessible levels of society, which display human relations with, and dependence on, the gods; although conventional, this material should be taken seriously (Baines 1991b, 176-78). In addition, a more expansive conception of divine provision for the cosmos can be found from the mid-third millennium on. In this view, people depend directly upon the gods. They—in particular, no doubt, the elite who have access to temples—may consult the gods and call on them for help. The creator god is responsible not just for the four principal categories of the cosmos, but for all living beings. The chief early source for this view is a Fifth Dynasty solar temple that seems to praise the sun-god by displaying the wealth of natural, and principally animal, forms which he sustains (c. 2400 BC; Edel 1961-64; Edel and Wenig 1974). The same conceptions can be seen in a list incorporated in a Coffin Text of the Middle Kingdom (discussed by Assmann, 1984a, 209-15) and in New Kingdom solar hymns (Hornung 1982a, 197-203; and see ahead).

The morality of nonroyal display texts of the late Old Kingdom, which are earlier than any comparable royal texts, includes provision for the unfortunate that has no explicitly theocentric formulation, except in terms of destiny in the next life, but fits well with the beliefs just sketched (Assmann, 1990, 106, sees this as relating to the king, the "Great God," but I prefer to understand that term as relating to a deity). In the succeeding First Intermediate Period, the local ruler Ankhtify of Moalla, who described his political and military exploits in immodest terms (Vandier 1950, 162-256; selection Lichtheim 1973, 85-87), presented a coherent nonroyal morality that may refer to direct oracular consultation as legitimation for political action (Fecht 1968, 53-56; Baines 1987a, 88-91). Such moralities would logically have drawn on the expansive view of the gods, although late Old Kingdom notables recounted their activities as priests in their biographies. Ankhtify's ideology was formulated without seeming difficulty soon after the collapse of centralized rule at the end of the Old Kingdom. His legitimations cannot have been very difficult to devise, and they retained the fundamental element of assuming that there is a single holder of power—in this case a small-scale, local power. Yet although in later periods kingship was perhaps never again as dominant as it had been in the central Old Kingdom, it was not rejected as the indispensable organizing and legitimizing ideology. Instead, the assumption that kingship was indivisible became less automatic, making the institution more flexible.

It is impossible to gauge the relative importance of the narrow, kingly view and the broader one that looked to "natural morality" and directly to the gods (Baines 1991b, 124-30, 137-46), but the tension between self-presentation through actions relating to the king on the one hand, and through individual exploits and moral stature on the other, is visible in nonroyal biographies of the Old Kingdom (Roccati 1982). The king is said to show concern for all his entourage (Kaplony 1968, 50-51). In the preserved material, which derives from the elite, he does not exhibit a more universal concern for humanity, but he probably claimed that too. If he did, there would, in theory, be moral competition both between the king and the more dispersed gods, and among human society between the king and other members of the elite.

To us there may seem to be no necessary connection between legitimation in terms of natural morality—which is in the broadest sense what the *maat* of wisdom texts offers—and of relations with the gods. The looseness of association of these two strategies probably helped nonroyal people to formulate their own moralities (see ahead); but the whole thrust of religious thought and state organization and tradition kept the two strands intimately linked and tended to obscure this point. Thus, a general social secularization was hardly an option and can be largely ignored in studying the development of the king's role. There was discourse about kingship and its legitimation and discourse about the gods, and the two competed while remaining linked; until the first millennium BC there was no significant royal legitimation in terms that did not relate to religion or lessened its significance.

Before reviewing different discourses about kingship and its slow marginalization, the relation between kingship, violence, and succession should be considered. Rules of succession, which are not well understood, are not in themselves significant here. What is relevant is that violent transition was not the norm, so that a disputed or violent succession, of which there were evidently many, created a need for legitimation.

Texts are seldom explicit about changes of ruler or dynasty. Most of the thirty dynasties of the Graeco-Egyptian historian Manetho (Waddell 1940) correspond to identifiable historical breaks, and there were numerous irregular successions within as well as between dynasties. In the Second Dynasty these tensions were expressed through allusions to the gods and through myth (outline: Edwards 1971, 29-35; see also chapter 3 §3.3). The Horus name of the first king, Hotepsekhemwy, means "The One Who is at Peace in respect of the Two Powers"—Horus and his perpetual antagonist Seth. Later in the dynasty Peribsen, whose name also refers to Horus and Seth, took the title Seth instead of Horus, while his probable contemporary Khasekhem "The One Who Arises in respect of the Power," seems to have defeated Peribsen and changed his name to Horus-and-Seth Khasekhemwy "The One Who Arises in respect of the Two Powers," sometimes expanded with "The Two Lords are at peace in him" (cf. te Velde 1967, 71-73). These devices exhibit conflict explicitly and legitimize it by referring it outside human society: the reconciling king manifests afresh the peace and order in which the gods are both present and content. Other early changes of dynasty or probable disputed successions show no such clear public evidence for struggles over the kingship. The Fourth Dynasty, the period of the great pyramids, included three very short reigns and the violent destruction of the pyramid complex of its third king, Redjedef (e.g., Smith 1971, 173). The only salient feature of the record that may reflect associated conflicts, which surely occurred, is the geographical dispersal of the pyramid complexes. While this crude indicator gives a sense of which kings wished to show that they belonged together, it does not explicate the ideological aspects of conflict, some of which are generally assumed to have been articulated through solar religion.

At the start of the Fifth Dynasty, a more literal legitimation than that of the Second Dynasty seems to have been formulated in terms of the king's Son of Re title. A later literary text presents what must be a tradition going back to the Fifth Dynasty, according to which its first three kings were sons of Re by a human mother (Lichtheim 1973, 219-22). Siegfried Morenz (1975, 83-94) claimed that this tradition mobilized the existing royal "Son of Re" title to adjust the king's position in relation to the dominant deity, and thus diminished the king's status. This view may, however, take the implications of earlier titles rather too literally (see also chapter 3). The king's dependence on the gods went at least as far back as late predynastic times, and any such diminution is quite uncertain. New Kingdom relief cycles presented the same conception as the literary text by showing the king as begotten by the principal god, Amun-Re, who took on the form of the predecessor to have intercourse with a royal wife (Brunner 1964; Assmann 1982). These cycles are often said to be legitimizing propaganda for particular rulers, but the mythical conception underlying the reliefs was probably valid for any king and the preservation of a record for particular ones may be a matter of chance. In the Late Period, the same material was transformed to create local cycles of the birth of gods from goddesses, appropriating its symbolism to the pantheon.

No royal name, text or representation from earlier periods states explicitly, or even implies strongly, that a king deposed his predecessor: legitimacy and continuity could not be separated. In several periods, notably the Thirteenth–Seventeenth dynasties, kings succeeded one another at great speed, but idioms and legitimations of kingship seem not to have been affected by this instability. Very ephemeral rulers evoked the grandest associations (e.g., Baines 1974). Almost the only public acknowledgment of instability was the occasional use of the title "God's Father" for nonroyal fathers of kings and for the nonroyal ancestor of the Eleventh Dynasty (Habachi 1977a).

Another mode of legitimation that could be related to instability and a loss of status for the king appears in a nonroyal context in the inscriptions of Ankhtify. The first political act Ankhtify recounted was his intervention in Edfu, which he stated to have been ruled by the "House (*pr*) of Khuu," evidently a line of local potentates (Lichtheim 1973, 85-86). In contrast with the mainly divine context in which kings presented themselves, this usage looks to a human founder rather than a kingly predecessor and can allow for competing genealogies of founders. Khuu was presumably the ancestor whose successors used him as a point of reference. The same usage of appealing to a "house" or its founder is known from the Theban Eleventh Dynasty (e.g., Habachi 1963, 44-50) and from the *Instruction for Merikare* (see ahead), which purports to depict the Ninth/Tenth Dynasty (contemporary with the Eleventh Dynasty: Lichtheim 1973, 105, 107).

Later "dynastic" usages and periodizations employed essentially similar "historical" legitimations (cf. Baines 1989a).

Middle Kingdom Discussions of the Role of Kings and Their Opponents

In the Twelfth Dynasty (*c.* 1991-1783 BC), literary texts focusing on kingship were composed probably for the first time, and royal inscriptions analogous with private biographies appeared. These texts present complex images of the king's role, allowing for dissent, disputed succession, and questions of motivation, responsibility, and policy (excellent presentation of phraseology: Blumenthal 1970). These issues were not novel, and the way in which they appear in texts probably had more to do with the evolution of writing and literary genres than with changes in ideas. Such developments can, however, have a self-sustaining character and may be difficult to control. The texts have been treated in terms of political propaganda (especially Posener 1956), but that approach neglects their literary complexity. Political persuasion is probably only one facet of them, and not necessarily the most important.

Some works with nonroyal protagonists or fictional authors, such as the *Story of Sinuhe* (Lichtheim 1973, 222-35) and the *Loyalist Instruction* (Posener 1976), exalt kingship strongly, and a cycle of hymns to the king is preserved as a work of literature (Lichtheim 1973, 198-201; Derchain 1987). The texts with the most critical content have imputed royal authors—principally the *Instruction for Merikare* (ascribed to a Ninth/Tenth Dynasty king but probably composed in the Middle Kingdom) and the *Instruction of Amenemhat*. Kings are presented irreverently or negatively in texts that are given the appearance of folk stories (Posener 1960, 89-103); these include a hostile view of Khufu, the owner of the Great Pyramid (Lichtheim 1973, 215-22), and a story about a corrupt late Old Kingdom king who has a love affair with a military officer (Posener 1957; analogous Late Period treatment of a king: Posener 1985). These stories show, unsurprisingly, that people knew of potential or actual failings of rulers, but whether they constitute serious criticism of kingship is uncertain. In some sense most or all Egyptian literature was "serious." However, works composed many centuries after the time of their protagonists probably say nothing authentic about the characters themselves, but rather relate to concerns of the time when they were written, or simply to a folk tradition or construction; in the case of Khufu, the same opinion is known also from Herodotus. Sneferu, the first king of the Fourth Dynasty, was treated favorably in the literature (e.g., Lichtheim 1973, 60), but his good reputation might derive from his not having built the Great Pyramid rather than from what he himself did. (Erhart Graefe suggests, 1990, that his reputation was due to the meaning of his name, which contained the root *nfr* "good.")

There is a comparable distinction among nonroyal and royal public inscriptions, which are nearly as literary as literature narrowly defined. The most varied image is in royal texts of Senwosret I (*c.* 1971-1926 BC) and III (*c.* 1878-1841? BC; Lichtheim 1973, 115-18, 118-20), which present royal aggression against outside forces, divine descent and relation with the gods, and the dedication of the fruits of campaigns to them (Farag 1980; see briefly Redford 1992, 78-81). In addition, the occasions for rebuilding temples, because of destruction by rebels (Helck 1985; Barbotin and Clère 1991), or through inspiration in a dream (Helck 1978), link the themes of dependence on the gods, the defense and maintenance of order, and the dedication of success to the gods (nonroyal parallel Habachi 1985, 36-37; Franke 1991). This diversity of topics and the admission of internal conflict disappear almost completely from later royal inscriptions.

Among the royal instructions, that for Merikare may not have been written to the prescription of a particular king, but its themes must have been acceptable to royalty (Lichtheim 1973, 97-109; see Baines 1989a, 137-38). The text has a complex, not necessarily unitary presentation of the king's role, moving from the pragmatic need to respect powerful factions and avoid executing people who lead them, through discussions of particular aspects of policy and of responsibility and accountability up till the point of judgment after death, to praise of the creator, who made and cares for people, including the weak (cf. Assmann 1984a, 201-04). The office is burdensome and solitary, and has more community with its other holders than with normal kin. The often harsh tone is legitimized by the king's assumption of responsibility and by the praise of the creator, both of which place the king within a global context in which more than human life on earth is at stake and the present order of things is reaffirmed as ultimately good and sustainable. The text seeks to integrate the expansive moral view of the cosmos with a strong statement of the need for kingly authority. In this way, it reclaims moral ground which the expansive view tended to assign to the gods and to humanity in general, perhaps including the elites of the First Intermediate Period, rather than specifically to the king. The presentation of the king's humanity and acceptance of judgment after death, which could have been evaded by recourse to a separate other-worldly destiny for him, may be a necessary concomitant of this integration of values; it may also register a change in belief, in which the king's seemingly quite separate Old Kingdom destiny was abandoned (for some components, see Krauss 1992).

In its discussion, the *Instruction for Merikare* rehearses politically significant issues on an ethical plane. The Twelfth Dynasty kings confronted entrenched elites whose aspirations were expressed in terms of care for their dependents, local lineage, and their own exploits (selection of texts: Lichtheim 1973). The king of the Instruction obeys the same moral precepts as these elites, but has a cosmic role and legitimation that they lack. Otto (1969, 386-87) remarked that the text's argumentation pointed logically toward a secular and rational legitimation of kingship. This view is valid in part, but neglects the cosmic overtones which set the king's position off against those of members of the elite. His further comment, that later developments constituted a step back from this position and that this is one of the enigmas of Egyptian history, is rather occidental and implicitly assumes a universal, unidirectional development toward the secular (e.g., Berger 1973). I argue, rather, that competing discourses and agencies which challenge sacral aspects of kingship need not be secular. Ancient Egypt is one of many instances of such competition.

The *Instruction of Amenemhat* (Lichtheim 1973, 135-39) is narrower in focus than the *Instruction for Merikare*. The deceased Amenemhat I (*c.* 1991-1962 BC), the founder of the Twelfth Dynasty, who succumbed to or possibly survived an assassination attempt (the text is deliberately vague), addresses his successor. Amenemhat seems to have introduced the institution of the coregency, in which a new king was installed in office toward the end of his predecessor's reign. Coregency is not mentioned in the Instruction and was never integrated into official royal ideology, but the argument of the text is probably in part a justification of the new practice, stating in a less central context what could not be said in royal display or in a royal inscription.

For later times, the Middle Kingdom was the "classical" period of literature and history. The manuscripts of these instructions are many centuries later than their date of composition, and they were still being copied in the Late Period (Burkard 1977, 6-8). The archetypal hero of the Egyptian history of the Greek Herodotus (ii.102-11) was "Sesostris," a name derived principally from the Egyptian Senwosret, perhaps a conflation of Senwosrets I and III. The latter king consolidated Egyptian rule in Lower Nubia, where he was deified, and set up copies there of an inscription presenting himself as a model of kingship (Eyre 1990). The exploits of Amenemhat III (c. 1844-1797 BC), who reclaimed land in the lakeside oasis of the Fayyum, were recalled, together with his first cartouche name Nimuaria (ny-mꜢꜥt-rꜥw), in the "Lamares" of Herodotus. These kings had themselves depicted in statuary in a unique style, with careworn faces whose obvious analogy is in the instruction texts (Evers 1929; Aldred 1971; Simpson 1982b; Tefnin 1992; Baines 1994: 80-83). This sculpture was placed in temples, offering its somber vision to the gods, but its character is meaningful chiefly for a human audience; the same style was used for colossal statues placed outside temples (Romano 1979, no. 40). Thus, the king fulfilled his royal role in his martial or constructional exploits, but also made public the responsibility weighing on him. This style did not recur in later times, and its display of the burdens of office has few parallels in royal materials, even though the Middle Kingdom instruction texts continued to be copied.

The New Kingdom Crisis and Erosion of Centralized Kingship
(c. 1550-1070 BC)

After partial foreign domination in the Second Intermediate Period (c. 1650-1550 BC), Egypt was reunited by the Theban Eighteenth Dynasty, which extended the boundaries of the state into Sudan and Western Asia. The maintenance of this "empire" involved a larger, more permanent and more separately organized military establishment than there had been before. Much of the wealth gained from conquest was donated to the gods in gratitude for success—a success which it was asserted the gods had granted in the first place. The resultant temple buildings and estates came very gradually to form the most significant economic force in the country.

The king displayed his dependence on the gods. Before campaigning, he would consult the god—normally Amun-Re—and receive an oracular command to go out and defeat the enemy. The god subsequently eulogized the king's successes (e.g., Lichtheim 1976, 35-38; 46-47). Such beliefs and practices may well have existed earlier, but if so, they did not have the same institutional consequences as in the New Kingdom. In parallel with the new military, a newly professional priesthood appeared. The three institutional spheres of the traditional bureaucracy, the military, and the priesthood were not separate and many careers encompassed more than one of them, but the newer institutions nonetheless came to diminish the power of the bureaucracy, creating a web of overlapping allegiances. The temples were integrated with the state, so that changes in relative wealth may have been almost imperceptible. By the end of the New Kingdom, however, the temples came to be almost separable from the state organization and to rival it in wealth and power.

Eighteenth Dynasty nonroyal biographies approximately parallel royal texts in their range of subject matter, and thus tend also to support the increased prominence of the temples. Early examples continue to narrate military exploits in relation to the king (cf. Baines 1986, 44-50). The texts present episodes conducive to the dedicatee's glory, but not continuous or comprehensive narratives. Military biographies contrast with other mortuary inscriptions, which seldom recount important "historical" events, being concerned more with their protagonists' civic role and moral worth in relation to fellow citizens, or with their religious actions. The other principal subject of royal display, the construction of monuments, was also recorded in nonroyal biographies (e.g., Helck 1961, 269-74, 328-30). Internal political affairs were not a subject for royal or nonroyal texts. This concentration on religion and morality during the period when temples were growing created a new focus of prestige and ideology, whose potential gradually affected the balance between king and temple.

An uncertain factor in this development is "popular" religion. From earlier periods there is hardly any evidence for popular participation in temple cults. In the Eighteenth Dynasty there were both changes in decorum that allowed religious topics to be more prominently displayed on nonroyal monuments than before and changes in religious practice. Notables set up intermediary statues in the outer parts of temples, through which others could address their requests to the gods. Large quantities of votive offerings presented by a wider range of people than the inner elite have been found around and within some temples (Pinch 1993). These practices, which kings both countenanced and positively promoted, nonetheless ran counter to the official iconography of the king as the intermediary between humanity and the gods. The inscriptions on intermediary statues do not display disloyalty, relying rather on king's favor. Royal permission was needed to set them up and was given only to leading people. Perhaps both they and the king wished to direct and influence people in their access to the gods, while also securing everlasting benefits for themselves. Yet as the position and wealth of temples changed in a development that ultimately escaped royal direction, people's expectations for the roles of temples and their gods in the lives of individuals also changed.

An example of complex royal motivation in relation to legitimacy is given by the stelae of Amenhotep II (c. 1427-1401 BC) and Thutmose IV (c. 1401-1391 BC) around the Great Sphinx at Giza (texts e.g., Lichtheim 1976, 39-43; Helck 1961, 140-43). Both inscriptions recount their owner's athletic and leisure activities in their youth and immaturity, before they came to the throne. Amenhotep II related this period explicitly to his being selected as successor (and probable coregent). During their outings, they rode their chariots from Memphis to the Sphinx and pyramids, where they rested their horses or themselves near the ancient monuments. Thutmose had a siesta and a dream that inspired him to clear the Sphinx of sand, a surprising statement when there was a well established secondary cult of the Sphinx flourishing in the area. Amenhotep simply acquired the intention to revive the reputations of the ancient monuments and their kings. These activities bring together ideas associated with the king's personal fitness to rule (cf. Hornung 1957), legitimation by reference to great monuments of antiquity—a widespread interest of the time (Helck 1952) and a scale of creation that could hardly be emulated by present kings—and semi-popular religious cults that had emerged around the monuments and evidently flourished with royal participation. While older views that these stelae specifically legitimized the succession of Thutmose IV in particular were surely mistaken, the implications of the monuments are strongly and diversely legitimizing, illustrating how kings who as yet could display few achievements of their own were able to draw on a wealth of other meanings.

Implications of the development of a focus on temples can be seen on the monuments. Royal mortuary provision, which had been the principal form of display in earlier periods, became less significant: the contrast between the massive pyramid complexes of the Old Kingdom and the smaller New Kingdom royal burials in the Theban Valley of the Kings is striking. Some New Kingdom mortuary temples were grandiose in the extreme, but they were not dedicated exclusively to kings. Instead, they were temples dedicated to the gods in which a particular king had a cult. Kings, who had themselves initiated or encouraged this greater prominence of the gods, could respond to it through detailed features of their own monuments and through making themselves more divine.

The most successful campaigning king of the dynasty, Thutmose III (1479-1425 BC), was the focus of a long-lasting assimilation of the king to Amun-Re. His throne name Menkheperre (meaning uncertain; the form early in the reign was Menkheperkare) became a decorative motif on innumerable scarabs made during the next millennium. The use of these scarabs probably outlived the memory of who Menkheperre had been. The scarab beetle was an ancient symbol of the sun-god Re, while Menkheperre was read cryptographically as Amun (Hornung and Staehelin 1976, 174-77; Jaeger 1982, 94); the object and name together related Thutmose and Amun-Re.

The same possibility was exploited in the throne name of Amenhotep III (1391-1353 BC), Nebmaatre (for the reign, see Kozloff and Bryan 1992; Cline and O'Connor forthcoming). Amenhotep III also went farther than earlier kings in self-deification, setting up a cult of himself as a god whom he was depicted worshipping (e.g., Habachi 1969, 48 figure 32). One of his texts describes him as taking on something like the role of the sun-god in his barque (cf. Yoyotte 1959, 25-26), an identification made closer by a new royal epithet "Radiant solar disc" (O'Connor 1980, 1175). Amenhotep III's massive building projects at Memphis and Thebes remodeled the cities as stages for the celebration of kingship (Hayes 1938, 20-24; O'Connor n.d.). Central to the program at Thebes were the king's vast mortuary temple on the west bank of the Nile and the rebuilding of the Luxor temple, the most enigmatic major religious foundation in the city. There was also a great palace complex at el-Malqata, with nearby temples and temporary structures for celebrating jubilees (O'Connor 1980). The ritual of the Luxor temple may have centered on the cult of the royal ka or "vital force," the most divine aspect of the king's person (Bell 1985a). Major temples were embellished with colossal statues of the king, many of them facing away from the structures and toward the outside world (Wildung 1973a, 551-54). These displayed his intermediary role in relation to the gods more grandly than nonroyal statues could announce the roles of their owners. They were also named with royal epithets which turned them into quasi-divine beings that could receive devotion on their own account.

In these constructions and activities Amenhotep III presented himself as loyal to Amun-Re. There is a tension between the development of his position and of those of the gods, and part of his intention may have been to balance the colossal monuments built for them with his own temple and with his dominating presence in the temples to the cult of the gods. The possibility that a king might construct an enormous funerary monument exclusively for himself, as had been done in the Old Kingdom, no longer existed, but Amenhotep's mortuary temple went as far as it could toward such monumentality (Kozloff and Bryan 1992, 90-93).

The same kind of tension between divine and royal and between different modes of access to the divine can be seen in more narrowly religious developments. The Cairo Hymn to Amun, some of which may date as early as the Middle Kingdom, is a key text for the Eighteenth Dynasty (Assmann 1975, 199-207; 1983a, 170-82; Barucq and Daumas 1980, 191-201). The hymn develops the "expansive" view of the creator god, presenting his creation of the world in all its aspects, his provision and care for it, and his kingly role in it—the last of these being the most relevant here. There are parallels for these attributes in early Eighteenth Dynasty offering formulas, but their full significance emerges in radical hymns, first attested from the reign of Amenhotep III, which remove the mythological trappings of the solar cycle, concentrating on the here and now and on the god's provision for all beings (Lichtheim 1976, 86-89; Assmann 1983a, 209-12). There was thus a convergence between a creator god with aspirations to be both royal and immanent, and a king with divine aspirations.

Amenhotep IV/Akhenaten (1353-1335 BC) launched a revolution formulated in terms of this convergence. His god was a purified adaptation of the all-caring solar creator; the Great Hymn to the Aten (the solar disc) from his reign has descriptions of the god that are similar to those in the other radical hymns. The most visible forms of his new dogma were the presentation of his god's name and changes in artistic style. The long and complex name, devised at the beginning of the reign, defined the nature of the jubilating sun-god. This name was then awkwardly enclosed like a king's name in a pair of cartouches, qualified by "giver of life" (e.g., Fecht 1960b, 91-118). Both god and king celebrated jubilees early in the reign (Redford 1984, 122-30). The idea of a god as "king" was ancient (cf. Hornung 1982a, 231-34), but it had seldom led to presentation with specifically royal symbols and iconography.

At first Akhenaten occasionally followed the logic of his god's explicit kingship and replaced part of the traditional, mythological opening of his own titulary with the title of "Chief priest" of the god; kings had never before used such titles (Gauthier 1912, 349, no. XIX; Sandman 1938, 144, line 5, cf. Wenig 1975, 212 with n. 28). For the most part, however, he attempted to raise his own status as king in relation to the god and to humanity. Akhenaten's early reliefs include figures of a chief priest of the cult of himself as king (Smith and Redford 1976, 95-99), something that is unknown for other kings, and the iconography of his sculpture displays his own divinity (e.g., Aldred 1988, pls. 33-35). He also emphasized his sole knowledge of his god, his principal epithet being "the Unique One of Re." This exclusiveness combined with new, and in part deliberately shocking, rules of decorum, according to which the god was represented only in the form of a solar disc with rays terminating in human hands that offered blessings to figures of the king and his family (see e.g., Hornung 1982a, 248). In the houses of elite adherents of the new cult were shrines with stelae showing the king with his family in domestic scenes under the rays of his god. Access to the god was through his unique royal representative on earth, whose queen, Nefertiti, and family provided a virtual replacement for the traditional pantheon surrounding the principal god (on the interpretation of these stelae, see Krauss 1991). Both the pluralism of traditional religion and the growing plurality of access to the gods were restricted. The king was depicted smiting his enemies, as was Nefertiti (Cooney 1965, 82-85; Aldred 1988, pls. 40-41), and he had a conventional foreign policy, but the deeper associations of championing order against chaos vanished along with solar mythology and the realm of Osiris, the lord of the underworld.

Akhenaten's artistic reforms were the most comprehensive in Egyptian history, extending through aesthetic ideals, subject matter and representational aspects, to reversals of decorum. In texts, Akhenaten made public both his rejection of the traditional gods (Redford 1981) and his alleged political problems, together with those of his predecessor Amenhotep III (Helck 1961, 365-68). His followers said they had been nobodies before being elevated by their king (Assmann 1980a, 9-19). Akhenaten violently destroyed the monuments of those who fell from favor and erased the name of the god Amun everywhere on the monuments, as well as occasionally the word "gods" in the plural. So far as these rejected beings were now inimical or disordered, some of this violence may have had a similar function to the king's traditional performance of his role of countering enemies and reaffirming order (as suggested by John Huddlestun). One of Akhenaten's most prominent epithets stated that he "lived on *maat*" and thus proclaimed his adherence to that central value; but it is not known how this assertion related to older conceptions of order.

Akhenaten's reforms have the character of a revolution—the only one in Egyptian history—but a revolution that was initiated by the central figure of the traditional order. This paradox is displayed in the king's ambivalence toward the wider society: his message was one of sweetness and light, proclaiming an all-caring god, but, like many creeds, its concomitant was intolerance and violence. His centrally driven revolution was articulated in terms of, and aimed in large measure to enhance, the defining institution of society, kingship. The pivotal role of the king as a single being between many gods and the many of humanity was to be replaced by a more problematic one to one—one god to one king—with the many of humanity hardly integrated into the new religion; separate human access to the god was denied.

Under Akhenaten's second or third successor, the child king Tutankhamun (1333-1323 BC), the revolution was abandoned, and with it the unique knowledge of the god or gods claimed by Akhenaten. The restoration inscription composed in Tutankhamun's name does not focus on kingship but states that the gods had been absent from the land because their cults were not being maintained (Helck 1961, 365-68). Military campaigns abroad had failed and gods did not provide advice (oracles?) or respond to prayers for help. The new king, however, revived cults, commissioning new cult statues, appointing new priests from reputable families, and increasing temple establishments. By implication, foreign campaigns now were or would be successful and so the king's traditional role as restorer of order within and outside the country was reaffirmed.

The narrowly religious reaction to Akhenaten is difficult to interpret because the dates of texts with new systematizations of the gods are uncertain (Zandee 1987, 127; here Hornung, 1982a, 217-37, and Assmann, 1983a, need revision). There was no new attempt to make cult and knowledge of the gods depend narrowly on the king and knowledge hitherto displayed only by kings began to appear in nonroyal sources (see range of sources for the text Assmann 1970; 1983a, 24-25; 1983c, 48-49; for the general context, see Baines 1990b). The idea of the kingship of the gods became widespread, but it was not commonly presented through the royal symbol of the cartouche. Amun-Re acquired as a constant epithet "King of the Gods (*nswt-nṯrw*)" which later fused with his name into the Greek word Amonrasonter. The growing economic, and ultimately political, power of the temples favored such an institutional analogy for the god's power. However, in slowly asserting its independence, the priesthood began by staying within its own context and used the kingship of the gods as an expression of praise and a metaphor, not as a pretext for action. In succeeding centuries this position changed greatly.

The last king of the Eighteenth Dynasty, Horemheb (*c.* 1319-1307 BC), was the chief military commander of the reign of Tutankhamun. Horemheb rejected the memory of Tutankhamun, erasing or annexing his monuments. In a "coronation" inscription which is significant as the earliest preserved royal text which states at length that its subject was of nonroyal origin, he wrote about his accession to the throne in a similar vein to that of Tutankhamun's inscription (Gardiner 1953). The text contains no simple criticism of Horemheb's predecessor, Tutankhamun's successor Ay (1323-1319 BC), who is not mentioned by name. The exposition moves from calling Horemheb the vice-regent of the land to recounting his selection for the kingship by Horus of Hnes, the god of his local town in Middle Egypt, whose "eldest son" he is. This Horus presented the future king to Amun in the Luxor temple at the Festival of Opet, the most important and probably the most public religious celebration in the religious center of royal legitimacy (the rituals performed within the temple itself would of course have been seen by few). Like Tutankhamun, Horemheb emphasized his restoration of the temples and reestablishment of the priesthood, this time drawing its new members from the elite of the army. The shift from citing people of repute to invoking the army is significant in pointing toward Horemheb's power base and, more generally, in suggesting how the traditional bureaucratic elite was in decline and the power of the newer institutions of army and professional priesthood was growing.

Horemheb's inscription shows a tension between his secular origins and religious legitimation. The legitimation is not expressed in terms either of unalloyed power or of the intrinsic power of the kingship, for the latter is shown to depend on the gods. The king serves the gods by securing their cult and cult personnel. This emphasis on cult performance is a specifically religious strategy. Although priests hardly presented themselves as kings before the Graeco-Roman Period, they themselves and the king stated that they were responsible for the normal performance of the cult. Here, the form of conventional temple iconography, in which the king makes all the offerings, tends to distract from the institutional and social significance of Horemheb's concerns. The text scarcely uses the general mythical legitimation of kings at accession through reestablishing order from chaos. The concentration on restoring the temples discounts martial overtones that a general might favor, and reduces the cosmic scope of the king's role. Although strongly religious in focus, the text is also very pragmatic. It is conceivable that this retreat from the notion of order reflected a failure of foreign policies—which had almost certainly taken place—but it is more likely that the choice of emphasis related to the king's nonroyal background and to the country's principal concern in the period.

In his use of the past, Horemheb exploited the aftermath of Akhenaten's revolution by demolishing his buildings, and interred blocks from them within his own constructions, incorporating in a material form the idea of an enemy within rather than beyond Egypt who was to be combated (such reuse of building material was, however, often neutral in meaning, cf. Björkman 1971, 11-21, 121-22). His annexation of the works of two predecessors presented him as responsible himself for rejecting the revolution. A Nineteenth Dynasty king list followed this lead and omitted Akhenaten and his successors (Redford 1986a, 18-20). An inscription of the reign of Ramses II refers to Akhenaten's reign as that of the "enemy of Akhetaten (his new capital city)," and gives Horemheb at least 59 years of rule, the majority of which were those of the kings who were removed from the record (Gaballa 1977, 25). This treatment of "history," which is not spelled out in discursive texts, mythologizes Akhenaten, associating him with general enemies of order but retaining his position in the succession of events.

The Nineteenth Dynasty (1307-1196 BC) saw the reign of one of Egypt's most famous kings, Ramses II (1290-1224 BC), whose aspirations to divinity and building programs resemble, and were probably intended to surpass, those of Amenhotep III. Ramses portrayed his relations with Amun-Re in a dramatized version of the cycle of affliction and divine mercy found in pious nonroyal texts (Lichtheim 1976, 65-66; von der Way 1984). This vision of royal dependence, which may have had a political dimension (Assmann 1983b) and mobilizes a similar divine–royal relation to that of Horemheb, could be seen either as tempering the ruler's divinity or as giving him a status separate from normal mortals since only the king could claim divine succor on such a plane. Whichever of these two is the case, the text provides a contrast with Ramses' claims to divinity.

Dynastic troubles left Ramses as a model for the next dynasty, in which every king after the first took the dynastic name Ramses (III-XI). Reflecting this subordination of the identity of the later kings, scholars term the Nineteenth–Twentieth dynasties the Ramesside period. This royal model weakened royal links with the gods. Before, the motifs of continuity and of descent from the gods had balanced each other, but now the this-worldly references in royal texts were stronger. Sethnakhte (1196-1194 BC), the first king of the Twentieth Dynasty, recorded his struggle for the country (Drenkhahn 1980). This was also commemorated by Ramses IV (1163-1156 BC) in a text which presents Ramses III (1194-1163 BC) posthumously describing his antecedents and works (Breasted 1906, 198-206; Erichsen 1933). Sethnakhte was vague in his references to predecessors who were enemies but, like Horemheb, he indicated that the conflict was internal while at the same time assimilating it to the old pattern of the defeat of the forces of chaos. The Ramses III/IV version of the narrative is more open,

seemingly—but probably not in fact—identifying the "Syrian" leader of the defeated faction by name (the name, *iir-sw*, probably
means "Self-made Man").

Between Horemheb and Ramses IV there was thus no single
treatment of opposition and its defeat. Variations in approach may
relate to different purposes served by particular texts as much as
to different attitudes to kingship and rebellion. Ramses IV erected
a stela containing invocations to Osiris and eleven other deities
which has been characterized as a "treatise on royalty" (Derchain
1980; Korostovtsev 1947). This text combines many motifs,
including legitimacy and royal descent (which are not identical)
and a set of ritual denials of wrongdoing similar to those which
deceased people were held to pronounce in order to be judged
favorably after death, as probably did priests when they were
initiated into office (Grieshammer 1974). The denials demonstrate that the king submitted to priestly codes, and their import
for the king's status is therefore comparable to Horemheb's
historical-priestly presentation of events and decisions. Ramses
states in as many words that he was not a usurper, something that
was true of few of his immediate predecessors, and this assertion
places added weight on the other legitimations in the text. As in
other compositions of this date, there is little legitimation in terms
of order, force, or foreign conquest, no doubt in part because of
political decline. In a period when writing and knowledge were
more widely disseminated than in the Third Millennium, the gap
between assertion and reality might have been too great to carry
conviction. Thus, in part through lack of achievement, the king
came to have a moral position and stature all too similar to those
of other human beings. In rhetorical terms the text of Ramses IV is
novel, being cast in the first person as an act of devotion to the
gods. Its general message and allusions to current conditions
appear to involve an audience much wider than this form would
imply. As often, the public who would hear that message is hard to
define.

During the Twentieth Dynasty, the position of the king became
progressively weaker and conflict began to center on the high
priest of Amun-Re, whose resources rivaled those of the king. The
central administration retained some coherence throughout, but
one high priest was temporarily removed from office, and under
Ramses XI (*c.* 1100-1070 BC) a civil war arose around the persons
of the high priest Amenhotep and the viceroy of Nubia (e.g.,

Helck 1968a, 203-05). Amenhotep and his predecessor Rames-sesnakhte created unprecedented temple reliefs showing themselves before the gods which were carved on walls in the outer parts of the great temple at Karnak (Lepsius 1972-73, plates 237b-d). Herihor, Amenhotep's successor, who seems to have been a military man who entered the priesthood toward the end of his career, went further. While Ramses XI still reigned in the north, he adopted limited kingly titles and iconography in reliefs in the main cult areas of the temples of Amun-Re and Khonsu (Bonhême 1979). He did not present himself as king elsewhere, and his first cartouche name was "Chief Priest of Amun," which ignored almost all traditional royal legitimation. This radical reduction of kingship was the culmination of the tendency I have traced from the time of Tutankhamun and Horemheb, but it was reached only by a usurper.

Herihor's successor Piyankh did not take the same formal step of assuming the kingship, but continued to use his military titles and waged a campaign against the viceroy of Nubia. A letter he sent to Thebes from Nubia ordering the murder of two policemen continues with the comment, probably in response to his correspondent's worries that the king might find out or attack: "As for Pharaoh, how can he reach this land (Nubia or Thebes?)?—And as for Pharaoh, whose master is he in any case?" (Wente 1967, 53, modified). Such opinions of the king—and, through reference to the office rather than the person, the kingship—are otherwise hardly preserved from antiquity. They could either have been part of the background to ideological change in this period or have been common in many periods.

The slightly later story of Wenamun, which has the form of a report by an emissary sent by Herihor to obtain timber in Lebanon for the barque of the Theban god Amun-Re, ignores Ramses XI entirely. The 21st Dynasty or slightly later manuscript of this text was found at el-Hiba (Gardiner 1932, xi), the frontier town of the domain of Amun-Re which had formed from the Twentieth Dynasty breakdown of central rule, encompassing much of the Nile Valley. One episode of the story narrates how during negotiations, the ruler of Byblos refers to the treatment of earlier envoys of Khaemwese, probably the birth name of Ramses IX (c. 1131-1112 BC), who were detained at Byblos until they died. Wenamun replies that the comparison is wrong because Khaemwese's messengers were men, as was Khaemwese himself—a marked slight for a king—whereas on this occasion Amun-Re King of the Gods has sent his divine messenger, Amun-of-the-Way (a portable statue) and with him Wenamun, his human messenger (Lichtheim 1976, 228). This exchange reads like a fictitious and probably retrospective legitimation of the splitting of the country and marginalization of the king, who has become irrelevant to power and authority. In a welter of endeavor and intrigue, the god alone counts. Twenty-first Dynasty Thebes was ruled by high priests, of whom one or two took the title of king for short periods (Kitchen 1986). But the acknowledged kings at Tanis in the Delta, whose rule was nominally accepted at Thebes, cannot have viewed things on the lines of Wenamun, and the ideology of kingship survived along with them. Priests had only limited success in taking over the position and authority of kings, but the withering of the traditional state centered on the king left them as the guardians of high culture, a role they retained to the end of Egyptian civilization.

The New Kingdom crisis of belief that culminated under Akhenaten attacked central elements in the definition of kingship, cosmos, and culture (see in general Assmann 1983a). Its short term effect was not to diminish the kingship but rather to focus on the restoration and consolidation of the traditional cult of the gods. In the longer term, the emphasis on the kingship of gods, both under Akhenaten and in the aftermath, as well as shifts in royal and divine power, raised the status of the gods in relation to the king on earth, while the plurality of their identities and manifestations in an increasingly divided society provided many possible avenues and modes of access to superhuman power, legitimation, and succor. Models of the primacy and hierarchy of the gods made the supreme deity or deities vastly superior to any this-worldly power (Assmann 1980b), and hence, partly through the use of metaphors of kingship, put the king in second place or lower. So long as the king wielded effective political control and could harness access to the gods, these developments need not have threatened his position, but over several centuries they weakened it markedly.

The First Millennium BC and Roman Period: Dissolution and
Reformulation (c. 1070 BC–AD 395)

These very gradual developments had long term successors in the later evolution of kingship and the state. I present this period extremely briefly.

For 350 years after the end of the Twentieth Dynasty there was seldom a dominant power in Egypt, and from the later Ninth century BC the kingship split progressively until the late Eighth century, when a high priest, perhaps five local rulers bearing the title of king, and numerous princes and other rulers called "Great Chief of the M(eshwesh)," divided the country (Kitchen 1986). The role of the temples and the gods in the affairs of this period is exemplified by an inscription probably from the end of the Twenty-first Dynasty, which shows an oracular decision of Amun-Re to grant a cult of an ethnically Libyan leader called Nimlot to his son, the Great Chief of the M(eshwesh), Shoshenq (Blackman 1941; Edwards 1982, 535-38). This procedure is doubly significant because the king of the day displayed exaggerated satisfaction at the result of the oracle. The Shoshenq is probably the future Shoshenq I (*c.* 945-924 BC), the founder of the 22nd Dynasty, and the king is his predecessor Psusennes II (*c.* 959-945 BC). Thus, oracles, which had confirmed the intentions of well established New Kingdom kings to carry out acts of expansion, were later used to legitimize a potential successor's status before he came to the throne or became the king designate. New Kingdom kings had referred to oracles that had supposedly designated them before-hand for extra legitimation during their reigns, but these accounts are evident fictions. By the Third Intermediate Period, kingship and succession may have been more directly dependent on gods and oracles.

A major force throughout this period was ethnicity (cf. A. Leahy 1985, 1990b; Baines in press a). Many leaders were ethnic Libyans descended from soldiers and prisoners of war settled in Egypt during struggles of the Nineteenth–Twentieth dynasties. The Meshwesh were the most important of these groups. By the end of the Twentieth Dynasty Libyans had penetrated the family of the High Priests of Amun, and one of the kings of the 21st Dynasty bore the Libyan name Osorkon. These people were culturally Egyptian but retained a defining ethnic and military identity. Despite their use of Egyptian symbols and adherence to general

Egyptian values, they seem, unlike traditional Egyptians, not to have had strong centralistic ideals, and this possibly ethnic aspect of their ideology may have contributed to the progressive splintering of kingship and rule.

In 730 BC the most powerful leader north of Thebes was Tefnakhte, the ruler of the ethnic Libyan heartland of the western Delta. During a raid through the country from south to north, the Sudanese 25th Dynasty king Piye (c. 750-712 BC), who ruled much of the Nile Valley, forced all the other rulers except Tefnakhte to submit to him (Lichtheim 1980, 66-84), but he did not remove them from office, and indeed depicted a number of them as kings on the triumphal stela recording his campaign (Grimal 1981, plates 1, 5). Piye emphasized that he was a traditional king who observed ritual prescriptions of purity, unlike rulers in Egypt. Purity is not prominent in earlier royal display, although it can be inferred from the text of Ramses IV cited earlier. Making purity into an issue might imply that even an obvious aspect of kingship, which is visible in numerous formulas in which the king instructs those who enter a temple to purify themselves four times, had been neglected by Piye's enemies. He seems thus to have presented them as "secular," in contrast with his proper integration with the world of the gods and the traditional service for them which he provided as a true king of Egypt. The strength of this emphasis could, however, also be an innovation of his time, and would be in keeping with general developments toward exclusivity that can be seen in the succeeding Late Period.

Piye presented his campaign as having been inspired by his god Amun-Re and occasioned by Tefnakhte's southward expansion in the Nile Valley. Perhaps looking back to New Kingdom traditions, Piye prided himself on his care for horses, as against the Egyptians of his time who maltreated them (Grimal 1981, 280-82). He exploited the divine associations of kingship, but contemporary kings, hardly any of whose inscriptions are preserved, may have done the same. Because so many Egyptian leaders displayed a notionally non-Egyptian ethnicity, the Sudanese Piye could claim that he was more Egyptian than they, whether or not native Egyptians accepted this.

In the aftermath of Piye's raid, Tefnakhte consolidated his power and he or his successor Bocchoris (24th Dynasty, c. 717-712 BC) took the title of king. Later history created a dynasty running from Tefnakhte to the powerful 26th Dynasty (672-525 BC), but this may have been a fiction ascribed to ancestors who had not themselves presented their rule in kingly terms. Although Piye's successor Shabaka (*c.* 712-698 BC) attempted to eliminate other kings and initiated a cultural revival throughout the Nile Valley, the Assyrian conquerors of Egypt in 672-664 BC found a political map that was little changed from the Eighth century. They applied the Akkadian term for "king" to many people, cutting across Egyptian categories (Oppenheim, in Pritchard 1969, 294-96). In another development that escaped both royal symbolism and long-standing attempts of kings to influence Thebes by dedicating their celibate daughters as "divine adoratrices" and principal personnel of Amun, the Fourth Priest of Amun-Re in Thebes and "Governor of the City" Montuemhat became more important within Upper Egypt than the kings of his time.

This wide variety of "royal" and nonroyal power was broken by Psammetichus I (664-610 BC), who declared himself independent from Assyria and reunited Egypt. Psammetichus constrained the Thebans to accept his daughter as the divine adoratrice's heiress, while ostensibly reaffirming her predecessors in office (Caminos 1964). Elsewhere, he displaced local rulers and attempted to centralize and secularize his rule. For earlier times, one might with qualification term "secular" the power of the elaborately supported, central, and symbolically legitimized kingship, together with its bureaucracy. The long dispersal of power and kingship had weakened the significance and the religious integration of these institutions, and Late Period kingship emerged as relatively secular in a Western sense. Although himself probably of "Libyan" extraction, Psammetichus pursued national unity by suppressing the ethnicity of the elites and by winning over those with military rather than religious authority. As had been true for centuries, the temples were the economically and culturally dominant sector of society, and this relative secularity of kingship existed in an intensely religious context. The other repository of power continued to be the military, among whom were foreign Greek and Carian mercenaries. These people were scarcely integrated into native Egyptian culture, which they did not affect as much as the Libyans had done.

From the Twenty-fifth Dynasty, through the Persian occupations of Egypt (525-404, 343-332 BC) and native rule in the Fourth century (404-343 BC), into Macedonian and Ptolemaic times (332-30 BC), there were frequent changes of dynasty, usurpations, and campaigns of destruction by rulers against their immediate or more distant predecessors. This pattern of events may not have been very different from that of the Third Intermediate Period (which is less adequately documented in this respect), except that there were not multiple concurrent dynasties in the Late Period. Much of this history is known from foreign sources, and some of the principal earlier periods might appear similar if similar evidence for them were preserved. The contemporary context does, however, seem to show similar patterns in the very few preserved royal inscriptions from the period.

Here, the earliest relevant text is a fragmentary inscription of the Twenty-fifth Dynasty king Taharqa (690-664 BC), in which he acknowledges a wrong that he had committed as king (Spalinger 1978a, 28-33). In the complete text this no doubt formed part of a pattern of guilt, affliction, and "atonement" comparable with Ramses II's use of the model of piety in his Kadesh narrative, but Taharqa went further in admitting guilt and thus in bringing royal self-justification still closer to human patterns. For the Twenty-sixth Dynasty, the crucial figure is Amasis (570-526 BC), a "nationalist"—that is, anti-Greek—usurper who later was conciliatory to Greek mercenaries, on whom he depended for defense against the Near Eastern empires, and perhaps also for internal stability. Amasis overthrew his predecessor Apries (589-570 BC), waging a three-year struggle in which Apries was defeated and killed (Edel 1978a), and then burying him with full royal honors in the royal cemetery at Sais in the Delta. Amasis recounted all these events in an inscription that does not use the name Apries but spells out the struggle clearly. Earlier usurpers may well have buried their predecessors in order to establish their legitimacy, since this was a fundamental Egyptian "filial" duty, but this record in a text of strikingly "objective" tone has no earlier parallel. In keeping with this broadening of official sources, later anecdotal material, in one case formed into a literary text, gives Twenty-sixth Dynasty kings a notably secular image (cf. Spalinger 1978b). The anecdotes, which dwell on Amasis' drinking and his treatment of everyday affairs, may have recalled legitimations disseminated during his time that would have presented the usurper favorably to the Egyptian people, and perhaps especially to the Greeks.

Nectanebo I (380-362 BC), the usurping founder of the Thirtieth Dynasty, took this candor a stage farther in a different context. An inscription commemorating rebuilding in a temple at

Hermopolis states that before his accession, when he was a military officer, he visited the place and was shocked at its condition; when he later became king, he undertook to restore it (Roeder 1954, 389). The motif of restoring a structure seen in decay before accession is common in earlier royal inscriptions (e.g., Helck 1961, 140-43) and occurs in the Late Period under Taharqa (Macadam 1949, 14-21), but previous kings who used this device had been the heirs to the throne before their accession. Nectanebo seems to have been concerned here about his legitimation through action for the gods—an appropriately traditional concern—but hardly about how he came to the throne. The casualness of the reference to his earlier position could, however, also be a way of defusing an issue and making his accession appear more natural.

This broadening of royal inscriptions continued into Ptolemaic times (305-30 BC; see in general Bevan 1927). The earliest preserved hieroglyphic inscription of one of the period's rulers is the Satrap Stela of Ptolemy I Soter. This was set up before Ptolemy took the title of king and records, among other matters, the return to Egypt of cult images removed during the second Persian occupation (see Lorton 1971, 162-63). Rulers of earlier periods would probably not have admitted that such statues had ever left the country, and this motif, which is known for all the first four Ptolemies, could be non-Egyptian in origin. Whether the achievements they claimed really occurred and whether, or how many times, the images were really removed, is quite uncertain. Later in the dynasty, "public" decrees were issued and inscribed in hieroglyphic, demotic (cursive Egyptian), and Greek. The decrees of Ptolemy IV Philopator (221-205 BC) and V Epiphanes (205-180 BC) proclaim the results of conciliatory meetings between representatives of royalty—the kings themselves were very young—and the native priesthood (no modern editions: Bevan 1927, 208-14, 232, 262-68). That of Ptolemy IV also celebrated the return of statues from abroad, while the decree for Ptolemy V announced the end of a rebellion and the king's Egyptian-style coronation. These texts represent a compromise between Egyptian and Greek ideas. The later ones specifically addressed the native elite (the latest preserved dates to Augustus, 30 BC-AD 14: Porter and Moss 1939, 253). In the complex, plural culture of Graeco-Roman times, where native tradition was concentrated in temples to which few had direct access, none of these texts can have addressed the native population as a whole; the kings were attempting to win the

people over by working through the elite. How their propaganda
to their own immigrant group related to their presentation of
themselves to Egyptians is an involved question, which Ludwig
Koenen (1983) has studied brilliantly (see also Préaux 1976). One
notable feature of the legitimation of the Ptolemies that is not well
paralleled earlier is the dominant emphasis in their Greek and
Egyptian titularies on descent from predecessors in office. This
went together with an elaborate cult of deceased and living
members of the royal family that is attested almost exclusively in
the dating formulas which form the preambles to administrative
documents (Clarysse and van der Veken 1983; Minas 1993). The
cult was an essentially Greek institution practiced in Alexandria
and Ptolemais, the Greek city which had been founded in Upper
Egypt.

Throughout the Late and Ptolemaic periods, the focus of elite
Egyptian personal display was in the temples. Its most important
form was the inscribed temple statue (Bothmer 1969). Secular
power and actions were rarely evoked. The owners of these statues
(Otto 1954) presented themselves in their texts as priests devoted
to their gods, subsuming action in the outside world within
religion. Such a presentation is analogous in important ways with
the conventional image of the king as the dutiful servant of the
gods, except that the king also predominates in the decoration of
temple structures, where the nonroyal were not shown, in part for
reasons of decorum. In the early Persian period (c. 520 BC),
Udjahorresne, who chose to serve the Persian kings, justified that
decision by the improvements he was able to bring to the temple
of Neith at Sais, the capital of the previous dynasty (Lichtheim
1980, 36-41; Lloyd 1982b). In Macedonian times, two men, one a
son of the last native king, Nectanebo II (360-343 BC), justified
their exile and, it seems, their joining the service of a foreign
ruler, more in psychological terms by attributing their motivation
to a god (Clère 1951, 152-54). Here, the presentation of such
events in biographical inscriptions (as against works of literature)
and the lack of direct reference to the king have no parallel in
earlier texts. This emancipation of foreign affairs from royal
participation no doubt related in part to the new conditions of
foreign rule and to the lack of a native king to whom one could
appeal.

The cultural focus of temples was paralleled in architectural
activity as early as the Twenty-first Dynasty. From then on, nonroyal

people did not build the massive tombs that had been their central display (Seventh–Sixth century BC Thebes provides a major exception). Kings did not have large separate tombs, but were buried in relatively small structures within temple enclosures, as were some other leading individuals (Stadelmann 1971; nonroyal tombs of this type at Memphis and Heracleopolis: Pérez Die 1990). Proximity to the gods had become the highest expression of special status, while also conferring greater security on tombs than could be achieved in any other way. In Late and Graeco-Roman times there was much temple building throughout the country. A higher proportion of the monuments of antiquity was created then than is now readily apparent, but in the southern Nile Valley, the major Graeco-Roman temples are still dominant, exceeding most predecessors in size and number. This massive outlay parallels the textual persuasion of the elite in the multilingual inscriptions and in whatever wider forms of dissemination they enjoyed, but the temples were more visible and persuasive for much of the population—even though few people entered them. It may be no coincidence that the largest preserved Graeco-Roman temples are in areas that have been backwaters since antiquity but were centers of anti-Ptolemaic feeling at the time.

The rulers who built these structures could not read their inscriptions and could have had little detailed understanding of the role of the king that was portrayed in them, beyond knowing that he articulated human–divine relations, and hence the Egyptian cosmos (which was different from the Ptolemies' own, Hellenistic cosmos). This generalization of the king's functions across cultural and ethnic divides was acceptable in antiquity, when people respected or worshipped other people's gods and believed that the god of a place might have preeminent power locally. Within the native temples, however, the living king or emperor remained an outsider, whose deification in other contexts in Egypt and in his wider domains followed Hellenistic rather than Egyptian models. For the Egyptians, the temples remained a vital and beneficent force in a way in which the kingship had ceased to be centuries earlier. The figure of the king presented in their reliefs continued to be crucial and was elaborated richly over more than five hundred years (Derchain 1962). Yet in subtle ways what was presented in the reliefs behind a façade of continuity shows a marked decline in his status and role, as has

been convincingly shown by Eberhard Otto (1964, 63-83) and
Erich Winter (1976; for a rather different view, see Quaegebeur
1988, 1989).

A crucial insight into Egyptian views of kingship in this period is
given by the Demotic Chronicle. This literary text purports to be a
set of oracular pronouncements about the latest native kings
(Johnson 1983; see also Lloyd 1982a), whom it assesses, finding
the majority who were usurpers wanting because they did not respect the gods. The ideals of the chronicle are not surprising. The
king should be the legitimate successor to the throne and should
have a proper coronation. He should protect the country from
foreign invasion and nurture its prosperity. His most important
duty, however, is to honor the gods and be generous to their
temples, and in this way to be a "man of god." In this crucial case
the king is referred to not as a god, but as a man. This rather
muted view of his status is a suitable conclusion to the fluctuating
fortunes of Egyptian kingship and kings; here, the king is clearly
subordinated to the higher power of the gods. In comparison,
contemporary Hellenistic ideals of kingship gave the ruler a more
central position in his rather more plural, and in some senses
more secular, state. For native Egypt, kingship and kings became
marginal and primarily symbolic during this period when the
rulers were culturally alien, even though they were the political
masters of Egypt and had their power base in the country itself.
The uneasy compromise between the originally all-powerful native
king and the dominant settler reflects many of the strains in the
Ptolemaic state.

Conclusion

In this chapter I have focused on royal legitimation, particularly
on aspects that relate to doubt and dissent; true statements of
opposition are almost absent. Legitimation can be studied more
easily for periods when continuous texts were written, but it is a
feature of most institutions and must have been a factor from the
beginning of the kingship. Over millennia, Egyptian society very
slowly became rather more plural and less focused on the king.
This change was not due to periodic collapses in the kingship,
which survived the intermediate periods without significant
diminution in its stature and remained so central that the
ideological crisis of Akhenaten was articulated in terms of

kingship. That crisis was, however, in some respects the first stage in the erosion of kingship as a central symbol, forming a development with both religious and political dimensions. During periods of weakness of the kingship and in its long final diminution, kings did not reject the divine associations of their offices or persons or discourage divinization, but their claims became more and more focused on temples to the cult of the gods. After the New Kingdom, kings had no temples to their own cult, although they had tombs with chapels in temple complexes and statue cults in temples of the gods (e.g., Otto 1957).

The foreign rulers of the Late and Graeco-Roman periods could not fully exploit local paths to divinity and were not accepted in local esteem as much as the Roman emperor was, for example, in the more "Classical" region of Asia Minor (Price 1984). Egyptian kingship was tenacious in its symbolic and political aspects but, like most kingships, it was specific to a single culture, and the new kings, who came from a civilization that was not coextensive with any one state, stood on the edge of it. The king of the native monuments ultimately became an almost entirely symbolic or theoretical figure who was explicated by the small priestly elite but was not the ideological or religious focus for the rest of the native population. Texts emanating from a temple environment but disseminated a little more widely propounded explicitly the ancient view that order was fragile and had to be maintained by the cult of the gods (Vandier 1961, 129-31; see Fowden 1986, 13-44). Whereas this had earlier been a royal duty, now it was formulated in relation to the temples and without specific reference to the king.

In terms of power, however, the king retained his position: some of the Ptolemies were among the most dominant central rulers of Egypt of any period, but they assimilated themselves to the local culture only to a limited extent. The temples could not dispense with the symbolic role of the king and his economic power as patron of their buildings and endowment, while for the ruler and the elite they had become more potent repositories of native culture and of social solidarity than the kingship. Thus, kingship was marginalized both by the foreignness of the rulers and by internal religious developments. During some earlier periods, ideologies that centered less on kingship and more on the roles of local grandees had acquired some prominence, but such tendencies were never important when the country was centralized. In the highly centralized Graeco-Roman period, king-ship remained the centripetal definition of native Egyptian civilization, but was nonetheless reduced to a definition rather than a living focus, and became centered on the temple, in con-trast with earlier times, when the temples had to a great extent depended on king and state. The foreign rulers were well aware of this weakened prestige but did not neglect the native office of king. The Roman prefect, an appointed official who served for a limited period and governed the country in the name of the emperor, was invested with some of the aura of kingship. He performed rites for the inundation which kings had earlier performed (cf. Bonneau 1964, 331-32, 448), and he was forbidden to travel by boat on the Nile during the inundation, a prohibition that has no apparent basis in Graeco-Roman times and may preserve a dynastic royal tradition (for discussion, see Bonneau 1961). It is difficult to say how far these practices went toward legitimizing Roman rule in Egypt and the emperor's almost com-plete absence from the country.

Developments in Egyptian kingship and its legitimation relate to change at a societal level, where significant patterns can be identified. Texts that provide evidence for these changes, however, derive almost as much of their meaning from the literary genre and from relations to the discourse of one another as from any unmediated response to social life—if there can be such a res-ponse. Studies of kingship and society become studies of works of literature and art, produced by the small elite that mostly focused around the kings, or in later periods, the temples. These legit-imations hardly spoke to the wider society in the way in which the great works of architecture of various periods must have done.

Attitudes to kingship are enmeshed in the interdependence of successive texts and cannot be approached directly. This per-spective of the material as forming a tradition allows interpre-tations of long-term changes, such as the "secularized" image of Late Period kings, that might not seem so significant for the short term, and could even not appear as innovations to the actors. Yet this perspective has elements in common with that of the Egyp-tians, in that they had the monuments and texts of the past before them and so constructed their present in relation to a past that was more immediate than any counterpart can be in Western society. The detailed implications for kingship of this use of the past, which included distinctions among earlier periods, have yet to be worked out for the Late Period, during which "archaism" was a salient phenomenon (Brunner's reading, 1970, is implausible; see further L. M. Leahy 1988, chapter 6). One detailed example of this evocation is the form of Twenty-sixth Dynasty royal inscriptions, such as that of Amasis recording his war with Apries. A number of these are written in vertical columns, recalling the format of Old and Middle Kingdom texts (even in the Middle Kingdom this was disappearing). This form contrasts with the content and may help to legitimize it.

Despite the recalcitrance of the sources, ritual and other forms of legitimation are vital avenues of approach to the reality of Egyptian kingship. Ritual, which I have not studied in this chapter, addresses continuity while supporting and constraining the king's role in his performance of his office; other forms of legitimation address more generally the problematics of rulership, power, and inequality. Because no discursive history or description from outside the ruling elite is preserved, rather little is known from Egypt of the anecdotal details of intrigue and assassination which are familiar from the Classical world and many other societies, but there is every reason for assuming that such events occurred. These events, and the orderly successions, achievements and conquests of rulers who did not suffer them, formed the background, chiefly among the elite, to the largely monumental and literary discourse I have examined. Legitimation is a crucial factor in the interrelations of all these historical and social currents.

Bibliographical Note and Comment

This chapter treats its subject very selectively, hardly considering, for example, modes of legitimation in terms of the past or of the king's own person and relations with his entourage.

Among previous studies, only Otto (1969) has a similar focus. I document specific points, but not normally current interpretations (Hornung 1982a, 135-42, gives an excellent summary). For texts I mostly refer to published translations; the originals can be found from there. Both the present volume and Bonhême and Forgeau (1988) have large bibliographies. Dates are those of this volume as a whole (alternative scheme: Krauss 1985).

Jan Assmann's major work *Ma'at: Gerechtigkeit und Unsterblichkeit im Alten Ägypten* (1990) appeared after this chapter was first completed. Since his book covers in depth areas related to those I review, a couple of sentences of comment may be useful; it is not practicable to offer an extended critique or to refer to it throughout much of my text. Assmann's work is focused around the concept of *maat* "order," but in presenting Egyptian ethics and social solidarity he also ranges very broadly through material in which the word itself does not occur. He discusses legitimation specifically in his chapter VII. The result is a remarkable tour de force and a compelling synthesis. In relation to my present topic, however, I see three difficulties in its approach. First, it does not take into account sufficiently the contrast between the inclusiveness of ethical statements—which I would see as a legitimation—and the extremely small audiences to which the texts were addressed. As a result, the social vision he presents is more filled with harmony than the material may warrant. Second, Assmann makes little allowance for possible variation in beliefs, for the likely size of the gaps in preserved evidence, and for sectors in society whose beliefs and orientations are unknown. Together, these two points mean that he presents the perspective of the elite actors on legitimation rather more than an observer's perspective of the kind attempted in this chapter. Third, Assmann's traditionalist image of the Old Kingdom as an integrated age followed by an intellectual crisis in the First Intermediate Period may take too long-term a perspective and, I believe, does not do full justice to possible and indeed attested complexities in Old Kingdom ideas.

Acknowledgments

This chapter was first prepared as a paper for a conference on divine kingship organized under the auspices of the Wenner-Gren Foundation for Anthropological Research by T. O. Beidelman, Gillian Feeley-Harnik, and Annette Weiner, and held at New York University in September 1988. I should like to thank them and the Foundation for the opportunity to participate in a most stimulating meeting. A version was also presented at the University of Arizona. The paper has been revised for this volume. I owe a great debt of thanks to David O'Connor and David Silverman for offering to include it here.

   I am very grateful to John Huddlestun, Helen Whitehouse, Norman Yoffee, and members of a seminar in Oxford for commenting on drafts. Ursula Rössler-Köhler most kindly showed me her *Individuelle Haltungen zum ägyptischen Königtum der Spätzeit* (1991) in advance of publication. Anthony Leahy is finalizing a book on *Aspects of Saite Kingship* which I believe will give a comparable, but altogether richer, view of that period's kings.

CHAPTER TWO

THE NATURE OF EGYPTIAN KINGSHIP

David P. Silverman

Periodic re-examination of the subject of kingship over the years has shown that the ancient Egyptians seemed to have viewed this concept differently at different times (Barta 1978, 478-481; Brunner 1978, 461-464; Barta 1979, 485-494; Blumenthal 1979, 526-531; Bell 1985a 251-294; Goedicke 1986, 989-992; and Silverman 1991a, 58-87).

While kingship as an institution may have continued fairly constantly throughout the more than three thousand year history of ancient Egypt, just what the office signified, how the holders of the position understood their role, and how the population perceived this individual do not constitute uniform concepts that span the centuries without change. Indeed, the very nature or personality of a particular ruler might precipitate a sudden alteration of a long accepted view, as was apparently the case with the pharaoh Akhenaten (Redford 1984).

Changes might also be effected because of economic conditions, as may well have been the situation toward the end of the Old Kingdom. Certainly, political circumstances might also be responsible for modifications; witness the status of kingship during the times just prior to each of the three Intermediate Periods. It is likely that other factors contributed toward these alterations. As the nation grew, it evolved, and it is reasonable to assume that many of its institutions would, therefore, develop likewise, and in turn be modified.

There are many ways to investigate the status of kingship, some of which are dealt with elsewhere in this volume. Some earlier studies have been encyclopedic in their choice of source material, while others have limited their sources by time period.

The present examination focuses on literature in its broadest sense and will include much of the written material that was inked, painted, or sculpted by the ancient Egyptians. The major emphasis will center on texts from the New Kingdom, but there also will be references to earlier sources. It seemed best to be liberal in choosing the genres of inscriptions to study so that as broad a picture as possible could be examined. Such an approach is preferred, since it has already been shown that references to pharaoh undoubtedly differed depending on the type of text utilized.

Goedicke studied non-religious texts of the Old Kingdom, and he noted that the king referred to was designated in terminology that ordinarily did not occur in other types of literature (Goedicke 1960, 87-93). Henri Frankfort came to the conclusion that divinity was an important element of kingship in Egypt, but he had relied in large part on religious inscriptions and coronation rituals for his ideas (Frankfort 1948 [1978], 36-197). Georges Posener's sources were more catholic, for he examined secular, religious, and literary works (Posener 1960, 1-2), and his resulting theories, therefore, differ from those of others. There are also other inscriptions such as titulary and epithets of the rulers, that undoubtedly should provide some clues as to the nature of the monarch (Posener 1960, 2, n. 1).

The variations in both terminology and perception were great. A pharaoh might be: named a god in a monumental historical text, called the son of a deity in an epithet on a statue in a temple, hailed as the living image of a god in a secular inscription, described as a fallible mortal in a historical or literary text (Posener 1960, 89-103; Jacobsohn 1939, 13-22), or referred to simply by his personal name in a letter. Each source, therefore, will help to provide the elements that together comprise kingship in ancient Egypt, according to the written documentation of the Egyptians themselves. A complete explanation of the concept, however, can be arrived at only after consideration of all aspects of the culture including art, architecture, iconography, government, socio-economics, etc., and these subjects figure in each of the other chapters in this volume.

The primary aim of this part of the study is to determine the nature of kingship through the king himself. The range of qualities of a royal figure is very broad. According to inscriptions on the walls of the temple of Seti I at Abydos and Ramses II at Beit el Wali, the king in the Nineteenth Dynasty is not only "the pharaoh, the breath of life who makes all men live when he has shone on them," but he is also a "good ruler and one who is loved" (Breasted 1988, 265 and 471; Ricke, Hughes and Wente

1967, 16). *The Bulletin* of the Battle of Kadesh portrays the ruler as a less than omniscient figure, when it records that Ramses believed that the treacherous spies before him were speaking the truth, when in fact, they were providing fallacious information about the Hittite host. Then, unaware of this deceit, the supposedly all-powerful sovereign led his forces directly into an ambush (Posener 1960, 77-79; Lichtheim 1976, 59-60; Kuschke 1983, 31-37).

Taken in the broader context of the whole story this episode can be viewed as a literary device, the function of which was to increase the dramatic impact of the events that were to follow. Because of his decision to believe the treacherous information, Ramses II subsequently found himself surrounded by the enemy and cut off from the few troops who could have otherwise offered him help. Therefore, despite overwhelming odds against him, he was able to bring about a victory from the jaws of defeat. He owed this accomplishment to his super-human valor which, in contrast to his role earlier in the report, now appears so much greater. As preserved on temple walls in several locations throughout Egypt, and on papyri, this record relates the devastation of pharaoh's forces and explains that, in the end, it was the might, the god-like physical abilities, and intelligence of Ramses that allowed him to vanquish the seemingly invincible Hittite enemy. Thus, in this single account, pharaoh appears as a fallible human being, a general, and a divine warrior. Of course, the emphasis is on the last part.

For our purposes, however, it must be noted that despite the eventual divine-like behavior of the king, the ruler does exhibit less than god-like omniscience in his poor judgment early on in the account, whatever the motive of the composer of the story.

It is important to point out that this event was recorded in hieroglyphs on a temple wall, and that such inscriptions were meant to last an eternity. Moreover, they ordinarily had both immediate and far reaching propagandistic value. For these reasons, the Egyptian rulers did not wish to record anything unfavorable about their land or their monarch. Interestingly, Ramses II inscribed this event, including the incident referring to his human frailty, not only on one monument, but also on the walls of the temples at Abydos, Luxor, Karnak, the Ramesseum, and Abu Simbel. In addition, it was also written on papyrus, and the presence of such copies suggests that there may have been also a transition from the monumental, non-literary, genre to the popular, literary one (Posener 1960, 97-98). The existence of these multiple records of what happened implies that the king approved of the text and must have assumed that his early lack of omniscience and poor judgment was more than compensated for by the positive resolution of what appeared to be an unavoidable disaster. All available records of the battle indicate that, despite the exaggerated boasting of the Egyptian ruler, Ramses II did not actually win—nor did he lose; the battle appears to have been a draw. Those who composed the text (which surely had to have the king's final approval) must have felt the need for dramatic tension and, therefore, they presented the pharaoh as a being who, by necessity, could transcend from one aspect of his being to another: from the human to the super-human, to the divine.

Ramses II was not the first pharaoh to be shown in a less than complimentary light; there are instances of both earlier and later rulers depicted in literary texts in less than flattering terms. For example, the *Westcar Papyrus*, which was composed in the Middle Kingdom, several hundred years after the death of the Fourth Dynasty pharaoh Khufu, portrayed him as a less than omniscient monarch (Lichtheim 1973, 217-219; Simpson 1972, 24-25; Simpson 1982a, 744-746). In one story, he wishes to learn whether it is true that a certain magician knows how to attach a severed head to a body. To test the ability of the magician Djedi, the king suggests that he use a human subject, but the magician displays what could be understood as royal benevolence when he suggests rather, that he should use a goose for the display. Khufu exhibits less than divine qualities, for he does not know whether such an act can be done by Djedi, nor does he have the knowledge to do it himself. In fact, most of the wonders described in this text are not those performed by the king, but by non-royal characters (Posener 1960, 94).

Examples from the wisdom literature, a genre that occurs throughout Egyptian history, indicate that royal figures often show human weaknesses, rather than divine strengths. In the Instruction of King Amenemhat I to Senwosret I, the king seems to warn his son about the type of treachery that was responsible for his own apparent assassination (Posener 1960, 5-7, 58-80, and 134-192; Simpson 1972, 159-241). In this text, the prince apparently needed advice from his royal father in order to perform adequately in his role as pharaoh; it did not come naturally.

Texts that contained such information were composed as early as the Old and Middle Kingdoms, and they were often re-recopied and used in later times in other versions. In each period, there were many non-royal versions, and all of these compositions can be grouped together in the category of instructions: those from a king to a prince, those from a vizier to a successor, or those from a man to his son. Such manuscripts contain many similarities in style, structure, and content. Some have been shown to have had some propagandistic value when referring to particular events, and some appear to have been used to justify specific behavior (Posener 1979a, 982, 984). Still, these texts all belong to a particular type of literature, and no matter what the rank of the advisor, the contents are all similar. Moreover, the "Instructions" never have deities as receivers, probably because that might indicate a lack of their divine omniscience. A somewhat rhetorical question in the "Appointment of Office" of the New Kingdom official, Kenamun clearly states why gods would be inappropriate: "Is it regarding sailing through heaven that Horus who is in the sky shall be guided? Is it to Ptah, the august one, who is master of skill, that one shall give instruction for knowledge? Is it concerning speech that Thoth shall be taught...?" (Silverman 1980, 78-79) The expected negative answers to these questions imply that in this type of literature, the gods apparently need neither advice nor instruction. On the contrary, royalty, administrators, nobles, and private citizens are all part of the group that needs to have such information. It is noteworthy that the immediate supervisors of these individuals act as the providers of the necessary knowledge, not the gods.

Seeing the ruler as a figure distinct from and less than a god is not an uncommon phenomenon in popular literary texts (Posener 1960, 98). During the Ramesside Period, in *The Tale of the Two Brothers*, the king plays a comparatively minor role, and this situation is fortunate, since his actions for the most part are inconsequential (Jacobsohn 1938, 13-22; Posener 1960, 95-96; Wente 1972a, 92-102 [translation of the story]; Lichtheim 1976, 203-211 [translation of the story]; and Brunner-Traut 1982, 697-704 [discussion and bibliography]). In what has been labeled the world's oldest fairy tale, *The Doomed Prince* (Bettleheim 1976; Lichtheim 1976, 203-211 [translation]; Wente 1972c, 85-91 [translation]; and Posener, 1960, 95 and n. 4), the king wishes to change the ultimate fate of his son, but he is powerless to do so.

Many different types of human frailties and weaknesses characterize all the figures in another New Kingdom literary text, *The Contendings of Horus and Seth* (Wente 1972c, 108-126 [translation]; and Lichtheim 1976, 214-223 [translation]), but here, the participating characters are neither royal nor private; they are divine. Such behavior amongst divinities is explicable, when one regards the history of Egyptian divinities. The gods were anthropomorphized from an early period in ancient Egypt's history, (Hornung 1982a, 105-107), and their portrayal both in figures and in text clearly is humanized. They have family problems; they bicker; they display moods; they exhibit ribald behavior; they can be insensitive, and they can be stupid. The Egyptians, in making concrete the more abstract concepts that originally comprised their early beliefs, attributed many human faculties to their gods, and in turn, they made them more recognizable and approachable (Silverman 1991a, 12-30). Therefore, ascribing more human qualities to the pharaoh would not in itself preclude his divinity, for the behavior among both men and gods was similar. Although the deities could act in such a manner, they functioned in their own realm; their activity occurred mainly in a world separate from that of man (Posener 1960, 99). They performed feats impossible to man, and their interaction with humanity was always one which depicted the divinities as a separate and superior group.

The Destruction of Mankind, a mythological tale found first in the New Kingdom is part of the *Book of the Celestial Cow* (Lichtheim 1976, 197-199), and it may well have originally been part of the literary genre. In one part of the text, the ruler of the gods, Re, instructs the goddess Hathor to destroy humankind as punishment for its plots of rebellion. He subsequently relents, but in order to reverse his directive, he must resort to subterfuge to fool the goddess who doggedly pursues her prey. In the morning following her carnage, she drinks what she assumes is blood resulting from her first foray, but it is in reality, beer-mash dyed red. After satiating her thirst, she becomes inebriated and is unable to complete her task. In this way humankind is saved from destruction. In the story, it is Re who orders his high priest to grind the red ochre, thereby dying the beer and effecting the necessary trick. It is perhaps also noteworthy that Re has the title of the King of Upper and Lower Egypt. There is even a later parallel to this story in the Demotic period involving the pharaoh Amasis, (Posener 1960, 98), and there, the king is referred to as the king of both gods and men.

Another struggle, this time between the divinities Isis and Re, occurs in a story where Isis manages to force Re to divulge his secret name to her. She is described as being "craftier than a million men, choicer than a million gods, and more discerning than a million of the noble dead" (Wilson 1955, 12-14; Hornung 1982a, 86-87). Although a powerful goddess, she lacks the knowledge she wishes. Moreover, Re, the supreme deity appears to be in total ignorance of the motives of his daughter Isis, and he apparently is unaware of the tricks she uses to gain her information. Again, it is clear that the divinities possess powers beyond those of man and his ruler, but that they are also subject to some of their weaknesses.

The Middle Kingdom story of the *Wanderings of Sinuhe* records the adventures of a self-exile from Egypt and his triumphant return home to the palace of Senwosret I (Lichtheim 1973, 222-235 [translation]; Simpson 1972, 57-74 [translation] and Simpson, 1984, 950-955). In the text, the king of Egypt is referred to in lofty terms, and he is even called a "good god" (Sinuhe R 12). Unlike a deity, however, he does not know the future, nor is he omniscient, since he had to be informed of his father's death. In a clearly rhetorical remark, Sinuhe makes the contrast between the two states clear: "Is god ignorant of what he has ordained?" (Sinuhe B126; Silverman 1980, 41 and n. 227)

As the narration approaches the conclusion, the traveler Sinuhe, who clearly wishes to end his days in his native land, receives an enthusiastic response from the king. He then formally, and in language one might expect in official texts, likens the king to several deities. It is not the only time in the texts that he uses such expressions; he had done so earlier in the story, in response to a question put to him about the situation in Egypt after the old king's death (Sinuhe B 45-74 and B 230-238). According to Sinuhe, it was his sovereign who had the ability to provide the air necessary for his servant to breathe.

These clearly exaggerated statements are unusual in literary texts, but they would not be out of place in the more formal language of the religious and official texts. The appearance here of such remarks, however, could be considered as rather exceptional. Perhaps they should be understood as quotations,

spoken excerpts of official language. They are in clear contrast to
the passages where the king's death and ignorance of certain facts
are described. Still, the tale, contains a reference to the almost
miraculous effect pharaoh's voice had on Sinuhe's senses (Sinuhe
B 254-56). Further, the royal children affirm that their father had
the power to give breath to the breathless (Sinuhe B 275). This
latter ability is well-attested in scenes found in temples and tombs,
but, there, a deity would provide it to a king. No religious scenes
exist wherein pharaoh is portrayed in such an attitude towards his
subjects (Posener 1956, 65-66).

It is possible that the *Wanderings of Sinuhe* may have been a
literary attempt to combine two views of the king, both an official
and a more realistic one. Moreover, the portrayal of the sovereign
in this story may have had propagandistic overtones and might,
therefore, have been in part an effort to depict the new king to
the best advantage—as a sensitive and compassionate ruler. Posener has noted that such nuances in literature are especially frequent in the Wisdom Texts (Posener 1956, esp. ch. 3). He would,
however, tend to see the story of Sinuhe as official literature from
the court of the king (Posener 1956, ch. 3 and Posener 1960, 89),
despite the fact that the "human" side of the king is clearly in
evidence (Tobin 1989, 89-91).

The Teachings of Merikare further indicates the different levels of
interpretation in Egyptian kingship. It distinguishes the aspects of
man, king, god, and royal office, and it may well reflect an
underlying sentiment prevalent among many Egyptians:

> ...the ruler of the Two Banks is a wise man, and a king who possesses
> an entourage cannot act stupidly. He is wise from birth, and god will
> distinguish him above millions of men. The kingship is a goodly of-
> fice; it has no sin and it has no brother who shall make its monu-
> ments endure, yet it is the one person who ennobles the other.
> (Simpson 1972, 190)

While it appears, at least officially, that the ancient Egyptians
viewed their rulers with respect, informally, they saw their mortal
weaknesses. The people continuously displayed piety for their
sovereign in words and action. There were numerous building
projects, statues, texts, and artifacts created in honor of or in the
name of pharaoh that are a testimony of their faith. The
architectural monuments often could be dedicated to the
reigning ruler, or could be specifically reserved for the cult of his

deified form, after his life on earth. There are even those structures, especially in the New Kingdom, that were built for the cult of the living deified king (Bell 1985a, 251-294). In contrast to these works in honor of the pharaoh, however, is contemporaneous evidence that shows that the living monarch was not always the recipient of the expected reverence and respect. For example, there is a pornographic graffito, apparently depicting Queen Hatshepsut of the Eighteenth Dynasty; it was found among textual graffiti that stylistically date to about the same period of time (Wente 1984, 48; Silverman 1982, 278; Romer 1984, 157-160; Manniche 1977, 22). All of them were inked on the walls of a grotto not far from the Queen's mortuary temple. In the scene, the reigning pharaoh is nude and depicted as the passive recipient of sexual advances, hardly a representation befitting the sovereign.

It is likely that this sexually explicit portrayal was intended as political satire. Hatshepsut was the daughter of one pharaoh and the major wife of another, and she broke with tradition when she assumed the throne of the designated heir Thutmose III (the son of a minor wife). Even though she had herself depicted on temple walls in full royal regalia as a male and often had the grammar of the official texts altered to refer to her in the masculine gender, her break with tradition was apparently, as is clear in this case, an object of derision among at least some of her subjects. They expressed their feelings extremely clearly in the sketch, and they placed their commentary in an area—not very far from her mortuary temple—that did not have a difficult access.

The artist of the sketch was undoubtedly the author of a nearby inscription in which he utilized only traditional funerary expressions in his prayer. According to the identification, he was neither a disreputable figure nor an iconoclast; he was a scribe attached to the construction work on the temple of Hatshepsut (Wente 1984, 48-52). His disrespect was not aimed at the office, but at the individual in it, and perhaps more specifically, only at the human element. It is interesting to note that other visitors to this spot, some of whom were priests, saw no reason to alter the depiction. The ancient Egyptians were not adverse to expressing satire, but they directed it more commonly against foreigners or enemies. This grotto has another example of a lack of proper respect for the office of the pharaoh in that one obviously private individual even wrote his name on the wall within a royal

cartouche. We may see some other examples of a lack of reverence or satire in the stories of the Middle Kingdom through some
of the negative characteristics attributed to the king. It is possible
that a statuette from the Amarna period that depicts monkeys
cleaning each other, may also belong to the same tradition; it may
be a satirical analogy for the intimate scenes of royal family life in
which Akhenaten, Nefertiti, and their daughters ordinarily were
portrayed (Silverman 1982, 280).

The artisans and writers who produced these items of parody
did not actually do any damage to the person of the ruler; they
merely continued a tradition of ancient Egyptian culture, that of
parody and satire. Even the gods were not immune from such
treatment, as seen in such stories as the *Contendings of Horus and
Seth.* The deities, however, were safe from physical harm for the
most part, the Amarna Period not withstanding. Pharaoh, in contrast, was susceptible to such attack, and there are several texts
that detail acts of aggression against the physical being of both the
living and dead king. Plots against reigning monarchs were known
to have taken place throughout history, and, while some were
discovered and prevented, others were successfully carried out.

Tomb robbery papyri describe more than the physical abuse
heaped upon the royal corpses; they record theft of valuables
from temples and royal tombs. The documents of the subsequent
proceedings in the court contain the captured criminal's description of his own actions against not only the physical and material
remains of the deceased sovereigns but also the cult temple
associated with these individuals:

> They [the officials] said to him: Tell us all the gold which you
> stripped belonging to the House of Gold of King Usermare
> Setepenre, the great god [probably the mortuary temple of Ramses
> II, the Ramesseum], and also every man who was with you and who
> went to strip the gold of the door jambs ... [and]... he said, I went ...
> along with my confederates ... [and] brought away two deben of
> gold ... and divided it among us (adapted from Peet 1930, 117).

and

> [We went to] his burial place(?) ... [and we] found the burial place
> of the royal wife Nub-Khaas in the place ... It was protected ... with
> plaster ... We forced it open ... and we found her lying there like-
> wise. We opened their outer coffins and their inner coffins in which
> they lay. We found this noble mummy of the king equipped like a

warrior(?). A large number of sacred-eye amulets and ornaments of gold was at his neck, and his headpiece of gold was on him. The noble mummy of this king was all covered with gold, and his inner coffins bedizened with gold and silver inside and outside with inlays of all kinds of precious [materials]. We appropriated the gold which we found on this noble mummy of this god and on his eyes amulets and his ornaments which were at his neck .... [We found] the royal wife ... and we appropriated all that we found on her too. We set fire to their inner coffins. We stole their ... objects of gold, silver, and bronze and divided them up among ourselves ... (adapted from Peet 1930, 48-49).

The robbers referred to the "noble mummy of this god," but the respect was in words, not actions, for the body was stripped of all valuables and then set afire. Such a fate was not destined for all rulers, and the officials of the necropolis were able to capture some thieves before excessive damage had taken place. The best example of their success would undoubtedly be the tomb of Tutankhamun. It is apparent that this tomb had experienced at least one intrusion and that some of the robbers were caught in the act. The disarray that Carter saw when he discovered the burial place of the young king was due in large part to the ancient priests who quite hastily put things in order and re-sealed the tomb after the robbery (Carter 1923, 188-189; Edwards 1977, 68). Despite the fact that magnificent treasures still remained inside, much of the jewelry not associated directly with the mummy probably had been looted. The unguents and oils apparently suffered the same fate, and greasy fingerprints found on some of the vessels may well be the marks of the ancient thieves.

In certain other cases, those in charge were too late to prevent the theft of royal burial objects because the criminals had successfully worked in secrecy for many years. Ultimately, however, these thieves too were discovered. While even some of the royal treasures were long gone, most of the mummies still survived. The bodies were re-wrapped, marked with identification, and placed in safer areas. There they remained undisturbed for centuries until modern tomb robbers discovered the ancient cache in which they were hidden (Harris and Wente 1980, xi). It is clear from these events that the pharaoh's final resting place was neither final nor a place of rest. In fact, most tombs probably were violated within a few years after their being sealed. Moreover, it is clear that such a robbery was not limited to the later New Kingdom; apparently it occurred throughout history.

It may seem difficult to understand the continuation of this blasphemous activity against the king while outwardly words and gestures of respect proliferated. It was the monarchy, however, that apparently survived these attacks, even if the individual monarch did not.

The record of the actions of the tomb and temple robbers of the Twenty-first Dynasty makes it perfectly clear that some of the people living at the time were quite aware of the vulnerability and mortality of their living king, and they were willing to risk repercussions by the royal police force. Those who were in charge of the necropolis, the judges who heard the cases, and the scribes who recorded them were among the individuals who were equally familiar with the attacks on pharaoh. Seeing such activity, they must have had some difficulty in accepting totally the traditional and official understanding that their ruler was divine.

Most of the population appears to have been involved in the continued royal funerary activities and the associated rituals that continued after the king's death, if one can judge from the archaeological and written remains. These people had participated in festivals, sung hymns, and served in the cults of the living king and then in the mortuary establishments of the deceased king. Yet the dichotomy persisted. There were continued violent assaults against the embalmed remains of royal figures and thefts of the valuables from the tombs and temples of kings and queens. These crimes occurred even though the concept of the divinity of the deceased pharaoh had been a tradition from early periods in Egyptian history. It was a part of the funerary religion, and texts attested that the ruler would join the ranks of the divinities after his death. Undoubtedly, the greed of the tomb robbers more than compensated for any fear the thieves may have had over the eventual vengeance of the new god. The practice of mummification and the associated burial rites continued throughout Egyptian history, and the ancient Egyptians must have placed much weight on the acts and rituals that were part of the funerary practices. In their somewhat intellectualized view, this process allowed the deceased ruler to become one with the divinities and transcend the earthly realm. What eventually happened to their mortal remains apparently was less critical than the assurance that all the correct and necessary funerary rites had been carried out (Wente 1982, 25).

There are other texts that record the activity of the citizenry who actually worked in the royal necropolis. In Papyrus Salt 124, which dates to the late New Kingdom, there are listed charges against certain workers including excesses with women, thievery, false swearing, and even sitting on the sarcophagus of a pharaoh (Černý 1929, 243-258). This last action might be considered blasphemous, since the coffin was for the king, and it may indicate an attitude that was less than respectful toward the pharaoh. It must be tempered, however, with evidence that shows that pharaoh was understood by his subjects to consist of several aspects. It is difficult to envision an ancient Egyptian treating a divine object in such a manner, but it must be remembered that the *Tomb Robbery Papyri* contain accounts of objects associated with deities that had been stolen from royal mortuary temples.

Another New Kingdom text records the world's first organized confrontation between labor and management. The *Turin Strike Papyrus* (Edgerton 1951, 137-145) relates the plight of unhappy workers who staged their protest at the rear of the mortuary temple of Thutmose III. Later they proceeded to demonstrate before the mortuary temple of Ramses II, the Ramesseum, into which they entered on the following day. To these people, their respect for the monuments of their deified rulers and the possibility of divine, not to mention pharaonic, retribution concerned them less than their need for the necessities of life on earth.

At the same time, this very culture produced an extremely large collection of inscriptions referring to and extolling the deified ruler, and examples from all periods abound. Early scholars were aware of these texts, and when they wrote on the subject of kingship they stressed the portrayal of the king as a divine entity, who undoubtedly was a god upon earth. Careful scrutiny reveals their sources to have been for the most part funerary in nature, and the validity of their view is seriously challenged by a broader approach that takes into consideration all aspects of the culture. Still, most scholars today would agree that interpretations based primarily upon funerary literature and related artifactual material would lead to the same conclusions.

In the Pyramid Texts, the earliest large collection of religious inscriptions, the king is usually addressed as the Osiris, King so and so, thus equating him with that deity in an implied metaphor. There are some spells where the identification takes places within the text, and they can take the forms of an implicit or explicit metaphor. For example, Utterance 219: "This one here is your son Osiris" (Faulkner, 1969a, 46); Utterance 258: "The king is Osiris" (Faulkner, 1969a, 67); and others such as Utterances 259 and 650. In addition, the pharaoh is identified with Re, the solar deity, similarly in, among others, Utterances 257 and 569. The Pyramid Texts identify other gods and goddesses with the sovereign, such as Horus (Utterance 478), Sia (Utterance 250), Sobek (Utterance 317), Thoth (Utterance 478), Satis (Utterance 439), and Geb (Utterance 599).

Specific body parts of the king can also be equated with a deity in metaphorical language: wing-feathers with Thoth (Utterance 524 and 724); flesh with Atum (Utterance 537); lips with the Two Enneads (Utterance 506); the face with Wepwawet (Utterance 424); arms, shoulder, belly, back, hind-parts, and legs with Atum; face with Anubis (Utterance 213); fingers with Shu and Mafdet (Utterance 385); and many more parts and deities in Utterances 215 and 539.

The simile is another literary device used in these texts. By means of the preposition/conjunction *mi* "like"/"as" the king can associate himself with all manner of divinities in the form of a simile, for example: "You have descended like a jackal of Upper Egypt as Anubis on the baldachin" (Utterance 659; Faulkner 1969a, 271); "I am girded as Horus ... I am on high as Wepwawet" (Utterance 559; Faulkner 1969a, 215; and "I shine in the east like Re" (Utterance 467; Faulkner 1969a, 156). The deceased royal figure is often in the company of deities, acting in a manner similar to them, treated the same as they, cared for as they, and engendered by them. There can be no mistake about the clear attempt to show and emphasize the divine nature of the king in these texts.

Later funerary literature is no less emphatic in indicating deification of the dead pharaoh and his exalted position in the company of deities. The walls of the royal tombs display many of these texts, such as the *Book of the Amduat* (*What is in the Underworld*) (Figure 2.1), *The Book of Gates, The Litany of Re*, and *The Book of Caverns*: "May the soul (ba) of (the) king pass into the following of He of the Horizon (Re)" (Piankoff 1954, 80). The mortuary literature in large part both illustrates and records the deceased pharaoh's divine place and identifies him with both the chthonic deities, headed by Osiris, and the solar deities, headed by Re (Wente 1982, 19 and 22-25). The former provide him with immortality based on an eternal rejuvenation and the latter with everlastingness, based on a daily cyclical rebirth (ibid, 1982, 19-26; Silverman 1991a, 72-73).

The existence and perpetuation of mortuary establishments for the pharaohs from the earliest periods throughout history would tend to support the notion that the deceased rulers could achieve immortality through the constant restating of their deification in both words and actions. The funerary literature was an integral part of this program which included the tomb, with its statuary, reliefs and equipment, the mortuary temple with its statuary, reliefs and associated rituals, and the bureaucratic organization established to operate the mortuary cult (Hawass 1987, 628-633, and Murnane 1980, 6-75).

The divine-like nature of the king can also be referred to in non-royal literature, associated with private funerary programs. For example, in the biographical inscriptions, the tomb owners attempt to record for eternity important events in their lives upon earth, and in so doing they make frequent references to the reigning monarch. In one case from the Old Kingdom the nature of the king expressed in the texts appears at first to be comparable to that found in the royal funerary texts (Urk. I. 39: 12-16):

> He knows, together with the entire retinue that if anything issues forth from the mouth of his majesty, it comes into being immediately. God has given to him wisdom already in the womb (or knowledge of things concerning the body) in as much as he is more noble than any god (Doret 1986, 88).

While the super-human quality of the king is in clear contrast to that of the author of the inscription, it is also somewhat differentiated from that of the god. Whereas divinities have their powers intrinsically, kings, as indicated here, receive them from the higher powers. The monarch's nobility, superior to that of the gods, is the explicit reason for his receiving his omniscience. Unlike the examples quoted from the funerary texts, where there is direct identification of the kings with divinities, the biographical inscriptions tend to make some distinctions between the two. This characterization would appear natural, since the former texts deal with the deceased deified pharaoh, while the latter refer to the deceased individual while he was on earth and to his relationship with the living ruler during that time.

Harkhuf, another Old Kingdom official recorded a letter the king sent him (Lichtheim 1973, 26-27). In it the ruler is portrayed not as a grand, removed super-human figure but an anxious, concerned individual:

> You have said in this your report that you were bringing a pygmy ... come northward to the palace immediately! Hurry! Bring this pygmy with you ... Inspect (him) ten times during the night (Urk. I. 128: 15-30).

What is important to Harkhuf was that he was in close contact with his king and that he had received a written communication from him. Apparently it was also desirable and noteworthy to record any instance of physical contact with the ruler. A contemporaneous noble Washptah was elated to record in his inscription: "Then his majesty said... Do not kiss the ground, kiss my foot." (Urk. I, 41: 15) Another official, Rawer, thought it important to record in his text that the scepter of his majesty struck his foot (see however, Allen 1992, 17).

Such incidents are further evidence of a multifaceted view of both the individual who ruled the country and the office that he held. Terminology referring to both was different for different genres of texts. The word *ḥm* which occurs mainly in biographical inscriptions and occasions when the physical embodiment of the pharaoh is referred to, is often translated "majesty." In the secular texts subjects can address their king through use of this term (Goedicke 1960, 51-79; Barta 1978, 478 and Allen 1992, 18 and the references in n. 20) or some other circumlocution, such as "the heart of" or "the wish of." The king, when speaking, uses the same expression *ḥm*: "My majesty (physical presence) has ...."

For the less personal, more abstract designations of the office, the term *nswt* "king" (ordinarily without the name of a specific monarch following it for this nuance) occurs. It was the *nswt* that was active in legal situations, official documents, certain decrees, specific events, and endowments. *Nswt* was also referred to in biographical inscriptions. That it was distinct from *ḥm* is quite clear. Whereas the latter is absent in the royal funerary literature, the former does, although rarely, occur: "Merenre has appeared as king" (PT 1138b). Considering the context of this passage, it would seem to denote the divine aspect of the office; a function not shared by *ḥm*.

The distinction is made even clearer in passages from two Old

Kingdom biographical inscriptions (Wilson 1947, 241-242). An inscription in the tomb of Ny-ankh-Sekhmet records that the false doors for this tomb chapel were to be produced through the authority (*r-gs*) of the *nswt* itself (*ds.f*) (Urk. I. 38: 16). In the inscription of Khufu-ankh a similar situation is recorded. Here, however, not only was the stone structure made under the auspices (*r-gs*) of the *nswt* itself (*ds.f*) the king actually came to see the work: "while his *ḥm* (physical embodiment) watched through the course of every day" (Reisner 1942, 65b). Generally the construction of false doors, offering tables, and other architectural elements of a private tomb or chapel were not events exceptional enough for use in a tomb biography. In these instances, however, the intercession of the royal office in regard to the production was considered important enough for inclusion, and *nswt ds.f* was chosen as the means of expressing it. Even more extraordinary was the record of the king's daily attention to the activity undertaken through an apparent order from the office (cf. Reisner 1955, 55-56), and it appears that the phrase *r-gs nswt ds.f* in these passages refers to it. (See also Urk. I. 232: 15 and Allen 1992, 15.) Other examples of *r-gs nswt* also occur, and there is even one text that has, in addition, a contrasting line with *r-gs ḥm* (Urk. I. 60: 4-6, and see also Urk. I. 43:11), again making the distinction clear between the office and the individual. (Goedicke, 1960, 31, prefers "kingship" and "its representative.")

Another designation *nswt-bity*, ordinarily translated as "King of Upper and Lower Egypt (See Figure 2.2)," appears to refer to the divine office, and it usually is followed by the name of the specific monarch. (See Figure 2.2) However, like *nswt* alone, it too occurs in the funerary literature, further evidence for associating these expressions with the divine/deified aspects: "It is because you have power over the gods and their kas that you have appeared as King of Upper and Lower Egypt" (PT 776 a-b). For the most part, however, *nswt-bity* and the royal name represented a combined phrase that occurs in the official texts when it was necessary to indicate more specifically that a particular royal office was responsible for the action, decree, document, or decision. This term seems to occur in the same range of literature as the simple *nswt*, but that was apparently a less general reference to the divine office.

The king can also be referred to as *nb*, "lord," and this term occurs in epithets and titles of private citizenry. In the Sixth

Dynasty, private individuals recorded in their biographies letters from the king, and he refers to himself in the same manner. In these texts, it is also that term which is used when royal praise for the tomb owner is given. In a few cases (Urk I. 61, 6; 63, 4; 129, 5; 179, 17) there seem to be parallel passages where ḥm or the personal name of the king, without any introductory terms, occurs, indicating perhaps that at this point in time, nb was becoming more related to the personal, rather than to the official side of the king (Goedicke 1960, 46-49 and 80-87).

Other expressions and circumlocutions do occur during this time period, and their quite specified use shows a distinct distribution among different genres of texts, at least as far as the Old Kingdom is concerned, and to some extent the later periods as well. This situation would seem to indicate that the Egyptians utilized different terminology to deal with the many aspects that they understood to be embodied in pharaoh: the human holder of the office, the office itself, the divine element, the administrator, the military, etc.

Clearly the individual who came to the throne could not hope to make the people forget or deny his human origins, but through ritual, the acceptance of an eternal office and an amalgamation with it, he could officially take on the divine attributes of the office. Such a concept is reflected perhaps in the Old Kingdom statue of Khafre, where the reigning mortal wears the royal garments, sits in (and is literally attached to) the royal throne of office. Behind his head and almost enveloping him in protective wings is the divine image of Horus, the symbol of the newly crowned king. (Figure 2.3) A further elaboration of this iconography is found in the Sixth Dynasty statue of Pepi I. In addition to the elements utilized in Khafre's statue, that of Pepi I incorporates also a serekh, a royal symbol on the back of the throne (see Figure 2.4 as well as below and Figure 2.5).

Political situations such as the power and/or personality of an individual ruler and the rising importance of the monarchy, military, bureaucracy, or priesthood might influence which aspect of the office might be emphasized at a particular time. Whether the people understood their leader to function in each role separately or they perceived him to be a multi-faceted composite being, they had seen him come from an origin similar to their own. Perhaps it was that fact that made it possible for them to consider him as an intermediary between them and the deities, beings who were clearly in a different realm.

Pharaoh was concrete; he could be seen; he could take an active and visible role on earth. The god's activities took place beyond the world of mankind and were perceived, not visualized. The divine images that stood in locations throughout the kingdom were merely temporary lifeless manifestations. The living pharaoh was a concrete being with a limited life span, while the gods were abstract concepts whose mythology endowed them with human (and, therefore, recognizable) qualities; they were for the most part, immortal (Silverman 1991a, 62-63; Tobin 1989, 89-102). The king lists visibly document this concept of the constant divine office animated by the individual, changeable ruler (von Beckerath 1979, 534-535; Barta 1979, 489), and they distinguish him clearly from the deities who are immutable. Yet there existed distinctions also between the new king and the rest of the living population. He was addressed differently than were others; his designations were changed; his persona was distinct; and his ultimate future lie in a world separate from that of humankind—one with the deities. In essence, it was his coronation, and hence, his accession to the throne that allowed him to transcend to another realm, but until death and his ultimate union with the world of the divine, he would be the link between the universe in which the ancient Egyptians lived and the one that they perceived, envisioned, and imagined.

It was the office of kingship that provided the ruler with that element of the divine that removed him from the sphere of mortal man. To a lesser degree of course but somewhat analogous, is the Presidency of the United States, the highest office of this land. The candidate who receives the greatest amount of votes is the one chosen to receive the title of President Elect. After participating in the rites of the office and taking its oath, the chosen one becomes the new chief of state; he has a new status; and reference to him in office is now Mr. President. Moreover, his place in history is then assured. His statements, decisions, comments, and views take on new significance, and they issue forth from the White House, his personified office/residence. Like this office, that of King of Upper and Lower Egypt was a constant; in theory, it existed forever and would continue in perpetuity. The individual within the office of pharaoh anthropomorphized it and allowed it to become a functioning authority

over the land. The concept itself was visualized from the early
periods as a *serekh*, a rectangular figure, ordinarily surmounted by
the divine symbol of the office, Horus. The lower part of the
rectangle has the form of the palace façade, while the upper
section contains the name of the reigning pharaoh (Figure 2.5).

It is unlikely, considering the evidence from a variety of written
sources, that the original mortal nature of pharaoh was ever
totally eclipsed by the divine aspect of the office. His subjects
treated him with the respect due his position, but not infrequently referred to him in a manner befitting his original human
status. We have already seen examples of political satire in graffiti
and literature. Evidence from private letters can sometimes rein-
force this view: "Another matter: As for Pharaoh, may he live, be
prosperous and healthy, how shall he reach this land (or perhaps
how has he reached this earth?)? and of whom is pharaoh, may he
live, be prosperous and healthy, superior still?" (Wente 1967, 53)
This actual letter from the Ramesside Period is clearly in contrast
to one of the model letters that indicate the traditional way of
referring to royalty: "May you be in the favor of the king of your
time, the Horus who loves justice" (Caminos 1956, 176).

Despite the lofty terms in this guideline, another real letter
appears to call Ramses II "the general" (Janssen 1960, 39; Silverman 1991a, 60 and Wente 1990, 31). Officially, however, he could
be ranked with the gods as indicated by oaths sworn in the name
of the king as well as that of the gods throughout most of
Egyptian history (Wilson 1948, 130; Silverman 1991a, 67-68). Letters exchanged between the rulers of Egypt and those of foreign
lands contain passages that deal with affairs of state and
diplomacy, and they are couched in such terms that indicate a
fairly close and familiar relationship among the monarchs.
Undoubtedly scribes recorded and read all these documents,
some of which touch on problems of hurt feelings, deliberate
snubs, or—far more politically sensitive—the need expressed by
an Egyptian queen for a Hittite husband (Campbell 1964, 50-60;
Redford 1984, 217-218). In regard to the affairs of state the
scribes might have been reticent to speak, but the mundane details of royal life may well have been communicated to others.

This dichotomy, the divine functioning royal office and the
human/mortal essence of its holder, is especially reflected in New
Kingdom texts and reliefs detailing battles. For instance, the
Kadesh inscription of Ramses II, referred to earlier, describes the

ruler in lofty, divine epithets, but it also relates his dependence upon the god Amun for aid in winning his battle:

> Do good to him who counts on you, then one will serve you with loving heart. I call to you my father Amun ... I know Amun helps me more than a million troops ... O Amun, I have not transgressed your command (Lichtheim 1976, 65-66).

It was not uncommon for pharaohs of the New Kingdom to ask for, receive, and then thank Amun for victories over their enemies. Temple walls are covered with texts and reliefs illustrating these dedications.

Just as the clear dependence of royalty upon the higher powers is clearly reflected in the iconography and texts of this period of time, so is the portrayal of pharaoh as a super-human figure. In regard to the latter is the increasing prominence of deification of the ruling king during the New Kingdom. We have already seen that divinity for the deceased king was an established belief in Egyptian theology, and this fact has been recognized and studied by many scholars over the last several decades.

Early artifactual evidence and passages from the Pyramid Texts substantiate that each royal figure upon death became one with the gods. Just to what extent that state existed for the ruling king has been the subject of much Egyptological research during the recent past. (Bell 1985a, 251-294; b, 31-59; and 1986; Moftah 1985, 198-265 and Barta 1975, and 1979; and Tobin 1989, 89-102 represent only a few of the references.) Indeed, much of the first part of this chapter has been devoted to the explication of the aspect of the divine that the king received from the office of pharaoh and the importance of the rituals associated with the coronation and accession.

It is clear, however, that there are other rituals that were enacted in order to imbue the king with divine powers. Among them are the celebration of the jubilee and the raising of the *djed*-pillar (Wente 1969, 90; Bleeker 1967, 116-117), and they occur throughout Egyptian history. It is, however, the ritual of the divine birth of Amenhotep III, as illustrated on reliefs and documented through texts on the walls of the Luxor Temple, along with the cult of the king's ka and the celebration of the Feast of the Opet (Bell 1985a, 251-294) that represent for us the best detailed records of any living king. Amenhotep II had this part of Luxor Temple constructed, but he clearly did not originate the concept.

Indeed, there are good indications that several earlier kings
attempted in similar manners to emphasize their divinity while
upon earth. But none prior to Amenhotep III appears to have
expressed it to the degree and the extent that he had.

Already in the earlier part of the Eighteenth Dynasty, during
the reign of Queen Hatshepsut, there were clear indications of an
emphasis being placed on this concept. She chose to have her
divine birth recorded in text and scenes and placed on the walls
of her mortuary temple. In addition to her divinity by right of
coronation and accession, she also felt the need to claim it by
divine birth. The Opet Feast (records of which do not predate the
Eighteenth Dynasty), which appears to be connected with the
deification of the king, was represented in her chapel at Karnak,
and fragments of relief indicate that it was also part of the
decoration of her mortuary temple at Deir el Bahri (Murnane
1981, 573-579; Bell 1985a, 290-291). It is possible that this
particular ruler felt it necessary to reiterate her divinity because
her accession to the throne was hardly routine. She may well have
been responsible for introducing the scenes of divine birth and
emphasizing the Feast of Opet and the cult of the royal ka in an
attempt to compensate for her unorthodox assumption of the
throne (Bell 1985a, 291). Indeed, if the satirical graffito nearby
(see above) can be accepted as evidence, she had good reason to
emphasize her divinity and thus reaffirm her position.

Whether this is the only, or ultimate, motive for the directions
she took remains to be seen. The reliefs illustrating the divine
birth of the queen on the walls of her mortuary temple in
connection with fragmentary reliefs of what appear to be scenes
from the Opet found in the same site are explicit references to
deification and the rites thereof.

But, like most other concepts, they may have had their roots in,
or were at least analogous to, scenes that were portrayed, texts
that were recorded, and rituals that were performed in mortuary
complexes throughout Egyptian history. For example, while she
did emphasize the cult of the royal ka, the concept had been
established previously, and earlier representations of, and textual
reference to, the royal ka are not uncommon. Cults of living kings
had been introduced much earlier. (Wildung 1979, 533-535; Kaplony 1978, 275-282; Jacobsohn 1939, 49-61; Bell 1985a, 255-258;
Greven 1952, 15-27 and 35-44). Moreover, Old Kingdom mortuary complexes incorporated in their decoration, not funerary

scenes, but programs of coronation and revivification that were inextricably linked with deification, divine birth, and divine kingship (Hawass and O'Connor discuss this point elsewhere in this volume [Hawass 1987, 492-536]). Recent excavation has provided information suggesting that palace structures may have been part of the mortuary complexes of some of the Middle Kingdom pharaohs at Lisht and Dahshur. There is the possibility that such edifices may also have existed at the Old Kingdom site of Abu Sir. It has also been observed that there are texts and scenes that depict the Eleventh Dynasty pharaoh Mentuhotep as Harsomtus, the son of the goddess Hathor, and that she is also pictured suckling the king (Gestermann 1984, 768-776). The implications with divine birth are clear. Hathor in bovine form is also pictured at Deir el Bahri several centuries later suckling Hatshepsut.

That the concept of divine birth of royalty was comprehended well already by the Middle Kingdom is made expressly clear in the *Westcar Papyrus*, a popular literary text:

> Who is she, the aforementioned Reddjedet? Then Djedi said: She is the wife of a wab-priest of Re, Lord of Sethebu, she being pregnant with the children of Re (Papyrus Westcar 9, 9-10; Lichtheim 1973, 219).

Later in the same text, when the three children are born, they are described in divine terms and identified as the first three rulers of the Fifth Dynasty. They are engendered by a male deity and a mortal female, the same god used later by Hatshepsut and other rulers for texts and reliefs on the walls of their temples. While political and religious implications may underlie this episode in the story, (Posener 1960, 90-92) the point remains that the concept of divine birth was apparently well-known already at that time (Barta 1975, 22-29 and Berlev 1981, 367-369; see, however, Kemp 1989, 197).

Moreover, the royal epithet *s3 R^c* "son of Re" (see Figure 2.6) had appeared already in the Fourth Dynasty with the name of the ruling pharaoh Djedefre (Kaplony 1979, 642), and the use of this term implies that the concept was conceived of quite early. In the royal titulary, the epithet occurs with the nomen of the king, suggesting that once coronation had taken place, that particular individual had become the son of a god and, he had, therefore, ascended to the realm of the divine. The later addition of *ḥt.f* "of his body," (WB III: 410, 11) seems an unnecessary edification.

Some scholars, however, would still classify this role as sub-ordinate to that of a god (Hornung 1982a, 142; Posener 1960, 34-35). It would appear, however, that the use of the expression *s3 Rᶜ* might support the notion that, once in his official position in the office of pharaoh, having ascended to the throne, the ruler received divinity retroactively (Hornung 1982a, 142).

The divinity of the ruling king may well have been conceived of early in Egyptian history, as the evidence noted above suggests, even though it may have been expressed more implicitly than explicitly. The material available today indicates that it was brought to new heights in the New Kingdom, when the depiction of the birth scenes in the temples of this period were coordinated with the rituals of the cult of the ka, and the newly introduced Feast of Opet. It was Amenhotep III who brought all the elements together at the temple of Amun at Luxor. Representations of the deified ruler from that time on were not uncommon at sites throughout Egypt and even beyond its borders. The birth scenes, however, remain rare outside the Luxor temple until their use in the Mamisi of the later periods. It has been suggested that the reason for this situation was that the special nature of the Luxor Temple allowed it to be utilized by all pharaohs (Bell 1985a, 280). Unfortunately, it is not possible to ascertain whether Amenhotep III's now destroyed mortuary temple contained scenes of divine birth, like that of Hatshepsut. Nor is it possible to determine whether Hatshepsut herself had birth reliefs commissioned at any place other than Deir el Bahri.

In the beginning of his reign, Amenhotep III's son, Amenhotep IV continued the tradition established by his father. However, it becomes apparent today, through archaeological, artifactual, iconographical, and textual evidence, that he quickly began forging new directions. Such a move can be seen in regard to the cult of the royal ka. The ka of the king, which had been part of the traditional beliefs for many centuries and had occurred in iconography and texts, was still utilized in scenes early in his reign. However, already in the Theban tombs of the officials Kheruef and Parennefer, which were executed before the king moved to Amarna, the royal ka is shown in a fairly abstract form, rather than in the more usual anthropomorphic one (Figure 2.7). Eventually, the latter type was deleted from the repertoire and it was omitted from any artistic expression at Amarna (Bell 1985a,

292). Ostensibly, this representation was avoided because it was considered part of the traditional views that the new king had now abandoned. It has been suggested (ibid.) that in an attempt "to deny any separation of the royal ka and the person of the king," the pharaoh decided to omit such depictions.

It has already been observed that proponents of the new religion attempted to remove the offensive figures from the Luxor Temple but left the hieroglyphic image, the upstretched arms, untouched (Nims 1965, 128; Bell 1985a, 291-292). By this act the pharaoh was perhaps trying to eradicate any visual reference to anything other than a single being incorporating the royal physical presence and the ka. It has even been suggested that "the king himself [was] the royal ka" and at the same time that the new godhead, "the creator Aten" now constituted the king's ka (Bell 1985a, 292).

It is possible perhaps to view the changes in another way. The fact that the figure of the king's ka was not represented at Amarna may indicate that the pharaoh (now called Akhenaten) introduced neither an implicit nor invisible royal ka in his own person, as has been suggested (Bell, 1985 and 1986), but rather he brought into being the concept of an explicit divine ka of the king. It is perhaps just this idea that Akhenaten intended to express when he added the phrase ꜥnḫ m mꜣꜥt "living on *maat*" to most of the examples of kꜣ nswt "ka of the king" that occur in some funerary formulae at Amarna (See for example Sandman 1938, 26: 5, 7, 15, 18). Since only gods as a rule, lived on *maat* (Hornung 1982a, 213-216), joining this epithet to kꜣ nswt would imply that the ka of the king, and hence, the king himself was divine. This interpretation is supported perhaps by the appearance of the same phrase after sꜣ.k, "your son," which is in turn followed by the king's name and the epithet pꜣy.i nṯr "my god" (Sandman 1938, 76: 9-10). The expression pꜣy.i nb, "my lord" (ibid, 76: 14-15), sꜣ Rꜥ, "son of Re" (ibid, 149, 2, among others) and nswt bity, "King of Upper and Lower Egypt" (ibid, 147, 12, among others) are other examples of royal designations followed by ꜥnḫ m mꜣꜥt (The expression, however, is not unique to Akhenaten and was apparently also used for Amenhotep I (WB II 20, 61; for further references and later examples see Keller, 1994, 151-152 and note 30.)

Interestingly enough, ꜥnḫ m mꜣꜥt does not occur after kꜣ nswt in the tomb of the official Parennefer (Sandman 1938, 140, 19), but

since this tomb was built prior to the move to Amarna the concept
might not yet have been introduced to the texts. The king's divine
ka, however, may well have been introduced into the reliefs in a
very simple form in the Theban tombs just noted above (See
Figure 2.7). Here the upstretched arms enclose the personal
name of the king that is encircled in a cartouche; above is situated
the solar disc. All of the necessary elements, although somewhat
abstracted, were present: the person of the king (through his
name), the ka (the transitional element for transformation into
the divinity), and the disc (the manifestation of the creator deity
itself).

Each of the components delineated in this rather abstract
image can also be recognized in a figurative representation that
becomes commonplace at Amarna (Figure 2.8). Again the disc of
the sun, now clearly the Aten, is at the top of the scene; the
physical presence of pharaoh, however, is represented now by his
image, rather than simply his name. An apparently new feature is
the series of rays that extend downward from the sun and end in
hands. These rays, however, also function as arms, and as such can
offer protection and nourishment to the king directly from Aten.
In other words, the traditional concept of the protecting and
nourishing ka (te Velde 1990, 94), as seen in the more abstracted
representation in the tombs of Kheruef (See Figure 2.7) and
Parennefer is incorporated into the new iconography. Previously
the ka had been represented by the hieroglyph with upraised
arms ⊔ ; now this concept is translated into the rays, which
according to nature must project down, from the sun to the earth.
These limbs are the new god's only anthropomorphic element,
and the hands are shown offering life and sometimes dominion to
the king. Akhenaten in physical form (rather than in the earlier
abstraction of his name) is again represented within the arms that
nourish him, provide life for him, and recreate him daily. Each of
these activities is recorded in many of the Amarna hymns. This
iconographic symbol omnipresent at Amarna represents the
interrelated elements of divinity: the Aten, the ka, and Akhenaten,
and it indicates the closeness of the relationship among them. Of
course other interpretations of this image are possible, and one
scholar has suggested that the image of the Aten with rays derives
ultimately from the hieroglyph meaning "light" (Assmann 1984a,
244).

Since Akhenaten's identification with the Aten and its "ka"

arms was so explicit in the iconography, it may well be that he no longer felt the need for the separate depiction of a royal ka, in the traditional sense. Earlier pharaohs had utilized that concept, combined with scenes of divine birth and the Opet Feast, for their own deification. Such ritual was unnecessary for Akhenaten, for in his theology he was the son of the disc that was reborn with his father the sun every day. He was called "your (Aten's) child who came from your rays" (Lichtheim 1976, 93). Akhenaten's theological changes allowed the living ruler to transcend the physical, earthly world which included his mortal origin and enter into a spiritual realm, wherein he intended to identify completely with his sole deity.

Traditional representations of the ka of the king are avoided at Amarna, but written references to it occur in the texts (for example, Sandman 1938, 5, 6, 17, 21, 65, 72). Many of these references are in regard to its divine nature; it is even worshipped, it lives on *maat*, and it is a creative force whose presence the deceased individual seeks to have (Lichtheim 1976, 94-95; Sandman, 1938, 26, 92-93). In his doctrines, Akhenaten tried to remove as much of the mortal element of the ruler as possible. His royal ancestors who had occupied this office acted, as has been noted above, as intermediaries between the gods and mankind. It was not Akhenaten's prime objective to be a mediator; he wished to be the focus of mortal interest and devotion. Support for this observation comes from both texts and representations. The scenes in private tombs reflect only those activities of the deceased that bear relation to the ruler/deity. No longer are the walls covered with traditional scenes of the afterlife—such as agriculture, fishing, fowling, and domestic activities. The iconography and texts of the underworld are also absent. No divine triads were referred to or represented. In the new theology, Osirian beliefs were unnecessary. Traditional eschatological scenes and texts and ancestor cults were apparently considered superfluous or inappropriate in the new repertoire for the private tombs.

In the place of all of these time-honored beliefs, texts, and iconographic elements was Akhenaten, his family and his deity— the Aten. Basically it was they who now replaced the entire pantheon of ancient Egypt. They would provide all that was necessary in this life and the next. In the past, myth had helped make concrete the original abstract concepts from which the deities

derived; myth anthropomorphized the gods; it put them in
human terms. In so doing, myth was essentially responsible for
helping the populace comprehend their supreme beings and the
forces that they represented (Silverman 1991a, 17-19 and 83-84).
Traditional mythology was not necessary during Akhenaten's
reign; in its place was the visual interaction and textual description of the relationship between the king and the Aten. The so-
called familial scenes of the royal figures and the deity should not
be understood as innovative iconography that provided glimpses
into the private life in the royal court; rather, they should be
viewed as emblems of the new mythology of the Aten. The myths,
stories, or relationships of triads of gods such as Osiris, Isis, and
Horus or Amun, Mut, and Khonsu were not compatible with the
new doctrines. Only the Aten and Akhenaten's family were
appropriate. Scenes and texts in private tombs reflect only the important events and activities of Akhenaten and the Aten. The
deceased is shown and referred to only in regard to the godhead
and his living representative. It is likely that the representations
were visual analogies to the (auto)biographical texts of the past,
where an individual would recall and record for posterity his
relationship with the king. The traditional formulaic inscriptions
requesting offerings are still present, but now they invoke only the
Aten, Akhenaten, or Nefertiti. Neither hymns nor prayers record
that the deceased would identify with either the Aten or Akhenaten in the next life, but rather that either or both were the
source of all that was needed by humankind. In the new doctrines
traditional funerary literature and vignettes were unnecessary.

The Egyptians had in the past come to expect a closeness with
and approachability to their deities while on earth and an
eventual oneness with them after death, provided that they had
met all of the necessary requirements. No such transformation
was possible now for humankind. The collection of helpful spells
inscribed on the walls of coffins and tombs, on the rolls of papyrus, and on the surfaces of images were now useless to them. Such
spells or rituals, interestingly enough, were also no longer
appropriate for Akhenaten or his family. He, however, did not
need transformation; he had already transcended to a unique
realm; he was a god upon earth, who was reborn every day to
become one with the only god. Mortals could apparently maintain
their former stations into perpetuity as entities subordinate to
and distinct from Akhenaten or the Aten. They would not become
one with the divine king nor the new godhead.

In order to record these new concepts, Akhenaten had the texts, including speeches, teachings, and hymns written in a style of language that was distinct from that previously used in such texts. Scholars have often seen in this apparently conscious change an attempt to express the language in a manner closer to the vernacular (Aldred 1973, 15), by recording more the patterns of speech. Indeed, the texts are not written in the classical style, but neither are they "written as if spoken" (Goldwasser 1990, 57-58), if one can judge from a comparison with the non-literary texts of the New Kingdom. Nor are they to be seen as an evolutionary stage or a simplified version of such later vernacular texts. True, the Amarna Texts make occasional use of some parts of speech that later become standard in vernacular Late Egyptian, such as the definite article, the possessive adjectives, the negatives *bw* and *bn*, circumstantial *iw*, and the pronominal compound. Occasionally, but to a much lesser extent, such features occur in texts as early as the late Old Kingdom. The category to which the earlier texts belong, however, is that of inscriptions which are to some degree closer to the spoken language than are the official texts of Akhenaten. The appearance of such grammatical features in the Amarna Texts is notable in that this was the first time that such elements occur with any regularity in more official texts. A few earlier official inscriptions do make use of such features (Kroeber 1970, XIX), but these elements occur neither with the frequency nor to the extent to which they do in Amarna texts. The Seventeenth Dynasty Stela of Kamose (Habachi 1972, 31-43; Smith and Smith 1976, 48-76) does employ the articles and possessive adjectives, but most constructions are written in the classical mode. It is important to note, however, that the overall style used in the Amarna texts hardly approaches that of vernacular language. Even though the definite articles, possessive adjective, and pronominal compound do appear, they are not used consistently. Moreover, the pronominal compound is not at all frequent. The Late Egyptian negative *bw* is sporadic, and most of the constructions in which it occurs are found eventually in later literary texts, not non-literary ones. Classical grammatical patterns and constructions predominate throughout the texts. This melange of styles is reminiscent of that used in the Late Egyptian stories; there, however, it is much more developed (Junge 1985, 1190-91). This similarity does not imply a direct link between the two; it does, however, emphasize the distinction between the grammar of vernacular-type (non-literary) texts and that of the Amarna inscriptions. It further emphasizes the uniqueness of Akhenaten's language, even though, as indicated above, such a composite system had been used before to a limited extent. [A successor for this style of writing may well be the language used in the *Bulletin* of the Kadesh Inscriptions of Ramses II (Lichtheim 1976, 60-62).]

It is clear that the language of the Amarna texts is less an attempt to introduce the spoken idiom into formal inscriptions than a move to develop a personal exclusive language tailored expressly for the new doctrines. Once it was introduced, its use spread to all types of texts.

The few letters surviving from this period (Wente 1990, 172-176), however, were composed in a different genre, one that was close to the vernacular and was quite distinct from that of the Amarna texts. This style may well represent an early developmental stage of the language used in Late Egyptian letters. (Silverman 1991b). This difference reflects the traditional stance between the genres of the non-literary and the more official texts. It also indicates that Akhenaten's changes were not all encompassing. A style similar to that found in these letters was apparently also used in a speech in the tomb of Parennefer (ibid.), the Theban official whose tomb was constructed prior to the move to Amarna. Later, such speeches that were inscribed in the tombs at Amarna used the "new" style of the more official texts.

The language that Akhenaten introduced was both distinctive and personal and appears to form an analogy with the mannered art produced during the same period. It too had some roots in the traditions of the past, but one glance reveals its differences. Based on the features and appearance of the king, the style eventually extends to all images, both royal and private. Some of these innovations hardly survive the reign of Akhenaten and his immediate successors.

Like his doctrines, the art as well as the other aspects of the culture had to reflect the focus on, and the importance of, the divine king. Recent studies have noted similar conclusions in regard to the city planning and architecture at Akhetaten (O'Connor, forthcoming, and this volume). The king's program included a new name, a new capital, new religious concepts, new architecture, new art, and it would seem, a new style of language to express his new doctrines. Such "regnocentric" artistic and literary styles would certainly be compatible with the interpretations of the Amarna theology given above and perhaps should be considered an integral part of the program. Akhenaten's writings portrayed the Aten as creator god and then identified the living king with the deity. He, like the Aten, was a cosmogonic divinity and, thereby, became one with the Aten and the cosmos. His physical form, however, made him accessible to man, and the deified figure could walk among his subjects as a living divine ka of the supreme power, the Aten. His designation $k\!\!\;\beta\ nswt\ ^\epsilon n\underline{h}\ m\ m\!\!\;\beta^\epsilon t$, "the ka of the king who lives on *maat*," would support such a conclusion.

Three dimensional images of the Amarna godhead, the Aten, have neither been discovered through archaeological excavation, nor observed in the iconography. It was apparently unnecessary to produce such icons, which, in the past were residences for the divine ka. Now there was the living embodiment of the divine ka in Akhenaten. Of course statues of the divine pharaoh could be created and the combination of him in the flesh and his images in stone would satisfy the public's need for access to their divinities (see also Assmann 1984a, 254-55). Moreover, the sun was visible to all humankind in the sky, although it was not approachable. Akhenaten must have assumed that his physical being and his statues would be adequate compensation to his subjects for their loss of the personal contact they had had with their traditional deities (Assmann 1984a, 24-30). The divine ruler had in fact, become a universal deity, who now had "eternal recurrence in kingship like the disc," and it is through him that humankind could continue to exist (Sandman 1938, 91; Allen 1989, 99).

One may well question Akhenaten's motive for this heresy. Others have clearly indicated that one can find, for many of the ideas, roots in the past (Redford 1984, 169-171). Some trends were already evident in earlier periods, and parallels and models can be shown to have existed previously (Aldred 1973, 11-79). It is likely, therefore, that, despite the revolutionary changes that took place during the Amarna Period, much of the philosophy derived from within the framework of traditional Egyptian thinking. This point of view does not diminish the impact of the strong presence of the particular individual Akhenaten and the cataclysmic effect his personality had on the developing themes. He had grown up in a relatively peaceful environment and may well have had sufficient time (from all indications, he certainly had the inclination) to observe and to theorize about the concept of deification of the ruling monarch. During the formative years of his youth he saw his father developing new ideas and establishing his own deification. In regard to the latter, he witnessed the building of the Birth Room and the celebration of the Opet Feast at the Luxor Temple (Barta 1975, 146). Moreover, he was aware that Amenhotep III extended his own deification to other temples (ibid, 162). Cults of this living king, his father, existed in Nubia, and certain of his statues were clearly deified aspects of the king (Kitchen 1982, 175; Bell 1985b, 35 and 51). As the son of a divine king, the young prince undoubtedly was quite involved with the philosophies he saw come into being. At court, he was exposed also to changes and developments in religion and politics, and these factors must have had a profound effect on the mind of Amenhotep IV.

Scholars over the last several decades have proposed a variety of reasons to account for the revolution that took place (O'Connor 1983, 220-221). It was specifically the king who was to benefit from the new structure of kingship that emerged under the new doctrines. He and the god were now united, and at the same time he was able to lessen the impact of the economically and politically powerful priesthood of Amun and its sizable organization. It may be a bit more difficult to rationalize Akhenaten's removal of the funerary beliefs that had already been so great a part of the Egyptian religious system and had been so important to the people.

For an answer, it may be best to examine again the situation during the early New Kingdom and the pharaohs who had begun to stress deification. With Hatshepsut, we saw the introduction of scenes of divine birth and the coordination of it with the Opet Feast, the cult of the royal ka, and the coronation. These ideas were elaborated under her successors, most notably Amenhotep III. While her unorthodox accession to the throne may have underlain her efforts, she may also have been influenced by a social/religious factor that may well have played an equal, if not more influential, role, i. e., the state of democratization of the religion.

Democratization of religion, however, is not an innovation of the Eighteenth Dynasty (Sørenson 1989, 109-123). With the recent discovery of Coffin Texts in a securely dated context of the late Sixth Dynasty (Valloggia 1986, 74-77), it is clear that by the end of the Old Kingdom, Osirian beliefs were no longer the sole prerogative of royalty. While no Pyramid Texts have been found in private funerary monuments this early (see, however, Silverman 1994), they begin to appear not too much later (Fischer 1963, 37; 1968, 88; Willems 1988, 244-249), as the First Intermediate Period begins. The Heracleopolitan Period sees private individuals being referred to as Osiris on false doors (Fischer 1962, 35-38), and within a short period of time, they can even hold the ankh, a symbol of their possession of eternal life; it was usually reserved for gods, but occasionally also for royalty (Fischer 1973, 23-27).

It is perhaps interesting to note that the reverse of this situation—private to royal—also apparently took place. Lector priests in a funerary scene of Hatshepsut recite two texts: one has an early parallel in inscriptions on Middle Kingdom coffins, and the other, originally a Pyramid Text, (118-133) is associated with an inscription on a Middle Kingdom stela, and it later evolved into Chapter 178 of the *Book of the Dead* (Wilson, 1944, 217). Examples of this type of fluidity amongst the recorded texts and rituals attest to the lack of exclusivity in the use of this type of material. It is likely, therefore, that the private people had some access to these texts. After all, they made up the work force of those who were involved in some way with funerary texts and rituals: scribes, line draughtsman, painters, sculptors, and lector priests, to name a few. By the end of the Old Kingdom, the citizenry apparently were formulating their own versions of funerary texts. Not too much later, they began copying and editing the original Pyramid Texts for their own use. Such acts meant that, prior to the First Intermediate Period, private people had access to—and were utilizing for personal use—texts and rituals that would allow for their identification with the gods after their death.

By the Sixth Dynasty, it was not unusual for private people to include in their biographical inscriptions a remark about being an excellent *akh*, followed by a statement regarding their having knowledge of the secrets, magic, or hieroglyphs necessary to be in a state of glorification in the necropolis (Edel 1945, 21-23). Royalty in their funerary texts claim no such knowledge, but perhaps it was self-evident (Friedman 1982, 146-147, but see also Sørenson 1989, 110-112). Information regarding the afterlife and its acquisition can be stated quite specifically by a private individual, such as "knowing that by which one ascends to the great god" (*Urk.* I: 88 and 121). At about this same period of time a similar phrase is introduced as one of the requests in the offering formulae (Barta, 1968, 31 [Bitte 31]). An analogous sentiment is expressed, perhaps more clearly, in the statement recorded by the Sixth Dynasty official, Sabni, in an inscription in his rock cut tomb at Elephantine: "I know the spell for ascending to the great god, lord of heaven" (Habachi 1978, figure 16).

There also came about during the same time period the rise of the cults of deified individuals. Primarily limited to great sages such as Hordjedef, Kagemni, Ptahhotep, and others (Goedicke 1986, 989-992 and D'Auria 1988, 95-96), these deified personalities were even included in the funerary prayer, where ordinarily a deity or the king would occur: after the phrase "revered before" (ibid; Barta 1968, 292). They can even be the subject of adoration and worship as was the case of Heqa-ib (Habachi 1977b, 1120-1122), as well as those individuals just noted.

One might also include in this discussion a remark about "the divine access through ritual imitation of mythical roles" (Sørenson 1989, 117) in regard to the representation of the hippopotamus hunt. This scene, in which the king alone battles the beast, symbolizes the mythical triumph of Horus (ibid., p. 112, and Save-Soderbergh 1953, p. 16), and scholars have traced the motif back to the First Dynasty (ibid. and Behrmann 1989, Dok. 53 and 54). They had assumed that the earliest reference to an analogy from the private sector was the scene from the Twelfth Dynasty tomb of Khnumhotep from Beni Hasan illustrating the tomb owner spearing fish (Sørenson 1989, p. 117, and Save-Soderbergh 1953, p. 21). It is clear now, however, that closer parallels from private sources existed already in the Eleventh Dynasty (ibid., Dok. 120, and notes 346-350), and that even earlier models may actually have occurred (ibid., Doks. 114 and 118, Valoggia 1986, plate XLI, and perhaps UM 29-66-683).

Each of these innovations represented another attempt to narrow the gap between the king and his subjects. The First Intermediate Period saw even more steps in this direction, as weak monarchs were unable to control the entire country. Pyramid Texts and versions thereof were eventually added to the increasing collection of spells in the Coffin Texts, and the collection was subject to wider distribution. Private people were using the name of the god Osiris before their own name with greater frequency, thereby indicating an identification with that deity, a formerly royal prerogative (Fischer 1963, 35-41). In Middle Kingdom tombs, there were representations of open private shrines that reveal a statue of the deceased inside, and the doors to it are referred to as the "doors of heaven" (Brovarski 1977, 107-110; Wente 1969, 88). One of these tombs and a contemporary parallel (ibid) contain the added phrase "that the god may go forth," apparently in reference to the statue within. There are further related labels such as "Following the statue to the temple" with an accompanying vignette (Newberry 1893, plate XXIX), and a passage from the same tomb owner's biographical inscription: "I followed the statues to the temple." (ibid., plate XXV, 83-84). The construction and movement of the colossal statue of the nomarch Djehuty-hotep at Bersheh is shown and described in great detail in his tomb (Newberry 1894, pls. XIV-XV). The graffiti at Hatnub contain remarks that indicate veneration of the statue of the vizier, Kay (Anthes 1928, plate XXIV). One of his epithets, one of his father's, and one of the nomarch Ahanakht refer to the individual as the seed of, or closely related to, a deity (Brovarski 1981, 18-21). On the walls of another Middle Kingdom tomb, the artist actually included a depiction of the king, a representation heretofore limited to royal monuments (Davies, 1920, plate XVI), and amongst the funerary cortege in the same tomb the artist has included individuals bearing statues with red crowns (ibid, plate XXI). Although a god is rarely shown in a private tomb, Sarenput I at Aswan is represented before Khnum (Simpson 1983, 428).

At the same time, we find references to royalty in divine terms, such as that which occurs in this hymn to Senwosret III:

> How great is the lord of this city; he is Re; little are a thousand other men ... How great is the lord of this city; he is Sakhmet to foes who tread on his frontier (Lichtheim, 1973, 199-200).

The official references to the pharaoh in *The Wanderings of Sinuhe*, as mentioned above, liken him to a god on earth. In a tomb at Beni Hasan, the king is called "Atum himself," and the sentence pattern is one of direct identity (Newberry 1893, plate XXV, 75-76). In another passage the divine identity is expressed by the more common prepositional phrase (ibid, 36-39). Perhaps it was coincidental, but whatever the reason, the situation seems to be quite clear. As the royal and private desires for a deified afterlife, as well as the means for obtaining it, grew more and more similar, the royal sector began to pursue new ways of distinguishing itself from the private. Deification while still alive was apparently one of the means. Perhaps that is why there are

allusions to the divine birth of kings already in the Middle Kingdom in literary sources and perhaps in iconographic ones as well.
After all, it was during this time that a private official makes reference to obtaining his own jubilees: "May you repeat a million *sed*-
festivals while Hathor gladdens you therein" (Wente 1969, 89).

It is likely that these attempts by royalty were only marginally
successful, for throughout the Middle Kingdom, it is clear that
private people continued to accumulate royal prerogatives. In
fact, the democratization was spreading further. In regard to the
funerary literature, the *Book of the Dead* (Heerma van Voss 1986,
641-643) of the New Kingdom was being developed, and once it
was coordinated, it provided a means for even more people to
have access to deification after death. The spells were inscribed
on papyrus and often had accompanying vignettes. In this form,
the information necessary for a divine afterlife could be disseminated to a larger portion of the population than before.

Royalty was also altering aspects of its preparation for the
afterlife as well, and, shortly after the advent of the New Kingdom,
kings changed their style of burial. They began to use tombs that
were cut deeply into the slopes of a valley on the west bank of
Thebes. In this Valley of the Kings, they decorated their tombs
with extremely detailed texts and iconography relating to a variety
of aspects of the next world. Some of this funerary material would
eventually be recorded on papyri and distributed, but that was not
the original intention. The decoration was for the sole use of the
king. Whether individuals among the many scribes, draughtsmen,
sculptors, painters, or other craftspeople who worked on the
tombs decided to utilize some of the information detailed on the
walls of royal tombs for private purposes is not a fact that can be
absolutely substantiated. However, the private tombs of some of
these people are among the earliest to utilize such decoration.
Funerary texts also begin to appear on the walls of private tombs
(Theban Tomb 82) by the reign of Thutmose III. Soon, the
traditional texts and scenes of daily life that had appeared in
tombs of the past were replaced by the iconography and accompanying inscriptions that detailed the afterlife and the means of
attaining it.

That private people were assuming more than royal funerary
texts and motifs is clear from a statement by the Eighteenth
Dynasty vizier Rekhmire. He goes so far as to claim qualities not
usual for mortals: "There is not that which the god shuts away

from him; there is not that of which he is ignorant in heaven, earth, or in any hidden place of the underworld" (Urk. IV: 8-9).

While such boasts were rare, the sentiment is clear and so are the implications. There were serious socio-political issues involved, and neither time nor the efforts of royalty had changed things. Faced with such a situation, it is not surprising that Hatshepsut (the efforts of her predecessors notwithstanding) went to such extremes to accentuate the divinity of the living pharaoh. It was clearly her intention to differentiate and thereby raise the status of royalty to its former heights with her strong emphasis on the concept of deification. Her interests were more than equaled by Amenhotep III who elaborated the process and coordinated the iconography, texts, and rituals at the Luxor Temple.

His son and successor, Akhenaten, however, must have sensed the need (or interpreted it thus) for a more dramatic change to separate his own being from that of mortal man. He identified only with the Aten, and his doctrine centered only around that deity (Allen 1989, 89-100). Unlike the concepts of deification used by his predecessors, his did not stress the royal ka, nor its cult. Akhenaten had a divine ka, complete with its exclusive iconography, and it incorporated his physical being and his newly interpreted deity, the Aten, bearing in multiple form, the arms of the ka. Akhenaten had entered the realm of the divine, and because of his transcendence, he required his own high priest. In theory, his subjects could worship only him, his divine ka, and/or the Aten. He completed his program of separation by omitting the gods of the underworld from his doctrines, thereby preventing his subjects from attaining deification after death by identifying with the deities. Other gods were also denied, and even the plural form of god(s) was erased from earlier inscriptions. All attention was focused on only the Aten and Akhenaten (and his family to some extent). Only through worshipping, adoring, and serving them could anyone hope for an afterlife. From the tone of the texts and the pattern of iconography in the private tombs, it is evident that this servitude was to continue in perpetuity. In the afterlife envisioned by Akhenaten, his subjects would serve and act for him and the Aten. In essence, this new afterlife consisted of an eternal distinction between the divine pharaoh and the Aten on one side, and his subjects on the other.

Much of Akhenaten's philosophy was deeply involved with fundamental issues (Allen 1989, 89-100), and all of his new programs were carefully and quite logically formulated and executed. His subjects, however, did not support this new way of thinking for a very long period of time; they apparently had difficulty accepting the radical ideas involving their religion and the office of kingship. In reality, the mortality of the king and his family must have been painfully obvious to all. Archaeological excavations have revealed that the citizenry may not have taken everything so seriously (Silverman 1982, 280-281) and that they retained in their homes memorabilia of their traditional beliefs (Peet 1923, 70-108; Gardiner 1966, 229). The few surviving personal letters from the period contain private addresses to the Aten without the king being invoked as an intermediary (Wente 1990, 89), an indication that, although the name of the god may have changed, the way of reaching it had not.

The political/religious experiment ultimately failed, and Akhe-naten's eventual successor Tutankhamun restored the orthodoxy and reestablished the cult of the royal ka. He had scenes and text relating to the Feast of Opet carved on the walls of the colonnade of the Luxor Temple. There, he also reaffirmed its importance in conjunction with the scenes of the Birth Room and the ritual of coronation in regard to the deification of the king. The cult of the divine living ruler continued during his reign and that of his successors. Tutankhamun, like his ancestor Amenhotep III, was worshipped at sites other than Thebes (Bell 1985b, 34-41). In the Nineteenth Dynasty, the pharaoh Ramses II re-emphasized and extended the scope of his own divinity (Kitchen, 1982, 177-178). He embellished Luxor temple and decorated it with statues, one of which is clearly dedicated to his deified form because the name "Re of the Rulers," is carved on it (Habachi 1969, 18-20). On the base, there is a relief of two priests, each of whom flank an inscription that seems to refer to the statue's use in the cult of the deified king: "... the offerings coming forth in front of your father (Amun-Re) for the royal living ka, Re of the Rulers" (ibid., 19). Ramses II utilized other names as well, for this divine manifestation of his being, and images bearing inscriptions of them can be found at various locations throughout the country (ibid, chs. 1-3). Reference to one such statue in his Delta residence can be found in a report recorded on papyrus:

> The youths of Great of Victories are in festal attire every day; sweet moringa oil is upon their heads...They stand beside their doors; their heads bowed down with foliage and greenery...on the day of

the entry of [the divine image of Ramses] User-Maat-Re Setep-en-Re, Montu of the Two Lands... (Caminos 1956, 74).

There is another text that describes this same town and the royal palace in explicit terms befitting the domicile of a deity, for it is said to be "... like the horizon of heaven. Ramses Mery-Amun is in it as a god" (ibid, 153-154). It is likely that when the king is referred to in the expression "Amun (or another god) of Ramses" it is another example of the living divine king (ibid, 2; Kitchen 1982, 177).

The temple at Abu Simbel has many examples of the deified Ramses among its reliefs (Habachi 1969, 1-16), and the representation of the barque, both here and elsewhere, is apparently a form of the deified king as well (ibid, 14-16). One of the four statues of deities in the sanctuary is the image of his deified form (ibid, 10), and the same is true for other statues of the king in this and other Nubian temples (ibid, 10-17). Clearly this cult was greatly extended during the long reign of this king, and there is evidence of it from the Delta in the north, to as far south as Nubia. It was far-reaching, and it was far from subtle.

Although Ramses II used the cult to proclaim his divinity throughout his empire, he employed existing frameworks; he did not attempt to alter the traditional eschatology of the ancient Egyptians. He allowed his subjects to continue their own preparations for a life in the next world, one that would include identification with, and life in the company of, the gods. He permitted the people to retain the traditional beliefs that affected them directly. Perhaps he felt that enlarging, embellishing, and extending the concept of the living divine king and the cult of the royal ka were sufficient enough actions to distinguish himself from his subjects and to emphasize his exalted status. He was a god in the temples and in his capital city; he was a royal living ka; he was "Re of the Rulers," throughout the land. Yet it was this very same individual—who much later would be the inspiration for Percy B. Shelley's *Ozymandias*, "the King of Kings"—he who during his lifetime, could be referred to simply as "the general," by his subjects.

2.1. Painting from the tomb of Thutmose III in the Valley of the Kings, depicting the Seventh Hour in the Book of Amduat. Photograph courtesy of David P. Silverman.

2.2. Hieroglyphs for *nswt bíty* "King of Upper and Lower Egypt." Illustration by Jennifer R. Houser.

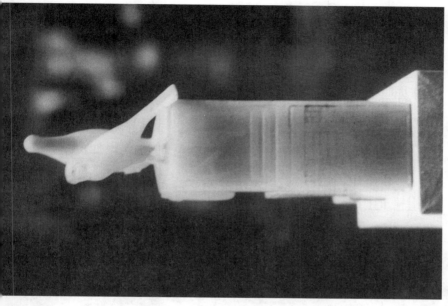

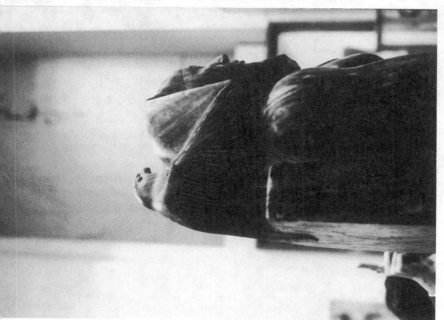

2.3. Statue of Khafre of the Fourth Dynasty with the divine image of Horus behind the king's head, now in Cairo Museum. Photograph courtesy of David P. Silverman.

2.4. Back of the statue of Pepi I of the Sixth Dynasty, now in the Brooklyn Museum. Photograph courtesy of Stephen R. Phillips and reproduced with the kind permission of the Brooklyn Museum.

2.5. Serkhs of three kings of the Archaic Period: Djer, Qaa, and Semerkhet.
Illustration by Jennifer R. Houser.

2.6. Painted relief of the titulary of Ramses III from his mortuary temple at Medinet Habu,
with the hieroglyphs *s3 Rᵉ* "son of Re" to the right of the cartouche on the left. Photograph
courtesy of David P. Silverman.

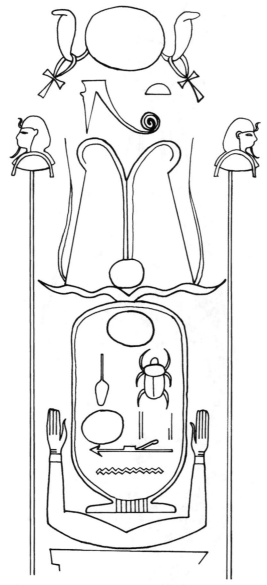

2.7. Relief depicting the royal ka from the tomb of the Theban official Kheruef of the Eighteenth Dynasty. Illustration by Jennifer R. Houser.

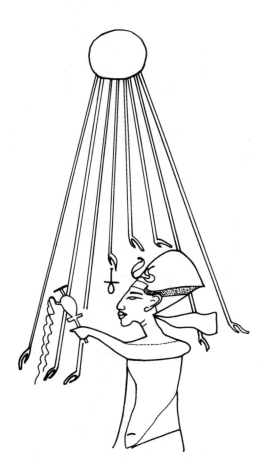

2.8.   Drawing of the painted relief on the
facade of the shrine of Akhenaten, depicting
the king and the Aten. Illustration by Jennifer
R. Houser.

PART TWO

HISTORICAL STUDIES OF KINGSHIP

CHAPTER THREE

ORIGINS OF EGYPTIAN KINGSHIP

John Baines

For much of Egyptian history, the monuments of the king and the elite presented kingship as the central institution of Egyptian society. In public terms, the king was more important than the gods. The state was unthinkable without kingship. In ideology, kingship formed the unifying apex of a host of dualities that constituted society, as well as forming the point of connection among human society, the gods, and the wider cosmos. Kingship can now be traced back into prehistory, much earlier than the "historical" events that have traditionally been held to mark the appearance of state and kingship. This change creates a less heroic, but more plausible image of the evolution of both institutions than had been current.

In this chapter I present a synthesis of those early institutions and of recent developments in analysis. Whereas older views were based primarily on later Egyptian texts, or on yet more remote Classical writings, the principal evidence for current interpretations comes from iconographic sources and the steadily increasing body of archaeological work. The iconography, in particular, can only be interpreted in the light of conventions; one of my main strategies is to assume that the initial evolution of developed Egyptian artistic conventions is reflected in the salient representational "monuments" of early kingship, most of which are quite small and hardly public objects.

1. Antecedents

1.1. The First Stages; Problems of Method

The oldest potential evidence for kingship is iconographic. A crown with the form of the later "red crown" of the king of Egypt is shown in raised relief on a fragment from a large jar of the

Naqada I (Amratian) culture of the mid-Fourth millennium BC (Figure 3.1). This is earlier than political or cultural unity in Egypt, even though Naqada I was rather uniform throughout the Nile Valley south of Asyut, as its predecessor, Badarian, also seems to have been. Werner Kaiser (1961, 39 n. 1) suggested that the crown might have been a symbol of a deity rather than of kingship, but in a sense this distinction is irrelevant, because most items of Egyptian divine insignia are animal or, as here, human in origin. The coincidence between the form of the relief and the later royal symbol, which is unlikely to be fortuitous, remains significant. Whatever the shape stood for—a deity or perhaps the emblem of office of a village headman—it was probably the formal ancestor of the crown (see further Midant-Reynes 1992, 174-75). Naqada I is the earliest period for which a patterned differentiation of wealth in the mortuary record, as against a variation in the wealth of individual tombs, has been identified. At Hierakonpolis there is a group of graves that are significantly larger than any others known, although they are not absolutely very large; these are at a site chosen subsequently for the area's most important late pre-dynastic tombs (see Bard 1989; see also Atzler 1981, 65-76, for other arguments for differentiation). Despite this coincidence of elite symbols and social evolution, Naqada I is a small-scale, relatively undifferentiated and certainly uncentralized village culture. By Early Dynastic times, the red crown was associated with Lower Egypt (Emery 1954, 102, figure 105, plate 35b)—the Delta and the northernmost section of the Nile Valley—but in origin this piece of insignia had been an Upper Egyptian symbol.

The crown is an isolated piece. The next evidence comes from the crucial period of state formation in the late Fourth millennium BC. This phase is known by various terms. It began in the later stages of the Naqada II (Gerzean) culture, and its continuation is termed Naqada III or, as a political stage, Dynasty 0 or Proto-dynastic (summaries: Needler 1984, 22-39; Midant-Reynes 1992; Spencer 1993). Research has lengthened this period greatly, and the implication that it is covered by a single royal "dynasty" is almost certainly misleading; it may better be termed neutrally "late predynastic." The Egyptian dynastic period, also known inappropriately as "pharaonic" (since kings were not termed "pharaoh" until a much later date) begins with the First Dynasty (c. 2920 BC). Both in antiquity and in modern discussion, the legendary King Menes has symbolized the division between predynastic and dynastic (§ 3.1 ahead).

The late predynastic period is the crucial one for the evolution of kingship. The interpretation of the period is changing rapidly as new evidence emerges, and it is worth contrasting current views with Henri Frankfort's classic *Kingship and the Gods* (1948, 15-23); his discussion of the king's position in the cosmos, and in relation to nature, is as stimulating as ever, but his historical reconstruction and picture of Menes describes a different world from that of later research—almost presenting a modern myth of origin.

Not all the royal material from this period is contemporary with the unitary state of Egypt: some will belong to its predecessors, a posited group of small polities or statelets in much of Upper Egypt (e.g., Kemp 1989, 31-46), and probably the Delta. The mid Naqada II wall painting in Tomb 100 at Hierakonpolis has, among other important motifs, a group of a man smiting three smaller enemies (Figure 3.2), who are tied together and arranged along a base line (for the date, see e.g., Kaiser and Dreyer 1982, 242-43, with references). The number three, which here may indicate simple plurality, is fundamental to later hieroglyphic writing, while the base line organizes all dynastic Egyptian painting and relief. This group has countless descendants among pictures of the king smiting his enemies (see e.g., Schäfer 1957; Swan Hall 1986). Thus, the painting includes a central symbol of kingship, conquest and domination, shown within later conventions but in a local context and a style far from that of dynasties 0-2. Williams and Logan (1987) have presented an integrated interpretation of the complete painting, relating the whole to the royal *sed*-festival (§ 2.2 ahead), but allowing for funerary meanings. If this is correct, it strengthens the tomb's claim to be royal, which had been argued on other grounds (e.g., Case and Payne 1962, 18; Kemp 1973, 42-43; Monnet Saleh 1987 [misguided]); it had royal successors not far away (Hoffman *et al.* 1982, 38-60; Hoffman 1986). The traditions and symbolism of kingship can then be traced deep into prehistory—Williams and Logan would follow them back to Naqada I—but this does not mean that the institutions of kingship, or of political units ruled by kings, were comparable with those of later times.

In terms of indigenous traditions, kingship originated during the time the Egyptians saw as what we would call prehistory (Kaiser 1961; Baines 1989a). It probably arose from the earlier small polities, as political unity must have done. There is no objection to the idea of a small-scale point of departure for kingship. In com-

parative perspective, the institution—if it is a single phenomenon—varies enormously. But the "kings" of the statelets would
hardly have recognized the paraphernalia and elaborate symbolism attached to their later successors of the First Dynasty, when
the dualizing ideology and iconography of king, state and cosmos
had been formulated in the mixed idiom of picture and written
caption. Even at that date, there was no continuous written record
of ideas of kingship; not until the second millennium BC were
such texts certainly composed (marginal Old Kingdom forerunners, e.g., Roccati 1982, 97-98).

The duration of the development from the proto-kingship of
the Hierakonpolis wall painting to the end of predynastic times
cannot be estimated closely, but it may have been two or three
hundred years. Werner Kaiser suggested that there could have
been ten to twelve kings of the entire country during this time
(Kaiser and Dreyer 1982, 261-69)—around 150 years on an ave-
rage reign length of perhaps 15 years; more recent work would
tend to increase this figure (see further, below). As pictorial
representation and writing advanced during this period, the
ideology of kingship came to be recorded, but the recording will
have changed the ideas, whose prototypes are lost with the verbal
and living contexts in which they arose.

In interpreting this early material I use later evidence, and I may
seem to imply that kingship does not need defining. These and
related issues of method should be sketched. The archaeological
evidence of differentiation of wealth and status shows a society in
transition from an acephalous, relatively unstratified type to one
with vast differences in wealth and power, but it is the use of
particular symbols, which can be identified only by hindsight, that
chiefly characterizes the type of rule as kingship; such symbols may
have originated long before kingship existed, because kings legitimize themselves by reference to antiquity. If the hazardous use of
hindsight in analyzing this evidence were excluded, much less
could be said about early periods, and their significance in
relation to later ones might be missed.

Reasons for not accepting that the Naqada I crown proves the
existence of kingship at that date relate to theory and definition.
Kingship is not characteristic of largely unstratified societies like
Naqada I, even if initial developments toward both stratification
and kingship may be suggested in them (Beattie 1968; n.d.). Thus,
the arguments of Williams and Logan (1987, 255-56) for iden-

tifying rituals of kingship on Naqada I textile fragments (Scamuzzi 1965, pls. 1-5) should be seen as relating to symbolic forms, not to the institution of kingship; the textile could also be later. A definition of kingship that excludes Naqada I would be that it is the reign of a single, mostly unelected person in a large-scale or state society—in terms of social evolution a complex society. The king normally rules but he may only reign—he may or may not exercise effective political power (e.g., Evans-Pritchard 1969). His reigning has symbolic and ritual aspects (Beattie 1968; Friedrich 1968) and he often has divine qualities, but his rule is not exclusively spiritual. Kingship often originates in conquest and expansion, and in cases of rapid formation is more typical of extended, territorial polities than of city states, where it frequently arises long after state forms. The normal mode of succession is hereditary, by primogeniture or other selection among the monarch's children, but nonhereditary selection also occurs (e.g., the Roman emperor). Violence often accompanies accession. Monarchs are seldom women.

The chief conclusion to draw from this rough characterization is that Egyptian kingship is typical. Egypt is not a special case or oddity, as the use of the word "pharaoh" rather implies. Among the principal aspects of kingship, the one that is most difficult to approach in early material is ritual (§ 3.2 ahead).

An essential difficulty in evaluating the relationship between early kingship and the state is the general lack of settlement sites of the crucial Naqada II-III periods; this hampers the understanding of social structure and complexity. No detailed trajectory toward social complexity can be seen, so that Egypt cannot be compared closely with early Mesopotamia or, for example, archaic Greece (cf. Runciman 1982). Features comparable with Egypt can be seen in the polities of chiefdoms known typically from Africa and Polynesia (e.g., material collected in Claessen and Skalník 1978; Sahlins 1985; see also § 3.1 ahead). Thus, there could be two points of departure for state and kingship in Egypt: the small, increasingly complex local polity; and the large territorial entity, whose complexity may have evolved at much the same time as it came into being. The two are not necessarily incompatible, because the organization of the extended state and the character of its complexity are different from those of city states. The second type seems more apparent in the record, but the paucity of sources makes evaluation difficult.

1.2. The Geographical and Ideological Coalescence of State and Kingship

Although kingship is typical of extended states, it is also locally based and relies ultimately on the presence and accessibility, or presumed accessibility, of the king, which give persuasive power to his rule and bring ruler and ruled into a moral community, even if there is hardly any real contact between them (compare Millar 1977, 3-12, on the Roman emperor). However little the king may acknowledge explicitly and present on the monuments his dependence on moral legitimacy and on the people (see also § 2.2 ahead), they remain vital. An Egyptian king might rule a small polity in a particular part of the country, as perhaps happened at the point of departure for centralized kingship, or he might rule the entire country, in which case the location of his capital was critical. He had to reconcile his local closeness to people with the need to create an administrative and symbolic center. A further Egyptian concern was with the country's duality. This was evident in the physical contrast of Nile Valley and Delta and was reflected in the final siting of the capital at the junction between the two; duality was also fundamental in ideology and iconography.

If Egyptian cults and legends of later times relate meaningfully to earlier traditions, some key places for the elaboration of kingship and development of the state were Hierakonpolis, Abydos (the probable capital of Dynasty 0), and Buto in the Delta. All were drawn into the ideology of kingship. Horus, the supreme god of the time who was also the one most closely associated with the king, was worshipped at Hierakonpolis, at Edfu nearby, at Tell el-Balamun in the northernmost Delta (Gardiner 1944), and in many other places. Seth, his rival, who briefly replaced Horus in the Second Dynasty, was the god of Naqada, north of modern Luxor, the type-site of the main predynastic Nile Valley cultures and the largest single site of the period (e.g., Hoffman 1979, 105-25). Three goddesses closely linked with the kingship, Nekhbet (whose name is not attested before the Old Kingdom), Wadjet and Neith, were associated with Hierakonpolis (with adjacent el-Kab), Buto, and Sais in the Delta. Hathor, who is also known from very early (Daumas 1977) and was later worshipped at Dendara downstream from Naqada, had cults in many places and came, with Neith, to be a goddess of the dynastic capital at Memphis. Both goddesses seem to have come from areas that lost importance, for which worship at the capital may have compensated.

In an earlier generation, such connections as those just men-

tioned formed the bases for "political" reconstructions of predynastic developments relating to the cults of dynastic times
(especially Sethe 1930), which were then rejected on the grounds
that their methods were reductionist and based on inappropriate
evidence. Yet, despite the pitfalls of reductionism, there is no
reason to deny that political circumstances have any influence on
religion; rejection of a relationship would go against evidence
from other cultures and would exclude potentially significant
evidence (see also Bard 1992).

There is, then, a remarkable congruity between the distribution
of major late predynastic sites and the gods who were later linked
with the kingship. Other archaeologically important sites should
be added to any list (Kaiser and Dreyer 1982, 244-45, with
references). Cemetery T at Naqada shows similar social differentiation to Hierakonpolis and Abydos (e.g., Kemp 1973, 42).
Among other places with major elite tombs is Abadiyya, while
Koptos, where Min was the god, represented by a group of early
colossal temple statues (e.g., Schäfer and Andrae 1942, 179), is a
significant city for which no early cemetery is known. The role of
the Delta in these developments is gradually emerging (van den
Brink 1992). Some impression of how Egypt may have been
divided into small polities before Dynasty 0 may be given by the
patchwork of late Third Intermediate Period territories (see
Kitchen 1986, 335-61; map Baines and Málek 1980, 47); the chief
difference is that at the later date the Delta was politically dominant (the dynastic administrative structure of nomes, which might
otherwise be used in comparison, is probably not closely related to
earlier times). During Dynasty 0, the size and significance of sites
around the later capital of Memphis increased, but these places
seem to have had no strong earlier traditions; the region was
economically and politically, but not yet historically, important.

The later hierarchical ordering of the gods within conceptions
of royalty and the cosmos cannot tell us anything about predynastic political hierarchies, but the spread of sites and its
consonance with the deities provides indirect evidence for local
polities as precursors of the single state. In late predynastic times,
the Egyptian state or states may have been imitated in A-Group
Lower Nubia, a development that had dire consequences for the
local culture, which soon became extinct, surely under Egyptian
pressure (cf. Williams 1987, 16-20). An Egyptian victory scene on a
rock from Gebel Sheikh Suleiman in the Second Cataract, which

was previously dated to the First Dynasty, has been shown to be rather earlier (Murnane 1987), demonstrating that the Egyptians raided through Lower Nubia in the same period.

The crucial change at the beginning of the whole development was from the Naqada I culture to Naqada II, after the rise of the separate Maadi culture north of the Fayyum (Rizkana and Seeher 1987-1990, vol. 1, 58-80); the Maadi culture seems to have extended over the entire Delta area and southward to the Fayyum. Maadi and Naqada II are wealthier, more densely settled cultures than their predecessors, with greater social differentiation and more connections to distant places. At first the two coexisted in their growing complexity, but the culture of the end of Naqada II (IId1-2) spread throughout the country, reaching the extreme north-eastern Delta at Minshat Abu Omar (Kroeper and Wildung 1985; for dating, see Kaiser 1987b) and displacing Maadi. Buto in the northern Delta has produced finds of the Maadi culture contemporaneous with later Naqada II that are succeeded by material characteristic of its unified latest stages (Naqada IId1-2; von der Way 1991, 1992). The final stage of Naqada II and all of Naqada III are uniform over the country to a degree that suggests large-scale organization and integration of the land and the economy, probably accompanied by some movement of people. Such uniformity, achieved at the expense of the Maadi culture's disappearance, could hardly have been brought about without military action, and was probably accomplished under one or more leaders or kings. This process must be considered the unification of Egypt, however long it took and whether or not it encompassed the entire later area of Egypt or led to the creation of a single polity (see § 2.3 ahead). As in some later periods, the north seems to have been in the forefront of the initial cultural development, but the south then took the political, and subsequently the cultural, initiative.

One vital premise for unification is the appearance of the idea of unity, which could have been seen in primarily geographical or cultural terms. Since later Egypt never conceived of itself internally as an "empire," unification may not have been envisaged as the conquest of "foreign" places, whether or not that was originally the case. In the south, the separate but closely related traditions of Abydos and Hierakonpolis may have merged in mid Naqada II, before a political coalescence. Thus, the south was probably where the cultural conception of unity emerged. This idea is in part given by geography, that is, by the isolation of the fertile land of Egypt and its distinction from the surrounding deserts, but such a conception is not inescapable.

The two possible points of departure for political unification are Abydos, where cemeteries go back to Naqada I, and Hierakonpolis, which is producing much evidence for royalty but is not tied very precisely to the sequence farther north. The kings of Dynasty 0 were buried in Cemeteries U and B at Abydos (§ 2.1 ahead). These cemeteries, which form a continuum, are separated from any communal necropolis by more than a kilometer of open desert; unlike Cemetery B, Cemetery U appears not to contain only royal tombs. This continuity of cemeteries and zoning fits an Abydene origin for the rulers and the kingship of Cemetery U, and possibly Cemetery B. Thus, it is rather unlikely that the earliest kings of the whole country originated at Hierakonpolis, which could perhaps have been a separate center that became integrated with the Abydos polity. Naqada seems to have been bypassed, although it too experienced the social differentiation visible in Cemetery T. In the Delta, places that might have been the centers of polities include Buto, Sais, Tell el-Balamun, Mendes, Bubastis (Beni Anir near Zaqaziq) or Hurbeit (Kufur Nigm) (for reports on several sites, see van den Brink 1992). The preservation of substantial amounts of evidence in the unfavorable environment of the Delta emphasizes the importance of its role. Finds at Buto in particular, as well as theoretical arguments for the derivation of architectural forms (Kaiser 1985b—problematic in detail), suggest that the predynastic Delta achieved high levels of material and artistic culture, to which its connections with the Near East probably contributed much. At Buto, the striking find of Mesopotamian-style Uruk period mosaic cones and plano-convex bricks reinforces this connection and provides impressive testimony to cultural complexity, even if derivative in character (von der Way and Schmidt 1987).

On the reconstruction just presented, kingship arose either before the centralized state or in the process of its formation, and before there was writing or any significant pictorial record of royal deeds. Therefore, less than has been assumed can be said about the original character of kingship, which must be seen as emerging in small-scale polities about which little is known. The Naqada I red crown suggests that the earliest forms of kingship owed much to the more remote past: during its formation, symbols of kingship may have been hallowed by an unknown antiquity. In theoretical terms, its point of departure was probably Weberian "charismatic leadership" (see e.g., Schnepel 1987). The most that can now be observed is the later, gradual institutionalization of that charisma. The material stimulus to unification and centralization can only be guessed at, but must have included economic growth within a uniform, easily traversed region, which has subsequently had a single government during most of five millennia. In addition, long-distance trade, known both from finds of exotica like lapis lazuli from Afghanistan (e.g., Porada 1980) and from rough Palestinian pottery in both Egypt and Lower Nubia (Maadi: e.g., Hoffman 1979, 201-14; Rizkana and Seeher 1987, 73-77; Minshat Abu Omar: e.g., Kroeper and Wildung 1985, 69-72; Qustul: Williams 1986, 78-80) and specialized Palestinian export wares (Hartung, in Dreyer 1993, 49-56), may have been significant, as well as other aspects of foreign relations with the Near East (e.g., Moorey 1987), Nubia, and the eastern and western deserts. Some of these developments could, however, have been consequences of the emergence of a large polity, which was the dominant power in the region and at that date the largest political unit in the world, rather than causes of it.

Bruce Williams (1986, 163-90; 1987; 1988) has proposed a different reconstruction of the unification, in which the period of the statelets would continue some way into Naqada III and the unification of the country may have proceeded from a polity whose rulers were of the Nubian A-Group culture and buried in Cemetery L at Qustul in southern Lower Nubia, rather than coming from Egypt itself. His central discovery, that there was a king-centered polity in Lower Nubia, extends greatly the range of early conceptions of kingship, and his conclusion that the destruction of the A-Group culture around the beginning of the dynastic period must relate to developments in the Egyptian state is convincing. His position does, however, involve difficulties in chronology, both in the succession of the Naqada II-III periods (see esp. Williams 1988a) and in the very long duration he proposes for the cemetery (1986, 167). In addition, there is an unresolved question of the scale of society implied by the cemetery and the wider archaeological context in Nubia, and hence the amount of pressure the region might have exerted on Egypt (Williams 1987 successfully rebuts W. Y. Adams here, but does not resolve this issue). I would prefer to see the Qustul cemetery as containing tombs of rulers of a peripheral statelet who adopted and adapted many features of Egyptian ideology and iconography, showing significant creativity and in some cases happening to leave for us earlier ideological evidence than is available from Egypt itself. It seems less likely that these are the tombs of the ideology's originators. Similarly, the objects Williams interprets as recording victories over Upper Egypt (esp. 1986, 154-55 with pls. 88-92) may be conventional, showing aspirations or events from the past, and not recording specific occurrences—a point that is significant also for material from Egypt.

Whatever the stimuli for the unification of Egypt may have been and wherever they came from, the institution that created, maintained responsibility for, symbolized, and later ritually reenacted unity was kingship. It follows from my reconstruction that the state, and especially the unified state of Egypt, was never envisaged without kingship. From the beginning the king could have said with foresight "*L'Etat, c'est Moi*," except that such a sentence is impossible in Egyptian, which lacks a word for the state. This absence points to kingship as the nexus of society: there is no separate state. Such a formation of a large polity is quite frequent and can occur rapidly over vast areas (e.g., Sahlins 1985, 32-54; Evans-Pritchard 1971), but these conquest polities often collapse as quickly as they formed, precisely because they are centered on one person and lack strong social differentiation, developed governmental institutions, and long-lasting complex organization. The context in Egypt and in other long-lived states and social forms is the surrounding complex society. In Egypt, the development of complex society appears to be inextricably associated with cultural unification, and the significant process is the institutionalization of a unifying charisma, not its occurrence. Despite the recession of kingship into prehistory as research has progressed, and despite the unanswered questions of whether pre-unification Egypt contained "states" and exactly how complex its societies were, this vital change of institutionalization can still be studied.

2. Aspects of Late Predynastic Kingship: Dynasty 0
(for list of kings, see Figure 3.3)

Three principal, interrelated aspects of early kingship can be identified—at the risk of some circularity of argument. These are:

associations with aggression, conquest, and defense; large-scale architecture; and general royal ideology (for the related area of ritual, see § 3.2 ahead). Aggression and conquest are exemplified by the unification itself—which can hardly have been completely peaceful—by motifs of smiting enemies and heroes warding off wild beasts (e.g., Gebel el-Araq Knife: Sievertsen 1992; in general Finkenstaedt 1984), and by large numbers of symbolic and real weapons found in some royal contexts (e.g., Adams 1974, pls. 5-6). Architecture is preserved in elite and royal tombs, which increased in size and were separate from those of other people. The king's chief presence must, however, have been in his residences. These cannot be studied archaeologically, but are visible in decorative motifs and in later survivals. The same motifs also constitute evidence for ideology. The earliest examples in all these categories are less informative than those from the end of the predynastic period.

First, the most distinctive prestige product of Naqada II provides additional context. This is buff, red-painted pottery commonly termed D-ware (Petrie 1920, 16-22; Bourriau 1981, 26-32; motifs: Monnet Saleh 1983). It has been found principally in graves (but see e.g., Fairservis 1983, 27 figure 6), and is much discussed because many of its motifs have parallels in later royal and divine decoration. The grave context suggests that the meaning of many designs may be mortuary. Typical representations are of boats, dances, animals, and emblem-like figurations of water, hills, and in particular, standards like later ones of Egyptian gods. Much of this is paralleled in the Hierakonpolis Tomb 100 wall painting (Quibell and Green 1902, pls. 75-79), on a textile (cited in § 1.1 here), and in rock drawings throughout the deserts and, for example, near the royal tombs at Hierakonpolis (Hoffman *et al.* 1982, 61-65; Hoffman 1986). The only pottery design that seems specifically royal is a group of three scorpions linked by a long straight line that may be a base line or a rope, associated with a barque; this is on a vase that is surprisingly primitive artistically (Asselberghs 1961, figs. 19-23; see also Williams and Logan 1987, 259-60). This may be compared with a rock drawing of a boat with prow in animal form, and "hovering" above it a charging bull that could signify a king by association with hovering figures of falcons (Hoffman *et al.* 1982, 62, figure I.18; second boat without a bull, figure I.19).

What is most relevant here about D-ware is its early disappearance, before the end of Naqada II (e.g., Finkenstaedt 1985), and its lack of direct successors. With the formation of kingship and state, prestige materials were progressively restricted as society became extremely unequal. Representation was a scarce, centrally-controlled resource, and pottery was emptied of symbolic significance in favor of extremely costly hard stone and metal vases (Midant-Reynes 1992, 179-83). D-ware was itself probably an elite product, but it gave way to those of a more restricted elite. Thus, the disappearance of types and patterns of finds, and their continuation and change and the introduction of new ones, are significant for the social context of kingship.

Cemetery U at Abydos, which dates to early Naqada III, after the disappearance of D-Ware, has produced the oldest material that may relate to kingship over all of Egypt. I review these finds before discussing the themes just enumerated.

The cemetery has a number of rich brick tombs (Dreyer *et al.* 1993). The most important so far discovered is the largest, Tomb U-j, whose furnishings include unquestionably royal symbols. The tomb has many chambers laid out as a miniature house or palace compound, with slits symbolizing doors between the rooms. The equipment included hundreds of pots, both imported Palestinian and local Egyptian wares, the latter often inscribed with single large signs. There was an ivory scepter in the form of the ruler's crook or *ḥqꜣ*. The most striking find is made up of more than a hundred inscribed miniature bone or ivory tags, perhaps originally attached to bolts of cloth. These typically have one or two signs, and often numerals. The signs can be read with values comparable to, although not identical with, those of dynastic times, but there is no certain correspondence. Objects represented by some signs were later associated with kingship, notably the "palace façade" (see §§ 2.3, 3.3 ahead; Dreyer *et al.* 1993, plate 7j), which provides indirect evident for large-scale brick architecture, and thrones, both of them in styles very close to those of the dynastic period. This complex use of manufactured symbols in an embryonic writing system implies that these were not the earliest inscribed objects.

Günter Dreyer, the excavator, proposes that the signs on the Egyptian pots, which include a falcon, a scorpion, a *pteroceras* shell (a Red Sea mollusk), an elephant on a sign for "desert," and a similar bull motif, are the "names" of kings—perhaps titles like later Horus names—and may indicate the provenance of the pots

and their contents from estates set up by those kings. He suggests
that the king buried in Tomb U-j was "Scorpion" (not the same as
the Scorpion of the period of Narmer). He connects these names
(Dreyer, in press) with a group of reliefs on panels on colossal
predynastic statues of the god Min from Koptos, one of which
Bruce Williams (1988) has identified as a palimpsest with the
name of Narmer; another monument with a comparable range of
symbols is the "cities" palette (Figure 3.4; § 2.2 ahead). Dreyer proposes that the owner of Tomb U-j came around the middle of a
sequence of kings whose names would be attested in the graffiti on
the statues and in other materials.

Tomb U-j predates the principal tombs in Cemetery B by
perhaps a century (see § 2.1). Dreyer argues from the inscribed
materials, some of which he attributes to the Delta, and from the
imported pottery, that the king buried there ruled the entire
country. While this cannot be proved, it is evident that Egypt was
culturally unified at this date. Thus, he presents a period when
royal names, writing, and symbolic forms differed significantly
from those evolving continuously into the First Dynasty. This
change in style is most easily seen as reflecting a change in ruling
house. If so, "Dynasty 0" was neither a political nor a cultural unity,
whether or not the group of kings around the owner of Tomb U-j
ruled the entire country.

The kings previously identified as belonging to Dynasty 0 are
attested both from tombs in Cemetery B—not all of which can be
assigned to specific owners—and from motifs scratched on sherds
and stone vases found over much of the country. These show a
rectangle, sometimes with an indecipherable sign inside, surmounted by one or two falcons (§ 2.3 ahead). These designs lead
directly toward the forms of dynastic kingship.

2.1. Architecture

The architectural remains of the earliest royal tombs are not
impressive in quantity or in scale, but they dominate other burials
(Kaiser 1964, 96-102; Kaiser and Dreyer 1982; Dreyer *et al.* 1990,
1993). They are out in the desert, away from contemporary burials
but perhaps near hallowed sites (Hoffman *et al.* 1982, 58-60), and
consist of rectangular brick-lined pits cut in the desert. They were
roofed with timber and matting, probably supporting coverings of
beaten earth. Some had light covering superstructures, perhaps of
reeds, skins, or cloth (Hoffman 1986); others, which seem not to

have been marked on the surface, may have been linked with undiscovered mortuary cult places nearer to settlements. Thus, their modest size was compensated for by their location and architectural form, and possibly by important separate structures. Among these elements, the crucial royal markers are location and small numbers, which suggest that only one person, or slightly more in Cemetery U, had such a burial at a time. Brick set the tombs off from their surroundings and gave them a rectilinear form. Unlike Mesopotamian brick, Egyptian always had a fully geometrical form; here as elsewhere, straight lines expressed order, becoming a vital element in royal and elite ideology (on possible symbolism of mud brick, see Wood 1987).

Cemetery B, which is adjacent to the First Dynasty royal tombs of Umm el-Qaʿab, contains several two-chambered tombs, a design which Dreyer suggests originated from the collapse of one chamber in the tomb of "Irihor" (B1/B2, Dreyer n.d.; Kaiser and Dreyer 1982, 224-25 are more cautious), in which case there would be no special ideological meaning to the layout, although it could quickly have acquired one, the obvious possibility being that it related to the duality of kingship. The tombs with paired chambers can be assigned to rulers whose throne names are conventionally rendered Irihor and Ka (Kaiser and Dreyer 1982, 232-35, 260-69), and to the famous Narmer. Despite their small size, it must be recalled that the chief purpose of the tombs was to accommodate the deceased's body and grave goods; many costly objects could have fitted in Narmer's tomb, which measured c. 3.2 × 5.6 m (B17/19, Kaiser and Dreyer 1982, 220-21). Nonetheless, neither the size nor the architecture of the tombs can be compared with the overwhelming elite predominance, and exploitation of the rest of society, which emerged in the Early Dynastic Period and reached a peak in the Old Kingdom. This formative period is distinct in its pattern of expression, and probably of rule, from later times.

2.2. Ideology and Aggression I: Relief Decoration

The fullest attestation of notions of ideology and aggression is in the group of late predynastic relief carvings on knife handles, slate palettes, and maceheads (collections: Ridley 1973; Williams and Logan 1987; Ciałowicz 1987, 1993, with very full bibliography; see also Dreyer et al. 1993, plates 6d-f). These elaborately crafted objects are royal and elite products. They are relatively small and some, at least, were dedicated in temples, where kings were later the almost exclusive benefactors.

Alongside such works of art are very fragmentary administrative records consisting of royal names and brief notes inscribed on pottery, probably as marks of ownership or of the destination of goods (tags comparable with those found in Tomb U-j happen not to be attested again until the First Dynasty). The historical importance of developed administration for prestige goods cannot be pursued here, but the inscriptions produce a clue to the institutional context. At least from Irihor they include information about the products in the vessels and their region of origin (Kaiser and Dreyer 1982, 232-33), chiefly oil from the North, that is, Lower Egypt (some still earlier inscriptions also go beyond royal names: ibid., 263 figure 14). Upper and Lower Egypt form a fundamental Egyptian dualism that is now attested in administrative sources earlier than the traditional dating of the "Union of the Two Lands" and the beginning of Egyptian "history" at the start of the First Dynasty. By analogy, the ideology on some knives and slate palettes may embody developed conceptions and institutions rather than their formation. The violent and aggressive subject matter can hardly relate to battles of unification fought by the latest predynastic rulers, for the country had, by then, long been politically unified—although internal conflict naturally remains a possibility—so that it must reflect other concerns. So far as the reliefs appear to show such battles, they may use the past to legitimize the present (cf. Baines 1989a). The message of these pieces is symbolic rather than realistic or historiographic.

The prestige significance of knife handles is fairly apparent. The knives themselves were large objects of pressure-flaked flint (Midant-Reynes 1987), whose manufacture achieved extraordinary virtuosity. These were highly valued products, some of whose associations must have been hallowed by antiquity; their forms were imitated in large copper knives by the First Dynasty (e.g., Emery 1961, pls. 42-45). The palettes are elaborate, ceremonial descendants of the commonest predynastic prestige objects (Petrie 1920, pls. 43-45), which were small slabs used for grinding cosmetics, especially eye-paint, a material that remained a status marker for much of the dynastic period and had divine associations. The latest palette, that of Narmer, is a votive, nonfunctional piece, as are a number of related objects. The small group of decorated maceheads comes from the "Main Deposit" at

Hierakonpolis (Quibell 1900, pls. 25-28; Adams 1974 pls. 1-4). Like palettes, maceheads were ancient prestige objects, mostly rather small and made of hard stone (Petrie 1920, pls. 25-26; Adams 1974 pls. 5-6; Hoffman *et al.* 1982, 145-46; Ciałowicz 1987). The ceremonial pieces are very much larger and covered with relief decoration. They seem to constitute a short-lived royal appropriation of a widespread form; nonroyal maceheads disappeared. Although maces continued to be symbols of royalty in the dynastic period, relief-decorated examples are not known from then; but details of the iconography of the early group can be related to later smiting scenes, suggesting some continuity of ideas.

The main decorative themes are animals—hunted or aggressors—warfare, and, on the latest objects, royal rituals (Williams and Logan, 1987, place the rituals earlier). An important motif that later occurs only in marginal contexts is that of fabulous animals; these extend the significance of animal combats into the mythical and emblematic (Altenmüller, 1980a, does not discuss these aspects; see also Westendorf 1966, 1-10 [interpretation problematic]; Baines 1993). Among many possible meanings, the hunting or domination of wild animals probably symbolizes the maintenance of order and containment of disorder (see e.g., Kemp 1989, 46-53) and is reserved for the elite in many societies, especially complex, stratified ones; even where hunting is functional, it is very often surrounded by symbolism. In an alternative presentation which implies that the king stands outside the mundane order of things, wild animals are a metaphor for his power. Objects that stand quite early in the group, such as the Brooklyn knife (Asselberghs 1961, figs. 39-42; Needler 1984, no. 165), the hunters' palette (Asselberghs 1961, figs. 122-24), and the two dog palette from the deposit at Hierakonpolis (Asselberghs 1961, figs. 127-28; Baines 1993, 60-61 figs. 1-2), exemplify the hunting theme in various ways. Royal interpretations of all are possible and elite ones necessary. Their iconography is not standardized, while that of the later objects—among which are palettes, the Gebel el-Araq knife (Sievertsen 1992), the maceheads, and some seals—moves toward the "classical" Egyptian and is contemporary with writing (some are inscribed). They gradually reverse the treatment of animals and eliminate fabulous ones. This material may span the period from Cemetery U to Narmer; only the latest objects can be sited securely within that time.

Some palettes decorated chiefly with animals have Horus names

(§ 2.3 ahead) at the top, or near the center among the animals (Asselberghs 1961, figure 170), and so were royal, as probably were several unidentified but artistically superior ones. The hunters' palette, which has no Horus name, has, offset near the top, a small reed building with a domed roof and a motif of the fused forequarters of two bulls facing in opposite directions (Figure 3.5). In late predynastic iconography the bull is a primary royal symbol, and this pair figure is likely to represent the king or kingship. Similarly, the building, which is out of scale and context with the rest of the relief, is symbolic or emblematic and may signify the same as the enclosure element in the Horus name. Alternatively, it could be a shrine similar in form to the heraldic shrine of Lower Egypt known from later times (Arnold 1982). Whichever interpretation is correct, the group of building and double bull probably symbolizes royalty with a device that later disappeared. Whereas the hunters around the edge of the palette appear to be equal to one another, on this interpretation the superior king is shown only indirectly, in a convention that anticipates dynastic developments (important "structuralist" reading: Tefnin 1979).

The chief victims on this palette are lions at either end of the enclosed area. On the later palettes, lions are symbols of kingship, as on the "cities" palette (Figure 3. 4), where seven heraldic animals hold hoes and stand on the brick enclosure plans of fortified settlements—at that date probably an idealized form. The order of the animals is: falcon and three lost in the upper row; lion, scorpion, pair of falcon standards in the lower. This gives primacy to falcon and lion, while the pair of standards is a royal element establishing that the whole is a distributed representation of the king. Animals which might have been among those lost are bull, catfish, vulture, cobra, and perhaps elephant (the Seth animal proposed by Schott, 1950, 20, is dubious). All the animals are dangerous ones symbolic of royal power. The representation is normally interpreted as the destruction of the settlements (e.g., Schott 1950, 20-21; Baines 1985a, 42 with figure 10; the interpretation of Bietak, 1986, ignores normal Egyptian conventions), within which are groups of proto-hieroglyphs and square shapes; this is paralleled on the Narmer palette (see ahead). The fragmentary bull palette (Asselberghs 1961, figs. 196-97), perhaps the artistic masterpiece of the group, has similar settlements on one side, while on the other side the supports for standards terminate in human hands grasping a rope holding captives (lost). The standards are two jackals, an ibis(?), a falcon, and the emblem of the god Min, introducing a symbolic or hieroglyphic sign (already ancient) in addition to the other "wild" elements. As a god of the eastern desert, Min could be associated with the wild, but such a unified interpretation may not be appropriate.

This ambivalence of wild animals, hunted and hunting, endured through Egyptian history and has many parallels. The lion, the "king of beasts," is the premier victim of the royal hunt, but tame lions are the most prestigious of all pets (de Wit 1951, 10-15), and were kept by King Aha of the First Dynasty and buried with him (Dreyer *et al.* 1990, 67, 86-87). In the late Eighteenth Dynasty, Amenhotep III issued scarabs with inscriptions commemorating the no doubt exaggerated numbers of lions and wild bulls he had killed in his first ten regnal years (Blankenberg-van Delden 1969, 16-18).

The wild animals which represent the king's power may also form his name (as Dreyer argues also for the group of names associated with Tomb U-j). The names of the latest predynastic kings include the scorpion and the catfish. The scorpion is often an aggressor without name on objects of the period (e.g., Quibell 1900 plate 19), while Narmer's catfish wields a weapon on a seal (Figure 3.6) and occurs separately on a later ivory tag (Schott 1950, plate 7 figure 16). Dreyer (1992) has proposed the existence of a king Crocodile, who might have been a northern rival, contemporaneous with Dynasty 0 (compare also the crocodile on the palette Asselberghs 1961, figure 157 [authentic?]). Associations of the king with the other animals enumerated here—but not with the crocodile—continued in dynastic times, while the scorpion became the goddess Selket, who was still related to kingship, and scorpions also occur in heraldic scenes; they are absent from royal titulary and epithets. The catfish was an archetypal agent of disorder that swallowed the penis of Osiris, which had been thrown into the Nile by the followers of Seth; it is also mentioned in an Old Kingdom fording song addressed to the god Bata, who was connected with Seth (Altenmüller 1974, 224-27). Almost all the royal animals are ones especially feared by people, and this can be linked to the position of the king in society (among relevant fauna only the hippopotamus is absent). In later times his moral community with humanity was less important than his cosmic actions and interaction with the gods; this imperiousness may have begun early.

The palettes can be seen as moving from a rather ambivalent celebration of the containment of disorder, in compositions both framed by and including figures of wild hunting dogs (Asselberghs 1961, figs. 127-28; Baines 1993), through multiple representations of the king, who is shown in the guise of wild animals subduing enemies, as the Horus name, or finally in full human depictions, which occur on the palette (Figure 3.7) and macehead of Narmer (Figure 3.8). Except on the macehead, the king towers over the other human figures as a different order of being. The Scorpion macehead (Figure 3.9; significant new reconstruction Ciałowicz 1993, 55-59 with figure 17) also has a fully human king (further maceheads Adams 1974, pls. 1-4; Ciałowicz 1993, 62-64, figs. 19-20). The existence and identity of Scorpion have been disputed and his exact chronological position is uncertain (cf. Baumgartel 1966 [arguments unconvincing]; Dreyer, 1986b, 41-43, suggests that Scorpion came between Narmer and Aha). The only other early human figures of kings are in rock drawings (de Morgan *et al.* 1894, 203; cf. Fairservis, 1983, 6, with figure 8; Winkler 1938, plate 14b; Kees 1961, plate 3a). These are of unknown date and peripheral in relation to major royal monuments.

This absence of early human representations of the king contrasts with the significant number of other human figures on the palettes. The best way of explaining this discrepancy may be to relate it to the lack of figures of gods, to which the only exception is the Horus name and the emblematic Horus falcon on the Narmer Palette and on a macehead (Adams 1974, plate 1; Ciałowicz 1993, 63 figure 19); no god is shown in a non-animal form (on emblematic representation, see Baines 1985a, 41-47, 277-305; 1989b, 474). In general, gods are depicted only in sacred contexts and are not common before the temple reliefs of the later Early Dynastic Period and Old Kingdom. The world of the palettes may then be a symbolic, emblematic world in which some animals stand for other actors and the only human figures are subordinates and enemies. Contrary to the view of Hornung (1982a, 103-05), this iconography need not be interpreted literally as showing that human beings were thought weak and defenseless in comparison with animals. Either some categories of being could not be represented, or lost contexts could have contained more direct representations of the king and the gods. The latter suggestion might seem implausible at first sight, but the developed form of the earliest iconography of kings could hardly have been achieved without forerunners, and for the following 1500 years, representations of kings were largely incompatible with full-size figures of human beings and animals; the same may have been true earlier. Unattested contexts of representation could have been in temples or on perishable materials. This incompatibility was a feature of the decorum which articulated the system of representation and iconography (Baines 1985a, 277-305). Other vital elements in the system include the base line or register line, which appears in Hierakonpolis Tomb 100 and is fully formed by the time of the Narmer palette. As in monumental brickwork, the rectilinearity of the line expresses order, in addition to the clarity it gives to a composition.

If this backward projection of ideas associated with base lines, decorum, and emblematic representation of deities and the king is justifiable, these monuments exhibit a thematic continuity which transcends apparent change. These can then be validly interpreted, despite the incompleteness of the sample. The later palettes deal with conquest and ritual. An innovation which can be read off the changing compositions is that the earlier pattern incorporated and contained disorder within the cosmos, whereas the later, rectilinear treatment banished it to the margins or removed it altogether. Such an ambivalence is found in dynastic period views of what is acknowledged as existing within, or lies outside, the ordered world (see te Velde 1977; Hornung 1982a, 172-85). The shift to the opposite pole of these possibilities during Dynasty 0 could relate to internal change rather than external threats. Whatever may have stimulated the presentation of order on the Narmer palette and the maceheads, it was normative for later periods. Order must be constantly defended against the encroaching and interpenetrating threat of disorder or of the uncreated world.

The hierarchies of decorum set the king apart from humanity as the only being who could be shown in the same compositions as gods and who was, with the gods, the sole protagonist of order. Activities of other humans were not depicted on royal monuments, while nonroyal ones did not include representations of the king until the New Kingdom; even the royal Horus name is absent from Old Kingdom private tombs. As a result, the monumental record is very one-sided. This commitment to discrimination and order, which implies that order is always under threat, goes with the rigidity of representational conventions in art; in later periods it was elaborated in written texts, but it probably had a verbal equivalent from the beginning. The search for order is paralleled in many societies which believe that the present world could cease at any time. These attitudes are the opposite of the assertions that might be read off massive Egyptian monuments, but those assertions were made in the apprehension that what they said might not be so.

Specific rituals can hardly be identified in the earlier palettes. Conquest can itself be a ritual, and the seemingly specific conquests of the later palettes could be used as analogies for the generalized containment or defeat of disorder on the earlier ones, as was done in dynastic times. As with the administrative inscriptions of Irihor, this material is best interpreted in the light of later evidence. Williams and Logan (1987) have suggested that a knife handle records a fusion of ritual and conquest in a representation of the royal *sed*-festival. This ritual of renewal, ideally performed after thirty years of a king's rule, was the archetypal celebration to which he aspired, often in the next world (the ritual is not well understood in detail; see Kaiser 1983, with references). Williams and Logan also trace forerunners of the scenes on the handle as far back as the painting in Hierakonpolis tomb 100, interpreting a wide range of decoration as belonging to a single cycle. This fusion of motifs is significant, but the themes they analyze had few successors and the identification of elements on some pieces is problematic. Their arguments do, however, supply a significant context for the latest predynastic presentation of conquest and royal ritual. In order to exemplify this, I describe three monuments.

The Narmer palette has on its principal side (the technical "verso"; see Figure 3.7) a large group of the king, who wears the white crown and is accompanied by a sandal bearer, about to smite a kneeling enemy with a mace. Facing the king is an emblematic group of a falcon with one human arm leading a personified "land" sign by a rope and perching on six papyrus stems that sprout from the sign. Beside the prisoner is a pair of hieroglyphs, perhaps his name. Beneath the register line are two captioned figures of limp enemies with their bodies as if spread across the picture surface. The other side has three registers. The top one shows the king wearing the red crown, preceded by four standards and with an attendant on each side, facing a spread of ten decapitated corpses. Above the corpses is a probable caption of a door leaf with a falcon behind it and a boat with a falcon on a harpoon hovering above. It looks as if the king is inspecting enemies who have been executed or killed in battle. There have been inconclusive attempts to identify the enemy through the caption (e.g., Kaplony 1958). The central register shows two keepers holding leashed interlaced felines whose elongated necks delineate the circular cosmetic depression. In the bottom oval, the king in the form of a bull butts down an enclosure wall with an enigmatic caption similar to those on the "cities" palette. Below is an enemy with splayed limbs.

The two principal scenes might be read serially as a military victory indicated by the decapitated corpses, followed by the ritual execution of the enemy leader. The groups at the bottom, which are emblematic in terms of later iconography, could have a similar sequence, but cannot be linked directly with the main part. The captions seem to refer to specific people, events and places, and the enemies have no clear foreign ethnic markers, so that an internal victory of south over north appears to be shown. Thus, Gardiner (1957, 7) interpreted the emblematic group as "The falcon-god Horus (i.e. king) leads captive the inhabitants of the papyrus-land ($T\beta$-$m\dot{h}.w$ 'the Delta')." This is plausible enough, but the "papyrus-land" had been part of the state for generations. Unless this is a rebellion—in later times rebellions were not depicted and hardly mentioned in texts—such an event does not fit the context. It is better to see the composition as a ritual affirmation of conquest, not a real event. The authentic-seeming detail could be derived from traditional sources, such as narratives about who was defeated in the unification of the country; in later periods too, Egypt or parts of it were included among the regions shown in subjection to the king. In the more bureaucratic Old Kingdom, captions on reliefs of defeated Libyans were transmitted with full accuracy from one inscription of the motif to the next (e.g., Hornung 1966, 18). This instance can be brought right back to the time of Narmer, whose seal showing the defeat of Libyans (see Figure 3.6) has a composition related to the reliefs of Sahure (though not the same figure types or names; Borchardt *et al.* 1913, plate 1; see further Baines in press a). Thus, the model for interpreting these scenes should not be the historical record or chronicle but something more like the Christian iconography of

Biblical events, which are not thought to occur again because they are represented repeatedly; the difficulties for Egyptologists have been that the king of the time was always named in the compositions, and the same forms were also used on occasion for recording genuinely new events.

The Narmer macehead (Figure 3.8) has a principal composition in several registers, with a second group set off by vertical dividing lines. The content is closely related to the *sed*-festival. The king, who wears the red crown and probably a long cloak, sits inside a canopy on a block-shaped throne (Kuhlmann 1977, 50-61) on a stepped dais, and is surrounded by attendants and fan bearers. In front, in the uppermost register, is an enclosure apparently containing a cow and a calf (a pair known in later mortuary rituals), with the four standards that accompany the king behind. Beneath is a register headed by a female figure inside a canopied carrying chair, an important but problematic *sed*-festival motif that is paralleled on the Scorpion macehead (see ahead), in the First Dynasty (e.g., Schott 1950, plate 7, figure 16), and later (full study, with partly different interpretation, Kaiser 1983; see further 1986). Three running(?) figures follow, set within a space defined by two sets of three crescent shapes shown in scenes of a royal *sed*-festival run (First Dynasty example: Schott 1950, plate 9, figure 18). Here the runners could be prisoners, but they may also be ritual performers. Below and behind is a large hieroglyph of a captive, with numerals for 120,000. In a rectangular space beneath are a bull and a calf, with numerals for 400,000 and 1,422,000; the bull and antelope could perhaps be the animals in the enclosure above. The separate scene shows a shrine, with a building, surmounted by an ibis, of similar form to that on the hunters' palette, a screen wall with a large cleft pole, and a jar on a stand. Beneath is an oval enclosure containing three antelopes(?). An archaeological analogy for this sanctuary, including the enclosure, has been found at Hierakonpolis (Hoffman 1986). Similar scenes without the enclosures are quite common on First Dynasty tags (e.g., Schott 1950, plate 7, figure 14; Baines 1991a, *passim*).

Thus, the macehead seems to show the presentation of captives and booty to the king in the context of a public *sed*-festival ritual. The whole probably relates to the separate shrine, which may legitimize ritual and conquest while also forming the ultimate destination of the wealth acquired. Captives and animal booty on the scale of the figures given are implausible; as on the palette, what is shown is made apparently precise by captions, but is a prospective ritual or a commemoration rather than a specific event. Numbers in ancient sources are in any case almost always suspect.

The Scorpion macehead (Figure 3.9), of which much less than half is preserved, is more elaborate than that of Narmer. The top register contains standards on poles, with lapwings, the emblematic birds of the "subjects," shown captive and suspended from the standards. Ciałowicz (1993, 55-59 with figure 17), building on an observation of Helen Whitehouse, has reconstructed a left-facing figure of the king wearing the red crown and straddling the top two registers, standing in front of a group of bows attached to standards that face those with the lapwings; I suggest that he could be holding a rope and leading the bows, who symbolize Egypt's foreign enemies. In the middle register, the king, wearing the white crown, holds a hoe, while in front of him a man bends with a basket and another holds out a staff-like emblem, perhaps a stylized sheaf of grain. Behind this scene are clumps of papyrus plants in two sub-registers, suggesting a marshy environment. A second, lost scene began in the same registers with two female figures in carrying chairs, similar to the canopied figure on the Narmer macehead, and a male attendant, with below four women dancing (Kaiser, 1983, does not mention the carrying chair figures, perhaps because they have no canopies; First Dynasty parallel Schott 1950, plate 7, figure 16; Williams and Logan, 1987, 265, 271, consider that they are captives). The bottom register is divided by waterways into a kind of map. People work on the waterways and a boat sails on the water; the enclosed areas of land include two buildings rather like the shrine on the Narmer macehead and the one on the hunters' palette, and a palm with a protective fence. The preserved decoration seems to be concerned with agriculture, fertility and the land, in the context of domination and the sed-festival. (Another fragmentary macehead seems to be associated with the sed-festival: Adams 1974, plates 1-2; Ciałowicz 1993, 62-62 figure 19.)

On these objects the king is overwhelmingly dominant, while their find context in the deposit at Hierakonpolis shows that his actions are dedicated to the gods, who are themselves absent. This absence, which is in keeping with decorum, gives the king more prominence than an abstract statement of his position in the cosmos might suggest, helping to project his status—especially in

relation to humanity—in a context where he is in theory subordinate. The Narmer palette implies more. The two human/
bovine heads at the top, which are probably vestigial successors of
the high relief animals on other palettes, are Hathor or Bat heads
(Fischer 1962) and allude to the supports of the sky, commonly
envisaged as a cow. The falcon completing the Horus name between them may be absent because it is conceived as inhabiting
the sky above (see § 2.3). Thus, the palette shows the cosmos, the
ordered world, outside and beneath which the prisoners are to be
cast. The king maintains the order of the world and dedicates the
fruit of his efforts to Horus, who hovers above.

The standards and attendants define and circumscribe the
king's presence. The most prominent people are his sandal
bearer, who also carries a jar and is probably captioned "servant/
attendant of the king," and a man wearing a leopard skin and a
long wig, captioned with an uncertain group (cf. Kees 1958); the
latter is probably a priest. Together with the fan bearers, they may
contribute to the ritual and attend to the king's person, protecting
him against harm from outside, and the outside from the harm his
person might cause (cf. Hornung 1982a, 139, 142). Several of
these motifs have later, explicit parallels; thus, the fans signify that,
in the words of a very common formula, "all protection and life"
are around the king (e.g., Baines 1985a, 74). The basic set of
standards, which consists of a jackal, a cushion-like object, and two
falcons (the standards vary in form), proclaims the king's power,
probably by associating him with protective deities. The falcons
may be the "Two Lords," Horus and Seth, given a single manifestation as the king's protectors. The jackal may represent
Khentimentiu, the local god of Abydos, or Anubis. A jackal is
common in First Dynasty inscriptions (e.g., Palermo Stone:
Schäfer 1902, 15-21) and was one of the principal gods of kingship, with a much more important role for royalty than jackals had
in later periods. The jackal's prominence can be seen as a transformation of the role of canines on the palettes (Baines 1993, 68-
69). The cushion-like object is the king's *nḥn* (Posener 1965a), a
word homophonous with the name of Hierakonpolis and perhaps
related to it. In later times the standards appeared at *sed*-festivals
and were called the "Attendants of Horus (*šmsjw-ḥrw*)," a term
closely related to the early kingship (Kaiser 1959).

The king's presence was surrounded by power and danger;
these had to be displayed and contained in the public contexts

depicted in the reliefs. A Fifth Dynasty text shows how inadvertent contact with an item of royal insignia was dangerous or life-threatening. Two others indicate that to be permitted to kiss his foot instead of the ground in front of him was a benediction (Roccati 1982, 102, 109). The paraphernalia of his appearance displayed and reinforced this aura, probably accompanying him constantly outside the palace.

One further aspect of the deposition of these reliefs in a temple should be considered. Only priests—many of whom were probably at the same time high officials and members of the inner elite—had access to temples, so who else saw or was persuaded by the depictions? The system of temple decoration, to which these objects are related, was not public, and there need not have been similar depictions on display. If the decoration of palaces was like that of later times, only the smiting scene would have been at home in them. So although the reliefs look like propaganda, correlates in the everyday world would have had to be in living ceremonial, in what was proclaimed about the king, and in the architecture of palaces. All of these could have conveyed similar messages powerfully. The reliefs, however, must be interpreted on their own terms, as objects with a very small audience who were deeply involved with their meaning and creation. If a wider repertory existed, it was probably not closely comparable with what is preserved, because its contexts would have been different.

2.3. Ideology and Aggression II: Royal Names

The irreducible evidence for royal ideology is in the king's names and titles (for the earlier group, see § 2 here). Because of the iconographic potential of hieroglyphic writing, these have more than linguistic significance, although the writing did not represent spoken forms fully. Like conventions of representation, those of writing were not at all standardized before the First Dynasty; the royal titulary continued to evolve until the Twelfth Dynasty (c. 1920 BC; on implications and development of early writing, see Baines 1988, 1989b; Vernus 1993).

The royal names of Dynasty 0 contain one or both of a figure of a falcon and a tall rectangle with a vertical pattern in its lower part (attested as early as Tomb U-j at Abydos, see § 2 here). To these is added a third, variable element, normally a flat rectangle above the pattern (Figure 3.10; Kaiser and Dreyer 1982, 263, figure 14: full range). The falcon represents the god Horus, with whom the king is in some sense identified, while the tall rectangle is the royal palace complex or residence (cf. Atzler 1974). In later Egyptian the rectangle, which was also used secondarily as a throne design, is termed a *srḫ* (Kuhlmann 1977, 60-61). The optional signs inside the flat rectangle are the individual king's "Horus name." This is an epithet or title assumed on coming to the throne, not the king's birth name, which remains unknown. The identification of palace compound and throne is a measure of the importance of thrones, while it also implies that wherever the king is, he manifests Horus, who perches on the palace enclosure, and, as he sits on the throne, creates a virtual "palace" (Baines 1990a, 1991a; Wilkinson's identification of the Horus name on a Naqada I pot, 1985, must be rejected, because the bird does not look like a falcon: Payne 1993, 40, no. 174, figure 25.)

Royal residences were symbolically vital places from which the king exercised power (compare e.g., O'Connor 1989b). The king ruled in the palace, where he had his normal being, or he went out from it to perform rituals, to progress through the country, or for political or military action. Later residences were named for particular rulers, but they too embodied the general institution of kingship. Words for palace came to be words for king, replacing the individual with the institution; this is the origin of the word "Pharaoh," that is "Great Estate/House," commonly used for the king from the mid-Eighteenth Dynasty.

In the earliest Horus names, the palace fuses the plan and elevation of an enclosure—the palace compound—with a distinctive, concave falcon's perch (Kaplony 1965, 152-55). The characteristic feature of the enclosure is the vertical pattern of its elevation. The later form of this is shown by the preserved mud-brick enclosure of a First Dynasty palace or temple in the settlement at Hierakonpolis (Weeks, in Fairservis *et al.* 1971-72, 29-33; see now O'Connor 1992), and by First Dynasty nonroyal tombs at Saqqara and Naqada. This general design later became extremely common in the form of the standard "false door" in royal and nonroyal tombs and temples. It consists of an elaborate pattern of recesses and salients and is closely paralleled in Mesopotamia (Heinrich 1982; for related mosaic cones found at Buto, see von der Way and Schmidt 1987). It has further parallels in unrelated brick architectural traditions such as that of medieval Islam, and may be a natural decorative use of brick, but it could imitate forerunners in such materials as reeds and wattle (cf. Heinrich 1982, figs. 1-43; see also Williams and Logan 1987, 270). Whichever of these possibilities is correct, brick was the prestige material of the time. Like other designs, the "palace façade" motif is strongly rectilinear and thus expressive of order. Large royal enclosures, probably plastered and painted white with colored patterning like that on First Dynasty tombs at Saqqara (e.g., Emery 1961, 130-31), would have dominated the floodplain and any settlements near them. The king must have had palaces in several parts of the country. Palaces were larger, above-ground, living architectural counterparts of the special forms and locations of royal tombs.

The falcon perching on the palace enclosure is a very powerful metaphor. What may be the earliest examples (Kaiser and Dreyer 1982, 263 figure 14 nos. 1-5) show two falcons facing each other. This pairing, which may express one of the dualities of Egyptian thought and is paralleled by the paired standards on palettes, emphasizes that the motif had abstract associations from the start (for the standards and "Two Lords," see § 2.2 here). The abode of the gods is primarily the sky (Hornung 1982a, 227-30), especially for a deity envisaged as a bird of prey. A god may descend to earth and inhabit a cult image in a temple, exercising power and receiving worship as long as he stays there (cf. Hornung 1982a, especially 135-38). Gods can be manifest in cult images or in living exemplars, which may or may not be of the same form or species as their principal manifestation. The falcon on the palace façade signifies the god inhabiting the palace or manifesting himself in the king.

The palace is consecrated by the divine presence and analogous with a temple. The Horus name written in the upper rectangle of the design describes the conjunction of Horus with a king, who manifests a named, mostly power-laden aspect of Horus—the "Mean Catfish," as Narmer can be translated (Dreyer 1986, 37), or more generally, the "Fighter," Aha (catalogue of names von Beckerath 1984; many readings are disputed). No god's being is exhausted by any manifestation, so that Horus exists apart from the king. Since the palace design presents the institutional aspect of kingship, this combination of god and king does not state that the king is intrinsically a god, or a god from birth—which would be nonsensical with high mortality—but that in his exercise of office he may manifest the god. A falcon perching or hovering behind figures is also a symbol of protection (as on the celebrated statue of Khafre, e.g., Lange and Hirmer 1967, pls. IV, 30-31;

Brunner-Traut 1971, 20-25; Baines 1990a, 19-27). Yet another
image, from the comb of the First Dynasty King Wadj, shows a pair
of wings with a boat and a falcon above it (Frankfort 1948, figure
17; Baines 1990a, 12, figure 4; partial parallel Emery 1961, 50,
figure 10, from the reign of Aha). This seems to present the sky
itself as a falcon—a motif later pervasive in the form of the winged
solar disc—with Horus in another form and perhaps representing
the sun, the king, or both, navigating across it. As the supreme god
of the pantheon, Horus hovers above the cosmos. In relation to
the king he perches above the palace in support, yet he is also
himself the king. The Horus aspect does not exhaust the king's
divinity (see § 3.1 ahead), nor does it proclaim that he is in any
simple sense a god.

The burials, iconography, and names of the kings of Dynasty 0
present an evolved system of rule, ideology, and iconography in a
well established state, but they also formed a prelude. Narmer is
crucial here. His name is attested from all over Egypt, from the
Eastern Desert (Winkler 1938, plate 11, 1), and from a number of
sites in Palestine (for background, see studies in van den Brink
1992, 345-425). His palette and macehead are crucial sources for
early kingship. By his time the southern frontier of Egypt had been
extended from Gebel el-Silsila, south of Hierakonpolis, to
Elephantine at the First Cataract (the graffito near Aswan, de
Morgan 1894, 203, may date to this period, while late Naqada II
material has been found in the town site: Kaiser *et al.* 1984, 170-
72). His tomb is, however, hardly larger than others in Cemetery B. On the basis of technical arguments and of literal interpretations of the apparent record of events on his palette, he was
long, and probably incorrectly, considered to be the Menes of the
king lists and of legend (e.g., Edwards 1971, 11-15, with references;
see also ahead). Recent evidence confirms that he was seen as an
ancestor (§ 3.1 ahead), but he was probably the last of his line and
not a great conqueror. The principal change of his period seems
rather to be that economic growth was harnessed both in
monuments that have been discovered and also in far-flung and
archaeologically visible networks. Aha was to transform further the
kingship's exploitation of the country's resources and establish
some characteristics of Egypt's development.

3. The Early Dynastic Period

3.1. Annals and Titulary; Royal Action and Ritual
(list of kings figure 3.13)

The assumption that Narmer's successor or second successor Aha (cf. Dreyer 1987a) inaugurated the First Dynasty is based in part on the reconstruction of the fragments of the Palermo Stone, which gives records of the kings of the First–Fifth dynasties (Schäfer 1902, cited here by page and number; Kaiser 1961, 42-53; Helck 1974b; object. probably later: Helck 1970; *contra*: Fischer 1976, 48). The first line of the stone has names of kings we would term predynastic, determined by hieroglyphs for king, some of which wear the red crown and some the double crown (Breasted 1930), the full symbol of royalty first attested in the First Dynasty (earlier examples cited by Kaiser, 1961, 53-54, are doubtful). The preserved names, all of which belong to rulers with the red crown, do not seem to be in the Egyptian language; they may derive from a tradition relating to remote ancestors (cf. Kaiser 1961, 39-40). Any known name such as Narmer would have stood on lost parts of the stone. As the first king of the First Dynasty, Aha is widely assumed to be equivalent to Menes, but his name is lost from the Palermo Stone. Apart from actions which support this identification, uncertain arguments have been derived from a sealing alternating Narmer and a name *mn*, which suggests that *mn* was a leading person of the reign of Narmer and so a plausible successor (Helck 1953; not necessarily a prince, see Fischer 1961), and from the group *mn* in a different context on a label of Aha (Emery 1961, 50 figure 10, fragmentary duplicate Kaiser & Dreyer 1982 plate 57c; these documents have also been used wrongly by some scholars to support the identification of Narmer with Menes).

For the first three dynasties (lines 2-4 of the Palermo Stone), the names of the kings stood in horizontal lines above rectangles giving either the "name" assigned to each year, which was known by a salient event or achievement, or, for incomplete years, chronological information. The level of the year's inundation was placed in a compartment below. The whole looks like an aid to administration—the inundation levels were necessary for calculating taxes—but events selected for year names are historically and ideologically motivated, giving insights into what was significant for the king and his role. The choice was presumably made just before a year and could record an event from the previous year or something in immediate prospect. This naming of years probably formalizes an oral practice that may have been loose, rather than organized in memorized lists, but the written forms are bureaucratic and impersonal. Wooden and ivory labels of the First–Third dynasties from royal and elite tombs fill out this material with additional examples, or with different and fuller kinds of records. Continuous language and connected discourse were not written until much later; the annals and year labels are confined to caption-like statements and pictorial representations.

The annals show a high degree of system. Part of this is probably due to later editing, because the frequent "first time" notations would be meaningful only when a sequence of years could be taken together (the label Spencer 1993, 87 figure 67, the only one with a "first time," may not be authentic, as noted by Swan Hall 1986, 6). The first year of a king's reign was termed "Appearance of the *nswt*-king; appearance of the *bity*-king; uniting Upper and Lower Egypt; encircling the Wall (Memphis)" (27 no. 7; 15 no. 3 has only "uniting ..."). This year retained this name until the end of the Old Kingdom, during which most other years were numbered; the "Appearance ..." element also occurs in year names that mention significant royal rituals, notably the *sed*-festival. The commonest year name, to which variable elements could be added, is "Following Horus (*šmst ḥrw*)" (e.g., 15 nos. 1, 4; 16 nos. 6, 8); this was biennial and came to be numbered (e.g., 22 no. 3, 23 nos. 5, 7). Its successor, which formed the basis of Old Kingdom year dating, was the mostly biennial "cattle count" (Gardiner 1945). The "Following of Horus" was probably a royal procession through the country conducting a census for taxation and displaying the king's authority. Legal functions of the king in hearing disputes and settling cases would surely have been involved, but are not recorded. This was the chief public administrative role of the king, but it was not an "appearance" in the same sense as an important ritual: in comparison, it would appear almost secular, although its formulation shows a typical emphasis on divine, as against human, activities. Most of the remaining annal entries concern the construction of temples, manufacture of cult equipment, and performance of rituals.

The chief legendary action of Menes recorded in later sources, including Classical ones, was the founding of the capital at Memphis (cf. Morenz 1973a); any record of this on the Palermo Stone is lost. The Memphite area had become important during

Dynasty 0, but Memphis—or the now inaccessible city's necropolis at Saqqara—was not yet its center. The earliest large tomb at Saqqara dates to Aha. The coincidence of this and his possible identification with Menes may be too neat, but very many rulers of new dynasties mark a beginning by founding cities and make administrative reforms, which is what year names and annals constitute. There is no reason for undue skepticism here (e.g., Morenz 1973a), but "Menes" is the founder of a dynasty and its city, not of the state. The nature of the transition from dynasty to dynasty is unknown. The dominance of the kingship did not make the ruler sacrosanct, and the change may well have been violent.

With the increased use of writing in the First Dynasty came developments in the royal titulary (Müller 1938; Barta 1975, 50-57), whose major components expanded to four. The first addition was the "Two Ladies" title, which related the king to the tutelary goddesses of the chief places at the extreme ends of the country, Nekhbet of Hierakonpolis and Wadjet of Buto (cf. § 4 ahead). These were the goddesses who protected the king, and through him the "Two Lands" of Egypt. The first probable appearance of Nekhbet is as a protecting figure hovering over the king on the Narmer sealing and macehead (Figures 3.6, and 3. 8), while Wadjet is not known before the reign of Aha, when she is paired with Nekhbet on ivory tags (e.g., Emery 1961, 50 figure 10; Kaiser and Dreyer 1982, plate 57c). As with the Horus name, what follows the "Two Ladies" was later an epithet proclaiming the aspect of the goddesses the king manifested, but in origin his personal name may have been placed here. This identification across the divisions of sex and of single/dual is not literal; only metaphysically could the king be a manifestation both of Horus and of Nekhbet and Wadjet.

By the mid First Dynasty, a third title was added, *nswt-bity* (reading uncertain, cf. Fecht 1960a, 17-30; Schenkel 1986). This proclaims the "dual" king, using the primary word for king, *nswt*, associated with the white crown and later with Upper Egypt, and the less prominent *bity*, associated with the red crown, Lower Egypt, and antiquity (cf. Otto 1960). The title is mostly translated "King of Upper and Lower Egypt," but in origin it probably fused two hierarchically ordered words for king and aspects of kingship. The places of origin and geographical associations of the words are unknown. After *nswt-bity* was written the king's own birth name, which naturally has little bearing on royal ideology. The later king lists from which the outline of history has been reconstructed used the birth names, including Menes (if it is authentic), so that there are problems in correlating the lists with the names on original material.

The fourth title, of which forerunners are known from the First–Second dynasties, is attested for Djoser in the Third. This became what is known as the "Golden Horus" name, a very uncertain rendering of a group showing a falcon on the hieroglyph for "gold." This title too is followed by an epithet which does not seem essentially different from that attached to the "Two Ladies" name. The Golden Horus name is the least understood element in the titulary (cf. Gardiner 1957, 73; Barta, 1975, 55-56 [problematic]).

The titulary stated who and what the king was in relation to a set of deities, and was probably accompanied in declamation by extensive eulogies, as are known in writing from later times (e.g., Blumenthal 1970; Hornung 1957). The Horus name proclaimed that his abode was the palace, presenting him to the elite and thence to society. Most of what was recorded in the annals had the opposite focus: the king acted for the gods and related to them, but in doing so he legitimized his exactions from society and solicited the return of divine favors to him and to humanity. The power of the gods was indefinitely great, superior to and more diverse than that of the king; he and humanity needed them. The cosmos consisted of the gods, the dead, the king, and humanity, all of whom stood together in their struggle to maintain order against the encompassing threat of disorder. The most succinct later definition of the king's role states that he performs the cult of the gods and the dead and "sets order (*maat*) in place of disorder" (Chapter 1 here). This fundamental idea is known from the epithet of the Second Dynasty king, Sekhemib "who goes forth for *maat*," that is, who champions order; it may have been basic to Egyptian royal ideology and religion from earlier.

3.2. Royal Action and Ritual

"Historical events" can hardly be recovered for a period as remote as that studied here. What can be studied is the king's embodiment of the ideas of order and of royal action, and how they were mobilized in monuments and iconography. An instance of the king's concern for the gods is the enormous deposit of votive offerings from Hierakonpolis (Quibell 1900; Adams 1974), which contained many objects discussed here and consisted principally of royal material of dynasties 0-II (dating controversial, cf. Dreyer 1986, 37-46; Whitehouse 1987). Expenditure on temple construction may have been quite considerable (contrast Kemp 1989, 65-107, with O'Connor 1992), and Hierakonpolis was one of the most important temples in the country; but similar offerings would also have been made in other places. Nonetheless, the level of offerings to the gods was probably below mortuary expenditure, particularly if the country's large numbers of major nonroyal tombs are taken into account. What is strikingly absent among early temple finds is royal statuary: except for a small ivory figurine and two statues of the end of the Second Dynasty (Figure 3.11), none is certainly known. It is unlikely that there was much in ivory or hard stone, because some should then be preserved (for a probable statue emplacement for the mortuary cult in the tomb of Den, see Dreyer *et al.* 1990, 76-78, plate 23b).

Within the palace, the king's life must have been enveloped in ceremony or ritual, while outside it, most of his recorded actions were rituals, which might be public to some extent. The kingship and the individual king's position in it were the focus of rituals (cf. Fairman 1958). The *sed*-festival, the most prestigious ritual after accession, predynastic evidence for which I discussed in § 2.2, is known from the First Dynasty (Hornung, Staehelin *et al.* 1974, 16-20; Dreyer *et al.* 1990, 80-81, plate 26) and through a statuette of a king in a *sed*-festival cloak (Spencer 1993, 75 figure 52). The ritual might not literally take place, but its representation marked an aspiration to a long reign and to its continued celebration in the next world; many examples relate to kings, such as Djoser of the Third Dynasty, who reign for less than thirty years (cf. Hornung, Staehelin, *et al.* 1974). The chief "real" kingly actions that are absent from this enumeration are those of political history: foreign affairs, the internal development of the country, responses to natural disasters, the suppression of internal dissent, and problems of succession. Some of these are implied by the ritualized events of the palettes and maceheads, while others are known or hinted at in much later royal inscriptions where they are subsumed within a pattern of rule (e.g., Vandersleyen 1967, 1968; Barbotin and Clère 1991, with references; Daressy 1900); some political issues never became fit topics to be recorded on the monuments. In summary, the king's entire sphere of action was a

ritual of rulership, laden with symbolism and drawing the maintenance of the cosmos into its patterns.

The ritualization of rule has advantages in demanding from the
actors a participation without which it could not continue, while
lightening the burden of decision and investing the mundane with
significance. "History" is a ritual (Hornung 1966; Rupp 1969;
Hornung 1983), while ritual events make history, as is amply
demonstrated by the annals. Here, those who view kingship as
being mobilized and reaffirmed by ritual understate their case
(e.g., Cannadine and Price 1987): kingship is ritual. Ritual is not
entered into and departed from, but rather constitutes a total environment, within which there are levels of ritualization. This does
not imply that there were no real events, or that the king would
have had little effective room for action (Assmann, 1984b, hypo-
thesizes this especially for earlier periods), but that events
acquired cultural significance through ritualization. The individual attitudes of a ruler are of no account here, while change is
quickly integrated into the ritual framework. For Egyptian kingship as a whole, these points are well known; what should be noted
is that they can be seen in the earliest material as well as in later
periods.

The gulf between the king and any subject is visible in the later
record of nonroyal actions. There are examples in Old Kingdom
"biographies" of people displaying their position in rituals
(Roccati 1982, 101-02, 108-11), not necessarily royal ones (Roccati
1982, 234-36); texts that narrate specific events are concerned with
their owners' careers, mostly in state service. All elite members
were officials, but the division between king and subject was so
sharp that subjects seldom presented actions that directly affected
royalty or might impinge on the king's special status (compare
McMullen 1987, 184-86, on Tang China).

In addition to the selection of "historically" significant events for
dating and recording, events themselves were adjusted. Some
rituals relate to the inundation levels: an abnormally low level in
one year would be followed by the ritual of the "Apis run" in the
next, which would be accompanied by a return to a good or
exceptional level (Helck 1966). This pattern is connected with an
evident concern about falling inundation levels that could have
threatened the country's economy (see e.g., Butzer 1976, 27-28),
but in its details it is clear that it cannot be taken literally. Exactly
how the records enhance reality is not known, but if apparently

factual statements like these, which would in theory have been used for calculating rents and taxes, were manipulated, the whole record is open to questioning. Its subject is not what did happen, but what should happen, what the king should do for the gods and for humanity, and what effect his actions and rituals should have.

In the annals, the pragmatic and programmatic record of "events" is combined with the names of kings and their filiation to their mothers. Fathers are not named, presumably because they should have been the kings' royal predecessors. The record of the succession of kings led in a continuous tradition to the *Aegyptiaca* of the Graeco-Egyptian historian Manetho (Third century BC; Waddell 1940), but must also have existed in a form separate from the annals. A late First Dynasty necropolis sealing from Abydos shows how the presentation of dynastic continuity and of the king's association with the gods was mobilized (Dreyer 1987; Dreyer *et al.* 1993, 61, mentioning another example, not yet published, which takes the sequence to the end of the dynasty). The seal names Khentimentiu, the god of the dead, and a sequence of kings. The order of the earlier example is problematic: Khentimentiu, Narmer, Khentimentiu, Aha, Khentimentiu, Djer, Wadj, Den, and King's Mother Meritneith. Dreyer suggests that it gives the names of kings whose cults were still celebrated in the reign of Den's successor, Anedjib. The occurrences of Khentimentiu after the beginning could replace the names of kings whose cult no longer functioned—perhaps Scorpion and "Athothis I," the posited ephemeral successor of Aha. The same could apply at the head of the list, where Khentimentiu might stand for a number of kings, or, as the patron of the necropolis, he could be the point of departure (for a different reading, see Kaiser 1987a). In any case, the seal balances completeness and the selection of significant figures. By including Narmer, it probably ignores divisions of dynasty and the introduction of written annals, while the King's Mother Meritneith breaks the rule of male kingship. Like some other early queens, Meritneith is prominent in the record, and she had a royal tomb of her own at Abydos, evidently with a separate cult. The explanation for this is probably that she was regent in Den's minority, at the beginning of his long reign; she was nevertheless placed after him in the list because she owed her status to his delegated power. This implies general respect for inherited dynastic institutions and for the successor to the throne, even if he was himself powerless.

This document is an instance of how, on a number of levels, the past and history are incorporated into the ritual of kingship, which is oriented primarily toward establishing and maintaining the cosmos, and hence toward the future. It has been suggested that the statue cult of Old Kingdom kings began as soon as they came to the throne (e.g., Baer 1960, 264-72; Posener-Kriéger 1986, 29, with n. 26); a cult of the living king would move the king's status still nearer to the gods, although the implications of a ruler's having his own aura of ritual at the same time as a cult to his divine/mortuary person are by no means straightforward.

It is possible to study the ritualization which was centered on the king's person in his basic abode, the palace. The commonest Old Kingdom term referring to the king is *ḥm.f* "His Person" (Spiegel 1938; Goedicke 1960, 51-68), whose symbolic ambivalence can be seen in the incident of the king striking an official during a ritual (p. 121 here). As Wolfgang Helck noted (1954, 15-28), many high-ranking official titles refer to personal and physical service of the king, including the care of his wigs, hair, and manicuring (cf. Baines 1985b, 467). On the palettes and maceheads, officials bear sandals, which are a potent symbol because they separate the king's purity from the polluting ground—and so are removed inside temples—while they represent aggression because he tramples his enemies with them or with the bare soles of his feet. That idea is attested in iconography from the Second and Third dynasties (Junker 1956; Firth and Quibell 1936, plate 58), but is implied already by the composition of the Narmer palette and by such objects as an ivory figurine of a captive that was perhaps the leg of a footstool (Quibell 1900, plate 11). Apart from personal service during life, many people closely connected with the king in the First Dynasty were put to death and buried either in his tomb complex (§ 3.3 ahead) or around a location dedicated to his cult at Abydos (Kemp 1966), or perhaps at Saqqara (Kaiser 1985a). These included human retainers of both sexes, dwarfs, and animals appropriate to a vast household, but few holders of high office (Edwards 1971, 58, with references).

On the largest private stela of the First Dynasty, from a major tomb at Saqqara, the owner's two principal titles, written in bigger signs than the rest of the inscription, are *iry p'̔t* "member of the *p'̔t*" and *sm* "*sm*-priest" (e.g., Kemp 1967, 27 figure 2). The *sm*-priest wears the same panther-skin robe as the priest on the Narmer palette, is identified as officiant on an early First Dynasty label (Schott 1950, plate 7, figure 14; O'Connor 1987, 33, figure 11), and was "in charge of clothing" in the fateful Fifth Dynasty incident when he was struck. By analogy with later practice, this title should correspond with its holder's highest function because it is written next to his name. His chief executive activities in the state may have been covered by his other, less prominent titles, but the most important one for his self-presentation related him to the king and to ritual.

'Iry p'''t points in a different direction. This is the highest ranking title in early Egypt (Helck 1954a, 55-56, 111-13; Baer 1960). It implies no function but asserts that its holder belongs to a social group; later it came to mean "heir" and was a title of queens (Helck 1950). The p'''t and the rhyt, the "subjects," are the duality which makes up Egyptian society (Helck 1960, 5-15). The rhyt are defeated and subjected, while and the p'''t are the "elite." The division between these two groups may have been notional, and in historical times the elite—the only sector of society accessible to us—was relatively open in composition, but the idea must originally have had meaning. The most plausible interpretation is that there was at first a small, probably kin group called the p'''t, which formed the inner elite and from which the king was drawn. Such a separation reinforces the inequality of society. If the typical iry p'''t owned a tomb like the major ones at Saqqara, there could not have been more than half a dozen of them at a time. The fact that retainer burials have been found around these tombs (e.g., Edwards 1971, 58-59), although not on the same scale as at Abydos, reinforces their special character and proximity to the kingship.

The king came from an inner group and was served by vast numbers of retainers. Power was delegated through proximity and access to him. This was made explicit particularly in cylinder seals which alternated his name and another person's (Helck 1953). Delegation distances the king from administration and reinforces the significance of his ritual presence in the palace. Probably the fundamental rituals of his life there, which formed the core ritualization of his office, were the essential daily ones of any life: rising in the morning, ablutions, dressing, eating, and so forth. Such, along with much praise, was the character of the daily ritual for gods (e.g., Barta 1980, 841-45; see also Blackman 1918; Gardiner 1938). In addition, by the late Second Dynasty (Smith 1946, 131, with references)—and no doubt earlier—the king was depicted in temples as the sole protagonist before the gods. This fiction will have corresponded with a heavy load of temple ritual.

While festivals like the *sed*-festival may have been public, the ritual of the king's existence was not addressed to humanity as a whole. Except in relation to his person, it did not use general human actions and needs as its model. It involved, and was addressed to, the elite. We cannot know how far the need for ritual was accepted elsewhere, but the institutions of a state that was necessarily headed by a king and embodied in rituals and in their concrete realizations in architecture endured throughout history, even though in some periods kings had little authority and during the Third Intermediate Period regional rulers did not always use the title of king (Kitchen 1986, 335-61). The Egyptian rituals do not easily fit the model of Maurice Bloch (1987; cf. Cannadine 1987, 15-18), who proposes that they must be based on common experience and offer benefit to all. What they offer is authority and a concern with matters in which human society is the element of least importance, as is the case with much of Egyptian elite culture (cf. Baines 1987a, 79-83). In taking on responsibility for maintaining order in face of disorder, the rituals claim to show a legitimizing concern for humanity and to integrate this-worldly action in its context of ultimate meaning. People must accept this responsibility of others and this function for ritual. They may have done so only because they were powerless not to, but they could look to no alternative form of rule.

This position of ritual, and later of colossal architecture (§ 3.3 ahead), raises the much debated question of whether royal ritual serves the state or the state exists for ritual, for the enactment of its meanings in relation to the ruler's person and thence to the cosmos. Pre-New Kingdom Egypt, in which expenditure of re- sources on divine cult was much less than later, poses this question acutely, and there is a difference between Early Dynastic times, when many leading titles and functions had a ritual character, and the Fifth Dynasty and later, when they were more bureaucratic. Nonetheless, the extremes of Bali, as presented by Clifford Geertz (1980; for criticism see Bloch 1987, 294-97), who states that there was little administration that was not connected with ritual, are not directly applicable to the large, centralized structure of Egypt. Other lightly ordered but intensely ritualized polities, such as those of Hawaii (Valeri 1985) or the Swazi (Beidelman 1966; Lin- coln 1987, with different view), are equally remote from Egypt's monolithic organization. Another phenomenon of a different character is the ritual participation of the Roman emperor, whose new institution intruded into existing state structures (Price 1984, esp. 234-48). Here, Egypt stands out as a case where, in the elite presentation, kingship constituted society to the fullest extent; it is not meaningful to ask what existed to serve what. In comparative perspective, the institutionalization of kingship and its rituals concomitant with the emergence of a complex society and a professional elite distinguish Egypt from other possible modes of state formation and create a fundamental contrast with the other African and Pacific cases just cited.

This comparative material is valuable in providing living, or more detailed, exemplars of what cannot be recovered for Egypt (see also Geertz 1983). Neither the king's biennial journeys through the country nor the mass of other rituals were necessarily accessible to many, but the journeys marked the extent of his domains and the passage of time, and must have been the principal events that arrived from the rest of the country among those who lived away from the capital. The meaning of ceremonies could be intensified by exclusion: rituals might not be known to those outside them, but their importance would be made evident by their remoteness. This whole living dimension of kingship can only be guessed at, but it is vital for the actors, both the included and the excluded. It is illuminating to view the escalation of mortuary display from the time of Aha, and continuing into the gigantism of the late Second to Fourth Dynasties, as a physical embodiment of ritualization for the larger society of the living and the dead which may have replaced some of the role of ritual. Such a shift of medium does not necessarily bring a great change in meaning: mortuary symbolism had insistent messages for living human society. I sketch some of these questions in the next section.

3.3. Royal Monuments, Mortuary Cult, and Names of the First to Third Dynasties

The tomb complex of Aha is a multiple of the size of its precursors and consists of three large square brick pits with 36 smaller ones in rows. Like the other tombs in Cemetery B, this one probably had no superstructure visible above ground. Only small, scattered fragments are preserved from the impressive mortuary equipment of any of the First Dynasty Abydos tombs and this aspect of the

burial cannot be reconstructed. The most significant innovation of
Aha, apart from the size of his installation, is that he was accompanied into the next world by many people who had been put to
death. The restudy of the complex yielded parts of skeletons of
more than twenty men of 20-30 years of age, too uniform a group
to have died naturally (Dreyer *et al.* 1990, 67, 81-86; for a possible
mid-First Dynasty parallel at Saqqara see Kaiser 1985a). They were
buried in the smaller pits, as perpetual attendants for their lord.
The number of skeleton fragments discovered suggests that there
was one burial in each pit. What destiny the king or they might
have had in the tomb is uncertain, but some material survival for
those who were buried is implied by predynastic and dynastic
burial practices. Aha probably had a mortuary cult place, with
further sacrificial burials around it, near the valley edge where later kings received such a cult (no trace of a cult place has yet been
found).

In its predominance of scale, Aha's mortuary complex manifests
the ideological implications of the palettes and maceheads, while
the killing of retainers demonstrates, among other things, the
submission of people to royal authority. Nearly six hundred were
buried with his second successor Djer or around his valley complex (Edwards 1971, 59). These were not sacrifices in which
people were offered up in order to bring benefits to human society, but are a more authoritarian practice of killing many for a
single person's benefit in the next world. The victims themselves
could have believed that they would join their master in a glorious
afterlife (cf. Geertz 1980, 98-120). People who were buried in large
tombs elsewhere must, however, have had equal and probably
higher status than those sacrificed (see ahead). Much later, in the
New Kingdom, a few people close to the king were buried in
modest graves in the Valley of the Kings, while the great of the
period had far more impressive tombs elsewhere (Hornung 1992,
185-90); here again, a shared destiny is an appropriate explanation. In Early Dynastic times, those who were not sacrificed could
have believed that the prosperity of the land depended on the
king's destiny, in comparison with which any other mortal's life
was of no account, but any strong version of such an idea would
undermine the position of the king's successor. There is no means
of knowing how the inevitable tension between living and dead
rulers was resolved, but the sealing discussed in § 3.1 demonstrates
the legitimizing force of the royal line by the mid-First Dynasty; the

idea was no doubt older. A less explicit presentation is in the myth of Osiris, where the successor must fight for the inheritance of his murdered father (e.g., Otto 1968, Part 1). A similar tension occurs in a non-royal context in the Middle Kingdom, where there is conflict between generations over access to the hereafter (Grieshammer 1975/76).

The killing of retainers at elite burials has occurred in many societies and is not in itself remarkable. The numbers must have been small in relation to society as a whole, so that the practice's wider impact might not be great. Life was cheap in most pre-modern societies and this was a striking example of that cheapness. What might seem surprising is that the practice should begin after a formative period, not in the setting-up of the centralized state and creation of a status for the kingship but at a later point of transition, although that too can be paralleled. Its motivation will remain unknown, but it occurred in the same period when the titulary proliferated, along with other assertions of royal status. For reasons that have not been established, the king's special nature and authority—but not divinity in any simple sense—were stressed to the utmost.

Apart from Aha's own tomb complex at Abydos, massive mud-brick mastaba tombs with visible superstructures at Naqada and Saqqara date to his reign (Edwards 1971, 17, 19, with references); other sites important later in the dynasty include Kafr Tarkhan, Helwan and Giza. These tombs are solid versions of the compounds with enclosure walls which would have been the normal residences of king and elite (on the form's origin, see Kaiser 1985b). They use the niched "palace façade" design of the Horus name, of which they are the most elaborate examples; by the end of the First Dynasty the paneling had become simplified. The existence and scale of the Saqqara tombs led to a continuing controversy over whether the kings of the period were buried at Abydos or Saqqara, but Abydos is now generally accepted (but see e.g., Stadelmann 1985c, 10-34). By the First Dynasty, the "palace façade" design cannot have been exclusive to the king.

The separation of Cemetery B and its continuation, Umm el-Qaab, from nonroyal burials, and the antiquity of the site, must have compensated, together with the cult places near the desert edge, for the inconspicuousness of the tombs. From the reign of Djer on, these had twin mortuary stelae (e.g., Figure 3.12; the best known is that of Wadj, e.g., Lange and Hirmer 1967, plate 6).

These stelae showed only a Horus name and were too small to dominate at a distance; they may principally have marked the position of the tomb, where offerings were perhaps made (cf. O'Connor 1987, 32). As pointed out by Dreyer, there may have been local religious meaning in the site, which is on the path up a low wadi from the floodplain to a prominent cleft in the escarpment, a feature similar to the later Valley of the Kings at Thebes. The chief prestige and cult of the dead king were, however, elsewhere, in the cult complexes near the valley, which were bounded by massive plastered and white-painted brick enclosure walls.

The Naqada tomb could be in part a final acknowledgment of the historical importance of the place, but it had no successors; a prince may have been buried in it (Seipel 1980, 11). The Saqqara tomb of the reign of Aha is more important, because it is the first in a series constructed at the new capital. Its unknown owner was perhaps the principal administrator of Memphis, probably a royal kinsman ranking second only to the king.

If Naqada and Saqqara are added to Aha's tomb at Abydos, there was a vastly increased expenditure on the burials of the inner elite. Late predynastic and Dynasty 0 mortuary display was significant, but it did not cross over into the truly monumental and there were probably larger buildings in settlements (e.g., von der Way 1992). The Saqqara tombs change this, because their location on the edge of the escarpment overlooking Memphis must have made them the dominant architecture of their time. No doubt the destiny of these people in the next life was very important and they believed that their buildings would help them to achieve it, but the tombs' implications go beyond that concern: at the beginning of the First Dynasty, the characteristic exploitation of mortuary structures as central architectural statements about power and the purpose of human society came into its own; it was to last at least 1500 years.

The architectural meanings of the royal and nonroyal tombs are different. The nonroyal tombs were virtual abodes in the hereafter and contained quantities of food offerings and other material goods suitable for a literal form of survival; some Second Dynasty tombs even have latrines (Edwards 1971, 54-56). This emphasis on the tomb itself is paralleled in Old Kingdom elite tombs, both in the decoration—a rather uncertain point in view of our poor understanding of the decoration's purpose—and in the texts, which speak of "walking on the perfect roads of the West" (the location of the necropolis and the normal euphemism for the hereafter), and of direct interaction between the living and the dead (e.g., Roccati 1982, passim). Royal tombs, by contrast, are not abodes, but rather point to a cosmic destiny. This destiny is not visually explicit in First–Second Dynasty royal tombs, but becomes so with the Third Dynasty pyramids. It is suggested by the hovering figure of Horus on a sealing of Aha and by the comb of Wadj (§ 2.3 here). More fully identified in death than in life with Horus or with the sun, the king would travel perpetually in the day and night sky. It is not clear how significant solar beliefs, later associated with Heliopolis, were in this context. The city was ancient and there are indications of associations with it in early material (Baines 1991c, 94-99), but the sun-god Re was not as dominant as he came to be in the Old Kingdom. However that may be, the king and his closest adherents, who were members of the same social group, had separate destinies which differed more according to their respective roles than according to their wealth: here again, the king was a being apart.

Several scholars assumed previously that the mortuary cult of the kings in the enclosures near the town of Abydos was performed in perishable structures of such materials as reeds and matting (e.g., Kemp 1966; Kaiser 1969). Until the recent excavations of the Pennsylvania-Yale Expedition, few solid remains had been discovered within the enclosures, most of them near entrances (O'Connor 1987, 35-39). The new investigations have revealed that the complex of Khasekhemwy of the end of the Second Dynasty had a range of brick buildings, and so open the possibility, now being tested in further excavation, that this was also the case earlier. Nonetheless, contemporary iconography and the architectural forms of later stone buildings suggest that the forms in flimsy materials, to which temple architecture and similar structures in later mortuary complexes looked back, incorporated positive values, probably conveying associations with hallowed religious forms like those of the sanctuary at Hierakonpolis (Hoffman 1986), and perhaps with contemporary divine cult temples (for representations see e.g., Schott 1950, plate 7, figures 14-15; Kaplony 1963, vol. 3, figures 144-71; solid enclosure Schott figure 13; Baines 1991a). The most elaborate form of such a temple is depicted as a brick enclosure with a flimsy shrine inside (Kaplony 1962-63, 7 figure 1). The annals record rather little about temple construction, perhaps because the dedication of equipment could involve as great an outlay as building (but see O'Connor 1992).

In addition to the enclosures, the area in front of Khasekhemwy's structure at Abydos contained at least twelve burials of large boats entombed in mud brick (O'Connor 1991; not yet fully excavated). These imply, at the least, the idea that the king and his entourage should voyage perpetually in the next world. So far, it is uncertain whether the boats belonged only to the complex of Khasekhemwy or were in a kind of symbolic harbor that was set up for all the kings who had cults nearby; the number of the boats allows either possibility.

The successors of the buildings in the complex of Khasekhemwy are preserved in the dummy structures of the Step Pyramid complex of Djoser at Saqqara (Firth and Quibell 1935). There, the form of the enclosure wall derives from brick, while the shrines look to perishable designs—the same distinction as in the examples just cited. If First Dynasty mortuary cult buildings were built of brick, they could have imitated perishable structures in the same way, incorporating the significant associations of those materials. The sealing with the list of kings suggests that the cults of most kings were not simply fused, so that as the dynasty endured the amount of cult activity increased. The enclosures at Abydos had massive and costly surrounding walls that gave them a dominant, monumental presence. All were destroyed to ground level, except for the latest one, and one now covered by a modern village and perhaps dating to Qaa, the last king of the First Dynasty. This pattern of destruction may have been progressive during the dynasties, with each ruler perhaps removing the preceding complex and transferring its cult and the earlier ones to his own, until the pattern was broken by a change of dynasty (O'Connor in press). Since Khasekhemwy's structure has stood without severe erosion for more than 4500 years, it is unlikely that the destruction of the brickwork of the others to ground level was due to chance and erosion.

The impact of this mortuary cult has to be seen in the context of its location. By the mid-First Dynasty, Abydos was probably a backwater. Its town site is not large and the necropolis contains no large nonroyal tombs, in contrast with the great numbers in the Memphite area. This maintenance of old practices at a remote location may have had its artificial aspects. Perhaps because so much ideology was at stake and expressed in a mortuary idiom, the practices did not change until the dynasty changed.

The Second Dynasty exemplifies two loci of conflict and ideology, in the king's burial and in his name. These may not reflect what was politically at stake during the period, much of which may have been disturbed, but it may rather constitute a form of discourse in which conflict was expressed; of that discourse, only what is archaeologically preserved can now be observed.

The first and third kings of the new dynasty, Hotepsekhemwy and Ninetjer, were buried in tombs at Saqqara with extensive underground gallery systems. The superstructures of these tombs, if any, have not been identified. The burial of the second king, Reneb, in the area is rendered likely by a stela probably found in the Memphite region (Stadelmann 1985c, 31). These tombs seem to move closer to the nonroyal type, but they were still physically separate from those of other people, being placed more than a kilometer south of the area with the great mastabas. As David O'Connor suggests (1989a, 83), they may also have had related mortuary cult areas in other locations. No royal tomb of the middle of the dynasty has been certainly identified. Peribsen, perhaps its second to last king, was buried back at Abydos in a tomb similar to those of the First Dynasty, as was Khasekhemwy, the last king, who occupied the largest tomb on the site. Peribsen and Khasekhemwy also built massive brick cult enclosures near those of the First Dynasty (O'Connor 1987, 1989a). Peribsen's is largely lost, but Khasekhemwy's stands to a height of ten meters or more and contained important structures within (Figure 3.13), including a brick-faced mound that appears to have been the model for the initial project of the Step Pyramid at Saqqara (O'Connor 1989b, 82; 1991, 9 figure 6). A similar enclosure at Hierakonpolis belonged to Khasekhem, a king known only from that site (Clarke in Quibell and Green 1902, 19-20, plate 74; Kemp 1963) who was probably Khasekhemwy before he altered his Horus name to mark a political change. Thus, Khasekhem seems to have originated from Hierakonpolis and planned his burial there, but when he had reunited the country he changed his throne name and prepared a new burial in the traditional royal necropolis.

Khasekhemwy himself was a transitional figure. The burial of his probable successor, the first king of the Third Dynasty, has not been found, but the next king, Netjerykhet, normally known as Djoser after his name in the king lists, finally moved the royal burial to Saqqara, planning a mortuary complex incomparably more grandiose than anything earlier (see Stadelmann 1985c, 35-72, with discussion of possible burials of Djoser's predecessors). As already implied, this complex was rooted firmly in the past except in the use of stone for all its structures and in its central feature, the pyramid; but even that had antecedents. Under Djoser the inner elite continued to be buried in large mud brick tombs, of which there are a number at North Saqqara and at Beit Khallaf north of Abydos. During the centuries since Aha, the number of smaller nonroyal tombs had reduced progressively; nonroyal tombs were few and large. In the Fourth Dynasty they became concentrated around the capital and the royal pyramid complex, and the country's funerary monuments bear witness to one of the most highly centralized states ever known. Royal dominance became total, and the population must have been mobilized almost totally to produce the great pyramids; the only aspect of royal exploitation that had lessened was that after the First Dynasty, royal retainers were no longer killed at burials.

This expression of power through architecture looks almost like an end in itself, but it should be related to other issues, among which the most important was the position of the king, the living embodiment of state and cosmos. The royal tombs were built for the king's next life, but they were central to this life. Changes in religious belief probably went with developments in funerary architecture, whose religious interpretation is, however, uncertain.

Royal names are a clearer expression of ideology. The Horus name of the first king of the Second Dynasty, Hotepsekhemwy, means "The One Who is at Peace in respect of the Two Powers (Horus and Seth)," casting in mythical terms a statement that conflict of the end of the First Dynasty had been resolved: Horus and Seth are the perpetual antagonists, but together they constitute the creative duality of order. This opposition was sharpened further after renewed discord of the middle of the dynasty. A king Sekhemib-perenmaat (see § 3.1 here), whose name means loosely "Valiant Champion," was succeeded by, or alternatively was identical with, the Seth Peribsen, the only king who ever used the title Seth instead of Horus. His name is of uncertain meaning, but alludes to "their" and so does not exclude Horus completely. Peribsen's monuments were unusually thoroughly destroyed; this could have been due to his espousal of Seth or to the savagery of his struggle with his opponent. Khasekhem, his antagonist, was the "One who Arises in respect of the Power (Horus)," and a stela fragment gives him the colorful epithet "efficacious sandal against evil" (Quibell and Green 1902, plate 58 [the context is Nubia]). He was the owner of the earliest preserved statues of Egyptian kings, around the bases of which are figures of slain captives together with exaggerated numbers (Quibell and Green 1902 plates 39-42; Junker 1956; Edwards 1971, 28). Khasekhemwy, the "One who Arises in respect of the Two Powers," used the unique title Horus-and-Seth, in which the animals of the two gods face each other heraldically on top of the "palace façade." Unlike other early kings, he added a comment to his name, making the conciliation expressed in the name clear and perhaps creating one of the earliest continuous written sentences in Egyptian: "The Two Lords are at peace in him" (Edwards 1971, 29). Contemporaries will not have missed the allusions in his name to the dynasty's first king.

These names mark a peak in the use of the Horus name for political and religious statements about the king. The kings proclaim that they are bringers of peace. The allusions in their names relate the conflict to the gods and do not present it as belonging simply in the human sphere. Rather similarly, architecture comments on, but does not give the full meaning of, events—except insofar as it constitutes them, which it must have done by the time of Djoser. Djoser's Horus name, Netjerykhet, may state that he is "the Divine One of the Corporation (of gods)," focusing directly on an issue that has been debated endlessly by scholars. Was the king a god? How far and in what sense was he one? Was he inferior, superior or equal to the gods? (See e.g., Posener 1960; Wildung 1973a.) The word "divine" is relatively rare in Egyptian (Hornung 1982a, 63-65) and praises a god to the utmost, so that it should be taken seriously here. Djoser's name, like his mortuary monument, expresses his overweening aspirations. He is the earliest king clearly identified with a word for "god;" in contrast, Ninetjer of the Second Dynasty may have been the "One who Belongs to the God." Djoser's monument also demonstrates his success in putting his message across: the organization, power, and creative potential of the country were harnessed in service of the idea that mainly its superhuman ruler (who was not simply a god), was of account. This was the final extension of the claims implicit in the decoration and deposition of the Narmer palette. In earlier times such claims must have been tempered in human society, in which there was a far less unequal distribution of resources than under Djoser.

Even Djoser's monumental achievements pale in comparison with those of Snefru and Khufu in the Fourth Dynasty. We can admire those achievements, but we need have no illusions about a society so exclusively and exploitively focused on a central living symbol and its architectural counterpart (cf. Baines 1988). There is a distinctive pattern in this development, as if Egypt had developed progressively for a number of centuries toward these ultimately unsustainable points. One may compare the emperor who first unified much of China, Qin Shi Huang (late Third century BC), who built an incomparable funerary monument within his own reign and linked up much of the Great Wall of China (e.g., Bodde 1986, 61-64, 82-83), but who came after more than a millennium of a widespread, differentiated, literate Chinese civilization.

4. Conclusion: Tradition and New Developments

An evaluation of the early Egyptian state and its kingship should not dwell upon the fact that these are among the earliest such phenomena known in the world. Rather, one should focus on the phenomenon itself and issues that arise in studying it.

The archaeological fieldwork and interpretation of the last generation, in which the outstanding figure has been Werner Kaiser, has made the evolution of Egyptian kingship appear less remarkable, but more comprehensible, than it once did. Attention focuses not on the first political events, which may have been as rapid as they ever seemed and which remain beyond reach of investigation, but on the development of a unified culture, state, and kingship. As Kaiser has remarked of Dynasty 0 (Kaiser and Dreyer 1982, 268), its increased length—which has been extended further by discoveries in Cemetery U at Abydos—gives a more human dimension to its achievements in creating the state and with it an enduring definition of its chief concerns. The period I have surveyed now extends to around five hundred years, more than fifteen generations. In studying developments over such a span, there is a danger of losing the human scale and the temporal perspective of the actors. The development in mortuary monuments of the First–Second dynasties must have been almost imperceptible to any except those directly involved, for whom it will have been the main commitment of their careers. In the case of Djoser, the development which produced his monument during his reign of around twenty years was rapid by any standards. It is much harder to assess the pace of change that led to the ideological formulations of the Narmer palette and macehead, because chances of survival can so easily affect the picture (compare the important new document presented by Williams and Logan, 1987).

The Egyptians distorted their perspective for the formative period when they, like most ancient annalists, multiplied reigns and totals for dynasties progressively up to the gigantic figures cited for the original rule of the gods on earth (cf. Redford 1986a). The development of this conception made kings before "Menes" into special cases and created a myth and a cultural, but not historical, caesura which scholarship has only slowly overcome (cf. Baines 1989a, 133-38; perhaps to be placed earlier than the post-Fifth Dynasty date suggested there). The separation of "history" from what went before brings the gods into the formation of human traditions. It also evinces a characteristically Egyptian concern with order and is influenced by the transition from oral to written recording.

In some areas, fieldwork has confirmed the validity of native Egyptian traditions against the skepticism of scholars. Thus, Wolfgang Helck (1951) and John A. Wilson (1955) used different approaches to argue that the importance of Buto and Hierakonpolis in dynastic symbolism could not be due to the real early significance of those places, but must relate to their position at the frontiers of the country's geography. Excavation has shown that this hypothesis was incorrect and I have ignored it. This does not mean that there is precise historical content or memory of specific events in later associations of deities with such places; the traditions are myths or mythical schemas. More generally, the point of departure for analyzing complex developments such as state and kingship should be human concerns and human society rather than considerations derived from the environment, as were those of Wilson, or other less immediate factors. Here, the gods are a human and direct factor because they were so closely integrated into Egyptian cosmos and society.

An opposite point can be made in another case. The "unification" of Egypt, which is recorded on the Palermo Stone as a ritual celebrated at the beginning of each reign but is described as an actual historical event in many text books, did occur—how else could the country have acquired a single ruler?—but we do not know whether it happened at one time, and it took place in a period before events were recorded in visible form or are accessible to research. What is recorded on the monuments is a fiction. Close attention shows that it is presented as such, but the fiction is culturally central, because it is the defining ideology of the king's relations with the outside world and the cosmos. Much later, it was also mobilized and modified to record a real event, as could always happen with such fictions: Nebhepetre Mentuhotep (c. 2061-2010 BC), who reunited the country in the Eleventh Dynasty, both changed his Horus name to "Uniter of the Two Lands," and devised a new iconography of the "Uniter of the Two Lands" motif (Baines 1985a, 229-38, 353-56).

I have taken as an essential premise that motivations and practices of a remote period should not be seen as any less complex than those of more accessible times. Contrary to such scholars as Wolfgang Helck and Jan Assmann, who use different approaches but agree in seeing early Egypt as suffused with a religious aura that almost abrogated rationality, I interpret the available evidence along similar lines to that from later periods. While this strategy brings the risk of anachronism, it may minimize that of condescension. Scholars have also often assumed that the ritual aspect of kingship emerged gradually and in a certain sense came to substitute for the direct exercise of power which had been possible in the institution's earliest stages. Comparative studies, however, suggest that kingship, like many other human institutions, is always strongly ritualized and conventionalized. I have attempted to show that the early evidence is more effectively interpreted as exhibiting the complexity, sophistication, and ritualization of later material than as almost inchoate.

This chapter has explored themes in early kingship that have general implications for Egyptian society, and for how it is studied. Kingship is so crucial that many further instances could be cited. Although Egyptologists try to get around the kingship to work on matters outside the elite, the king constantly reappears, because for millennia the Egyptians made him the focus of how they organized and presented the world. Kingship is fundamental to approaches to Egypt on the terms of the actors. From before "history" began, Egyptian society centered on kingship.

Bibliographical Note

The literature relating to the origins of Egyptian kingship is large, but I have not cited it extensively, instead presenting evidence directly together with arguments derived from it and from theoretical considerations. Differing views are not documented systematically, while references for iconographic evidence are kept within bounds by citing illustrations in more recent works rather than original publications.

Since Kaiser's fundamental reevaluation of evidence for the "unification" and presentation of Dynasty 0 (1964), there has been no synthesis on early kingship; his later short article (1990) is extremely valuable for the background of state formation. Atzler's work on the genesis of "forms of rule" in Egypt (1981) does not focus on kingship, which comes at the end of the period he considers, but contains useful material for the origins of the Egyptian state. Despite the subtitle of his book (1975), *Ritus und Sakralkönigtum nach Zeugnissen der Frühzeit und des Alten Reiches*, Barta addressed different questions from those I consider. There is also little contact with Janssen's more anthropologically informed contribution to *The Early State* (1978). The survey of Bonhême and Forgeau (1988) is concerned primarily with later periods; their scattered remarks on early kingship no longer reflect current knowledge.

My initial draft was made before the appearance of Williams and Logan (1987), which restudies many pieces I cite, and before Williams (1986, 1988) became accessible. I have attempted to take into account these works and many later ones (notably Kemp 1989, although seldom cited), but I may not have succeeded entirely; the pace of publication is such that it is very difficult to give a fully up-to-date presentation. Eiwanger (1987), the abstract of a promised book, uses a different perspective from mine, emphasizing environment, agriculture and trade, rather than political or ideological questions, and arguing from the perspective of the Delta; our studies scarcely overlap. For the late Predynastic and especially the Early Dynastic Period, Helck's *Untersuchungen zur Thinitenzeit* (1987) is a valuable collection, but it does not focus on kingship; his interpretive methods are very different from mine. The best available synthesis on predynastic Egypt is Midant-Reynes (1992), while van den Brink (1992) assembles an important collection of papers on the transitional period; Spencer (1993) is a useful brief treatment with excellent illustrations. I have unfortunately not seen Largacha (1993). Two further works I have not been able to take properly into account are Pereyra (1990) and Endesfelder (1991). Both, however, were written before the most recent discoveries, and Pereyra's article is based on generally superseded sources. Endesfelder makes useful comments on administrative aspects of the First–Second dynasties.

Since first writing this chapter, I have published several studies on the same period (Baines 1989b, 1990a, 1991a, 1993). Excavations at Abydos in Cemetery U and around the cult enclosures continue to extend our perspective on the origin of centralized rule and our understanding of its dynamics. For preliminary reports, see Dreyer *et al.* (1993), O'Connor (1989a, 1991). So far as possible, I have taken these findings into account.

Because my argument uses hindsight, there may be some overlap with other chapters in this volume.

Acknowledgements

I should like to thank the organizers of the 1987 Symposium in Denver, David O'Connor, David Silverman, and Barbara Stone, for their invitation to participate, and for making the event so rewarding. I learned much about the period, especially about Abydos, Hierakonpolis, and Minshat Abu Omar, from two July symposia at the British Museum in 1987 and 1993. Günter Dreyer has graciously permitted me to refer to the interpretation of finds from Tomb U-j at Abydos which he presented there and has made available a relevant article (Dreyer in press). I owe a debt to Christopher Eyre, Helen Whitehouse and Norman Yoffee for commenting on drafts, and to Roger Moorey and Donald Starr. I am very grateful to Krzysztof Ciałowicz for sending me an English translation of a crucial section of his work on royal symbolism (1993).

3.1. Relief red crown on a fragment of Naqada I period pot from Naqada. Oxford, Ashmolean Museum, 1895.795. Photograph courtesy of Ashmolean Museum.

3.2. Two groups from wall painting in tomb 100 at Hierakonpolis; drawing by Marion Cox from Quibell and Green 1902, pl. 76.

Dynasty 0 (c. 3100–2920 BC; Naqada III)

early group, related to Cemetery U at Abydos: names uncertain later
group, perhaps associated with Cemetery B
    at Abydos: three or more kings
"Irihor"
Ka
Na'rmer
Scorpion
Dynasty 0 may consist of more than one ruling house and could
extend for a longer period than that indicated.

Dynasty 1 (c. 2920–2775 BC)

Aha (= "Menes"?)
    "Athothis I" (possible king, Horus name unknown)
Djer
Wadj
Den (regent Queen Meritneith)
Anedjib
Semerkhet
Qaa
dynastic conflict; Seneferka, absent from
    lists: Edwards 1971, 29

Dynasty 2 (c. 2775–2650 BC)

Hotepsekhemwy
Re'neb
Ninetjer
dynastic conflict; various names, including Weneg,
    Sened, Nubnefer
Horus Sekhemib Perenmaat = ? Seth Peribsen
    Horus Khaekhem = ? Horus-and-Seth Khasekhemwy

Dynasty 3 (c. 2650–2575 BC)

Zanakht
Netjerykhet (Djoser)
Sekhemkhet
Khaba
"Huny" (Horus name unknown, possibly Qahedjet)

3.3. King list, Dynasties 0–III. Except where indicated, names are Horus
names. The reading of many is uncertain and the order of some disputed.
Doubtful names are omitted; there may have been additional kings in
Dynasties II–III.

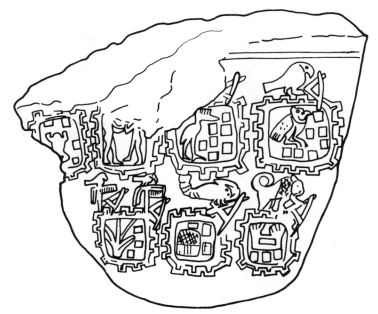

3.4. The "cities" palette, verso. Cairo Museum, CG 14238. Provenance
unknown, said to be from Abydos.
Drawing from photograph by Marion Cox.

3.5. The hunters' palette, London, British Museum
20792, 20790, and Paris, Louvre E 11254, detail from
recto of BM 20790. Provenance unknown, said to be
Abydos. Drawing from original by Christine Barratt,
kindly supplied by the Museum. I am grateful to T.G.H.
James for arranging this new drawing.

3.6. Narmer in the form of
a catfish smites Libyan enemies: design on ivory cylinder seal from main
deposit at Hierakonpolis.
Oxford, Ashmolean Mu-
seum 1896–1908 E.3915.
Drawing from original by
Michele Germon Riley, to
whom I am also grateful for
discussing the piece.

3.7. The Narmer palette, verso and recto. Cairo Museum, CG 14716. From Hierakonpolis main deposit. Drawing from the original courtesy of Jennifer Houser.

3.8. The Narmer macehead. Oxford, Ashmolean Museum 1896-1908 E.3631. From Hierakonpolis main deposit. Drawing from the original by Pat Jacobs, courtesy of the Ashmolean Museum.

9. The Scorpion macehead. Oxford, Ashmolean Museum 1896-1908 E.3632. From Hierakonpolis main deposit. Photograph courtesy of the Ashmolean Museum.

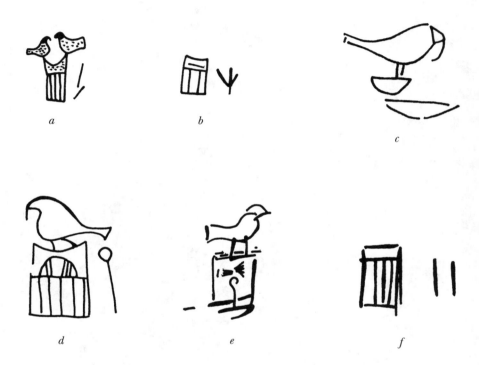

3.10. Selected early royal Horus names. After Kaiser and Dreyer 1982, 263 fig. 14. Kaiser and Dreyer's numbers beneath examples: *a–b*: earliest types; *c*: Irihor; *d*: Ka; *e*: Narmer; *f*: reign of Aha. Redrawn by Marion Cox.

3.11. Limestone statue of Khasekhem. From Hierakonpolis main deposit. Oxford, Ashmolean Museum 1896-1908 E.517. Photograph courtesy of the Ashmolean Museum.

3.12. The mortuary stela of Qaa. From Abydos, Umm el-Qaab.
Photograph courtesy of the University Museum.

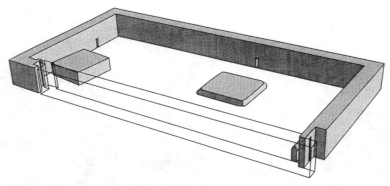

3.13. The Shunet el-Zebib at Abydos: the funerary enclosure of
Khasekhemwy, showing the enclosure, the cult chapel, and a mound or
proto-pyramid, taces of which were discovered in 1988 by the University
Museum, University of Pennsylvania-Yale University to Abydos. Recon-
struction by David O'Connor and Josef Wegner; drawing by Bridget
O'Rourke.

CHAPTER FOUR

THE CONCEPT OF KINGSHIP DURING THE EIGHTEENTH DYNASTY

Donald B. Redford

It is often difficult for us to conjure up in our mind's eye a picture of an urban landscape on the Nile, or the mind-set of its inhabitants before the Ramesside age, whose monstrous constructions so often conceal an earlier building behind it or, more often, in ruins underneath. Similarly, for those whose research has familiarized them with the preceding Eighteenth Dynasty, it is an exercise of imaginative effort to try to conceive the city of Thebes, the aspirations of its citizens, or even the spirit of the age, before the building boom of a Hatshepsut, the conquests of a Thutmose III, or the cultic renewal of an Amenhotep III. But we must, in fact, wipe the awareness of the Eighteenth and Nineteenth Dynasties from our consciousness if we are to grasp that moment in time when the New Kingdom concept of kingship took shape. Not that it sprang full-blown from the brow of some Protean deity. While the Eighteenth Dynasty certainly did contribute something new to the concept, she equally inherited a great deal from the past, even while discarding much from the immediate past. That past, both as model and object-lesson, laid down the broad limits within which the phenomenon of the Eighteenth Dynasty monarchy was so rapidly to evolve and even more rapidly to discredit itself (in general, Brunner 1956; Hornung 1957).

The Debt to the Past

The Second Intermediate Period was characterized by an abnegation of two fundamental principles of Egyptian kingship. First, the concept of "sonship," which in the context of the king's mythological pedigree had constituted the kingpin of his solar affiliation, had suffered a serious debasement. A myriad of unknowns, ephemeral in length of reign and vulgar in origin, clog the sixth through tenth columns of the Turin King-list, very few the offspring of their predecessors (Von Beckerath 1965). The very term "son" rapidly lost a strictly biological reference, and became also a "hierarchical" term denoting simply the highest rung in the command structure on earth, powerless but for the approbation of the god. While formal inscriptions continue to cloak the individuality of the monarch in a timeless mythological attire, the choice of prenomina and Horus names during the Thirteenth Dynasty betrays unmistakably a preoccupation with the agency of the sun-god in elevating a person to the kingship, and also the civic role of the head of state in benefiting the state. From the plethora of causative forms of prenomen during this period, one can say that *vis-à-vis* the incumbent Re was expected to "empower" (*swsr*), to "enable" (*smnḫ*), to "authorize" (*sḫm*), to "ennoble" (*sḳnn*), to "create" (*sḫpr*), to "establish" (*smn*), to "enliven" (*sᶜnḫ*), to "prosper" (*swꜣḏ*), to "nourish" (*sḏfꜣ*), etc. Horus names abound in such phrases as "protecting, calming, enlivening, uniting, pacifying, founding, prospering," all with *tꜣwy*, "the Two Lands" as object. Concepts such as these may be found *passim* in all forms of ancient Egyptian literature, but never in such concentration as during the Thirteenth Dynasty. Gone are the high-flown theological concepts hinted at in the glorious Middle Kingdom names, such as *Ḥr-kꜣ-Rᶜ*, *Nbw-kꜣw-Rᶜ*, *Ḫᶜ-ḫpr-Rᶜ*, *Ny-mꜣᶜt-Rᶜ*, etc; and in their place the lector-priests (who framed titularies), with only a few exceptions, concentrate on essentially human qualities predicated of Re; his calmness, goodness, happiness, contentment, peace, power, beneficence, etc.

The second principle of kingship that had been violated was the purity of the mythological descent of the god-king who sat on the Horus-throne, and by virtue of his ancestry, lawfully inherited the earth. In the second quarter of the Seventeenth Century BC, the unthinkable had happened. Egypt had suffered invasion and occupation by miscreants, those vile *ᶜꜣmw* from Western Asia whom for centuries kings and commoners alike had vilified in the most pejorative terms. Now, for a century the throne was to be occupied by rulers who, with but one exception, continued to worship their own god, to speak their own barbaric tongue and to ignore Egyptian culture almost completely. The Hyksos view of what a king should be and how he came to be king differed, we may be sure, in every respect from the Egyptian view. In keeping with the contemporary kingships of the Middle Bronze Amorite states in Mesopotamia and the Levant, the Hyksos dynasty laid great stress on a long table of human ancestors, and devotion to a Baal-type hero-god (Redford 1986a, 199-201). They were inter-lopers who, by and large, made no attempt to acculturate them-selves, with the notable exception of Apophis. As such, they could never be accepted, and the Egyptians could only rationalize the period of their rule by construing it as a grand interregnum in which the close association between the sun-god and kingship had been ruptured, or by denying its very historicity. The ancestral offering-lists knew them not, and the Thutmosids either ignored them or bestrewed their memory; and if the King-list had to enter them, it did so by indelibly stamping them "foreign rulers" (Redford 1970).

If the dismal prospect of the immediate past prompted a chastening disavowal of that model, the Eighteenth Dynasty had every reason to regard another ancestral house with much more favor and admiration, the Twelfth Dynasty, the "House of Sehtepibre." The achievements and standards of the Twelfth Dynasty had already exerted a powerful influence on the non-entities of the Thirteenth Dynasty. The Eighteenth, sharing as it did with the Twelfth both the Theban base of operations and the devotion to the parochial deity Amun, fell equally under the spell. The first two reigns of the Eighteenth Dynasty, especially that of Amenhotep I, are characterized by a faithful, if not slavish, adherence to Middle Kingdom models in sculpture, inscriptions, and basic concepts. This indeed was taken to the point of mechanically copying such material as calendrical texts in which the position of the Sothic Rising reflects the period of Amenemhat II without changing a thing! Sculpture, in treatment and execution, models itself so closely on Twelfth Dynasty archetypes that, without a cartouche, one is hard put at first glance to decide between Senwosret I or Amenhotep I! In the veiled threats in royal texts one can hear more than an echo of the loyalist literature of the Middle Kingdom (Redford 1967, 78); and the description of the royal audience harks back to Middle Kingdom prototypes (Urk. IV, 164ff; De Buck 1938, 54; Goedicke 1974). The common grizzly vocabulary of Eighteenth Dynasty mili-tary records, delighting in such clichés as "crushing all their chiefs throughout their valleys, wallowing in their blood, (the corpses stacked) one on top of the other" (Urk. IV, 1666) finds ante-cedents in the idiolect, say, of a Senwosret I, that "throat-slitter

and headsman." The contempt of a Senwosret III for the lesser
breeds without the law is mirrored in the similar attitude of an
Amenhotep II towards the same Nubians as well as the Asiatics.
Temple layout and decoration during the early Eighteenth
Dynasty recalled prototypes of five centuries past. The
administration of the country had scarcely changed from the days
of Senwosret III and Amenemhat III; and Middle Kingdom legal
traditions continued to live on (Kees 1938, 118).

Ahmose and Amenhotep I also fell heir to a concept of
kingship six centuries old, at least if taken from its initial
formulation. The hypostasis of pharaonic monarchy as we see it in
its pristine form in the high Old Kingdom, betokened by such
terminology as "Horus eldest of the eldest, pure of seats, who
dwells in the horizon for ever and ever," was effectually defunct. It
would never live again as the sole and appropriate means of
presenting the king of Egypt to his contemporaries and to posterity. After the turmoil of the close of the Old Kingdom, the
Egyptian view of kingship came to demand of the king basically
three roles, not one. One derives from the age-old mytho-
logization of monarchy, the second is implicit in it, while the third
is new. For all time the Pharaoh would wear the garb of Horus son
of Osiris and heir of Geb, descendent of the sun-god, primarily as
celebrant of the cultus. Whether the expression of the king's
divinity had anything to do with his ritual function is a moot point
(Blumenthal 1978). Certainly as time went on, the mythological
jargon of kingship tended increasingly to pass into the realm of
extended, albeit potent, metaphor. The second role brings us
down to earth, although it derives nonetheless from a celestial
mythology. More and more, from the close of the Third Millennium BC, Pharaonic kingship is described as an "office," or
"function" on earth (Barta 1975, 45), and the occupant as the
earthly surrogate of the god. As the god's plenipotentiary on
earth, the king replicates the deity on a terrestrial level, even to
the point of becoming the physical image of the god. He may, in
the jargon of mythological fiction, have been "wise while yet in the
womb," yet he still required instruction like any young man; and,
like any commoner would face the judgment after death. An
appreciation of the continuum of kingship through many generations becomes something worthy of expression, and is reflected
in both the ancestral offering cult and incipient King-list (Redford
1986a, 144-63). While stress is laid on the kingship as the lawful

inheritance of the incumbent, paradoxically he was nonetheless selected by the gods, sometimes out of millions! A human surrogate, successor to a long line of office-holders (*sti*), selected by the god and instructed by his father is at a distinct remove from the absolute god-king of the halcyon days of the Fourth Dynasty!

The third role that circumstances thrust upon the Pharaonic monarchy comes to the fore with the rebellion of the Eleventh Dynasty. In their quest for the approbation of contemporaries through the use of the biographical statement, the Antefs betray unwittingly their common origins (Redford 1986a, 148-9). Their speech resounds with all the clichés of the "worthy commoner," like the latter "who spoke with (their) mouth(s) and acted with (their) arm(s)," these were kings "who speak and act," "mighty men who act with their biceps." They have taken power by force and will retain it by force. The measure of their legitimacy is their ability to succeed, both by wiping out opposition and by benefiting their people. And the concept does not float in some ethereal form remote from the real world, but appears in a very personal and very physical interpretation. Pharaoh is literally a strongman prone to violence, and therefore excels on the battle-field. He rages at the enemy, he lassos them, tramples them, smites them, cuts their throats, crushes their skulls and deca-pitates them, all by himself, without assistance. Pharaoh gains understanding and support from his people because, in dealing with internal dissidents and wily foreigners, his patience has been exhausted.

Because of the general state of preservation of Eighteenth Dynasty monuments, it may seem at times as though these empire Pharaohs were innovators. The more evidence that comes to light, however, the more clear becomes the conclusion that numerous elements in the Eighteenth Dynasty "theory" of kingship derive from centuries past. On the other hand, the momentous events of the Fifteenth and Fourteenth centuries BC offered the kings of the time full scope to develop what they had inherited.

The three roles described above proved difficult to maintain and virtually impossible to bring together. Was the king of Egypt a mythological figure in touch with the very beginning of time and the foundations of the earth; or was he an autocrat, who main-tained himself through the exercise of raw power? Was he the image of god, a divine deputy on earth, or a self-made potentate with only a human lineage? Did the Egyptians themselves sense any mutual exclusiveness?

Egyptologists nowadays, when faced by such contradictions, are apt to deny that they are contradictions, ashamed perhaps that the ancients might be accused of muddle-headedness. And so out pop such convoluted rationalizations as the "multiplicity of approaches" (Frankfort 1948), or "complimentarity" (Wilson 1949, 54), or the "many-valued logic" (Hornung 1982a, 237-43), all in an effort, desperate at times one feels, to explain away the apparent contradictions in ancient Egyptian religious expression. (Why the whole exercise is restricted to Egypt is puzzling as, *mutatis mutandis*, ancient Canaanite, Mesopotamian or Indian religions display similar characteristics.) In fact it seems a basic step remains to be taken, namely, a close, form-critical examination of our sources (Egyptologists have traditionally suffered from poor training in form-criticism). The vast majority of ancient Egyptian religious texts whence comes the raw material providing us with our sole insight into Egyptian religious beliefs, fall under only two categories: liturgy/prescription and hymnody. (Magical texts are here excluded as being doctrinally derivative.) Almost wholly missing in the haphazard of preservation, the absence of sympathetic selection, are such genres as devotional literature, theological treatises, dogmatics, and commentaries. The midrash on an ancient dramatic ritual that masquerades under the title "The Memphite Theology" shows what we are missing. Now if one were to peruse, in the gamut of Christian literature, only those pieces that can be classed as liturgy and hymns and virtually nothing more, imagine the distortion that would result in one's view of this religion! Christ is at one and the same time "the Lamb of God," "the Light of the World," "the Word," "the Son of God," "the Son of Man," "the second Adam," and so forth; the abode of the Blessed is at one and the same time "heaven," "Abraham's Bosom," "The New Jerusalem," "Paradise," and so on; the abode of the Damned is variously, "darkness," "the Lake of Fire," "She'ol," etc. Contradictions abound here, but historians know the reason. It is due in part to the historical coming together of micro-systems of belief originally quite independent of each other within a larger whole, and partly due to the syncretistic typology for which we have to thank a Philo or an Origen. In any case, in the history of religion one need not postulate a prior climate accepting of contradictions; contradictions come in the very nature of the evolution of a system of human thought, and then are either expurgated or accommodated by reducing them to the status of extended metaphor. Egyptologists should ask themselves whether it is not the presence of the latter, rather than a peculiar mind-set, that has produced the alleged confusion.

For the early Eighteenth Dynasty, the insistence of recent history on the hierarchical principle as the chief informing element in the cosmos finds eloquent expression in the position of the king *vis-à-vis* the gods. Before the close of the Middle Kingdom, the historicization of the times of the gods had issued in the description of the *floruits* of such gods as Re, Ptah, and Osiris in terms of specific reigns, albeit of gargantuan proportions, in remote antiquity (Luft 1978; Helck 1975a, 23: 12-14). The very essence of god could be conceived of as a "King of Upper and Lower Egypt at his emergence from the womb of Nut" (Helck 1975a, 23: 1). Drawing on a doctrine of Middle Kingdom currency (Lacau and Chevrier 1969, plate 12, 14, 15 and passim), originally designed to enhance the prestige of an erstwhile parochial family of rulers, the Eighteenth Dynasty laid great stress on the supernal kingship of Amun, the dynastic patron and guarantor. As Pharaoh was Horus of the Living, so Amun was King of the Gods. The earthly kingship was but a reflection of the heavenly one; Pharaoh was Amun or Re's representative on earth, on "the Throne of Amun" and in "the Office of Atum" (Urk. IV, 563).

Selection is stressed in the texts, in spite of the fact that the god had fathered the king. Re or Amun-Re had chosen the king (Urk. IV, 553, 1359, 1722, etc.), "elevating (him) above millions" (Urk. IV, 1722), often because he "loved him more than any other king" (Urk. IV, 162, 553, 554, 1359, 1552, 1686, etc.); occasionally the boast is added (especially under Amenhotep II) that the king was "stronger than any other king who had ever been" (Urk. IV, 1290, 1363). Sometimes the choice had been "prophesied" or "proclaimed" in advance (Urk. IV, 180; Lacau and Chevrier, 1977, 133). Often the selection was made with specific ends in mind: "to guard Egypt" (Urk. IV, 361), "begotten of Re to provide him with good progeny on earth" (Urk. IV, 362; cf. 1285), to refurbish the cultus (Urk. IV, 553, 1320), "to perform what his ka desires" (Urk. IV, 1324), "to rule what the sun-disc encircles" (Urk. IV, 1667, 1702), "to direct the common people" (Urk. IV, 1722). Though the king was "begotten" or "fashioned" by the god, still an appointment or promotion was necessary, and the same verbs are used as would appear in the records of the appointment of magistrates to office. "Re has appointed him (Ahmose) king of the Two Lands" (Helck 1975a, 104 line 2; cf. Blumenthal 1970, 64 [B.1.8]); Amenhotep II is "he whom [Amun] himself has appointed as chief of that which his Eye encircles: (Urk. IV, 1286); "he is a king whom Re has made to rule, whom Amun has exalted" (Urk. IV, 17). The god also has the lead role in the first "appearance" or "coronation" of the new king: the latter is "the one that Amun himself has caused to appear on his throne in Southern Heliopolis" (Urk. IV, 361, 389, 1324, 1348, 1690, 1749).

The appointment and coronation of the king took the form of a true induction to office. The same verb, *bsi,* is used as would be used of a commoner's induction into a priestly function (Wb. I, 473; Redford 1967, 18). The image is drawn from the induction of the king by the gods into a temple, a scene frequently depicted in art (Mysliwiec 1978, 174 n. 1). While elsewhere the verb might contain a nuance of initiation (Bleeker 1965, 58 n. 1; Vernus 1979, 182 n. n), when used of the king it rapidly came to mean simple "enthrone." *Bs.tw.s,* "she was inducted" (used of a queen) is eventually translated in Greek by a simple 'απεδέχθη, "she was appointed" (Daumas 1952, 191). *Bsi r nswt* means simply "to be inducted into the kingship," and *ḥḳꜣ n bs* is "a (duly) inducted (and therefore legitimate) ruler" (Wb. I, 473: 8-9).

Consequently, if one considers the relationship here propounded, one can only conclude that in the Eighteenth Dynasty view the cosmos is ruled by a dyad of which the members are unequal, namely, the high god, the sun, in heaven, and his earthly representative on earth. This is made quite explicit in contemporary literature. There is "the Unique One in heaven, and the 'Second' upon earth" (Urk. IV, 15; contrast Westendorf 1984); "Thou (the sun-god) art in heaven, illuminating the earth, while he (Amenhotep III) is upon earth, exercising thy kingship" (Urk. IV, 1676).

The Influence of Empire

The terrestrial position of the king of Egypt during the Eighteenth Dynasty was enhanced by the role events forced him to play in the creation of an empire. Egypt's relations with her neighbors during the Old Kingdom had never been well-defined or rationalized, beyond the vague realization that Nubians, Libyans, and Asiatics combined constituted a "sphere of influence." In the parlance of the times "the foreign lands belong to the king," and existed solely for Pharaoh's exploitation. With impunity he could dispatch expeditions to mine, quarry, trade or pillage, or deport *en masse,* as the situation demanded. No king felt the need to justify such action. It was the obligation of the aliens to remain "on the water of Pharaoh," and his duty to see that "the fear of Horus be placed in the foreign lands" (Redford 1986b).

All this was in process of change within two centuries of the collapse of the Old Kingdom. Pharaoh of the Middle Kingdom shows great sensitivity towards the position of his frontiers, and his ability to extend them means that the gods favor him (Blumenthal 1970, 187-89). Imperial dominion is construed as an ever-expanding homeland, not the attaching of individual provincial units to a mother-country. The king is now conditioned to the exercise of brute force, and "seizes" both Egypt and the foreign lands violently; he embraces and unites them, ties them up, crushes them, and pacifies them (Blumenthal 1970, 189-98). Nor is the king indulging in gratuitous brutality: it is all described within the context of a lawful inheritance. Pharaoh, moreover, acts in this manner with justification. In the civil war, just prior to the inauguration of the Twelfth Dynasty Egypt had been laid waste by opposing forces, a sizable element of which had been foreign. In a progress throughout his realm Senwosret I viewed the damage caused, and in two surviving speeches describes the devastation. His brutal treatment of the foreigners turns out to be, in the king's view, justifiable punishment of wrongdoers: "as for them that had transgressed against this house (the temple at Tod). My Majesty made [a great slaughter among them ...] both men and women, the valleys being filled with rows (?) (of cadavers), the mountains bearing sheaves (of corpses); the enemy from the 'Terraces' were placed on the brazier—it was death by fire because of what they had done against it ... the young were sawn up, the children of the enemy were like sacrificial victims" (Redford 1987). It is the punitive function of the king that turned the image of the king of the Middle Kingdom into a *sḥm-ir.f,* "a potentate who acts."

Egyptian mythology could accommodate the arbitrariness of a potentate by recourse to the topos of Horus's championing of his father. The god, says Senwosret I, "appointed me protector of this land, (for) he knew who would bring it together for him ... I am a king of his creation, a sovereign l.p.h. who needs to be given nothing. I seized as a youngster, I was mighty even in the egg, I governed even as a child ... He appointed me to be lord of the commons, [I] was created in the sight of the Sun-folk ... To me were given its length and its breadth, and I was hailed as a born conqueror ... I am his son who champions his father: he has commanded me to seize what he seized" (P. Berlin 3029; Goedicke 1974). The violence of the king thus finds a pattern in the archetypal actions of the god, his father.

The Seventeenth Dynasty shared with Amenemhat I and Senwosret I the destiny of rescuing Egypt from the depredations of foreigners. Like Amenemhat I, Tao I could point to no illustrious pedigree, being an upstart southerner possibly of Nubian extraction (Harris and Weeks 1972, 123), who began life in vassalage to the Hyksos. The entire history of the family, prior to the final victory, constitutes a story of struggle against enormous odds—a superior enemy, limited manpower and resources, and an attenuated base of operations. Events transformed the king of Egypt into a commander-in-chief of troops, a "mighty king," a "strong ruler" who had to "act with his (own) arms," in imitation of Middle Kingdom jargon (Redford 1967, 37: Urk. IV, 1551, 1559, 1761, 1762, etc.). He was a "Horus, beloved of his army, a potentate ... who repels all foreign lands and rescues his city (Thebes)" (Mentuhotep stela, own copy). Significantly, Kamose seldom alludes to the agency of the gods in his two stelae; only in the preamble and in the stereotyped description of the start of the campaign is there a perfunctory reference to "Re [who set him] up as king himself and that decreed him victory in very truth" (Stela I, line 2), and to "the command of Amun, regular-of-counsels" (Stela I, line 10). Thereafter he talks of his own might, his own decisions, and his own skill. It is he who "punishes crimes" (Stela II, line 24), his is the "hot breath" that terrifies the enemy (Stela II, line 26), and he, the one that "seizes the land by force" (Stela II, line 35). This was a man "aware of his strength" and proud of his own accomplishments. As a "strong-man king," he conforms to a pattern familiar in the Eighteenth Dynasty. Thutmose I provides another excellent example. Neither in the Tombos stela, nor in his address to the priests of Abydos, is there any reference to Amun's authorization or help in winning the victory. The king does it on his own; his is the decision to "wipe out civil strife throughout the lands and to stem the influx from foreign parts" (Urk. IV, 8). He speaks of his major campaign into Syria as undertaken "to slake his heart's thirst throughout the foreign lands," i.e., to indulge himself (Urk. IV, 9); "he has captured the limits of the land in its entirety, he has trodden its ends in might and victory, seeking a fight, but he found no one (on the battlefield) who could stand up to him" (Urk. IV, 85). A feeling of parochial patriotism comes through in Thutmose I's inscriptions, centered not simply on Egypt, but on Thebes in particular (again foreshadowed in Second Intermediate Period texts), and a flush of pride in having but recently turned her fortunes around: he had come to the throne "to broaden the boundaries of Thebes, the confines of Her-that-Faces-her-Lord ... I have made the boundaries of Egypt as far as the circuit of the sun-disc, I have strengthened those who (formerly) were fearful ... I have made Egypt mistress, with every land her subjects" (Urk. IV, 102).

The feeling of independence of action and confidence in one's own strength translates easily into the informing element of the concept of the "performing athlete" (Decker 1981; 1984; Edel 1979). From Ahmose on, nearly every king of the Eighteenth Dynasty used the excuse of his presence in Asia on campaign to indulge himself in the hunt after the battle was won. Although it is true that the royal hunt in ancient Egypt often carries cultic significance (Altenmüller 1980b), the present practice was nothing more than an act of calculated insouciance for popular consumption. The same is true of the other feats of strength which continued to be devised with increasing novelty into the reign of Amenhotep II: archery with metal targets, boat-racing, and daredevil acts in battle. These were broadcast far and wide on stelae, the wording of which suggest the currency of a parallel oral tradition cultivated by the administration.

The dissemination of the mighty acts of the king throughout Egypt and the empire was a consciously adopted policy of the Eighteenth Dynasty designed to admonish and chasten. As such it continued the tradition and purpose of the loyalist literature of earlier times, presenting it in the guise of new genres, namely, the "compilation of mighty deeds," and (slightly later) the royal encomium in the form of a "song" (ḥst) to be sung to the harp. One senses underlying these texts a lively oral transmission that has left traces of itself not only in Egypt, but as we shall see, in Canaan as well.

Besides capitalizing on the new "Strong-man" image, the Eighteenth Dynasty monarchy also sought to promote the age-old notion of the wise and erudite king. Again, the experience of winning and maintaining an empire contributed in practice as well as theory. Thutmose III had, in fact, skillfully pre-empted the attempt of the Kadesh coalition to march on Egypt, and would celebrate his success ever afterwards in such epithets as "he who smote the foreign rulers who (would) attack him" (Barguet 1962, 161), and "who repelled all lands as they moved against him" (Urk. IV, 1230) ... they that had intended to bring destruction upon Egypt" (Urk. IV, 1254). Again, he had hit on the brilliant expedient of using prefabricated landing-craft on the Euphrates in a surprise attack which defeated the Mitannian forces. This was indeed a king to be boasted of! "There was nothing at all that he did not know. He was 'Thoth' in everything, there was not any subject of which he was not knowledgeable ... (he was) more conversant with the regulations than the scribes" themselves (Redford 1986a, 166-67)!

The empire made an additional contribution to the figure of the Eighteenth Dynasty monarch and one which, because of its alien origin, did not serve to bolster traditional concepts. Pharaoh was now classed internationally among the kings of the earth: He is referred to as a "Great King" (šarru rabû) in the Akkadian diplomatic language of the times, on a par with other world leaders such as the kings of Babylon, Hatti, and Mitanni. This had no currency at all in the traditional view from Egypt. The monarchy in Egypt constituted a unity, a single function, with universal application. There was but one nswt, "King (of Upper Egypt)." The mythology rationalizing kingship did not accommodate a plurality of nswts. The case with Akkadian šarrum or West Asiatic malkum, both "king," however, was quite different. These were terms which had basically terrestrial reference, and did not suffer the burden of mythological baggage inherited from the period of formulation. A Hammurabi or a Yarim-lim, or a Shamshi-adad, great kings themselves, were served by lesser kings, and the terms šar šarri or melek mᵉlakim, "king of kings," arose spontaneously. Pharaoh, on the other hand, thrust as overlord into the Asiatic sphere, could not conceive of, or tolerate, degrees of kingship. All foreign heads of state, whether they called themselves kings or not, were but "chiefs" (*wrw*) to him. "King of kings" (*nswt nsyw*) or "ruler of rulers" (*ḥḳ3 ḥḳ3w*) were simply mechanical translations of alien locutions (Urk. IV, 15, 1292, 1325, 1568, 1756).

Kingship and the Sun-god

Akhenaten's view of kingship cannot be divorced from his comprehensive program, especially from that part of it which he assigned to the sun-god. Amarna studies tend sometimes to bog down over the question of the correct characterization of the new cult: monotheism, henotheism, monolatry, or something else. Regardless of whether one credits Akhenaten with being a monotheist, at first glance it might seem strange that it was the physical disc of the sun that attracted his enthusiastic and single-minded devotion. The "Disc of the Day" had long enjoyed a place in the lower echelons of the pantheon, as an avatar of the sun-god; but this solar icon had never been widely referred to, nor had it achieved any important role in mythology. Together with the sunbeams that radiate from it (See figure 4.1), the sun-disc becomes here and there in the mortuary literature the object of the deceased's desire for eternal union (Redford 1976).

But, if the sun-disc was a novel object of devotion at the close of the Fifteenth Century BC, the sun-cult in all its forms and practices had long since exerted a powerful influence on the monarchy (Radwan 1975b).

The coming of the Empire conjured up and resuscitated a wealth of imagery wherewith to embellish the figure of the imperial Pharaoh in literature; and much of it proves to have celestial reference. Here the sun-disc wins a little more attention. The imperial king is one who is "content with victory, leader of his army, the head of myriads—he is patient, sharp-witted and intelligent ... speedy like the sun-disc ... an electrum star when he flashes by, chariot-mounted, strong-armed bowman, deadly shot" (Urk. IV, 1723). He is "a runner, like the disc when he moves, a star of electrum when he shines in a chariot" (Urk. IV, 1684), "... like the Disc, a Horus beloved of his army," "with a sharp spear, like Anhur, shining brightly in the eyes like the Disc" (Redford 1976, 49). The picture of the king leading his troops into battle inspires the image "a dazzling sun-disc appearing at the head of his army" (ibid., 50), or "a dazzling sun appearing in the war-crown" (Habachi 1954, plate 26). Also, the monarch "in the holiness of his palace" in his resplendent accouterments appears to the awe-struck courtiers as "the Sun-disc in his horizon" (Urk. IV, 1016).

This imagery is the somewhat superficial response of the exuberant court poets of the day, bedazzled by the new common appearance of Pharaoh, decked out in his imperial finery at numerous state functions. But the sun occupies a more fundamental position in the Egyptian concept of empire.

The sun-god, as creator of the world and primordial king, retains the absolute right to bestow, or to remove kingship whenever he pleases. From this right stems the notion of the selection of the king-to-be by Re; and, conversely, those who claim to rule in ignorance of Re are not kings at all (Gardiner 1946, 55). Now, in states widely separated in time and space, the sun-god is accorded an elevated position when an Empire comes upon the scene, mainly, it can be contended, because of an element of universal applicability in the worship of this heavenly luminary. One may point to the part played by Shamash in the bestowal of kingship and imperial authority in the empires of Western Asia during the Second and First Millennia BC. It would be difficult to deny seriously that the "Amorite" regime known in Egyptian history as the Fifteenth "Hyksos" Dynasty, did not similarly rank the sun-god as the author and guarantor of their far-flung dominion, although it is a moot point to what extent Hyksos beliefs had any lasting influence on the Egyptians. Certainly the few surviving texts from the Fifteenth Dynasty prove, in contradiction of Hatshepsut, a startling devotion to Re. Apophis is a "scribe of Re" and "living image of Re on earth" (Helck 1975a, 57-58). Equally compelling examples are to be found in the imperial histories of Iran, Rome, and South America. With the incipient formation of the world empire of the Medes, Ahura Mazda found a potential, if not immediate, fulfillment in the role of the universal, sole deity (Olmstead 1948, 195-99). In the waning years of the still united Roman Empire, when the government felt keenly the need to find a way to stop the fragmentation of the provinces, both Aurelian and Julian promoted the "Unconquered Sun" to the head of the pantheon, virtually as sole god; and the result was a humorless state cult, remarkably similar to that of Akhenaten's sun-disc in method and broad outline (Rose 1970, 999). With similar purpose, and again in an imperialistic setting, the Incan sun-god was placed at the head of the pantheon by the emperor Pachacutec in the early Fifteenth Century (Toynbee 1962, 25-27).

Since he is chosen by the sun-god "to rule all that which the sun-disc encircles," and since he is already son of the solar deity, whether Re or Amun-Re, it should come as no surprise that this surrogate on earth should resemble the high god he represents. Sometimes the notion is expressed within the high-flown imagery of poetry. The king is "Re by whose beams people see, one that brightens the Two Lands more than the Sun Disc" (Blumenthal 1970, 100); he is "glimpsed like Re when he rises, as when the sun-disc shines and Khepri appears to view" (Urk. IV, 19). He is "Re when he shines like the horizon-dweller, that people may live" (Urk. IV, 1695). The king's dominion over all peoples, Egyptian and foreign, finds expression in such phrases as "Sun of Egypt," "Sun of the plebes," "Sun of the Nine Bows," "Sun of the foreign rulers," etc. (Urk. IV, 1652; Brack, 1977, 39 [28]; Meeks 1982, 167). The Universalist expressions investigated here, involving *n ḫ3swt*, are not new with the Eighteenth Dynasty, but were current already in the Second Intermediate Period, and are probably much older (Redford 1970, 12 n. 5). All perhaps are influenced by the very ancient "Re of the foreign lands," a figure attested from the Old Kingdom (Montet 1929, no. 57). In the expression *Rᶜn ḥḳ3w*, "Sun of the Rulers," *Rᶜ* approximates in position and meaning *nswt*, "king," in the parallel *nswt nsyw*, "king of kings," or *ḥḳ3* in *ḥḳ3 ḥḳ3w*, "Ruler of Rulers." "Sun of the Nine Bows" also parallels the more common *ḥḳ3 n pḏt psḏt*, "Ruler of the Nine Bows," predicted especially of Akhenaten, Tutankhamun, and Horemheb (Urk. IV, 1963, 2033, 2135, and passim).

But imperialist phraseology made the physical resemblance of monarch to sun-god even more explicit. From the Middle Kingdom come such expressions as "the great god, the likeness of Re" (predicated of Senwosret I: Blumenthal 1970, 99), an epithet to be taken up by Hatshepsut, Amenhotep II and Amenhotep III to name a few (Urk. IV, 275, 279, 362, 1287, 1676). Already the Hyksos Apophis knows and uses of himself the phrase "living image of Re upon earth" (*twt ᶜnḫ n Rᶜ tp t3*: Helck, 1975, 58), as does the roughly contemporary Ikhernofret at Thebes (Vernus 1982). Amenhotep III is addressed by Amun-Re as "my living image who fashioned my limbs" (Urk. IV, 1655), and the morphology of the name *Twt-ᶜnḫ-itn* is derived precisely from this locution. Much more popular, however, in the Eighteenth Dynasty was the word *tit*, "picture, replica," the same word as was used to designate hieroglyphic signs (Redford 1986a, 167 n. 12). Thutmose I is called "offspring of the Bull of the Ennead, splendid replica of the divine limbs" (Urk. IV, 84), and Hatshepsut "faithful picture of the Eternal Lord" (Urk. IV, 361; 244, 275), or of Amun or Re (Urk. IV, 552); Amenhotep II and Amenhotep III become variously "holy replica of the Lord of the Gods" (Urk. IV, 1319, 1324, 1348) or of Atum (Urk. IV, 1359, 1687). Amenhotep III is termed "Picture of Re, pre-eminent over the Two Lands" (Urk. IV, 1667; cf. 1702), or "his beautiful godly replica" (Urk. IV, 1724). Less popular choices of vocabulary convey essentially the same meaning: "living image (*šsp ʿnḫ*) of the eternal Lord" (Thutmose IV: Urk. IV, 1540), "thy shape (*inw*) partaking of his goodness ... thou having indeed arisen in the form of his sun-disc" (Hatshepsut: Lacau and Chevrier 1977, 120). Pursuant to the imagery that translates Pharaoh into the image of the sun-god on earth, the falcon-icon of Re-Horakhty insinuates itself into the mode of representation of the king: he is depicted wearing a "falcon-suit" as it were (Redford 1976, n. 79 & 101), and described as "the divine falcon emerged from the divine limbs" (Amenhotep III: Urk. IV, 1701, 1743), and "divine king, like the horizon-dweller who brightens the earth like him that came forth from the Nun" (Amenhotep III: Urk. IV, 1703).

The locale where the choice of the king was made and published, and where the god, at least ideally, placed the crown on his head, was Heliopolis, city of the sun-god. Here, "in the Great Mansion" it was that "his father Atum published his 'Great Name' as enduring king" (Urk. IV, 591). The holy *išd*-tree, an ancient cult feature of the city, attested in an inauguration myth as early as the Coffin Texts, bore the new king's name upon its leaves already in the Twelfth Dynasty, in the writing of Thoth; and the same god drafted the annals of the coming reign either on the same foliage or under the tree (Helck 1957; Mysliwiec 1980). Re-Horakhty-Atum affixed his crown, and the king became, in truth, a "Heliopolitan."

The Humanizing of the Good God

The new personae events had conspired to thrust upon the head of Pharaoh during the Eighteenth Dynasty—the strong-man king, god's representative on earth, the image of the high-god, the superior intellect—combined paradoxically to humanize this erstwhile god. His feats of strength were performed, not in the maximum privacy of the palace, but in full view of the entire land; his daily functions on behalf of the gods made plain his essential distinction from the gods. The daily exercise of his intelligence and superior judgment exposed him unmercifully to the risk of failure, and the state to the risk of a discredited head. The popular expectancy, enshrined in the motif of king-in-council, in fact even demanded that the king make a habit of opting for risky action against the sober advice of more cautious counselors. There is a striving, indeed a posturing, in the antics of the Eighteenth Dynasty monarch. One is made to feel that, in the failure of older forms, the king must invent new guises or develop unusual roles to maintain himself in the scheme of things.

The function of empire-builder had awakened in the collective consciousness of the nation the expectation that every king would turn out to be a paragon of strength and intelligence. Unfortunately, the chequered history of Egypt from 1600 to 1400 BC did not prove conducive to turning expectation into reality. The kings of Egypt had set themselves an unattainable goal. No sooner had legitimacy been won by force of arms in the struggle against the Hyksos, than the royal family plunged unwittingly into a feud over the rule of the empire, with all the crass hallmarks of a family quarrel at the human level. The great victories of Thutmose III arrested the process of discreditation that such feuds entail; but because of their very success these conquests deprived his successors of the chance of emulation. The frontiers simply could not be further expanded. "Moreover the monarchy was now made to sustain new stresses, never experienced before. In place of absolute conquests of foreign states, treaties were now entered into which even involved .... marriages with non-Egyptian ladies! A crop of able officials had grown up, functioning more independently than their counterparts of earlier periods; and new institutions (the temple, the army), although still in incipient stages of development, rivaled the king's house in influence. What room was there for Pharaoh?" (Redford 1986a, 186-87).

The monarchy's response to the gradual weakening of its divinity was not entirely successful. In an effort to enhance claims to legitimacy when rivalry beset the succession to the throne, the Eighteenth Dynasty invoked the idea of the juridical oracle, and placed the dynastic god, Amun, in the position of delivering it. The texts maintain that the oracle was wholly unexpected, although the god had long intended it. By making the delivery of the oracle at a public spectacle where it could be witnessed by a great throng, the dynasty acknowledged its need for popular approbation; and by deferring to Amun in so theatrical a fashion, it placed a power in the supreme god's hands that he would not easily relinquish (Berg 1988).

The juridical oracle, as employed by Hatshepsut and Thutmose III may have been new, but the "Divine Birth" motif derived from an ancient prototype. Chastened by the awareness of the conflict that might arise between a claim to divinity and an all too evident humanity, the dynasty from time to time resorted to the myth of the miraculous birth of the present incumbent (Brunner 1964). Religious literature from time immemorial had dwelled extensively on the divine birth of the king, but it had consistently located the event in the timeless realm of the gods and within the undefined limits of myth. Even folklore made no bones about the paternity: Re was the father of Userkaf and his "brothers," not Re in the disguise of a human being. The motif of the "Divine Birth," however, as it appears in the Eighteenth Dynasty exemplars, begins with an ostensibly human birth which everyone acknowledges took place in present time; and characterizes it arbitrarily as a mystery, not apparent to the eye of man. It then reveals and explains that mystery in a statement of dogma: it was not Thutmose I that begat Hatshepsut, but Amun in the guise of Thutmose I. The "Divine Birth" is thus not myth in form, but is better classed as a revelatory midrash, or commentary, on a historic event. Whether any court ritual lies behind the text is beyond our ken in the present state of the evidence (Morenz 1973b).

Another attempt to rehabilitate the role of divine king lay stress on affirming his position in the cult. Amenhotep III, to judge by his constant allusion to it, had made temple restoration, and the refurbishing of the divine service, the cardinal goal of his reign. He not only built and rebuilt temples on a vast scale all over Egypt and the empire, but he also engaged in a thoroughgoing pro-

gram of fashioning the gods' images and renewing cult
paraphernalia to the extent that gods are made to say in one
inscription that now they are "seen existing upon earth" (Urk. IV,
1676). And one thousand years later the folktale circulated in
Egypt about the king "Amenhotep (alias Hor)" whose one wish
had been "to see the gods" (Redford 1986a, 248-51).

It was the same king that breathed new life into that ancient
and most "royal" of celebrations, the *sed*-festival, or jubilee (Frankfort 1948, 79-89; Hornung and Staehelin 1974). Amenhotep
claims to have rediscovered the archives an old and unadulterated
order-of-service for the festival, which brought the three performances of his reign into line with the pristine form of the
observance. Whether this is true or not—I believe there is some
truth to it—the *sed*-festival celebrations turned out to be the most
important events (from the viewpoint of contemporaries) of the
last decade of the reign, lauded in royal and private inscriptions
alike. The festival brought gods and commoners together, on the
spiritual plain to reaffirm the kingship of Horus, the inheritance
of Geb; on a more mundane level to enjoy the king's largess at a
continuous feast over several days.

Akhenaten's View of Kingship

In a nutshell, the affect (if not the purpose) of Akhenaten's
reform was, by denying the present existence of all other gods, to
focus all attention on the role of himself and his father, the sun.
Epithets and topoi that contributed thereto were retained; those
which did not were discarded.

As we have seen, the image of Pharaoh on the eve of the reign
of Amenhotep IV-Akhenaten (See Figure 4.2) had undergone a
subtle but considerable evolution over eight generations since the
expulsion of the Hyksos. A physically powerful likeness of the sun-
god sat on the throne of Egypt, engendered, selected, and duly
appointed by the sun-god himself. He signalized his function by
daring plans that always came to fruition, he performed feats of
strength renowned the world over. He was pious and wise: he kept
up the cults and worshipped his ancestors, and instructed his
subjects in what they should do. But if this persona was his native
inheritance, he also donned a guise forced on him from outside.
He now wore the mantle of a king of kings who had to deal with

monarchs of equal rank whom native mythology would never credit; he signed treaties with them, corresponded with them, sent them presents, and even married their daughters.

If all these demanding functions comprised the "inheritance in office" of Akhenaten, an inheritance that his immediate predecessors had already learned, took an exhausting toll, it is certain that he either could not, or chose not, to fulfill them *in toto*. The fundamental iconoclasm which informed the movement had swept away most of the cult and its attendant mythology, and consequently the Pharaoh of the Amarna Period could never appear in the traditional mythological role of Horus-son-of-Isis, with all that that relationship entailed. His ability to function as a *shm-ir.f,* "a Potentate," sustained largely by his ruthlessness and success, suffered from Akhenaten's physical limitations. He could not credibly step into the role of the "strong-man," and although he is shown frequently in a chariot, he apparently never led, nor intended to lead, a military campaign. (This at least was the impression conveyed to Canaanite kings: cf. EA 53). Not that he shrank from ruthless policies. In the few surviving letters from him to his vassals in Asia, Akhenaten threatens malefactors with death by fire or the ax (EA 162), orders mass deportations (Edzard, 1970), and authorizes impalement (Schulman 1982). However, his retirement from an active life in administration (Redford 1984) and his championing of an art form imbued throughout by a feminine spirit, detracted in an obvious way from the traditional role he was supposed to play.

It was contemplation of the relationship between Pharaoh on earth and the god in heaven that enlivened the creative imagination of the king. Here he made a signal contribution. The "sonship" of the king was not only stressed above all else, but was described in a number of novel ways. The king was the Disc's son "who came forth from (his) limbs," "thy sole son who came forth from thy body" (Sandman 1938, 54, 59, 75, 78, 96, etc.). He was "the beautiful child of the sun-disc" born "as the sun-disc is born" (ibid., 17). The birth was effected through the radiance of the sun: "thou gives birth to His Majesty as thou givest birth to thyself daily without ceasing; thou hast fashioned him with thine own rays" (ibid., 75). "The Disc gives birth to him whenever he rises" (ibid., 84). Nor was the notion of the king as god's image on earth given up. "Thy limbs are like the beams of thy father," says Tutu, "thou art like him" (ibid., 84); "Thy beams (are shed) upon thy good image, the ruler of Truth" (ibid., 59).

All the other attributes of the god's representative on earth followed naturally. The king had been selected by the Sun-disc and placed on the throne by him. The king had been "[given] the kingship by his father Re" (Karnak 1972: 3). The god had "set him up as king like the Sun-disc" (Sandman 1938, 59). Akhenaten is ensconced "upon the seat of the living Sun-disc who fabricated [him]" (Redford 1982, 126). The "office" of king itself belonged to the Sun-disc: "thou hast established him in thine office of King of Upper and Lower Egypt" (Sandman 1938, 75); "thou (the king) art established in his office for ever" (ibid., 80). The king's universal dominion was granted directly by the Sun-disc (although in this connection the texts are banal and stereotyped): it is the Disc that "extends [for me my frontiers] to the limits of heaven on every road, bequeathing [to me the foreign lands of] Syria and Kush, all lands together being beneath my feet" (Karnak 12610-17).

In contrast to the preceding reigns, the link between god and king in the Amarna Period was significantly strengthened by the priestly and didactic functions the monarch adopted. Akhenaten reserved for himself the role of principal priest and celebrant of the god, and because of the centralization of the cult at Amarna this priestly position loomed much larger than it would have done otherwise. Akhenaten became "First Prophet of Horakhty" (Habachi 1965, plate 25a; Kees 1956, 371), "who offers the great hecatomb to his father," the Sun-disc (Urk. IV, 1983), and "proffers *maat* to thy beautiful face" daily (Sandman 1938, 59). "I am the one," he says, "who makes [offering] myself [to the Sun-disc my] father in the house of the Sun-disc in Akhetaten" (Urk. IV, 1977). The king maintained his centrality as prime worshipper of his father even in cult iconography. On the diagonal slopes of the great Re-Horakhty altars, the recumbent figures of bag-wigs adoring the sun in the company of baboons, are those of Akhenaten (Smith and Redford 1977, plates 78-80), and on the *ben-ben* stela, it is the king that is shown kissing the earth before the sun-disc.

The intellectual union between god and king marks a significant and new departure. Even in the "Karnak Period" there are scattered allusions to the special communication between the two: "[it is my father the Sun-disc] that puts (it) in my heart," says

Akhenaten (Karnak 909: 11); "[Thou knowest (?)] thy father's heart," says an un-named interlocutor, "he leads thee" (Karnak 118: 11). At Amarna, the passages are better preserved and consistently aver that it is only to the king that the Sun-disc has revealed himself: "There is none other that knows thee except thy son .... thou hast made him skilled in thy plans and thy strength" (Sandman 1938, 95). Akhenaten was "thy son who knows thee" (ibid., 65), and the Sun-disc in return will "obey whatever he wishes for him" (ibid., 59). Akhenaten, therefore, stood between mankind and the godhead (although private worship was not interdicted), and acted as sole spokesman for the god.

The "teaching" of Pharaoh, often alluded to but never made explicit, probably consists simply of the king's utterances, both hymnic and didactic, decrees as well as *obiter dicta*. That it took the form of face-to-face oral communication to an entourage or the intoning of set pieces during ritual, is strongly suggested by the oft-repeated desire to hear the king's voice. "Thou (the king) art the light! I live at sight of thee, I thrive at hearing thy voice!" (Berlin 20375; cf. 20376). "May I hear the voice of the king when he performs service for his father!" (Mahu: Sandman 1938, 52). "My lord promoted me because I did his teaching, because I listened to his voice without ceasing" (May: ibid., 60). "My arms are raised in adoration of him, my ears hear his voice .... He used to rise early to teach me every day, so thoroughly did I execute his teaching!" (Tutu: ibid., 75-76). "How prosperous is he that carefully listens to thy teaching of life!" (ibid., 92). Tutu is "one who listened to what thy son said" (ibid., 16), and Ay craves burial "in the seat of the blessed who hearkened to thy sweet voice in the Mansion of the *ben-ben*" (ibid., 92).

Vincent Tobin has placed us all in his debt by recently undertaking a close analysis of the Amarna hymns, and establishing in detail the dependence of the various exemplars. The stemma he sets up not only proves the primacy of the "Great Hymn" and the tertiary dependence of such pieces as those of Huya, Ay, and Mahu, but he has also unwittingly demonstrated that the form of composition and transmission was oral and formulaic. The evidence is thus consistent in suggesting that Akhenaten's "Teaching" was spoken, even extemporized, and was directed at the circle his voice could reach. Tobin correctly concludes that it constituted a rigid, unbending system of belief within which the worshipper, other than the king himself, could show originality, if at all, by stylistic variation only (Tobin 1986).

Whether any part of the "Teaching" could be termed "doctrinal"—and what "doctrine" can we point to apart from that which lurks among the poetic imagery of the hymn?—a good deal was apparently preceptoral in a crass, self-serving mode. Some statements couple reference to the "Teaching" with simple, ethical concepts, while others indicate that obedience to the "Teaching" brings rewards (Davies 1908a, I, plate 30). While Akhenaten could not realistically make use of literary genres celebrating the mighty acts of a "Sportsman king," the old "loyalist" tradition lives on and melds into the "Teaching." Ay, *mutatis mutandis*, lives very much in the tradition of a Sehtepibre and his precursors when he advises, "Ho all living upon earth and those who shall be young men someday! I shall tell you the way of life .... Offer praises to the Living Disc and you shall have a prosperous life; say to him: 'Grant the ruler health exceedingly!' then he shall double favors for you .... Adore the king who is unique like the Disc, for there is none other beside him! Then he will grant you a lifetime in happiness of heart, with the sustenance he grants" (Urk. IV, 1998-99).

All the mechanisms of Akhenaten's system, as we have seen, conspire to direct and focus attention on the god-king axis, and allow no private initiatives. The king was the image and representative of the deity; what was the deity?

No one, perhaps, has made so succinct and precise a statement as Barquet nearly two decades ago: "the Aton of Amenhotep IV would stand for the royal principle, essentially a divine principle, but enlivened and made tangible in a sort of way and worshipped under the form of the solar disc" (Barquet 1968, 29). The Sun-disc was a great icon of kingship, elevated into the heavens and treated as a universal, archetypal Pharaoh. At the outset, the god seems to fall victim to the new art style, so that he physically resembles Akhenaten (Redford 1976, plate 8; Smith and Redford, 1977b, plate 86: 9); but from the Second or early Third year he began to partake of the accouterments of royalty: cartouches, titulary, equities, and circumlocutions.

Although we cannot say that Akhenaten had not had this aspect of his god in mind from the start, the dramatic evolution of the Sun-disc to celestial king took place at the time of the first *sed*-festival. The excavations of the *Gm-pꜣ-itn* in East Karnak have demonstrated the overriding importance of this celebration to the new king. Almost the entire repertoire of relief decoration in this vast structure was given over to a lively and non-stereotypical depiction of the jubilee. Another significant discovery lay in store. Although the art had changed drastically, the order and identity of the individual acts of the ceremony followed the sed-festivals of Amenhotep III closely, at least where the rigors of the new system permitted. Scholars have long expressed puzzlement as to why Akhenaten should have decided on a jubilee, normally a "30-year celebration," in the second year of his reign! The growing awareness of how close the young king patterned his own performance on the revised liturgy of his father, excites the imagination, and may well point the way to new interpretations. Was the sed of Akhenaten simply the prolongation of the "jubilee-series" of his father? Falling at the end of his Second or the beginning of his Third regnal year, it would have coincided with the fortieth year since the accession of Amenhotep III, precisely when a fourth jubilee would have been celebrated, had the old king lived. Although the jubilee is said specifically to be that of Akhenaten ("the first sed-festival of His Majesty which [his father, the Sun-disc(?)] granted him"), the god himself is called, from the moment of the celebration on, "the great living Sun-disc who is in jubilee" (Redford 1975, plate 1). Does the god in fact share vicariously with his son in the performance of the sed? In the light of the proximity, bordering on identity, enjoyed by the pair, this is quite likely. In the hymn of the "king's-children" (msw-nswt), the king appears to be addressed variously as Re, Horus, and "our father," and his celebration of the sed and (prescriptive?) writings therefore are somehow compared to the sun-god (Spalinger 1988).

If Akhenaten's purpose was to rehabilitate the monarchy by stressing the unity of supernal and earthly kingship, and eliminating the distractions of the roles based upon mythology and empire, he failed miserably. The institution might have sustained a modification, even a radical one, in its theological underpinning; but to discard the imperial function which through victory and wonder-working had brought untold esteem to the person of Pharaoh, however difficult to maintain, was shortsighted. While he yet lived, Akhenaten had won a reputation for not wanting "to go hard against" the land of Canaan, and for desisting from military activity; and significant failure to achieve military success in Asia figures prominently in the list of shortcomings of which Tutankhamun accuses the previous administration. If the Pharaonic monarchy survived, as indeed it did with some vigor, thanks must go to the intervention of the very military Akhenaten had shunned. It was the verdict of this military that officially branded the Amarna period for all Egyptians as "the time of the doomed one," or "rebel," military pejoratives both (Gardiner 1938).

Concluding Remarks

The concept of kingship that the Eighteenth Dynasty inherited was a very old one, and it must be admitted that, in sum, it changed relatively little over three millennia. Because so much is preserved from the New Kingdom in contrast to what preceded, the Theban kings may appear to us as innovators. However, the more evidence one adduces in this matter, the more it seems a fair statement that it was the solar concept, in the form shaped by the Twelfth Dynasty, that the Eighteenth Dynasty adopted intact.

It is sometimes maintained that Akhenaten's movement should be more correctly characterized as a "throw-back" to an Old Kingdom type of orthodoxy. Nothing could be further from the truth.

If Akhenaten inherited any concepts from the Old Kingdom they were of the most general sort, filtered through all the intervening centuries and no different from what was available to his immediate predecessors and successors. The relationship between sun-god and king in the high Old Kingdom is only a part of a fully integrated system in which Horian, Butic and Abydene roles predominate (to mention only a few). Moreover, the father-son axis involving king and sun-god is not nearly as developed and central in the Old Kingdom as it is in Akhenaten's program. Pharaoh in the Pyramid Texts plays a variety of roles vis-à-vis Re, often more as a suppliant than a son. Again, the pronounced monarchism of the godhead under Akhenaten is looked for in vain in the Old Kingdom. Again, the didactic function of the king at Amarna, so prominently filled by Akhenaten, is absent from the Old Kingdom role of the "perfect god!" One could multiply the list of contrasts to such an extent that the original contention that prompted the rebuttal would appear what it is: superficial and misleading.

It fares no better with the belief that Akhenaten attempted "to impose orthodoxy" (Baines 1987c). The mutually beneficial relationship between god and king in Ancient Egypt can be construed as the maintenance of the "God and His Shrine," and all that this entailed: 1. The periodic renewal of the deity, his images, his chattels and his house according to the prescriptive texts; 2. The performance of the daily cult; 3. The re-enactment in the mysteries of the mighty acts of god. These constitute the accepted and traditional practices of a true king of Egypt; they are by definition orthodox. Anyone who disregarded these traditional practices and chose for himself was, again by definition, heretical. Anyone who totally disregarded the mighty acts of god and committed their very form to oblivion (scarcely a process of "demythologizing!"), anyone who refused to commemorate the godhead, anyone who reduced the daily cult to one act, anyone who refused to renew the deity and literally destroyed his chattels and his house, cannot by any stretch of the imagination be called "orthodox." Such a one was Akhenaten.

Most scholarly treatments of kingship in ancient Egypt tend to devote most space to Pharaoh's mythological status and function within the framework of the pantheon, (which is something like describing medieval kingship solely in terms of its relationship to papal institutions). In defense, it should be pointed out that in concentrating on the mythological setting of kingship in Ancient Egypt, we are only dealing with the texts as they have come down to us. We must address the themes of the Birth of the God-king, Horus-the-Avenger, the Osirian connection, the Ennead, etc.; we cannot conjure up a reasoned treatise on Pharaonic monarchy if none has been preserved for us! But by the same token, if both haphazard of preservation and the nature of ancient propaganda have conspired to close off from us a view of kingship in its mundane, day-to-day setting, our work will inevitably turn out to be lopsided and possibly to a certain extent, irrelevant.

In this regard it would be of great value to have been vouchsafed a perspective on Egyptian kingship from outside Egypt. For the latest period of Egyptian history, such a perspective can be reconstructed, but makes its entry on the stage already laden with Hellenic preconceptions on the ideal king (Murray 1970). Even contemporary Demotic disquisitions owe a greater debt to foreign views on monarchy than to autochthonous ones (J. Johnson 1983).

For the period under discussion, however, there luckily exists a sizable corpus of texts directed to Egypt and composed almost exclusively for the perusal of Pharaoh. This is the Amarna archive.

Since the king of Egypt is the addressee, and since an elaborate form of address was expected, one should be able to discern in what form the Pharaonic colossus appeared over the horizon to the majors and regents of Canaan, and the great kings of Asia. As mentioned above, the West Asiatic protocol is favored in which a "great kingship" with all its attendant attributes is predicated of all major rulers, Semitic, Egyptian, Aryan, and Aegean. We should have expected this, since Asian rulers naturally corresponded in native forms; and in the few letters coming from the Egyptian capital, Amenhotep III and Akhenaten follow suite.

But were the native attributes of Egyptian kingship recognized at all? To a certain extent they were. No Asiatic ruler ever alludes to the king as "Horus," "Son of Osiris," "heir of Geb," or uses any other epithet that betrays familiarity with his mythological function. However, they do reflect usage which is undoubtedly of Egyptian origin. Most frequently, vassal mayors address their Nilotic suzerain as "my god, my sun, the Sun who is in heaven" (EA 301-6, 314, 320-26, 328-29, 331, etc.); the "king is hale like the sun in heaven" () (EA 99: 23-24, etc.). Elsewhere he is "the son of the Sun" (EA 55: 1, 320: 23), or the "Sun of the Lands" (EA 84: 1, 92: 2), a direct translation of the Egyptian (), and source of light (EA 266, 296, etc.). That this is not the coincidental concurrence of concepts of, say, Hittite or Hurrian origin, is proven beyond a shadow of a doubt by the extended context in which these images are used in Abi-milki's letter EA 147: 5-13: "My lord is the Sun-god who rises over the foreign lands every day, as his gracious father the Sun had ordained, one who gives life by his sweet breath, and languor when he is hidden, who pacifies the entire land with the power of his mighty arm, who emits his roar in heaven like Baal and the whole earth shakes with his roar" (Albright 1937).

It is not surprising that the one royal association which proved strong enough to make a lasting impression in the world was that which derived from Heliopolis: Pharaoh was the son of Re and even Re himself, and could reveal his power both as a cosmic force and as political might.

(The substance of this paper is the product of research undertaken by the Akhenaten Temple Project, sponsored by the University of Toronto, and funded by the Social Sciences and Humanities Research Council of Canada.)

4.1. Painted relief from the facade of a shrine of Akhenaten, now in the Cairo Museum. Photograph courtesy of David P. Silverman.

4.2. Collosal sandstone statue of Amenhotep IV from Karnak, now in the Cairo Museum. Photograph courtesy of David P. Silverman.

CHAPTER FIVE

THE KINGSHIP OF THE NINETEENTH DYNASTY: A STUDY IN THE RESILIENCE OF AN INSTITUTION

William J. Murnane

The very subject of Ramesside kingship lends itself all too easily to triviality or misrepresentation. For all the retrospective glory the Egyptians bestowed on the great Ramses II, there is no evidence that they recognized a distinctively Ramesside style of kingship. To be sure, the second Ramses was notable for the sheer length of his reign (Kitchen 1983, l9: 12-15; Stadelmann 1981b). The grandeur of its architectural legacy and memories of its overall prosperity combined to make this one of the golden ages of ancient Egypt. Later ages came to regard "Ramses the Great" as a model for all that was admirable in the exercise of the kingly office (Kitchen 1982, 226-231). Nothing extraordinary, however, was seen in his embodiment of that office *per se*, and thus any study that concentrates on kingship in the later New Kingdom is under a particularly stringent obligation to define *what* is being studied. More than one approach is possible. The religious underpinning of the ideology, for example, is a rich subject with a vast literature (e.g., Frankfort 1948; Moftah 1985). Since the spiritual dimension of kingship is part of a continuum, however, an investigation that confines itself to the Ramesside period poses troubling questions about the distinctiveness of the phenomena: are they peculiar to the Ramesside age (Dynasties XIX and XX), or were they merely given their clearest statement at that time? The worship of the living Ramses II is a case in point. Many features of this king's "deification," while they are explicitly attributed to him (e.g., Habachi 1969; Wildung 1972, 1973a), are now seen increasingly as reflections of earlier usage (see Bell 1985a, 1985b). It seems preferable, therefore, to approach the question from a more overtly historical perspective. The political circumstances of the earlier Ramesside age, unique in themselves, present many points of contrast and congruence with the preceding Eighteenth Dynasty. The grandiose monuments of the period, moreover, often betray tension as well as harmony with the timeless ideological statements they purport to make. By considering these anomalies we can hope to avoid the twin pitfalls of irrelevance and banality in our attempt to understand the practice of kingship at this midpoint of the New Kingdom.

By the age of Ramses II, it is generally agreed, the king had regained the prestige that had been so seriously compromised in the later Eighteenth Dynasty. The Amarna episode, while it did not discredit the monarchy altogether, had exposed the limits of its power. The failure of Akhenaten's reforms had made it brutally clear that the king could not remake Egyptian society to his liking. Not even support from significant blocs of the "establishment" (including the most influential elements of the civil bureaucracy and the army) could force acceptance of the king's more radical programs. These were ultimately checked by dissident interest groups (most obviously the dispossessed clergy) and, not least of all, by the sullenly passive resistance of the Egyptian people. In the years following Akhenaten's death, his feeble successors were forced into concessions that demonstrated, if only by virtue of their existence, the dynasty's capitulation to the governing classes of society. It was clear, as the religious policies associated with the heretic were abandoned and state patronage returned to the Amun cult, that the king's agenda and his person were in the hands of his chief advisors (see most recently, Redford 1984).

It has also been recognized that the monarchy began to regain its effectiveness near the end of the Eighteenth Dynasty, when the ruling family died out and the throne passed to the "king's representative before the Two Lands," Horemheb. It was not enough, however, for the new pharaoh to succeed at the practicalities of government. Kingship in Egypt was more than a political office; it was an institution compounded of social and religious duties—a complex fabric of traditional and latter-day symbols that had been evolving as recently as the Eighteenth Dynasty. Political effectiveness made Horemheb's rule possible, but by itself it could not square the new king's position with his institutional identity. Seen from this standpoint, and not simply in terms of the political *fait accompli*, a change of dynasties was a very delicate operation; given the complex nature of kingship, the eclipse of the previous royal house imposed a very careful path on any of its would-be successors.

By the earlier Eighteenth Dynasty, at the latest, the ruling family at Thebes had developed particularly close ties with the premier god of its district, Amun of Karnak. This relationship was symbiotic, and it may have been more intimate than the traditional ties that bound the Pharaoh to his "fathers and mothers," the deities of the Egyptian pantheon. From remote antiquity, the king's legitimacy had been grounded in a god's paternity, and to this extent his filial connection with Amun was nothing new (e.g., Barta 1975, 21-22, 42-43, 82). Especially noteworthy in the New Kingdom, however—and perhaps unusual, although we lack virtually any means for making a comparison with other periods— was the manner in which this connection involved other members of the royal family, and also the ways king and god reinforced one another's divinity. An annual festival, the "beautiful feast of Southern Opet (Luxor)" was the regular medium through which the relationship between the king and Amun was affirmed (Murnane 1981, 576, and idem, forthcoming; cf. Bell 1985a). During these ceremonies, Amun of Karnak visited Luxor Temple and there (re)generated his son, the divine king. Episodes in this ritual were enacted probably by the king and queen, perhaps with other members of the royal family in subsidiary roles. The king, however, was not the sole beneficiary in this "sacred marriage." While begetting his royal son upon the queen, the identity of Amun himself underwent a significant change: for, at the very moment his living essence passed into the queen's body, the god of Karnak was transformed into the resident Amun of Luxor, "Amun-Re, Lord of his Harim," var. "Lord of the Thrones of the Two Lands, pre-eminent in his Harim" (see Brunner 1964, plate 4). By virtue of this apparent fusion, Amun of Luxor became, along with his alter ego at Karnak, the father of the king; and it is as the lord of Luxor that we see him giving instructions to Khnum, the potter god who fashioned the royal child and his Ka before they were born (ibid., plate 5). Once the king had (re)entered the world, Amun reverted to a more ambiguous identity as "Amun, Lord of the Thrones of the Two Lands" (ibid., plate 10) or "Lord of Heaven, King of the Gods" (ibid., plate 14). Quite possibly these were forms of the Amun of Karnak; but while these epithets could refer to the lord of Karnak, and indeed often do, they are not as specific as Brunner apparently believed (ibid., pp. 23 [II D a], 34 [III L a]; cf. Sethe 1929, 12-14), and it is likely that the Egyptians themselves left this point open. What is important, however, is that this pattern is not confined to the divine birth reliefs in this temple. The "Luxor" and "Karnak" forms of Amun are frequently juxtaposed there in a manner that suggests their fundamental identity (e.g., Murnane 1985a, 136-137, 148). More significantly, it appears that the king was responsible for the mortuary cult of his divine father, the Amun of Luxor: this is the only reasonable construction to put upon a scene inside the god's shrine chamber, where the king presents the ceremonial adzes for the "opening of the mouth" to Amun (Brunner 1977, plate 118), or upon the lengthy offering sequence devoted to this ritual on the walls of large vestibule outside (ibid., pls. 9-15 = Room XVII, scenes running from the east wall [north] onto the north and west walls, and concluding on the south wall [west]). The interdependence that these tableaux suggest is striking: Amun was clearly required for the continued existence of the divine king—but the royal "son of Amun" was equally necessary for the cyclical resurrection of his father.

These rituals, and the ideology they embodied, had a number of political implications. As Amun's son, the Pharaoh was not only confirmed in office by the "King of the Gods," but shared in his father's divine nature. The ram's horn that occasionally forms part of the royal headdress was the visible symbol of this connection, equating the king's status as *deus praesens* in society with his identity as the heir of Amun-Re (Bell 1985a, 266-269). Since the mechanism that brought this connection into being, the Opet Feast, was an Eighteenth Dynasty creation, Amun's royal sons had always been scions of the royal family. Even Ay, who held the throne for a few years before Horemheb's accession as king, may have claimed the throne by virtue of an indirect connection with the family of Thutmose IV (Reeves and Taylor 1992). So long as the royal succession remained within one family, the element of divine paternity reinforced the principle of descent by blood; it supplemented the lineal, dynastic succession without offering it any competition.

With accession of Horemheb, however, the close fit between religious and dynastic legitimacy broke down. To be sure, Horemheb joined himself with the family of the now defunct Eighteenth Dynasty by marrying Mutnedjemet, the sister of Queen Nefertiti (see Hari 1985, 68, n. 8; Martin 1982). The political utility of this union may even have depended on more than Mutnedjmet's collateral relation with the now-discredited Akhenaten; for, if Nefertiti herself became "king" at her husband's death (as now seems probable: see Samson 1978, 107-139, as modified by Allen, forthcoming), Horemheb could boast a physical connection with a ruler of the recent past—an ephemeral and controversial ruler, true, but one whose legitimacy had not yet been denied by orthodox revisionists. What is far from clear, however, is the practical value of such a connection. Claims that Mutnedjmet played an overtly political role (Hari 1965) are not convincing, and it is far from clear that this marriage gave Horemheb much more than a convenient alliance with a fading but potentially troublesome faction. In any case, the precedents for claiming the throne by marriage were not reassuring. Most recently, when the founding family of the Eighteenth Dynasty had co-opted the Thutmoside family by marriage, the result had been a long-festering crisis. The prestige of this particular connection could hardly have been worth such trouble—and more to the point, Horemheb seems to have made very little of his ties with the Eighteenth Dynasty. It is true that he usurped the names of his two predecessors on the processional colonnade at Luxor, including Tutankhamun's claim to have renewed the monument of his "father" Amenhotep III (Epigraphic Survey, forthcoming; see, for now, Bell 1981-82, 17-18). At Karnak, however, Horemheb laboriously avoided giving the false impression that he was connected with Amenhotep III when he revised a relief of that king which Tutankhamun had originally restored (Murnane 1979). Nor can it be said that he falsified his antecedents on any of his own monuments. The past, it seems, was not a conspicuous crutch of Horemheb's regime.

Horemheb's accession also disrupted the "genealogical" link between Amun and the royal family. Indeed, in his coronation inscription (Gardiner 1953) Horemheb goes out of its way to put that connection on a new footing. From the beginning, it is made clear that Horemheb is the son of the Horus of his hometown in Middle Egypt (lines 4, 5, 12); but although the youth's divine nature is said to be evident from the start (lines 2-4), the god is content to promote his son's career among the royal officials "until should come the day of receiving his office" as king (lines 4-9). Such an acknowledged hiatus between the appearance of a god on earth and his recognition as king is highly unusual: the only precedent—again, not one which would commend itself late in the Eighteenth Dynasty—was the interim alleged between Hatshepsut's divine birth and her "forced" coronation by Amun (Murnane

1977, 32-34). The parallel is instructive, however, since in both cases it was necessary to explain how someone so plainly predestined for kingship could have assumed it so tardily. The answer, also in both cases, is that this person's pre-royal career could be treated in no other way. Hatshepsut's regency and Horemheb's offices supported their claims to such an extent that these episodes could not be ignored; they could only be woven into the royal myth. Thus Horemheb's steady advance to the top of the administration, his calm competence—in notable contrast to the hysterical behavior implied for his royal master "when the Palace fell into rage" (lines 6-7)—are all incorporated into the god's dispensation. Describing the situation in these terms also avoided too bald a connection between Horemheb's accession and the death of his unworthy predecessor—although this is surely implied, for it was only at this point that Horus could take the next step "to establish his son upon his eternal throne" by escorting him to Thebes and presenting him to Amun at Karnak. This is not the first time Amun has been mentioned in this text. He was described, among the gods who presided over Horemheb's extreme youth, as the one "who nurtured him" (line 2 [rnn]; cf. Gardiner 1953, 16, n. d); but although this passage is preceded by a fragmentary reference to Kamutef which might allude to this god's role in bringing the future king into existence (ibid., 16, n. c), the coronation inscription avoids being too specific in describing anyone but Horus as Horemheb's father during his pre-royal career. Horemheb's filial relation to Horus persists, in fact, up to the moment when, during the Opet Feast, Amun caught sight of "Horus. Lord of Hnes, his son (Horemheb) with him ...." (line 14). Once Amun had singled out Horemheb for himself and arranged his coronation, however, we are told that "Amun is come, his son in front of him, to the Palace ...." (line 17; cf. similarly line 20). In other words, the identity of the divine king's father shifted, during this celebration of the Opet Feast, from Horus to Amun, just as it regularly oscillated between the Amuns of Karnak and Luxor during the normal course of these rites.

The account of the coronation of Horemheb illustrates the capacity of the royal myth to adapt itself to extraordinary circumstances. The eclipse of the Eighteenth Dynasty line meant that the kingship could not be transmitted "normally." Both the regular process of the royal succession (from one generation of the royal family to the next), and the mechanism that legitimized the chosen mortal as the god's heir were disrupted. To resume, they would have to be reconciled with Horemheb's position as an outsider. To be sure, the adjustments we have been discussing were not at all inconsistent with traditional royal ideology. Horemheb's position as the "eldest son of Horus" (albeit the local Horus of his native town) dovetailed nicely with his identity as Horus, the royal god *par excellence*. Even so, the creation of a divine genealogy for Horemheb exposed an alarming arbitrariness in the principle of divine election. The gods had made one choice outside the hitherto closed circle of the royal family: might they not do so again? Precisely such an eventuality was already enshrined in a popular myth regarding the alleged origins of the Fifth Dynasty (in Papyrus Westcar: see Simpson 1972, 25-30). Although Horemheb's practical mastery was unquestioned, the double-edged potential of the device which legitimized his kingship might well give a thoughtful ruler pause.

If the reign of Horemheb is so much of an anomaly that its very placement at the end of the Eighteenth Dynasty is a matter of debate (e.g., Phillips 1977), the advent of the Nineteenth Dynasty is generally seen as the reassertion of normality. This impression is based entirely on historical hindsight. The highly successful reigns of Seti I and Ramses II, which conferred such a solid sense of accomplishment on the Nineteenth Dynasty, were still in the future when Ramses I ascended the throne. This man, like his master, arose from within the administration: as is well known, he was Horemheb's vizier. His family, however, had even less of a claim to the throne than did Horemheb. The very tenuous connection which Horemheb had established with the previous royal family is something which the Nineteenth Dynasty apparently did without. The founders, in fact, were as frank in admitting their non-royal antecedents (Kitchen 1982, 15-18, with bibliography on p. 247; cf. Cruz-Uribe 1978) as they were consistent in *not* claiming family ties with their predecessors. Neither Ramses I nor his son and successor, Seti I, seem to have married into Horemheb's family: either this group had as few eligible females as it did viable offspring, or so little was made of the connection that it vanished without a trace. Continuity of royal blood, clearly, was not the element that gilded the new dynasty's prospects. Moreover, if the succession of the Nineteenth Dynasty was due to Horemheb's childlessness, as is commonly surmised, the entire question of dynastic continuity became moot. In such a situation, the most potent argument for Egypt's continued stability under a new dynasty would be that the vizier Ramses had a family that already stretched forward into the third generation. This hypothesis, plausible in itself (Kitchen 1982, 17-18), can now be supported more convincingly. The most recent examination of Ramses II's mummy suggests that he died at the age of eighty or, at most, eighty-five years (Balout and Roubet, 1985, 83). Since his reign lasted sixty-six years and approximately ten months (Wente and Van Siclen 1976, 235), Ramses II would have been at least thirteen, and perhaps as old as eighteen years of age when he became king. For the reigns of Ramses I and Seti I together we can reckon a minimum of twelve years, with fourteen being the more generally accepted figure (ibid., 232-233). In other words, while we cannot be certain that Ramses II had been born before Horemheb's death, it seems likely that he was. The presence in one family of three potential heirs, two of them already grown men of proved ability and experience, would obviously not have prejudiced Horemheb against it.

Although the future Ramses I seems not to have been granted the title "king's son," he probably received an eminently practical grooming for power. The foundations for this supposition consist of two statues from Karnak which belonged to a vizier named Paramessu (Helck 1958a, 2175-76) and what are apparently this man's sarcophagi, later re-used by a Prince Ramses-Nebweben (Kitchen, 1979, 912-913). While these monuments are widely attributed to the future Ramses I (e.g., Kitchen, 1982, 17), this identification has also been denied or accepted with strong reservations (Goedicke 1966, 37; Zivie 1984, 101-103 with notes; Stadelmann 1984, 912). A third document, the "Stela of the Year 400" (Kitchen 1979, 287-88), refers to a vizier Paramesses as the father of another vizier named Seti, but the identities of these persons are even more strenuously questioned (see Stadelmann 1986, for a convenient overview). To date, they have been equated with the future Ramses I and Seti I (Drioton and Vandier 1962, 328; Gardiner 1961, 247-248); with the father and grandfather of Ramses I (Goedicke 1966, 23-24); or with two otherwise unknown viziers who functioned during the later reign of Ramses II (Meyer 1904, 1, 65-67; Habachi 1975, 41-44). Limits of space and my overall subject keep me from penetrating the thickets of these arguments too deeply, but my interpretation of the evidence may be stated briefly as follows:

(1.) The Paramessu who owned the Karnak statues and the

sarcophagi employed variants of ordinary titles that are otherwise associated only with Horemheb during his pre-royal career. Notably, Paramessu was "His Majesty's deputy in Upper and Lower Egypt," which is identical in scope to Horemheb's pre-royal title, and just as uncharacteristic: titular "deputies" were normally assigned to a specific institution (e.g., Helck 1958a, 2068: 17, 2164: 15). The only other instance where such an official had charge of a wide area was in the case of the "deputy of Kush/Wawat," who was the Nubian Viceroy himself (e.g., ibid. 2067: 12-13, 2068: 15-16), and thus acted in his province with an almost regal authority. Paramessu also held an extended variant of the title $iry-p^ct$ (conventionally translated "hereditary prince"), which had been at once the most anomalous of Horemheb's titles and the most characteristic as well. What set it apart was its use in isolation from its normal companion, the title $h3ty-^c$: when employed together, both were merely indicators of high official rank, but $iry-p^ct$ alone was used by Horemheb to express his unique standing in post-Amarna court circles. It was in this fashion that it was used by Paramessu, who defined it even more specifically on one occasion as "$iry-p^ct$ in the entire land." This man's extraordinary titles, and their similarity to those held by Horemheb, suggest that Paramessu was no ordinary vizier. Overall, the likelihood that he was the future Ramses I seems greater than not.

(2.) If this Paramessu was the future Ramses I, then the viziers Paramessu and Seti on the "400 Year Stela" could not be his grandfather and father (as suggested by Stadelmann 1965, 54; cf. Goedicke 1966, 37), because the father of the Karnak Paramessu was a low-ranking military officer named Seti. His titles are given as "judge" and "commander of a host" ($hry pdt$) on one of his son's statues (Helck 1958a, 2176: 10) and similarly on another piece from an earlier stage in his son's career (Cruz-Uribe 1978). Since the Karnak Paramessu would not have degraded his own father in rank, and certainly not to this extent, it seems clear that the vizier Seti and his father belong somewhere else.

(3.) The alternative placement of these men in the later reign of Ramses II (see Stadelmann, 1986, 1043, n. 21 for the date) also seems improbable in the light of the pronounced military character of their background: titles such as "commander of a host" ($hry pdt$), "group marshaller" ($ts-pdt$), "fortress officer" ($imy-r3 htm$), and "cavalry officer" ($imy-r3 ssmwt$), which testify to a career in the armed services for these two viziers and for the future Ramses I, are duplicated for none of Ramses II's known viziers (see Kitchen 1980, 1-67). On the contrary, the titles which these later officials bore in addition to the vizier's normal sequence are priestly or administrative in nature, and the same is true for all the known viziers of the later New Kingdom as well (see Helck 1958b, 458-465). Moreover, the independent use of the title *iry-pʿt*, which characterizes both viziers on the stela, as well as the future kings Ramses I *and* Horemheb, is quite exceptional in the protocols of any later viziers. The handful of examples (Kitchen 1980, 34: 2-3 [Paser]; 47: 6, 50: 8 [Neferrenpet]; 53: 10, 14; 54: 5, 11; 55: 5, 56: 5 [Parahotep 'B']) can be explained as abbreviations of the more usual sequence *iry-pʿt, h3ty-ʿ* ... in these men's titularies, or as religious allusions (e.g., "*iry-pʿt* on the throne of Geb, eyes of the king....": Kitchen, 1980, 13: 8 [Paser]). In sum, while the carving of the "400 Year Stela" must have been done late in Ramses II's reign, as Stadelmann has shown, the careers of the two officials mentioned on it were probably earlier.

(4.) There are other reasons for believing that the events described on the "400 Year Stela" (if not the monument itself) predate the time of Ramses II. For instance, the abbreviated titulary of Seti I that precedes the protocol of "King" Seth (Kitchen, 1979, 288: 5-6) has not been adequately explained. Not only is it very baldly inserted into the text, but it has no obvious equivalent on the lunette—and this is odd, considering Ramses' stated purpose of making this monument "in the great name(s) of his fathers (ancestors), in order to set up the name of the father of his fathers," i.e., "King" Seth (note the determinative, apparently a royal figure, between the words *it* and *itw*: ibid., 288: 5). Behind Ramses II on the lunette we find, not King Seti I, but the figure of an official who must be the vizier Seti, the main actor in the events described in the inscription. Regrettably, the upper edge of the stela is worn away, taking with it the figure's head—a pity, since the presence or absence of a royal uraeus on his brow would have placed the matter of his presumed identity with Seti I beyond all dispute. The bull's tail hanging from the back of the figure's kilt is, alas, no proof of royalty (Stadelmann 1965, 48; idem, 1986, 1040-41); but even a professed critic of the vizier Seti's regality (ibid., 1040, 1043 [n. 21]) has been forced to admit that it is highly unusual to find an official portrayed at the same scale size as his master this early in the New Kingdom. Identifying the vizier Seti with the later Seti I, an attractive option in my opinion, would provide one explanation for the protocol of Seti I and the reference to the "great name(s) of his fathers" on the stela. The apparent discrepancy between the name of the vizier's mother (given as "the lady of the house and chantress of Pre, Tiu": Kitchen, 1979, 288: 9) and Seti I's mother (generally assumed to be Queen Sitre, wife of Ramses I: e.g., Gaballa and Kitchen 1968, 259 with n. 4; Stadelmann 1984, 912 top) is not decisive, and it can be explained on the assumption that Tiu changed her name to the grander-sounding Sitre when her husband became king. After all, Ramses I himself assumed a more classic form of his earlier name at the same time; and one of Ramses II's daughters was named Tia-Sitre—perhaps after her grandmother (Zivie 1984, 106, n. 15)?

Plausible as all this may seem, there is an alternative explanation that cannot be disproved: the titulary of Seti I may not connote his identity with the like-named vizier, but may refer instead to the date when the vizier Seti visited the temple of Seth at Avaris. The earliest re-occupation of the site following the Hyksos Period came under Horemheb (Bietak 1986b, 322; cf. idem, 1979, plate xxxviii. 2), which provides a *terminus post quem* for the event described on the stela—and which, parenthetically, also suits an identification of the vizier Seti with Seti I. Alternatively, though, if this king's titles connote the reign during which the four-hundredth "anniversary" of Seth took place (probably some sort of cultic jubilee: Stadelmann, 1986, 1041), the vizier Seti could have been the Lower Egyptian vizier, the colleague of the vizier Nebamun or Paser (Kitchen 1975, 283-301) who served under Seti I. Postulating this "dynasty" of northern viziers brings with it its own historical implications, but it is intrinsically no less likely than the presumed identity of the vizier Seti and Seti I.

At the end of this lengthy digression, I would conclude that (a). the Karnak statues and the sarcophagi of the vizier Paramessu did indeed belong to the future Ramses I, but (b). the further identification of the viziers on the "400 Year Stela" with the first two kings of the Nineteenth Dynasty is hazardous, though not improbable. Even so, it is still possible to get some idea of Ramses I's pre-royal career from the inscriptions reasonably credited to him. Not surprisingly, his titles are strikingly similar to those which Horemheb laid claim before he became king (Hari 1965, plate xxiv, a-c), although there are important differences as well. Unlike Horemheb, who never held the office of vizier but outranked its holders by virtue of his personal influence (Schulman 1965),

Paramessu was entrusted with the highest office in the land. Possession of the vizierate gave him entrée into the various branches of the administration (see Helck 1958b, 51-64 for an overview), and Paramessu's titles indicate specifically what some of these areas were: as an "overseer of foreign countries," he participated in the administration of Egypt's imperial territories (Helck 1971, 247-249); and his responsibilities as "overseer of priests of all the gods" brought with them some measure of supervision over the clergy (though see Helck 1958b, 48-49; cf. idem 1939, 32-33). A number of military titles are also indicated, but these could belong to an earlier stage of his career, since none of these offices compares to Horemheb's role under Tutankhamun and Ay. More significant, however, is the title "fan-bearer at the king's right hand." In recent times, it had been awarded very sparingly, being known only for Huy, Tutankhamun's Viceroy for Nubia (Helck 1958a, 2066: 11, 2069: 12) and for Maya, the powerful treasurer who had bridged the reigns of Tutankhamun and Horemheb (ibid. 2163: 9, 21; 2165: 10, 2166: 19, etc.; cf. Helck 1958b, 405-407). Beside this prestigious honorific, moreover, Ramses could boast the extraordinary rank conferred by the extended offices of "deputy" and *iry-pʿt*—dignities which raised him above his colleagues in office and effectively marked him as the future king.

These conclusions are not new, but I have restated them to define, as clearly as possible, the antecedents of the Nineteenth Dynasty's progress to the throne. Most notable in this "grooming process" was its grounding in the highest rank an official could obtain in the traditional *cursus honorum*. No doubt this was an attempt to regularize what was still a highly irregular means of transmitting the crown. If so, it implied that the vizier, since he could go no higher, stood next in line of succession to the childless king—by no means the usual understanding, though it was not unprecedented either (as, for example, when the vizier Amenemhat had succeeded Mentuhotep IV of the Eleventh Dynasty). Besides, the vizier's office was by no means the worst training a future king could have; it provided both experience and a hierarchic superiority that would accustom subordinates to his government and thus might ease his transition to the throne. Since the vizierate was not a normal stepping-stone to kingship, however, Paramessu was also given those titles that had marked Horemheb's exceptional position under the Amarna Pharaohs.

Even this, however, was a matter of outward form, since the heir-presumptive did not possess the overbearing influence Horemheb had once been able to command. Nor did Paramessu, for all his family's military background, hold the titles that denoted Horemheb's control over the Egyptian armed forces, i.e., "generalissimo" and "overseer of generalissimos;" Paramessu was "general of the Lord of the Two Lands," "overseer of the fortress," and "overseer of the river mouths," but these may belong (as suggested above) to a previous, purely military stage of his career. Such a modest role in army affairs, during what must have been the high point of his official career, suggests that control over the armed forces remained a kingly prerogative that Horemheb was loath to delegate, even to a trusted subordinate.

If this last point evokes the Nineteenth Dynasty's bourgeois background, it should also serve as a warning against the presumption of normality that the start of this period usually draws from historians (e.g., Wilson 1951, 239-240; Gardiner 1961, 246-249; Drioton and Vandier 1962, 354; Helck 1968a, 181; O'Connor, in Trigger et al. 1983, 222). As I have tried to show, the succession of Ramses I to Horemheb was anything but "normal" by the standards of the Eighteenth Dynasty; and the new dynasty's lineage was a political imponderable. Seti I's vigorous military policy is often cited as an instance of the Nineteenth Dynasty's security and drive, demonstrating the empire's vitality in Western Asia after the troubles of the Amarna Period (e.g., most recently, Murnane 1990, summation). But the major achievement of Egyptian policy during Seti's reign—the recapture of the former border provinces, Kadesh and Amurru—occurred at the expense of a peace treaty which, very probably, Horemheb himself had negotiated with the Hittites (ibid., ch. 1. 3). The contest for mastery in central Syria, which had gone poorly for Egypt since the time of Akhenaten, had been ended with an agreement that recognized what was already a *fait accompli* a generation earlier. Seti's reconquest of Kadesh and Amurru reopened this dispute, setting the two empires on a collision course that in the long run would be of no profit to either one. In Seti's defense, it may be argued that he was presented with an opportunity that no king of Egypt could afford to miss. For all the militaristic rhetoric of Seti's battle scenes at Karnak (Epigraphic Survey 1986, pls. 22-23), it appears that Amurru, at least, re-entered the Egyptian fold of its own accord, an act for which the Hittites later punished its ruler

(Murnane 1990, ch. 3). Yet the Egyptians had very little to gain by reasserting their old claim to Kadesh and Amurru. The empire had been secure enough without them, and it would continue to function effectively when they returned to Hittite control under Ramses II. The Hittites, for their part, would certainly not brook the loss of their own southern border territories. Apart from any strategic considerations, they were bound to the rulers of these lands by treaties that they took with utmost seriousness. The fact that the first Hittite revanche was a failure should not have lulled the Pharaoh or his advisers into believing that victory was finally won. Hittite tenacity had earlier fought the Egyptians to a standstill, and the likelihood of a fresh challenge (which in fact came in the fifth year of Ramses II's reign) could not have been unexpected. Seen from this perspective, Seti I's abrogation of Egypt's treaty with Hatti, far from being an unqualified demonstration of imperial vitality, emerges as being more than a little foolhardy, and one wonders if a purely military explanation is satisfactory. Rulers both ancient and modern have known that there is nothing like a foreign war, and especially a successful war, to distract attention from internal problems and build support for the government. Could the foreign policy of the earlier Nineteenth Dynasty, so long seen as typical of its strength, be a sign of uneasiness instead?

In one other area, also, the early Nineteenth Dynasty was singularly "abnormal" in practice. Throughout Egyptian history coregencies had been infrequent and exceptional. An ideological anomaly (Frankfort 1948, 101, 372 [n. 4]), although cf. Lorton 1986), they occurred most often when the succession was threatened or otherwise in doubt. The background of the most notable and perhaps the earliest examples of coregencies, in the Twelfth Dynasty, is too well known to require elaborating here (see Murnane 1977, 1-23, 245-256). Although they faced internal opposition far graver than anything the Nineteenth Dynasty had to deal with, these first rulers of the Middle Kingdom shared with their later congeners a non-royal background and (in the case of the founder) a distinctly irregular succession to royal power. Amenemhat I, like Ramses I, had probably served as his predecessor's vizier, and while historians have tended to doubt that he was his master's appointed heir, it is not impossible that the circumstances of his succession were similar to those between the Eighteenth and Nineteenth Dynasties. Evidence that the Eleventh

Dynasty's last king took the founder of the Twelfth as his co-regent is as ambiguous as it is for Horemheb and Ramses I, but a coregency is not implausible in either case (ibid., 23-24, 182-83, 227-28, 234). Amenemhat I, like Ramses I, came to the throne late in life, and although he lasted far longer, he was eventually compelled to co-opt his son as the "strong arm" of the partnership, just as Ramses I would later employ Seti I as his agent in foreign wars (Simpson 1956; Murnane 1977, 183). After Ramses II, admittedly, the parallel breaks down, for the interlocking chain of coregencies found through the Twelfth Dynasty was not duplicated by the kings of the later Nineteenth. The pattern was consistent, however, for the first three generations (being most clearly attested for Seti I and Ramses II: see Murnane 1977, 57-87). Even while allowing that the New Kingdom pharaohs were never the victims of the sort of disloyalty that plagued Amenemhat I and Senwosret I, it is proper to wonder whether some of the same factors motivated coregencies both in the Twelfth and Nineteenth Dynasties. In more recent Egyptian history, coregencies had also accompanied "growing pains" within the royal house. Apart from the controversial case of Amenhotep III and Akhenaten (now widely disbelieved: see Redford 1967, 88-169; Murnane 1977, 123-169; but cf. Johnson 1990), the only clear examples under the Eighteenth Dynasty had involved Hatshepsut, Thutmose III and his son, Amenhotep II (Murnane 1977, 32-57)—another transitional situation, involving what was in effect a new royal line emerging from beneath the shadow of the Eighteenth Dynasty's founding family.

One further indication of the new dynasty's unease has been known for some time, but only recently was it properly interpreted. In a number of scenes on the north exterior wall of the Great Hypostyle Hall in the temple of Amun at Karnak (Figure 5.1), a figure attending the king has either been expunged or replaced by that of Prince Ramses, the future King Ramses II (see Epigraphic Survey 1986, pls. 6, 10, 12, 23, 29, and commentary *ad loc.* for the raw data of what follows). The original figure, long believed (on the authority of Breasted 1899) to be an elder son of Seti I who was superseded and consigned to oblivion by Ramses, is now recognized as belonging to a "group-marshaller [*ts-pdt*] and fanbearer [*t3i-ḫw*]" named Mehy (see Murnane 1977, 60-61; idem, 1985, 163). Of the scenes on the east wing of Seti's war monument, where Mehy's identity was apparently superimposed upon attendant figures that were an integral part of the relief as it was first carved, little can be said, for the inscriptions in their primary version(s) are either lost or illegible. On the better preserved western wing, however, it is clear that the presence of an attendant in these scenes was an afterthought. Mehy's figure was carved over the minor epigraphs at the sides of these scenes (Epigraphic Survey 1985, pls. 23 and 29 [the figure at the left originally was shown following the king in the scene to the left]). Two of these last figures (ibid., plate 29) and at least one on the east wing (ibid., plate 6, although probably also on plate 12) were eventually usurped by Prince Ramses (Figure 5.2). The others were either erased entirely (ibid., plate 23) or adapted for an anonymous "fanbearer on the king's right hand" (ibid., plate 10).

Gratifying as is this access of reliable information, the discovery of Mehy raises fresh questions that still cannot be answered. His name, as given, is merely a hypochoristicon of one that, in its full form, would have been "(DIVINE NAME)emheb" (Fecht 1960a, 75-79; Sethe 1907, 89-90), but no convincing candidate has yet been found among the known contemporaries of Seti I or his son (Murnane 1985b, 170-171 with n. 17). As a "group marshaller" he held a military rank of some responsibility (note Schulman 1964, 72-73; but see, however, Helck 1988, 147; and Murnane 1990, 109-111), and the fanbearer's title is also a notable status, borne out both by the surviving text (Epigraphic Survey 1986, 23: 17, 29: 9) and by the tall ostrich feather fan that is one of Mehy's common accouterments. By itself, however, the title "fanbearer" was hardly a very exalted rank: often held by foreigners (Helck 1958b, 281; Schmitz 1986, 1162-1163), it applied most characteristically to the multitude of nameless officials who escorted the king on public occasions (e.g., Davies, 1905, pls. viii, xiii; Epigraphic Survey 1940, pl. 197). The expanded form, "fanbearer at the king's right hand," was on a different level altogether. Initially the preserve of officials whose duties brought them into close contact with the royal person, it had been extended by the later Eighteenth Dynasty to such high-ranking members of the administration as the vizier, the overseer of the treasury, and the viceroy of Nubia (Helck 1958b, 282-283). Mehy's texts describe him as a mere "fanbearer," but it is remotely possible that he held the higher dignity, since the title can be abbreviated thus in other sequences (e.g., Varille 1968, 151). In addition, his exclusive attendance on the king (not to mention the extraordinary honor of his insertion into the finished war reliefs) suggest a loftier standing than his titles otherwise imply.

The ambiguity of the evidence has elicited more than one estimate of Mehy's true place in history. Helck (1981, 1988) suggested that he had been the heir presumptive in the early part of Seti I's reign, but this seems unlikely. As I have argued above, it is exceedingly probable that Prince Ramses had already been born when his father became king (cf. Murnane 1990, appendix 6) and with the advent of the Nineteenth Dynasty all reason for the adoptive principle in the royal succession would have ceased. Only if Mehy himself had royal blood in his veins—if, for example, he were a son of Horemheb, born at about the time his father died—could his claim to the throne have rivaled that of Prince Ramses. One might then see Ramses I and Seti I acting as "caretakers" for their master's heir: Mehy's anomalous position would be consonant with the progress of their dissatisfaction with this assigned role—from ambivalence, which would have governed the very limited but real prominence which Mehy enjoyed so briefly, to his ultimate suppression and the confirmation of the family's dynastic ambition in Ramses II. It hardly needs saying that this scenario is a fantasy: we have no evidence that Mehy was anything more than he seems, and no grounds for imagining that the Nineteenth Dynasty stole its way into history. More realistic is another interpretation (Murnane, ibid.) which has seen in Mehy a pretender to the role of "chief subject" that had been filled to such effect earlier by Ay, Horemheb, and (most recently) Paramessu. In contrast to these men, however, Mehy's standing is modest, and while he may have been the actual manager of Seti I's wars in Asia, it would be fatally easy to overestimate both his personal influence and his true standing at court.

Elusive as Mehy is in the records of his time, there is scarcely any ambiguity in the response he elicited from Ramses II. The significance of that response goes beyond what Ramses did to Mehy's figures on his father's war monument, however, and embraces all that he did thenceforward to promote his interests and those of his family. Since our theme is the practice of kingship in the early Nineteenth Dynasty, it is necessary to go beyond the general treatment given to this question (e.g., Murnane, ibid.) and to consider the dynastic policy of Ramses II in some detail.

When Prince Ramses (or King Ramses II) usurped Mehy's figures at Karnak, he substituted for Mehy's titles two sequences of his own that defined his position as heir apparent. Both strings share the title *iry-pᶜt*, a much discussed honorific that is usually seen as conferring hereditary rights of succession upon the holder (Kitchen 1972, 186 [but cf. n. 5]; Schmitz 1976, 315-316; Kaplony 1980, 177-180; but cf. Roemer 1980, 817-818). Of the two remaining titles, "first king's son of his body" (Epigraphic Survey 1986, plate 29: 10), probably denoted the prince's status as 'first born' by a particular queen (Kitchen 1972, 186, with n. 4) rather than of the king himself (as suggested by Sethe 1896, 59, n. 1; Schmitz 1976, 316-317); while "eldest king's son" (Epigraphic Survey 1986, plate 29: 11-12) is self-explanatory and would apply, along with the unadorned variant "king's son," to whichever prince was currently the heir apparent (see Roemer 1980, 816; Schmitz 1975, 297-298 is not convincing). In the one other surviving usurpation from Mehy, on the east wing (Epigraphic Survey 1986, plate 6: 33-34), the official's and prince's titularies are uncomfortably blended, for only the last two columns have been adapted for the king's son (ibid., p. 22 [n]) and his titulary ("king's son of his body, his beloved") is less distinctive than in the scenes on the west wing. What is preserved overall suggests that the titles Prince Ramses surcharged on Mehy's were not only representative for a king's son, but were designed to stress his rights as heir presumptive: in particular, "first king's son" and "eldest king's son"—both otherwise attested for Prince Ramses (Schmitz 1976, 315-316; Murnane 1977, 60 [a, b])—are unambiguous statements of his position within the royal family. The meticulous fashion with which these points were made is surely relevant to the nature of the threat which Mehy was perceived to be.

Prince Ramses' usurpation of Mehy's place on Seti's war monument wrought changes not only to the epigraphs of these scenes but also to the figures they described (Epigraphic Survey 1986, pls. 6, 19). The significance of these changes lies both in the substitution of princely for private features (e.g., the royal sidelock for the official's wig which Mehy wears) and in the iconographic elements which Ramses took over from his rival. The insignia of Mehy's low military rank, his bow and quiver, were suppressed, but it is interesting that the prince retained the tall ostrich-feather fan that defined Mehy's status as "fan-bearer." While this emblem continued in use by non-royal fan-bearers, as in the past (see ibid., p. 29, and especially the references in nn. 5-10), it became a notable part of the "uniform" which Ramses II's sons, and later princes of the New Kingdom, habitually wore in their official portraits. Princes were now shown wearing a distinctive costume, and the senior members of the family were set off from their younger brothers by means of a more elaborate court dress (e.g., Lepsius 1972-1973, 168; Epigraphic Survey 1957, pls. 299-301). In the official hierarchy the princes outrank the heads of the civil, military and religious administration—something we may assume was theoretically true in earlier periods, but which is only explicit as of Ramses II's reign (Kitchen 1979, 608). In addition to the ubiquitous feather fan, the princes also bear other insignia, e.g., a long handkerchief, together with other items generally associated with the military escort of the Pharaoh (Epigraphic Survey 1986, 30-31 [references in nn. 14, 16]). The conferral of these insignia on kings' sons implicitly extended to them the rank these insignia implied. The standing of royal princes was thus formalized, bringing them unambiguously into the highest circle of officials at court.

The conspicuous display of the princes' position, both within the official hierarchy and in close association with the king, is something that is not seen before Ramses II. In fact, the appearance of Prince Ramses in Seti I's war reliefs marks the beginning of a new trend, since princes were only sporadically represented on public monuments before then. In the Eighteenth Dynasty, king's sons had been shown most often in the company of their tutors and generally in the latters' tombs (See Figure 5.3, and note also Rosellini 1832, xxix [3]; Wilkinson [ed. Birch] 1878, I 406, No. 176; Davies 1933, plate xxx [E]), although they made an occasional appearance in more formal environments as well (e.g., Gitton 1976, plate 14). None of these earlier instances is comparable with the Ramesside examples: the very young children, while shown wearing the royal sidelock, are either naked or are arrayed in court dress without the insignia that become common in the later period. If older princes are set off from adult officials at all, it is by the richness of their costume rather than any distinctive markers (excluding, of course, the regalia that occasionally denote a prince's succession to the throne: e.g., Lepsius 1972-1973, III 69a). Not much evidence bears on the pre-royal careers of princes who later became kings. The "Sphinx stelae" of Amenhotep II and Thutmose IV (Helck 1958a, 1276-1283, 1539a-1544), for instance, do not suggest any regular pattern of honors and responsibilities for these youths. To be sure, it appears that a

son and grandson of Amenhotep III held the office of High Priest
of Ptah before the outbreak of the Atenist heresy (Kees 1953, 66-
67; Wildung 1977, 1259-1260); and it is possible to argue that the
king's younger children generally vanished into the ranks of the
bureaucracy once the royal succession was assured. Even so, it
seems hard to escape the impression that little fuss was expended
on princes of the blood during the Eighteenth Dynasty (cf.
Schmitz 1980, 628-629 [especially n. 17]). Nothing indicates that
the king's children had regular roles to play in court ceremonial.
The role of Akhenaten's daughters is the obvious exception that
illustrates the general rule. Although a fragment from the later
Amarna Period does preserve part of a small fan-bearing royal
figure, wearing a uraeus, who follows a larger individual that can
only be the king (Newberry 1928, 8, figure 4), this arrangement is
so unusual that it seems safest to hazard that the smaller individual
was adapted from an originally non-royal person who, given his
accouterments, was probably an official rather than a prince
(Murnane 1977, 173, n. 313).

In contrast to this overall pattern of obscurity for princes in the
Eighteenth Dynasty, the reign of Ramses II witnessed a proli-
feration of princes and princesses, both as attendants and actors,
in royal monuments. Processions of the king's sons and daughters
graced temple walls and statue bases throughout the Nile Valley,
from Ramses II's delta capital down into Nubia (see Kitchen 1979,
858-868 for texts and sources). In addition, the king's sons were
now depicted regularly in their father's battles and triumphs (e.g.,
Ricke, Hughes and Wente 1967, pls. 8, 14, 15; Kitchen 1979, 141-
145, 171-175, 182-183, 187-188, 210, 222 [texts and references]),
and they were increasingly visible in practical affairs as well.
Khaemwese, the most energetic of Ramses II's sons, was high
priest of Ptah at Memphis for many years. In this he followed in
the tradition of Amenhotep III's son five generations earlier (see
above), but his tenure in office was far longer and he also
undertook a number of highly visible commissions before his
death late in his father's reign (Gomaà 1973; Kitchen, 1982, 103-
109). The other princes, less well known to us but no less
ubiquitous in public life, held responsible positions in other
branches of the administration (e.g., Kitchen 1979, 906-907
[Meryatum], 909-910 [Merysutekh]). This was by no means a return to the royal monopoly on high government office that had
prevailed in the earliest dynasties: the royal house could not afford

to alienate the official classes by blocking too many avenues to advancement. Thus the vizierate, the viceroyalty of Nubia, most positions in the higher clergy, and the overwhelming bulk of lower offices remained in non-royal hands (see Helck 1958a for civil administration; for the viceroys, Habachi, 1980 with references; and for the priesthoods, see Lefebvre, 1929; Kees 1953, 89-158; cf. Bierbrier 1977, Schmitz 1977, Wildung 1977, with references). Even so, it seems hard to deny that Ramses II's tribe of sons played a more conspicuous role in public affairs than had their counterparts in the Eighteenth Dynasty.

While the visibility of the princes is easy to establish, it is more difficult to determine their political role in government as a group. It is tempting, for example, to read significance into the "generalissimo" title used by Ramses II's two elder sons and by his heir (Kitchen 1979, 860-861; see Gomaà 1973, 9-11 ; and cf. Edel 1978b, 134 on Sethherkhepeshef [ibid., 914-915]; for Merneptah, see Kitchen 1979, 902-905). Could this role for these three sons, as well as the military functions of a number of others (e.g., ibid., 862, 871 [Preherwenemef], 899 [Montuherkhepeshef]), imply that the royal family monopolized these the commanding ranks in the army? This tantalizing possibility, alas, cannot be demonstrated in detail. High-ranking commanders are scarce among the army personnel of Ramses II's reign, but records of these officials are also very sparse (Kitchen 1980, 234-239). While the evidence does suggest that the senior princes, at least, held posts at the highest level of the military hierarchy, their domination of this sector is far from clear. Ramses II's eldest son, Prince Amonherkhepeshef, is once called the "generalissimo of his majesty" (Kitchen 1979, 860: 11); and his younger brother, Prince Ramessu, is described as the "first generalissimo of his majesty" and "generalissimo of the Lord of the Two Lands" (ibid., 861: 10-14)—but since these expanded variants occur only sporadically in princes' processions and are not otherwise used for those princes, the significance of these titles is not clear. The evidence does not show that Ramses II's sons controlled the army nor that they monopolized the highest ranks at the expense of career officers. Given the absence of a discernible pattern in these princes' careers, as well as the enormous gaps that occur even in a reign as well documented as Ramses II's, it may not be possible to form a very clear idea of the political role which accompanied the royal family's new prominence in the Nineteenth Dynasty.

It may be possible, however, to go beyond the obvious fact that royal princes, so irregularly in the public eye before Ramses II, were constantly on view thereafter. As we have noted above, one of the regular iconographic markers associated with princes in the later New Kingdom is the tall ostrich-feather fan. This feature marches with an inscriptional commonplace found with princes, namely, the title "fan-bearer at the king's right hand." The iconography of the princes suggests that this honorific rank was implicitly awarded to all princes: even though the title itself is specifically attached only to the older sons in the processions (e.g., Kitchen 1979, 860-862), it occurs sporadically for more junior members of the family as well (e.g., ibid., 909 [Merysutekh]). The fan is a well nigh universal feature of princes' figures, not only in relief (see Figures 5.1 and 5.2), but also in the round (See Figure 5.4, i.e. the figure on the façade of the smaller temple at Abu Simbel: Porter and Moss 1952, 100). The title "fanbearer, etc.," which Ramses himself seems not to have held as crown prince, granted to its holders not only a traditional closeness to the king's person, but an equally historic prestige and flexibility: as we have seen (above, p. 00), full-fledged "fan-bearers on the king's right hand" had been important officials in all branches of government. Conferring this regular status on princes of the blood could have been seen as associating them with this select cadre without limiting the range of other positions open to them. Apart from the high military titles held by most of Ramses II's heirs, the status of the premier princes was defined outside the normal *cursus honorum*. With the notable exception of Khaemwese, who came to be crown prince after his priestly career had been in progress for a number of years, none of Ramses II's heirs held any substantive office other than "generalissimo." Even Merneptah, the last heir-apparent, defined his position not by service titles, but primarily by means of rank indicators. Apart from "generalissimo," his only title from the regular *cursus* was "chief of the Two Lands" (*ḥry-tp tꜣwy*: see Kitchen 1979, 902-905), an honorific that belonged also to the viziers in the later New Kingdom (Helck 1958b, 452 [Neferren-pet], 453 [Rahotep], 458 [Panehsy]) and defined the holder's rank at the head of the Pharaoh's government. Overall, the pattern of rank and title that emerges for Ramses II's sons suggests that they were given the status that went with high office without being bound by its limitations.

As I have pointed out elsewhere, the link between Mehy's eclipse and the rise of the princes under Ramses II is too close to be entirely coincidental. The stereotyped environments of King Ramses' earliest war scenes, which resemble the campaigns which Prince Ramses usurped from Mehy, no less than the participation in these scenes of princes too young to have borne arms both suggest a rhetorical answer to the issues which Mehy's intrusion into Seti's battle reliefs had raised (Murnane 1990, appendix 6). The extraordinary honor Mehy received from Seti I is undeniable proof of his influence, even if we cannot know its precise nature and extent. Equally clear is the threat Prince Ramses saw in Mehy's position—and considering his background, this is not very surprising. Even granting that Prince Ramses was born near the end of Horemheb's reign, he would have been very young—not even an adolescent—during the early part of his father's reign when Mehy's influence was apparently strongest (ibid., 165-168; and see above, p. 192). The existence of a so powerful a "right-hand man" as Mehy might well be alarming to a young crown prince who lacked the maturity and experience, well seasoned in office, that his father and grandfather had enjoyed at comparable stages in their careers. The true mystery in this affair—the reason why Seti I permitted Mehy to rise so far above his station—eludes us now, but the implicit menace of such a situation, coming at such a time in the young dynasty's career, is not mysterious at all.

It would be useful to know the date of Mehy's suppression—whether in the later years of Seti I or after Ramses II had become sole ruler of Egypt—since this episode raises fresh questions about Ramses II's accounts of his own early reign, and particularly his coregency with Seti I. It is no help that the main textual support for this partnership, the "dedicatory inscription" from Abydos, was composed at Ramses' behest, years after the fact, and celebrates his filial piety with the customary exaggerations. Contemporary monuments can be interpreted to reflect a period of joint rule, but this evidence is also ambiguous (Murnane 1975). While I do not believe that Ramses II invented the coregency for his own purposes, the historical passages of the "dedicatory inscription" now seem all the more self-serving in the light of the contest with Mehy. In particular, Ramses' claim to have "reported concerning the [affairs] of the Two Lands as commander of the infantry and the chariotry" (Kitchen 1979, 327: 14-15) bears a suspicious resemblance to the more expansive statement put into the mouths of the royal entourage in the stela of his third regnal year from Quban (ibid, 356: 1-6):

Everything has come to your attention since you have been governing this land. While (yet) you were in the egg you managed affairs
by means of your office of child-heir. The business of the Two Lands
was told to you when you were (yet) a child with the sidelock. No
monument came to pass without being under your supervision. No
commission came to pass without you. While you were (yet) a lad of
ten years you acted as chief of the army.

While most Egyptologists have tried to treat these effusions
seriously (e.g., Gardiner 1961, 257-259), I now believe they should
be taken for what they seem to be: blatant propaganda, designed
not merely to flatter but to conceal the implied question that
Mehy's competition had raised about the young prince's
competence. Ramses may not have been totally inexperienced, but
the only dated reference to him—an indirect one, as "his (Seti's)
eldest son" (Habachi 1973)—comes relatively late in the ninth year
of Seti's reign. By this time, Ramses could have been anywhere between eleven and sixteen years old (see above, p. 192); and while it
is possible that he began his practical training for kingship earlier
in his father's reign, none of the other contemporary monuments
we have for Prince Ramses show the high military and
administrative titles which he later claimed to have held during his
minority (see Murnane 1977, 60 [a. b]). In the light of his rivalry
with Mehy, it is at least as reasonable to believe that Ramses II
exaggerated his earlier training as it is to credit him with such high
responsibilities at so young an age.

In all, the experience of the Nineteenth Dynasty up to Ramses
II's accession seems not to justify the degree of confidence
historians have tended to assume. The dynasty was less than twenty
years old when Ramses became king. Its political power, grounded
in Horemheb's adoption of the family and in the administrative
experience of its members, was equally shallow—shallow enough
for it to fear competition in the very ranks from which it had
sprung. These factors, hitherto neglected by historians, make up
the setting in which the achievement of the Nineteenth Dynasty
must be measured. They also shed light on the policies of Ramses
II as seen in his monuments, and they deepen our appreciation of
the ways in which he used his resources—and, when necessary, his
mistakes—to shape the grandiose façade that posterity has
accepted as the essence of Ramesside kingship. At the outset,
however, the future that lay before the young Ramses II could not
have inspired the greatest confidence. The young dynasty was still
haunted by the possibility of failure, and the likeliest source of that

failure lay on the volatile northern border of Egypt's empire in Western Asia.

Much of the credit Seti I has received from historians depends, as we have seen, on a foreign policy that seems questionable in its implications over the long term. The historic advantage that Seti had regained—possession of the two former border provinces, Kadesh and Amurru—was achieved at the cost of disrupting a viable status quo and precipitating a fresh confrontation between the superpowers. The instability of this inherited situation would be driven home shortly following his accession, when Kadesh re-entered the orbit of the Hittite Empire. The reasons for this change of allegiance—military conquest or defection?—are unknown and, in the end, unimportant, for the loss of Kadesh drove a wedge into the northern border of Egypt's Asiatic empire and placed the neighboring territories of Amurru and Upe at risk.

The oft-told tale of the debacle that followed—the faulty intelligence of the Egyptian army scouts and foreign service, the Hittite surprise attack at Kadesh, the king's desperate rallying of his routed armies until relief forces came up, the retreat following the inconclusive fighting on the next day, and the subsequent loss of Amurru and Upe—need not detain us here. We must, however, pay some attention to the ongoing debate over the nuances of the propaganda campaign which followed. At issue is the significance of the official version of events, which was widely distributed both on the walls of royal monuments and on papyrus. One of these handwritten copies shows that the main literary account—or "Poem," which is the version most eulogistic and defensive of the king—was in circulation by Ramses II's ninth regnal year, barely four years after the events it described (Kitchen 1979, 110: -11-14). Obviously this propaganda was circulated in the general interest of Ramses II, but to what end? Was it to draw attention away from the king's failed generalship, or for some other purpose? A recent attempt to probe the mystery has seen the Kadesh battle monuments as part of Ramses II's strategy to outflank opponents within Egypt itself: according to this view, they reflect the king's effort to contain an all-too-powerful military establishment, paving the way for a Hittite-Egyptian peace made impossible up to that time by this war party (Assmann 1983b; von der Way 1984, especially 379-398). As I have suggested, however (Murnane 1985b, 24-51, 177-242), this understanding of events does not coincide with the overall pattern of events in Egypt prior to the Battle of Kadesh. What

we know of the army's behavior, especially during the Amarna
Period, does not reveal an overwhelming desire to fight; and the
assumption of a war party's dominance over Egyptian foreign
policy after the Amarna Period is contradicted by the peace treaty
that Egypt concluded with Hatti, either in the later Eighteenth
Dynasty or by the start of the Nineteenth. Barring the equivocal
career of Mehy, whose titles now locate him in the upper echelons
of the army, nothing shows that the first kings of the Nineteenth
Dynasty were in any sense prisoners of their armed forces. Seti I
himself had led the army into Western Asia even while his father
was on the throne (Kitchen 1975, 111: 7-15), and he seems also to
have led a campaign in his own first year as king (Epigraphic Survey,1986, pls. 3-8; Murnane 1985b, 55-59, 65-76), just as Ramses II
would later act as supreme commander during the Kadesh
campaign.

It is also doubtful that Ramses held the entire army accountable
for the debacle before Kadesh. The high-ranking officers of the
army are indeed mentioned in Ramses' indictment of his army's
behavior, but they are not singled out for abuse: rather, they share
the blame with the rest of the infantry and cavalry (Kitchen 1979,
27 [74-75], 32-33 [88-91], 41-42 [117-119], 55-65 [168-204], 68
[211-213], 78-84 [251-275], 96 [323-326]). Moreover, the Kadesh
reliefs and inscriptions as a whole stop short of a blanket
denunciation of the army. If the purpose had been to discredit the
entire military establishment, it is hard to see why Ramses would
have mentioned the crucial role played by the $Na^{c}rn$, whose arrival
actually saved the day (ibid., 131-133 [11]). Moreover, the
indictment is not confined to the army, but extends also to the
"overseers of foreign countries" (var. "garrison commanders") and
the "princes [*wrw*] of the lands of Pharaoh," i.e., the native rulers
of imperial territories together with their supervisors in the
Egyptian foreign service, which includes but is not confined to military officers (ibid., 113 [54-56]; Gardiner,1960, 33 [B55]). The
terms of this catholic denunciation are at once too wide and too
qualified to have had any practical effect (although for another
view, see Goedicke 1985, 99-104), and as tactical weapons in a
political struggle, they appear to be meaningless.

The purpose of the propaganda campaign following the Battle
of Kadesh is, I believe, more obvious than is generally assumed. Its
prevailing tone, moreover, cannot have been negative: such an
egregious self-defense could hardly have fooled many in the

audience to which it was addressed, and Ramses' policy in the years after the Battle of Kadesh depended on the very forces which, following the conventional interpretation, were being vilified back in Egypt. The true rhetorical point of the Kadesh composition, I suggest, is not the sin of the king's servants but its obverse: namely, Ramses II's personal heroism, which had snatched honor, if not total victory, out of the jaws of disaster. The central premise of the Kadesh inscriptions, implicit both in the layout of the reliefs and in the more explicit terms of the "literary record," is that the young king's valor saved the Egyptians from total defeat. Only thus was it possible to achieve the military standoff that had led to the Hittite king's proposed disengagement and the orderly retreat of the Egyptian army. This position must have been credible, at the very least, although Ramses II's actual role in the fighting is open to legitimate doubt. Despite the verisimilitude of certain details—the Hittites' despatch of reinforcements (Kitchen 1979, 49-51 [147-153]), for instance, or the sixth charge led by the king (ibid., 70 [221])—the actual course of events just after the Hittites attacked the Egyptian camp is so obscured by rhetoric that a consensus on what actually happened may never be possible. The skepticism of modern commentators, who have minimized the significance of Ramses' actions on the battlefield (e.g., Faulkner 1958, 98; Helck 1971, 206; Assmann 1983b, 192-207), is as unproveable, however, as its opposite. All that remains is the account issued after the fact, which emphasizes the king's valor in the face of his army's sudden disintegration and his tenacity until the danger was past. Although the literary accounts (the "Poem" and the "Bulletin") omit the contribution that the *Naʿrn* division made to the final outcome, they are not incompatible with it. As a unit, the written and pictorial elements of the composition permit the army's role in events (both creditable and otherwise) to emerge. The emphasis, however, is firmly on the king—"a stout rampart around his army, their shield on the day of fighting" (Kitchen 1979, 6 [11]), "like a fierce lion in a valley of desert animals, who goes out in valor and returns when he has triumphed ... one whose counsels are effective and whose plans are good ... who saves his army on the day of fighting; great protector of his chariotry, who brings (back) his followers and rescues his soldiery, his heart being like a mountain of copper" (ibid., 9-10 [19-23]). The rhetorical preeminence of this theme, which is universally conceded, leads inexorably to the only constructive purpose this propaganda campaign could have served in Egypt: namely, the rallying of Egyptian society behind the heroic figure of its king.

In the years that followed the Battle of Kadesh, Ramses II's armies repeatedly challenged the Hittites' dominion of central Syria. The history of these encounters cannot be written. Although the later wars of Ramses II are comparatively well documented, they are only sporadically dated; and while a plausible sequence has been suggested for them (Kitchen 1964), even the duration of the active hostilities remains uncertain. Beyond the well-documented campaign of year 8 (idem, 1979, 148-149), we have the "southern stela" at the Nahr el-Kelb (ibid., 149 bottom), which is too badly damaged to reveal anything about the circumstances in year 10 it was designed to commemorate. Since it dates so soon after a known campaign, however, it seems likely that the Egyptians were still actively engaged at that time—during which, as we know (see p. 209 above), the propaganda campaign about the Battle of Kadesh was in full swing back in Egypt. On the other hand, the single-minded rhetoric of the stela of year 18 from Beth Shan (ibid., 150-151) might be consistent with a state of guarded peace, but it tells us nothing beyond the fact of an Egyptian imperial presence at this site (Černý 1958). Fighting seems eventually to have given way to cold war, but we have no way of knowing just when this took place.

The war's very inconclusiveness, however, would have motivated a change in policy. Although the Egyptians did recover their province of Upe, they were unable—for all their efforts, which included at least two forays deep into Hittite territory—to regain control over Kadesh and Amurru. Yet, despite this standoff, a state of war continued to exist between Egypt and Hatti for almost sixteen years after the Battle of Kadesh had been fought. What turned the tide were developments in Western Asia: the rising power of Assyria, challenging the Hittites on their eastern border, and the struggle within Hatti's royal family, which came to a head when King Murshili III (or, as he is better known, Urhi-Teshup) was deposed by his uncle, who assumed the throne as Hattushili III. Once Urhi-Teshup had escaped and taken refuge at the Pharaoh's court, moreover, the Hittite monarch had even greater reason for concluding a peace with Egypt (for all this see Kitchen 1982, 68-74, with references on 250).

Egypt and Hatti had been at war for at least two decades when

Hattushili III overthrew Urhi-Teshup (see Rowton 1960, 16-18; idem 1966, 244-245 for the date of this last event in Ramses II's reign). Paradoxically, now that Urhi-Teshup had taken refuge in Egypt, Ramses had also acquired an incentive to come to terms. It is a curious but undeniable fact that the threat this deposed monarch posed to Hattushili III was used, not in further military adventures, but in pressuring the Hittites toward peace. Hattushili III's interest in reaching an accord is obvious, but some writers (notably Rowton 1959; Schulman 1978) have called attention to the comparatively weak military advantage the situation had given to Egypt. From the Pharaoh's perspective, however, I would argue that the incentive was not primarily military, but rather a question of face. Ramses had little to show for the long years of war with Hatti. Admittedly, he had restored the empire's northern border to its pre-war limit, but the attempt to reclaim the wider boundaries of the Eighteenth Dynasty was a failure. In this situation, Urhi-Teshup was not only a bargaining chip, but a key to regaining the high ground which Egyptian diplomacy had lost in the wake of the Battle of Kadesh. Possession of the deposed monarch gave Ramses II a lever against the Hittites that everyone knew he had; this was what lay behind the vassal king of Mira's untimely question about Urhi-Teshup, which the Pharaoh was able to answer so brusquely once an accord with Hatti had been reached (Cavaignac 1935; Kitchen 1982, 81). Possession of Urhi-Teshup, moreover, gave Ramses a continuing leverage in maintaining the agreement he ultimately made with the current king of Hatti. Urhi-Teshup was not handed over to his uncle once the treaty had been formalized, but remained as a guest at the Egyptian court. He was still living there more than a decade afterwards, during the negotiations that preceded the first diplomatic marriage between the two superpowers (Helck 1963; Schulman 1979, especially 186-187). Moreover, Urhi-Teshup was able to bring his immediate family from Hatti or to start afresh in Egypt, for his descendants were among the parties with whom Hittite vassals were forbidden to associate in the next generation (see Ünal 1974, 172-174). Fear that Hittite vassals might treat directly with Egypt or refuse to acknowledge their suzerain's heir remained vivid enough to be enshrined in the prohibitions of Hittite vassal treaties (e.g., Kühne and Otten 1971, 9-13 [Vs. II 1-48]), even after the treaty between Egypt and Hatti had guaranteed that Hattushili III's heirs would be supported by Egyptian arms, if necessary (Pritchard, 1969, 203 [obv. 40 ff.]; cf. Schulman 1978, 117-120, 126-130). Further, since the guarantee to the Hittite dynasty's posterity is the only part of the treaty that was not reciprocal, the implication is clear: Hattushili III had need of such assurances, Ramses II did not. All told, control over the person of Urhi-Teshup, deposed son of the Pharaoh's old opponent, Muwatalli of Hatti, gave Ramses II the precious advantage he needed to negotiate peace from a conspicuous position of strength, something he had not been able to do since Kadesh had revolted in the early part of his reign.

Out of such unpromising conditions was built the great kingship of Ramses II, which so many of his own and his contemporaries' monuments trumpet so proudly. Starting his reign with shaky antecedents and comparative inexperience, Ramses' problems were soon compounded by the confrontation with Hatti, beginning with the near disaster before Kadesh and dragging on through years of inconclusive warfare. Given these conditions, it ought to be surprising that the second Ramses' reign did not end ingloriously. That it waxed so splendidly might well be regarded with something close to astonishment and admiration. While most historians have allowed Ramses some honor for this achievement, they have generally scanted the difficulties he faced, taking for granted the Nineteenth Dynasty's strength as the heirs of Horemheb (e.g., Breasted 1905 [1967 ed.], 334-370; Wilson 1951, 236-252; Gardiner 1961, 247-268). Yet, as I hope I have shown in this paper, even the stability of Ramses II's reign was no foregone conclusion. So uncertain of itself was the new dynasty that it first permitted the advancement of an interloper such as Mehy, then realized the danger his career might pose to a royal family whose roots also lay in the military sector. Ramses II, as we have seen, quickly redressed the balance by promoting his own sons to an unprecedented position in public life, then maintained that policy so successfully that it became standard practice throughout the later New Kingdom. When the war with Hatti turned against Egypt it was Ramses, once again, who was the linchpin of his country's response. Extricating his armies from Kadesh, he managed to divert his countrymen's attention from their defeat and to lead them back into Western Asia continuously until they had achieved all that was possible on the battlefield. Next, when armed struggle had given way to cold war, Ramses was able to wait until circumstance had given him a winning hand, and then to play it brilliantly. None of these achievements was inevitable. None of them could have succeeded without the imagination to conceive such plans, together with the energy and steadfastness it took to carry them out. For these qualities, no less than for the conspicuous glamour of his reign, one might reasonably call him Ramses the Great.

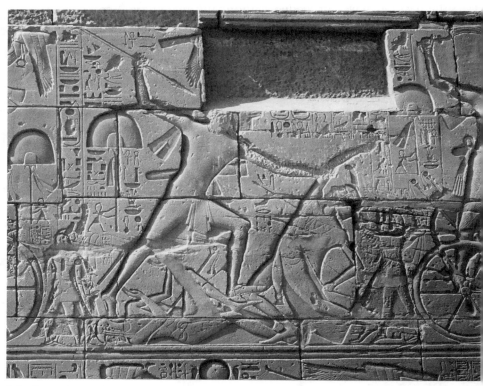

5.1. Karnak, north wall of the Great Hypostyle Hall of the Temple of Amun: the figure of Seti I killing a Libyan is flanked by figures which originally represented the military official Mehy and which were lated usurped by Ramses II to portray himself as crown prince. Photo courtesy of William J. Murnane.

5.2. Reconstruction of two superimposed figures on the north wall of the Great Hypostyle Hall of the Temple of Amun at Karnak that were reworked by Ramses II (See Figure 5.1.). Redrawn by Jennifer Houser and reproduced here with the kind permission of the Oriental Institute of the University of Chicago.

5.4. Abu Simbel, facade of the Temple of Hathor with a sculpted figure of a prince in full court dress. Photograph courtesy of William J. Murnane.

5.3. Prince Ahmose-Sapair stands behind King Amenhotep I in a cult scene from a tomb at Thebes. Redrawn by Jennifer Houser.

PART THREE

ANALYSIS AND INTERPRETATION OF ROYAL ARCHITECTURE

CHAPTER SIX

THE PROGRAMS OF THE ROYAL FUNERARY COMPLEXES OF THE FOURTH DYNASTY

Zahi Hawass

The royal cemetery at Giza is one of the best excavated, documented, and studied of all the royal pyramid sites (Figure 6.1). Nevertheless, there is no clear consensus about the actual function of the pyramid complexes at Giza. In fact, the same could be said about the function of pyramid complexes throughout the Old Kingdom (Figure 6.2).

Ricke, Schott, and many other scholars have suggested that the pyramid complex was used for the burial procession of the king and that the lower temple was used for the mummification ritual and process (Ricke 1950, 60-109; Schott 1950, 149-214; Hawass 1987). These theories have been brought into question because their evidence is based on parallels with scenes from private tombs, whose architectural layouts differ from those of royal tombs, and from an analysis of pyramid texts, which record religious beliefs and do not contain any information about actual function.

Moreover, there are architectural features in the temples of the Giza necropolis that do not agree with the theory that the pyramid complex was used for the king's funeral procession. For example, the doors of the upper temples that led to the pyramid court are too narrow to have allowed the king's coffin and the funeral procession to pass through to the burial chamber inside the pyramid. In Khafre's lower temple, the corridor and the door that led to the causeway are not wide enough to have accommodated the procession of the king. In addition, the layout of the Old Kingdom causeway does not indicate that it was necessarily a ceremonial way for the procession of the king.

Further, the lower temples do not appear to have been designed for either the rituals or the process of mummification. The holes on the roof of the lower temple of Khafre were not for the poles of the washing tent, as some have suggested (Grdseloff

1941, 22-49; Drioton 1940, 1013-1014), but, rather, were associated with the construction of the temple. The ground plan, wall reliefs, cult objects, and statuary programs found in the lower temple do not indicate any association with the process, or ritual, of mummification either.

If previous theories regarding the function of the pyramid complexes at Giza are called into doubt, what then might be a more logical explanation of their function? This is what I hope to answer in this chapter by revealing the organization of the kingship of Khufu, Khafre, and Menkaure through a study of the textual, architectural, and archaeological remains of the three pyramid complexes at Giza.

Arnold had rejected Ricke and Schott's theory that the pyramid complex of the Old Kingdom had a ritual function, suggesting instead that pyramid temples served to promote the corporeal afterlife of the deceased king through the mortuary cult, as well as the continuance of his kingship, his victories over his enemies, and his deification (Arnold 1977b, 1-14). Arnold's functional analysis, which was based on the study of wall reliefs, architecture, statuary and relevant inscriptions, dealt with the pyramid temples of Dynasties V and VI. In this chapter I will use the same approach and apply it to the pyramid complexes of the Giza Plateau.

I will first examine six discrete elements of the Giza necropolis: (1) the architectural features of the Giza pyramid complexes, such as the upper and lower temples, the causeways, and the pyramids themselves in comparison with other Old Kingdom complexes; (2) the program of the wall reliefs in Dynasties V and VI and how it relates to the reliefs of Khufu's temples; (3) the statuary program of the upper and lower temples of Menkaure; (4) the program of cult objects in the Giza temples; (5) the personnel of the cults of Khufu, Khafre, and Menkaure; and finally, (6) the additional archaeological remains attached to the pyramid complexes of the Giza Plateau. Following this, I will attempt to synthesize these individual elements to understand their interrelation and explain what I see as the purpose and function of the pyramid complexes at Giza.

Architectural Elements of the Pyramid Complexes at Giza

While the exact function of the three main architectural elements of the pyramid complex at Giza is a matter of debate among scholars, the layout of the elements is well established. The three elements are: the upper temple (mortuary temple), the lower temple (valley temple), and the causeway.

The Upper Temples

Although the upper temples of the three pyramids at the Giza necropolis share similarities, they are not identical. The main feature common to these three temples is the existence of the open court. Textual evidence confirmed that Khufu's upper temple had five statue niches; four niches for the four names of Khufu, and one niche for a statue of Hathor. Each of these statues was served by a priest (*Urk.* I, 154; *PM* III[1], 177; Hassan 1936, 46-64; Hawass 1987, 646-756) (Figure 6.3). In Khafre's upper temple, five statue niches were also found. However, as only three of his names had priests associated with them, it is probable that only three niches would have contained statues for these names (Baer 1960, 96-97; Hawass 1987, 680, Table 13 B). The other two niches may have contained statues of Khufu and of Hathor (Figure 6.4). The presence of Hathor is suggested through the existence of priests and priestesses of Hathor, at least as early as Khufu's reign. The name of Hathor is also written on the southern door of Khafre's lower temple. In addition, statues found in the lower temple of Menkaure represent the goddess, together with Menkaure and a nome goddess. Menkaure's upper temple, in contrast, has a completely different layout. Instead of including five niches, it contained only one long niche (Reisner 1931, 25; Maragioglio and Rinaldi 1967, 50-52), which, I believe, contained a statue or a cult object of Re (Figure 6.5).

There were rooms in each of the three temples that contained cult objects as well as other rooms that were utilized as treasuries. The temples of Khufu and Khafre were decorated with scenes, but Menkaure's temple was not (Goedicke 1971, 1; Hayes 1953, 63; Reisner 1931). This may have been because Menkaure died before the completion of his monuments, and his pyramid complex was then completed by his son, Shepseskaf. Menkaure's temple was the only one in which many of the original statues and possible cult objects, such as flint instruments, offering pottery, stone vessels, and other items, were found (Reisner 1931, 42).

A cult offering place existed between the base of each pyramid at Giza and the rear walls of the upper temples (Stadelmann 1982, 82-87; Ricke 1950, 49, 65). Khufu and Khafre's offering places each contained an altar and two limestone stelae while Menkaure's contained a false door.

The Lower Temples

The lower temple of Khufu was recently discovered. In 1989, the Sphinx Emergency Sewage Project was inaugurated at the request of the Egyptian Antiquities Organization as an inevitable necessity to drain the water away from the monuments of the Giza Plateau by equipping the nearby village of Nazlet el-Samman with a modern sewage system (Figure 6. 6. (See also Figure 6.1)).

During March 1990, a black-green basalt pavement was discovered during the construction of the sewage system of the village located at the foot of Khufu's pyramid. This area has been identified as the lower temple of Khufu. The excavation trenches opened for this drainage project in the streets of Nazlet el-Samman provided an unprecedented opportunity to examine the remains of monuments belonging to the lower level of Khufu's pyramid complex at a number of points comprising parts of the causeway, as well as the remains of a building that may be identified as his lower temple.

The location of the lower temple of the Great Pyramid of Khufu has been a matter of speculation ever since serious interest in the Giza pyramids began. The early maps produced of this area from the Eighteenth and Nineteenth centuries show traces of the lower part of the causeway still clearly visible on the contemporary ground surface, with a conspicuous change in direction towards its eastern end. The site of the Valley Temple, however, was never indicated, and it may be assumed that already by that period anything surviving from it had been buried and its location lost. In more recent times, the expansion of Nazlet el-Samman and surrounding villages from small hamlets at the edge of the Nile valley to the suburbs of Cairo has made it increasingly apparent that whatever remained of these monuments was irretrievably lost beneath the urban sprawl (Norden 1757, plate XLIII; Perring 1839; Vyse 1842, plate opposite p. I; Jacotin 1822, plate 6; Lepsius 1849-1859, figure I, plate 14).

The levels of the black-green basalt blocks that were discovered ranged between 14.20 -14.00 m. above sea level and 4.5 m. below the present ground level. The basalt pavement was neither continuous, nor complete. Removal of blocks in antiquity had reduced the original layout, although some of the apparent gaps in the pavement may represent the positions of dividing walls, either of mudbrick or stone, which were themselves either destroyed or intentionally dismantled. The overlying strata of pure

Nile alluvial silt sealed the basalt blocks in their current condition and extended as far as the foundation of the modern Mansuriyh Street (Figure 6.7).

There were no cultural inclusions noted in this material, only very rare flecks of limestone (natural) and no indication that pits or trenches had been cut through the silt to extract blocks. Therefore, it seems safe to assume that the destruction was ancient. Further evidence of this was present in the form of one typically Roman amphora sherd (ridged surface, Nile silt, red-brown fabric) found among a group of basalt flakes.

At the south edge of the basalt blocks archaeological excavation revealed part of a mudbrick wall possibly as much as 8.0 meters wide (although its south side is not definitely defined). Five additional test trenches dug on the west side of the original trench gave further valuable details about the configuration of the basalt blocks.

Additional confirmation of the mudbrick work at the south end of the site was supplied by careful excavation in the southern test trench. The monumental building discovered here is certainly to be interpreted as the lower temple of Khufu's pyramid. This identification is confirmed by the discovery of a wall inside the village. Unfortunately, it is impossible to complete the plan of the temple because the extension width of the temple is located under a modern house in the village. At least, however, the temple length has been recorded, as well as its location (Hawass and Jones, forthcoming).

Khafre's lower temple is the most complete temple from the Old Kingdom. Of the two entrance doorways. that of the north was inscribed with the king's titles and the name of the northern Lioness goddess, Bastet (Otto 1973, 628-630)while that of the south was inscribed with the king's titles and the name of the southern goddess, Hathor, Lady of the Sycamore (Hassan 1960, 17; Maragioglio and Rinaldi 1966, 78). The presence of the two goddesses representative of the North and South is indicative ofthe power of the king as ruler of the Two Lands (Figure 6.8).

The temple had a T-shaped hall with pillars and statues of the king. The latter were found broken into small pieces, suggesting deliberate damage, perhaps for reasons of revenge. The lower temple of Menkaure is interesting because of the intact cult objects found within it. The presence of these objects proves that the cult of the king was maintained inside the temple as late as the end of the Old Kingdom.

The Causeways

Both Khufu and Khafre's causeways were decorated with scenes and covered with roofs. The causeway of Khufu was also discovered during the recent construction of the sewage system in Nazlet el-Samman. At six points along the streets of the village, excavations revealed elements of monumental limestone architecture on axis with the extended direction of the causeway of the Khufu pyramid. Previous excavation by Goyon in 1968 in Abdel-Hamid el-Wastani Street successfully identified another part of the causeway in an area in a direct straight line on the eastward projection of the causeway from the upper temple and Sinn-el-Aguz (the desert edge) (Figure 6.9). Goyon postulated the end of the causeway and the location of the lower temple at this spot. The work of 1990 enlarged upon Goyon's discoveries and connected his location to the lower temple. The major discovery regarding the causeway is that at the point of the excavation in Abdel-Hamid el-Wastani Street, the causeway turns 32 degrees to the North of its original direction and continues from there an additional 125 meters to the lower temple. The overall length of Khufu's causeway from the upper temple was approximately 825 meters. During the work, a fragment of the south wall of the massive limestone revetment constructed to support the causeway east of the desert edge (Sinn-el-Aguz) was revealed in Khaled Ibn el-Walied Street. This is the first time that a clear view of the south side of the embankment had been drawn and photographed although a considerable part of the north side remains exposed at the Sinn-el-Aguz (See Figures 6.6, 6.10, and 6.11).

Menkaure's causeway was uninscribed. The entrance to his causeway followed the plan of the Dynasty V causeway, and is different from that of Khufu and Khafre.

The only complete causeways that exist from the Old Kingdom are those of Khafre, Sahure, and Pepi II. All the causeways are similar in plan (Goyon 1971, 11-41; Hassan 1955, 136-144; Raslan 1973, 151-169; Drioton 1942-3, 45-54; Goyon 1969, 51 ff.; Goyon 1977, 140-142). The plan indicates that it was simply a corridor linking the upper temple to the lower one. The entrance on the lower end of each temple is narrow and therefore scholars have suggested that it would have been unsuitable for the passage of the funeral procession of the king. It's shape and architecture confirm this idea. Furthermore, the temple of Neferirkare has no causeway, and this implies that the pyramid complex continued to function after the procession and the burial of the king took place.

The Sphinx

The statue of the Sphinx at Giza is unique; nothing comparable has been found at any other Old Kingdom site. I believe that the Sphinx represents Khafre, as Horus, giving offerings with his two paws to Khufu, as the sun-god. The latter is in the form of Re who rises and sets through the two temple niches over the temple in front of the Sphinx. The presence of Khufu (as Re) in the Sphinx Temple has been explained by Stadelmann. He suggested that the cult of the king changed and Khufu became Re himself, since the name of Khufu's pyramid, *3ḫt Ḥwfw*, "the horizon of Khufu," indicated that Khufu was to be equated with Re, whose natural location was on the horizon. Furthermore, he noted that Djedefre and Khafre, the sons and immediate successors of Khufu, were the first kings to bear the title *s3 Rᶜ*, "son of Re," suggesting that their father, Khufu, was Re (Stadelmann 1982, 126 ff.) (See Figure 6.8).

Further support for this idea, in my opinion, is indicated by the enlargement of the upper temple of Khufu. When Khufu became Re in year 5 of his reign, changes occurred to accommodate his new cult. Moreover, the kings of the Old Kingdom who had a pyramid were buried beneath it, with the exceptions of Khufu and Sneferu, who were buried within it (Hawass 1993a; 1993b; 1990; Lehner 1985, 72-74). The pyramid shape is clearly related to the *ben-ben*, the symbol of the sun-god. This *ben-ben* was thought to be the true pyramid. From the Third Dynasty, the normal burial chamber was placed under the *ben-ben* (except for those of Khufu and Khafre). A burial chamber within the *ben-ben* would identify the king with Re because both the god and the king would be on the horizon (Fakhry 1969, 8; Edwards 1961, 290-293; Hawass, 1990).

Furthermore, Khufu (Figure 6.12) and Khafre (Figures 6.13) were the only two kings of the Old Kingdom who had five boat pits around their pyramids. At Khufu's pyramid, the two boats on the South were solar boats for Khufu, as Re, and the eastern boat pits were for boats connected with the king, as Horus. Their axes were directed North to South, because the king, as Horus, had power that extended from North to South (Maragioglio and Rinaldi

1965, 70). The location of these pits near the upper temple of
Khufu suggests that they were connected with the living king
whose activities are recorded in the reliefs of the upper temple
which, perhaps, to some degree, corresponded to his palace as the
living or, "Horus" king. The fifth boat pit flanking the causeway
may have belonged to the cult of Hathor at Giza. Thus, the above
points indicate that the monuments of Dynasty IV represent a
transitional stage between earlier temples and the later Fifth and
Sixth Dynasty temples.

The Architectural Program

The study of the architecture of the monuments at Giza can reveal
the following: Khufu and Menkaure's upper temples introduced
the portico, or recess, located on the west side of the court. This
portico does not occur in the Fifth and Sixth Dynasties. The *pr-wrw*
was introduced in Khafre's temple and continued in use throughout the Old Kingdom. The *pr-wrw* was a vestibule with twelve pillars
found in all of the Old Kingdom upper temples. The word was
found in the Abu Sir papyri in association with the upper temple
of Neferirkare. Khafre's *pr-wrw* had pillars, similar to those in the
temple of Neferirkare (Von Bissing and Kees 1922, plate 18;
Jéquier 1936, plate 22; Altenmüller 1972, 173). Khafre's temple
had five doors leading to the five niches, a feature different from
all other temples. Menkaure was the only king at Giza to have had
one niche instead of five, and the remains of the temple walls
south of this long niche cannot be used to reconstruct five niches
(See Figure 6.3, 6.4, and 6.5). The *zḥ*, "booth" or "shrine" (a term
also known from the Abu Sir papyri) was an offering hall in the
temple containing statues of the king and the god. In Dynasty IV,
the *zḥ* was located between the pyramid base and the temple wall,
except for that of Khafre, which had two different locations (Posener-Kriéger 1976, 503).

There are seven lower temples that have been excavated from
the Old Kingdom. These temples belonged to: (1) Sneferu; (2)
Khufu; (3) Khafre; (4) Menkaure (of Dynasty IV); (5) Sahure; (6)
Niussere (of Dynasty V) and (7) Pepi II (of Dynasty VI). Arnold
noted that the lower temples of Sahure, Niussere and Pepi II
differ in their plans and permit little generalization (Posener-
Kriéger 1976, 503). The same situation occurs in the three temples
of Dynasty IV. There is no archival information from any lower
temple to explain the function of this temple. The complex of

Neferirkare does not have a lower temple, a divergence from the Old Kingdom pyramid plan.

In the Abu Sir Papyri, the entrance to the upper temple of Neferirkare was called the *rwt-ḥ3t*. It had four pillars in front of the temple (Posener-Kriéger 1976, 496). Posener-Kriéger suggested that this unique structure could be the designation of the lower temple of Neferirkare (Posener-Kriéger 1976, 496). Therefore, possibly *rwt-ḥ3t* is the general name for the lower temple in the Old Kingdom.

In all the Old Kingdom temples that have one entrance, the entrance, in general, is almost identical. The temple of Khafre, in contrast, had two entrances, and Sneferu's temple had a different plan altogether. The portico, however, was the same in all the temples, except in that of Khafre, where the shape was different. There was no portico in Sneferu's temple. Additional rooms existed in the temples of Sahure and Niussere. A portico was located in the temple of Menkaure. However, in Khafre's temple there existed a long hall with pillars located at the temple forepart.

Magazines were numerous in the temples of Menkaure and Pepi II. The other temples did not have as many magazines. Khafre's rooms, located behind the five niches, had a different layout from the others and cannot be identified as magazines. Magazines in Dynasty IV were not as numerous as in Dynasties V and VI and they had a different location.

Menkaure's lower temple was similar in plan to the later Old Kingdom temples, except for the presence of the court and magazines. Its unique court was similar to the Sphinx Temple. The significance of this courtyard in Menkaure's temple doubly emphasized the worship of Re, rather than Osiris, who did not appear in the monuments of the Old Kingdom until the end of Dynasty V (Baer 1960, 297; Griffiths 1966).

The lower temple served no function either in the mummification processes or rituals (Hawass 1987, 431-486; Arnold 1977b, 12), nor did it have a connection with Anubis, as suggested by Altenmüller (1971-1972, 307). In addition, it should not be identified with the so-called *mrt*-building of Hathor, as proposed by Helck (1965, 2207-2208).

The Program of the Wall Reliefs of the Old Kingdom

The general pattern of the wall reliefs from the royal temples of the Old Kingdom can be divided into a number of categories:

1. Scenes involving foreigners.
2. Scenes involving Egyptian officials and courtiers in front of the king.
3. Scenes showing the king hunting and fishing in the marsh.
4. Scenes of the royal estates of Upper and Lower Egypt.
5. Ritual scenes.
6. Scenes relating to the gods.
7. Scenes of ships under sail visiting foreign countries.
8. *Sed*-festival scenes.

These are the main themes of Old Kingdom wall reliefs. They were repeated from one royal temple in the pyramid complex to another, as well as within each temple itself. The scenes, therefore, must have followed a program, as did other aspects of the funerary establishment. By program, I mean a systematic organization of the relevant elements (scenes in wall reliefs, statuary, objects, architecture and personnel) organized in such a way as to fulfill a set of specific functions. The overall purpose of every program was to confirm the perfect nature of each king's governance, and to emphasize his special relationship with the divine world which thus created the idea of the program.

The wall reliefs of Khufu's temples (the only ones of Dynasty IV for which there is detailed evidence) have never been studied as a program. The recent study of the Fifth and Sixth Dynasty scenes concerning subject matter did not analyze the pattern of these scenes, nor how they related to their location within the temple. To clarify this pattern, and to better understand the rather incomplete remains of Dynasty IV at Giza, I will concentrate on the scenes of Sneferu of Dynasty IV, Sahure of Dynasty V and Pepi II of Dynasty VI. The scenes in Khufu's temples will be studied separately in comparison with these reliefs because his reliefs were not found *in situ*.

The program of Sneferu's wall reliefs from Dahshur included scenes depicting royal estates to ensure offerings from Upper and Lower Egypt for the king's cult. In the same location, the reliefs depict the king in front of the gods showing his relationship to the divinities. The royal estate scenes were repeated in the same building in the portico. Following these scenes, the king was shown celebrating the sed-festival illustrating his victory over enemies, establishing offerings, and asserting his divinity. In the same area of the sed-festival scenes, the king was shown with depictions of himself and the gods who also attended the sed-festival. Finally, the king was shown together with his titles and names on the final register (Fahkry 1961, 19-58; Fahkry 1969, 80; Fahkry 1954, 563-594).

The most remarkable aspect of the program of Sahure's wall reliefs is that the same scenes were repeated in different areas of the pyramid complex. For example, the scene of the king and the gods capturing Libyans and Asiatics is found on the lower end of the causeways as well as in the lower temple (Borchardt 1913, pls. 15, 45, 64, 69).

The scenes from Pepi II's wall reliefs were set in a program that illustrated different subjects that asserted the king's divinity. The repeated scene of Libyan captives in both Sahure and Pepi II's wall reliefs indicate that the artisans had a preconceived notion of this program before beginning the decoration of the pyramid complex. Therefore, it can be seen that the scenes did not necessarily record historical events from the king's life, but simply followed a well-defined program (Jéquier 1938; Jéquier 1940, 4).

The program of the royal reliefs seems to have been fixed at the time of Khufu and was used in other monuments during the Old Kingdom (Goedicke 1971, 151-157; 9, 13-17, 18-20, 22, 29-30). Most of the fragments from Khufu's pyramid complex were found reused at Lisht. The fragments that were found beside the upper temple at Giza indicate that this temple may have housed scenes of the sed-festival and scenes of the king accompanied by his officials. In the reconstructed plan of the lower temple of Khufu, based on the reliefs of Sneferu, Sahure and Pepi, there were scenes of the representatives of the royal estates bringing offerings. Khufu's titles would have been depicted on the walls in the first hall of the hypothetical plan of the lower temple. The scenes in the second hall would have included scenes of royal activities, such as: the king sporting and hunting in the marshes, ships under sail, and scenes of the members of the royal suite.

The causeway of Khufu should have had, in its lower end, the king's titles, and a scene repeated from the lower temple. In addition, one would expect a scene of representing Libyan captives, illustrating the king's victory over foreigners. In the middle of the causeway there was a scene of a procession of oxen, representing foreign offerings as an indication of the extent of the king's power. The royal estates of the lower temple and the foreign representations would have been depicted in the lower end of the causeway.

The Program of Statuary in the Menkaure Pyramid Complex

Few Old Kingdom pyramid complexes contained intact statuary comparable to that of Menkaure. The upper and lower temples of Menkaure contained statues and statuettes in different areas within the temples. Seven statues and statuettes made of slate and alabaster were found in the upper temple (Reisner 1931, 108-114). Only two of these should be considered statues because of their large size. These statues may have been made for the original program of Menkaure's cult.

The first statue, a seated image of the king, is larger than life-size and made of alabaster. It is inscribed with the name of Menkaure and was found broken in many pieces. It is now restored and exhibited at the Museum of Fine Arts in Boston (Smith 1981, 44). There is no doubt that this large statue was originally made by the king for his program, because such a statue would not have been produced after the death of the king. Moreover, the workshops in the Old Kingdom would have provided the cult of the king with cult objects and statuettes, not with large statues.

The statue was found in an unlikely location in the northern magazine. It must have been placed in the temple and subsequently damaged, the pieces then being collected and stored in the rooms of the northern magazine. Smith felt that this statue would have been placed in the upper temple in a niche (1981, 116; 1946, 35), a feature that Reisner suggested was in the granite casing of this room (Reisner 1931, 29; Maragioglio and Rinaldi 1967, 52). I do not feel that this room would have contained this huge statue because the proportions of the statue are too big for the proposed architectural setting. Rather, this niche would have contained a smaller statue, or a cult object of Re and Hathor. The statue is better suited to the temple portico, in the offering room entrance. It is also possible that there was another statue of the same size.

The other statue that must be considered is another seated

image of the king. On the basis of on Ricke's restoration of the statues around Khafre's upper temple court I suggested that this seated statue was part of a similar program in Menkaure's court (Hawass 1987, chapter 5).

The statuary program of Menkaure's lower temple, whether initiated by him or executed by his successor, Shepseskaf, is clearer. However, there has been no systematic study of the statuary program in the Old Kingdom due perhaps to the lack of a complete set of statuary in the Egyptian temples of the Old Kingdom. Since there was a clear program for the wall reliefs, there undoubtedly would have been one for the statuary.

It is uncertain how many of the statues and statuettes that were found in the lower temple were part of the original temple program. The small statuettes are not discussed here because they could have been made later in the Old Kingdom.

Five complete statues and many fragments were found in the lower temple of Menkaure. The most important of these are the triads, representing Menkaure, Hathor and one of the Upper Egyptian nome goddesses. Except for five triads, most of these statues were found in fragmentary condition. These five triads are the best preserved and show a high artistic style typical of the Old Kingdom (Wilson 1947, 231) (Figure 6.14).

These triads from the lower temple were found in the corridor of the southern magazine, in the so-called "thieves hole." Another triad was found in the court of the temple; and fragments of three more triads were also found (Reisner 1931, 35-42). The third, made of alabaster, was found in small pieces, and Reisner listed them as belonging to a nome triad. However, the pieces could have been from small ka statuettes. Thus, I cannot take this information into account. Therefore, there are seven triads that are securely allotted.

The characteristic style of the four well-preserved triads represents the king always wearing the crown of Upper Egypt. None have been found with the king wearing the crown of Lower Egypt, accompanied by a Lower Egyptian nome representative.

Another important iconographic aspect of the characteristic style of the triads is that they consistently depict the king on the left side of Hathor. In one triad, Hathor is shown holding the king's shoulder with her left hand; in another, she is embracing him. In the third triad, Hathor is touching his hand. Finally, the fourth one depicts the hands of the king and the goddesses away from each other. These different attitudes indicate a relationship among the triads.

In these triads, the king is shown equal in size to Hathor. The inscriptions on the triads identify the king: "He is beloved of Hathor, Mistress of the Sycamore shrine in all her secrets" (Reisner 1931, 109). Fischer noted that Hathor, as Mistress of Dendera, is different from Hathor, Mistress of the Sycamore shrine (Fischer, 1968, 26). However, Allam indicated that the two are the same, since he found inscriptions at Giza giving Hathor both epithets (Allam 1963, 21-22). During the Old Kingdom at Giza, therefore, Hathor may have held both of these epithets. Smith and Edwards suggested that Menkaure may have intended to have forty-two triads, each one showing the king with a different nome goddess or god (Smith 1981, 44; Edwards 1961, 138). Wood offered two objections to this theory. First, she noted that all the triads show the king wearing the crown of Upper Egypt and questioned why none of the Lower Egyptian triads survive in the temple. She pointed out that, if the Lower Egyptian nome statues existed, then they should have been made of limestone, not alabaster, referring to the alabaster fragments Reisner found. The second point that Wood makes is that the suggested number of life-sized triads is unlikely to have existed in the court (Wood 1974, 82-83).

Wood also believed that the eight chapels placed at the beginning of the temple would have been the likely place for the four complete triads, as well as the fragmentary ones (Wood 1974, 82-83; Terrace 1961, 40-49). She based this reconstruction on the existence of the representatives of the estates in the entrance corridor of Sneferu's lower temple (Wood 1974, 87). There is no doubt that either the northern corridor, the portico, or the long hall could have been a place for the triads. Wood has suggested that the most likely place for the triads would have been either in the eight chapels or the court. I feel that the eight chapels would have been an unlikely setting because it is difficult to imagine that the triads represented only Upper Egyptian nomes. The inscription on one of them reads: "I have given to you all things which are in the South, all food, all offerings, since thou art appeared as king of Upper and Lower Egypt forever" (Reisner 1931, 109). This inscription indicates that these depictions of nome representatives have the same function as the representation of estates on wall reliefs. Their purpose was to provide the king with offerings for the continuation of his cult and the cult of the gods. The estates applied not only to the lower temple but also to the upper temple as well.

In general, I believe that throughout the Old Kingdom reliefs and statues formed part of a consistent program; however, due to historical accident, there are no reliefs in Menkaure's temples. It seems that in Menkaure's complex, the triads are related to the royal estates and show the relationship between the king and the gods, since both nome representatives and the goddess Hathor appear.

Therefore, I suggest that there was a fixed program for the Lower Egyptian nomes as well, and all were placed in the court of the lower temple. This hypothesis is likely because of the size of the court: 19 meters east-west, and 41 meters north-south (which could accommodate any number of statues). The number of triads should not be restricted to forty-two because a complete set of forty-two royal estates of Upper and Lower Egyptians nomes is never seen in the wall reliefs of the temples. The number of the estate representatives of Upper and Lower Egypt differs. It is impossible to know for certain how many triads were originally in the court. Undoubtedly, there were at least sixteen, judging from the eight remaining Lower Egyptian triads and the eight proposed Upper Egyptian parallels. The fragments of the triads that were found in the court would seem to support the assumption that the triads were originally located there. Shepseskaf decorated Menkaure's pyramid complex with statues instead of reliefs presumably because it would have been less time consuming artistically, and the statues would have conveyed the same ideas that reliefs did.

I argue that Menkaure did not follow his father and grandfather's new cult. Through the influence of the priests of Heliopolis, he returned to the worship of Re. For this reason, Menkaure planned his lower temple to have an open court to emphasize his link with Re. This solar court was not a regular architectural feature of the Old Kingdom lower temples. It is unique to the sun-god, and its plan may have influenced Menkaure in the design of the Sphinx Temple which is nearby and also has a solar design. The statues of Hathor with the sun-disc are a further illustration of the link among Re, Hathor, and Menkaure.

The anteroom, located before the sanctuary hall, was intended to house four seated alabaster statues of Menkaure. The bases of

these statues were found *in situ* (Wood 1974, 85). Wood suggested
that the paired statue of Menkaure and his queen should be in the
central chamber, or the offering chamber beyond the anteroom.
This arrangement is unlikely, since this room is an offering room,
and should contain an altar for offerings or a triad of the king,
Hathor, and Re. The proper place for the pair statue would have
been the vestibule at the temple entrance.

Wood also suggested that the wooden statues that were found in
the temple could be part of the original program of the temple
dedicated to the goddess Hathor, Mistress of the Sycamore. She
based her hypothesis on the opinion that wooden statues were of
royal workshop origin rather than private (Wood 1974, 93; Lucas
1962, 121).

I suggest the following program of the statuary: the triads
represent the king standing with his queen (identified as Hathor);
further, they represent the estates and the divinity of the king as
Horus, together with Hathor and Re. The standing and seated
statues, as a whole, represent the king in his palace. The seated
statues in the temple anteroom and the offering room illustrate
the king's relationship to the gods. One might expect that there
would have been statues showing the king smiting his enemies in
parallel with wall reliefs with the same motif. The king's names in
the reliefs are among the inscriptions that are found on the triads.
There are 15 statuettes of the king left unfinished in the lower
temple. As I indicated before, it is difficult to assign them to the
original program of the king.

Edwards calculated that the pyramid complex of Khafre alone
contained between one and two hundred separate statues
(Edwards 1961, 149). In addition, three to four hundred fragments of royal statuary made of alabaster and diorite were also
found (Hassan, 1946, 61). The only statuary program that I
suggest for Khafre is in the lower temple, which contained 23
seated statues of the king placed in the T-shaped hall of the
temple. One of them was found almost intact in a hole at the
temple vestibule, which seems to have been cut in a later period.
This hole can be compared with the "thieves hole" of Menkaure's
lower temple.

No statuary program can be established for Khufu because no
statues have yet been found at Giza, except for the alabaster bases
found inscribed with the king's name (Smith 1946, 20).

The discovery of the triads of Menkaure and Hathor might

suggest that every pyramid complex was dedicated to the deities of Re, Hathor and Horus. In the triad, the king is Horus, Hathor is the wife of the living king and the mother of the future king. She is also the eyes of Re, who is represented as the sun-disc above the head of the goddess. Schott indicated that there was a special relationship between Neith and Hathor at the Giza necropolis. The two goddesses were considered Re's daughters (Schott 1969, 127). A greater amount of evidence is available for the existence of a Hathor cult at Giza, rather than for Neith, who is associated with the necropolis through only a few titles. (Neith may have had priests because she was the daughter of Re.) Hathor had both priests and a priestess at Giza who maintained her cult. Hathor's name is also inscribed on the entrance of Khafre's temple and the symbol of Hathor is shown in the reliefs of Khufu at Lisht (Goedicke 1971, 38-39). Since the earliest times, there was a relationship between Hathor and Re. She acted as the sun's eye and exercised the function of Re (Bleeker 1973, 53; Buhl 1947, 80; Wente 1969, 83-91). Furthermore, the name of Hathor in Egyptian was *Hwt-Hr* which means "the house of Horus." She was called "the royal mother," and was linked with the king's life (Bleeker 1973, 25, 51). She was the king's guardian and assisted him in the ceremonies of the *sed*-festival (Bleeker 1973, 52). Re was the universal god of the Old Kingdom, rising and setting every day. Thus, the upper temple faces east towards the sun, further associating it with Re (Winter 1957, 222-223; Kaiser, 1956, 104-116; Hornung 1985, 100-142). The triads of Menkaure are the strongest evidence to support the existence and importance of the gods Re, Hathor, and Horus at Giza.

The Program of Cult Objects of the Menkaure Pyramid Complex

Two kinds of objects were stored in the pyramid complex of Menkaure. One group was to be used in the cult of the king and the gods; the other was to be used by the king after his death. The pyramid complex of Menkaure is uniquely suited to the study of this particular program because his is the only pyramid complex at Giza in which such objects were found within the temples. Furthermore, one can observe a pattern in the distribution of these objects throughout the magazines in the upper and lower temples. This pattern may be used as a model for the Old Kingdom. As I

indicated above, there was a program assigned for the architecture, wall reliefs and statuary. It follows, then, that there would have
been one for the cult objects as well.

Most of the cult objects found in the pyramid temples of
Menkaure have been dated to Dynasty IV. Menkaure's lower
temple contained the majority of these objects (Reisner 1931, 45).
The cult objects that were found in the northern magazines
consisted of: stone vessels, pottery, flint wands, flint implements,
sets of model stone vessels, and other objects (Reisner 1931, 42).
Reisner, who indicated that these objects were broken and were
from disturbed contexts, believed that many objects of the same
type were missing (Reisner 1931, 42).

Statues were found stored in the southern magazines. However,
no cult objects were found there (Reisner 1931, 42). Above, I
suggested that these statues were originally set in the court and
other areas in the lower temple. Therefore, these statues were not
originally placed in the southern magazines or "statue rooms" as
suggested by Reisner. These magazines would have contained
objects other than statues.

In the court of Menkaure's lower temple, 537 stone vessels and
other objects were found (Reisner 1931, 104). Steindorff suggested that some of these stone vessels may actually have come
from Khafre's pyramid complex. He based this hypothesis on the
fact that very few stone vessels were found in Khafre's temples and
that some of these vessels bore the name of Khafre (Hölscher
1912, 104).

Reisner, however, felt that none of these objects bore Khafre's
name. He disregarded Steindorff's theory and believed that all
these objects belonged to Menkaure's temple and should be dated
to Dynasty IV (Reisner 1931, 104). I concur that the objects found
scattered in the lower temple of Menkaure are dated to Dynasty
IV. The cult objects among them, however, must have come from
the southern magazines, as was the case in the upper temple.

The archaeological circumstances of the cult objects in the
northern and southern magazines of the upper temple of Menkaure are clearer and may suggest the pattern for the placement
of cult objects. The southern magazines of the upper temple
contained Old Kingdom jars, bowls with spouts, small model
dishes, coarse red jars, fragments of two alabaster offering
tables, a thick diorite bowl, fragments of a slate cup, a fragment
of an alabaster slab, fragments of alabaster and copper statues,

and numerous fragments of stone vessels (Reisner 1931, 15-16).

In the northern magazines of the upper temple fragments of four flint knives, three flint flakes, a flint scraper, a flaring pot of mud ware, model jars and saucers, a large stone hammer of black granite, a tall stand of red pottery, fragments of two large trays, 50 small model dishes and jars, a few pottery jars, a bowl stand, broad flint knives, and fragments of alabaster statues were found (Reisner 1931, 17-18). Similar artifacts were found scattered in the court and the inner part of the upper temple. Because of their similarity, they may have belonged originally in the northern and southern magazines (Reisner 1931, 19-24). These artifacts of the upper temple were dated by Reisner to the Fourth Dynasty (Reisner 1931, 103-105).

The type of objects in the southern magazines, namely offering tables, suggests that the southern magazines served a function different from that of the northern ones. It also suggests that the objects found in the court of the lower temple were originally in the magazines before the second temple was built. The chronology of the deposits, as Reisner suggested, dated the majority of the upper and lower temples artifacts to the original temple of Dynasty IV.

The interpretation of the cult objects in the royal temples, as discussed by Reisner, is that the objects served to supply the spirit with the daily necessities of life in the other world (Reisner 1931, 98). Therefore, such items would have been stored in jars to be ready for the king to use at any time—a type of magical supply. There were also other objects needed in the temples to maintain the daily offerings, such as: flint implements for the opening of the mouth ceremony, stone offering slabs, and stone bowls. Recently, Arnold has agreed with Reisner concerning the necessity of these supplies in the king's afterlife (Arnold 1977b, 11-12).

The results of the excavations of the royal temples of Dynasty V show that similar equipment was found in temple magazines. It can be seen that these objects were not necessary for the ordinary food offerings and magical recitations, but may have been intended for special ceremonies and formulae (Posener-Kriéger 1976, 514-515; Reisner 1931, 101).

The records in the Abu Sir Papyri also indicate the importance of magazines in the upper temple of Neferirkare (Posener-Kriéger 1976, 514-515). Objects that were found recorded in the inventories of the temple included: gold cups and plates, an offering table (ḥtp), and another offering table (called ḥrt), a ḥȝṭs-vessel, ḥnwt-cups, and cloths used as offerings in front of the statues (Posener-Kriéger 1976, 171-187). These objects were inspected daily (Posener-Kriéger 1976, 162-187). At the same time, fresh offerings were brought to the temple for use in the sanctuary, namely, beer, bread and freshly slaughtered beef. After their use in the cult, these provisions were served to the personnel of the temple (Posener-Kriéger 1976, 634).

There are no distinctions in the Abu Sir Papyri between objects to be used by the king in his next life and objects used for offerings. The objects mentioned in the Abu Sir Papyri imply, however, that there was a division between those objects destined for use in the palace, and those being used for the offering cult. It is possible that the more expensive items, such as the gold cups and plates, as well as the ḥn-box, were the palace objects. The careful documentation of the these objects indicates that the temple personnel wanted to be sure of the constant existence of these objects for the king's use in the afterlife. In addition, there are numerous objects mentioned in the Abu Sir Papyri that were used for the offering cult, such as: offering tables, ritual knives, offering plates, vessels and basins.

The function of the northern and southern magazines during the Old Kingdom has not been identified by scholars. Unfortunately, the Abu Sir Papyri do not aid in this determination either. However, the plan of Menkaure's magazine and the objects found within may help clarify the program of the cult objects.

The types of objects found in the southern magazines of the upper temple, such as: offering tables, model dishes, and stone vessels, indicate that the magazines in the south of the upper and lower temples stored items that were used for the daily offerings and other rituals performed in the temple sanctuary. The pots in these magazines would have contained fresh offerings such as beef, beer, and bread from the funerary domains. The pots with the offerings were not kept in the magazine, but were used directly for the offerings. The fresh offerings were then used as payment for the personnel of the cult after their use in maintaining the cult. The objects that were stored in the southern magazines were taken to the sanctuary for offering purposes, and were returned and stored in the magazines after being used. The fresh offerings would have been stored in the magazines of the workshop of each pyramid.

The objects that were found in the northern magazines, such as:

objects for magical use, stone vessels, pottery, and flint knives, indicate that they would have been used by the king in his afterlife. These objects were the same as those the king used in the palace during his lifetime. In order to have a prosperous afterlife, the king would have needed all the objects he had possessed during his lifetime. Further, it is possible that these northern magazines would have contained tables, games, boxes, chairs, clothing, writing materials, weapons and beds. Wooden fragments that were found in the upper and lower temples of Menkaure seem to suggest the existence of such objects.

In conclusion, the analysis of the objects of Menkaure's temples indicates that the southern magazines contained material intended for the offering cult of the king and the gods. The northern magazines, in contrast, held objects that were used by the king in the palace and, consequently, were required by him for use after his death.

The Personnel of the Funerary Cult of Khufu, Khafre and Menkaure

The analysis of the titles of the personnel who were involved with the cult of Khufu, Khafre, and Menkaure can be summarized as follows. The organization of the cult of Khufu, Khafre, and Menkaure in the Fourth Dynasty was very uncomplicated. There were no compounded designations, simply: ḥmw-nṯr, wꜥbw and ꜥd-mr grgt (which occurred only in Khufu's cult). The titles ḥmw-nṯr and wꜥbw occurred only in the cults of the three kings in Dynasty IV. The ḥmw-nṯr had an elevated place in this period and served only Khufu. This simplified structure may be due in part to the lack of preservation, or the lack of securely dated tombs of the Fourth Dynasty. It would seem, however, that during this period the entire bureaucracy of the country was less complicated, and the cult followed a simplified organization as well. There is a false door panel from Giza (G1727) which has the title: shd wꜥbw Ḥ.f-Rꜥwr. It could be dated either to the Fourth or the beginning of the Fifth Dynasty (Strudwick 1985, 37-52).

By the Fifth Dynasty, the organization of the funerary cult was no longer as simple. Ranked offices appeared for the first time and high level titles were developed. The organization of the wꜥbw became more complex in Dynasty V. For the first time, the wꜥbw of the pyramid occurred with all three kings at Giza. The wꜥbw nswt of the pyramid, however, did not replace the earlier $w^c b$ $nswt$. It is possible that the titles were considered variants of each other. For the first time, the $w^c bw$ had a supervisor, the $imy-r3$ $w^c bw$, who was assisted by a $ḥrp$ and a $sḥd$.

No hierarchy appeared, yet, for the $ḥmw-ntr$. However, the $ḥmw-ntr$ of the other names of the king appeared for the first time, although they are attested only for Khufu. In the case of Khafre, there was the new title of $ḥm-ntr$ of the statue of Upper Egypt of the pyramid of Khafre. The title $ḥrp$ $imyw$ $z3$ of the pyramid of Khafre, also appeared for the first time, which suggests the phyle organization was now in operation.

The administrative office, $imy-r3$ $niwt$ $3ḫt-Ḥwfw$, first appeared in Dynasty V. There is no $imy-r3$ of the pyramid city of Khafre and Menkaure known for that time. It is possible that the $imy-r3$ of Khufu's pyramid city was also in charge of the other two pyramid cities.

Four new titles appeared in Khufu's cult in Dynasty V: "the overseer of the king's workshop," "the director of the Sed-festival palace," "the overseer of the fields," and "the overseer of the milk herd of the pyramid of Khufu." The titles $^c d$-mr $grgt$ and $imy-r3$ $niwt$ in Dynasty V may argue against the theory that the $^c d$-mr $grgt$ was in charge of the pyramid city.

New titles also appeared in Khafre's cult such as: "the overseer of the Sed-festival palace of Khafre's pyramid," "privy counselor" of Khafre's pyramid and the $^c d$-mr tn rsy $Ḥ^c.f$-R^c wr. The latter may have been in charge of Khafre's funerary domain. This last title became necessary because the bureaucracy of the country was extending and the number of funerary domains that were needed for each pyramid cult was increasing. The funerary domains of Menkaure were still organized by Shepseskaf's personnel.

The cult of Menkaure remained uncomplicated in Dynasty V. The only change in this period (parallel to that in Dynasty IV) is the presence of the title $w^c b$ of the pyramid of Menkaure. The simple structure of his cult may be a matter of preservation, since the archaeological evidence shows the continuation of the cult until of the end of the Old Kingdom.

The organization of the cult in Dynasty V was the same as in Dynasty IV. The priests performed the daily service in the temple and they celebrated the yearly feasts of Re, Hathor, and Horus. The only differences were: an increase of the number of offices, and an increase in responsibilities given to a greater number of people.

In Dynasty VI, the use of the two older titles from Dynasty IV, *ḥmw-nṯr.* and *wꜥb nswt* continued. The organization of the cult, however, became even more complex, paralleling the increasing complexity of the bureaucracy throughout the country. *Wꜥbw* were still found with the name of *nswt* and the pyramid. The ranking of the *wꜥbw* in Dynasty VI was: *ḥrp wꜥbw, sḥd,* and *wꜥbw.* There is no *imyrꜣ* attested. However, the title may have existed since it is already known in Dynasty V.

In Khufu's reign, the hierarchy of the *wꜥbw* was: *ḥrp wꜥbw nswt, sḥd wꜥbw, wꜥbw* and *wꜥb nswt;* that of the *wꜥbw* of the pyramid was: *ḥrp wꜥbw nswt ꜣḫt-Ḫwfw* and *sḥd, wꜥbw ꜣḫt-Ḫwfw.* The hierarchy of the *wꜥbw* in Khafre's reign was: *sḥd wꜥbw* and *wꜥbw nswt.* For the pyramid the only title was *sḥd wꜥbw Ḫꜥ.f.Rꜥ wr.* However, in Menkaure's reign, the hierarchy of the *wꜥbw* was: *sḥd wꜥbw Mn-kꜣw-Rꜥ* and *wꜥb nswt.* No *wꜥbw* of the pyramid of Menkaure seems to have existed.

Ḥm-nṯr of Khufu, Khafre and Menkaure still remained. For the first time, the office of *ḥm-nṯr* of the pyramid appeared. There was a completely new hierarchy of the *ḥmw-nṯr* in Dynasty VI that was as follows: *imy-rꜣ ḥmw-nṯr, sḥd ḥmw-nṯr, imy-ḫt ḥmw-nṯr, ḥmw-nṯr.*

The title *imy-ḫt ḥmw-nṯr* appeared for the first time in Dynasty VI. The complete set of *ḥmw-nṯr,* of the four names of Khufu; and *ḥmw-nṯr* of the three names of Khafre appeared for the first time.

A new title also appeared and was held by three individuals. This title is *ḥm-nṯr Ḫwfw ḫnty ꜣḫt-Ḫwfw,* "priest of Khufu who presides over Akhet-Khufu." The office of *ḥm-nṯr* of the king was not replaced by that of his pyramid, as has been suggested by other scholars. Indeed, the new office of *ḥm-nṯr* of the pyramid and the older office of *ḥm-nṯr* of the king, evidently existed side by side.

The complete standard sequence of the titles of *ḥmw-nṯr* in Dynasty VI suggests that by the Sixth Dynasty, every office in the hierarchy had acquired a new and elaborate ranking structure. Whereas in Dynasty IV, only the son of the king or his daughter served the cult, by Dynasty VI, the size and increased complexity of the bureaucracy made it necessary to have a more extensive organization of the cult. For the first time in Dynasty VI, the title *ḥntyw-š Ḫꜥ.f.Rꜥ wr* appeared and the sequence of titles of the *ḥntyw-š* in Khufu's cult was *imy-rꜣ* and *ḥntyw-š.*

The office of the head of the administration of the cult, that is, "the overseer of the pyramid city," continued. Now, for the first time, there were overseers of the pyramid city of Khufu, Khafre, and Menkaure. In addition, there were the administrative titles of *smsw ḥ3it* of the pyramid of Khufu and Khafre and *imy-r3 wsḫt* and *ḥbt* of the pyramid of Menkaure. These changes not only took place in the king's cult in Dynasty VI, the hierarchy of titles in the queen's cult was also affected. For the first time, for example, the titles *imy-r3 ḥmw-k3 mwt nswt* appears.

Menkaure's cult in Dynasty VI was completely different from the cult in Dynasties IV and V. His cult had a hierarchy within the *wˤbw* and *ḥmw-nṯr* titles and new offices were introduced for the first time that are not paralleled in Khufu or Khafre's cult. However, it is clear that as the Old Kingdom progressed, the organization of the cult of all three kings became increasingly complex.

One title connected with Menkaure's cult, *imy-r3 ḏ3t Mn-K3w-rˤ nṯri*, "overseer of council (jury) of Menkaure's pyramid," is dated to Dynasties V and VI (*PM* III[1], 294; *PM* III[2]/3, 736 Title No. 796, *ḏ3ḏ3*, should read *ḏ3t*). The increasing elaboration witnessed in Menkaure's cult in Dynasty VI, however, suggests that this title also belonged to Dynasty VI.

Khufu also had two titles that are not previously included in the organizational chart, these were: *imy-r3 zšw 3ḫt-Ḥwfw* and *zš imyw-z3 3ḫt-Ḥwfw*. Both date to Dynasties V and VI. It seems impossible to date these two titles based on the organizational chart because of the increase of offices in Dynasties V and VI in Khufu's cult (Hawass 1987, 558-627, 734-756). It is important to note, however, that these two titles existed in this period and were related to scribal offices; one of them being the scribe of the phyle of Khufu's pyramid.

The service and the function of the cult of Khufu, Khafre and Menkaure can be understood through an examination of the duties of the personnel listed in the Abu Sir Papyri. There were daily and monthly services, as well as yearly feasts. It is important to note that the titles of *wˤb* and *ḥm-nṯr* were not merely honorific titles but were actual functioning designations for people who performed services in the temple. In addition, the Abu Sir Papyri also list laundry men and other servants who were assigned to work in the temple (Posener-Kriéger 1976, 588-601).

The *ḥm-nṯr* of the king in Dynasty V (who was, at the same time, a *ḥm-nṯr* of a king in Dynasty IV) had to participate in the temple rituals. They took part, at least, in the monthly or the yearly festivals of Re, Hathor and Horus. The previous discussion can suggest that it is possible that there was a program established for the personnel of the cult of Khufu, Khafre and Menkaure, just as there was a program for the wall reliefs, statuary, cult objects and architecture.

Additional Archaeological Remains on the Giza Necropolis

Several types of building complexes should be discussed in connection with the cult at Giza. One of these, the funerary domain, was an establishment located on the flood plain near Giza that produced agricultural and animal products. However, no archaeological evidence shows its existence. These products and those of more remote estates were delivered to the *r-š*, which allotted them to the funerary establishment or to the palace. The other complexes were: the pyramid city, the rest house and the workshops. These can be expected to appear separately, but in connection with each of the pyramid complexes. One example, namely, the workmen's camp, most likely served the entire plateau. There were also other installations near the Giza plateau, such as a harbor and canals.

The terms *grgt* and *tn* were the designations of the funerary domains of Khufu and Khafre, located on the nearby flood plain. In Khufu's time, *grgt* was established as the main funerary domain of the king. In Khafre's period, this area, *grgt*, consisted of *grgt mḥty* (north) for Khufu, and *tn rsy* (south) for Khafre. Parts of these funerary domains were given to the royal residence at Memphis and the rest were given to the cult of Khufu and Khafre at Giza. *R-š* Khufu was the site of the delivery of the products from the funerary domain (Hawass 1987, 322-336; Helck 1957, 93; Jacquet-Gordon 1962, 457-477; Edel 1956, 67; Kees 1948, 77-81; Stadelmann 1981a, 69; Lehner 1986, 16-17).

One can wonder why scholars do not assign *grgt* and *tn* as funerary domains, even in instances where there is clear evidence that points to that function. In one of the scenes from the tomb of Nesut-nefer at Giza, the two titles of *ꜥd-mr grgt* and *ꜥd-mr tn rsy* are listed one under the other. Below the two titles are scenes arranged in registers, showing males and females bringing offerings to the deceased from the funerary domain (Junker 1938, figure 30). Nesut-nefer's tomb shows, through the list of domains, that he was a person who controlled many of these foundations. Therefore, he had strong connections with the funerary domain. Furthermore, many of the officials who were in charge of *grgt* or *ṯn* transferred their offices to their children, and control of the funerary domains would have been an office that officials would have transferred to their families more frequently than any other office.

There is no known list for Khafre's funerary domains during the Old Kingdom (Jacquet-Gordon, 1952). The funerary domains discussed by Jacquet-Gordon were of two types: a royal *ḥwt* and *niwt*. Khufu had one *ḥwt*-domain and four *niwt*. The number of titles that Khufu had can explain the need for this number of domains. I argued, in the previous discussion, in favor of the relationship between Khufu as Re and his son Khafre, as the son of Re. In addition, the *grgt*, or funerary domain of Khufu, was a single entity of which the southern portion became *ṯn rsy* and was assigned to Khafre. This would explain the texts that mention only *grgt* and the fact that there were seven *ꜥḏ-mr* who were in charge of it. One person was *ꜥḏ-mr grgt mḥty* and, at the same time, there was a *ṯn rsy* of the *grgt* because Nesut-nefer was in charge of both *grgt* and *ṯn rsy*.

From the Abu Sir Papyri it is known that the *R-š* Khufu clearly functioned as an economic unit. It was a place to organize the delivery of the products from the funerary domains to the temple and residence. Therefore, it was an area for the delivery of commodities, such as corn, fruit, bread, beer, meat and fowl. All of these items would have come from the funerary domain (Kemp 1983, 90; Helck 1974a, 66; Kaplony 1972, 56-57).

Textual and archaeological evidence indicates that each pyramid complex at Giza had its own pyramid city and that their location would have been at the foot of the lower temple of each pyramid (Figure 6.15). The name of each pyramid city was combined with the name of the pyramid. The determinative of the pyramid city occurred as early as the Fifth Dynasty, not the Sixth Dynasty, as indicated by other Egyptologists.

During the construction of the sewage system for the village of Nazlet el-Samman, a large settlement about 3 kilometers square was found. It is located about 50 meters south of the recently discovered lower temple of Khufu. During the excavation, the sequence of occupation was found to have been as follows: first, there were mudbrick buildings laid out over natural desert sand.

Then there was a destruction of the mudbrick buildings and leveling of their remains (indicated by a layer containing very dense pockets of pottery, bone, charcoal and layers of ash). This destruction layer is between 15 and 80 cm. thick. Thirdly, a second level of mudbrick buildings was built over the previous layer. These were also later destroyed and leveled, as is indicated by a layer of ashy rubbish containing much pottery. Finally, natural desert aeolian sand was deposited over the mudbrick building and completely buried in the Old Kingdom levels (Hawass and Jones, forthcoming). This settlement area contained two distinct ele‐ ments: the pyramid city of Khufu and the workmen's camp, located south of the wall called Heit-el-Ghorab (Kemp 1977, 185‐ 200; Trigger 1983, 71-174; O'Connor, unpublished paper; Petrie 1899).

It is likely that the palace and the administration of the king were at Giza. The $^c h$ was important as a ritual palace for the sed-fes‐ tival because the $^c h$ played a significant role at this feast. It served as a resting place and changing room at various points during the ceremony. The $^c h$ was strongly associated with Horus, the king. There is evidence that more than one $^c h$ may have existed at Giza. The second may have been a temporary rest house. The existence of two $^c h$ palaces is supported by the existence of two different titles associated with this building. The recent discovery of a settlement at Giza may support the theory that the palace and the administration of the country existed at Giza.

Three workshops were connected with Khufu, Khafre and Men‐ kaure. Textual evidence has revealed the names of Khufu and Menkaure's workshops, and the archaeology proves the existence of three workshops. The function of the workshop was to produce materials, to maintain the cult in the temples of the pyramid com‐ plex, to produce food for the personnel who lived in the pyramid city, and finally, to store the items that arrived from the funerary domains. There was only one workmen's camp that served the three pyramids at Giza. There is no textual evidence at Giza recording its name. Archaeological evidence, through Kromer's excavations and other test trenches by Hassan, indicates the existence of the workmen's camp on the far eastern side of the Giza necropolis. The workmen's community at Giza, which was found recently served the three pyramids and consisted of a number of institutions including: the workmen's camp (Figure 6.16); the bakeries and storage areas; the tombs of the workmen,

the artisans and their overseers; and finally a large limestone wall
known as "Heit el-Ghorab" (Figure 6.17) which separated the
aforementioned areas from the royal pyramid.

The camp (Figure 6.18), which was located in the recently discovered settlement, apparently had a permanent section for the
artisans and a temporary one for the workmen. This hypothesis is
based on the layout of the tombs. (Figures 6.17 and 6.18) Recent
excavations have revealed over 600 tombs for the workmen and 30
for their overseers. In addition, about 40 tombs for the artisans
were found just west of the institution area and the camp.

A bakery with two rooms was also discovered in this area. It is
possible that this bread factory supplied bread for the whole work
force. Large containers that could have held thirty pounds of
dough were found. These baking pots were apparently covered
with coals in large vats, as part of the baking process. A large cache
of Old Kingdom bread molds was also discovered. These are
identical to those depicted in the daily life scenes in the Fifth
Dynasty tomb of Ti at Saqqara. The grains unearthed in the bakery
suggest that the bread was made of barley, making the dark loaves
heavy and dense. The vats used for the dough and the bread
molds were stick-heated on open hearths of the bakery rooms.
Bread and beer were the common staples of ancient Egypt. (The
protein was available from beef and swine.) Another structure
located in this area has been tentatively identified as the storage
area for the grain. A seal impression was found which showed the
incised term $w^c bt$. This word means "to embalm," or refers to
metalworking (Lehner 1993, 56-67).

All three structures were separated by a 200 meter long wall
with a height of about 10 meters. In the middle of the wall there
was a tunnel allowing passage between the camp and institutional
area (Hawass, forthcoming). (Figure 6.19) The 1978 excavations
and drilling proved the existence of a harbor East of the Sphinx
Temple. This harbor may have been connected to the Nile by
means of a canal. In ancient times, the Nile was near the pyramid
sites and has gradually shifted throughout time to its current
position. The theory of the existence of a grand canal, parallel to
the Nile on the west side, to serve the pyramid site at the Memphis
region is unlikely (Hawass and Lehner, unpublished manuscript;
Smith and Jefferys 1986, 91). The harbor and the canal served for
the transportation of stones, laborers and officials from the capital
during the pyramid construction. It linked the pyramid site with

the capital and transported products for the maintenance of the cult of the deceased king.

Correlating the Elements

In conclusion, the function of the pyramid complexes at Giza can be established by looked at the programs of the following elements: architecture, wall reliefs, statuary, and cult objects. These elements were discussed above separately, but here it can be seen how they correlate to give a comprehensive explanation of the function of kingship.

The program of wall reliefs, and its development, can be seen through the study of the reliefs. In the time of Sneferu, the program occurred only in the lower temple. In Khufu's time, it was used throughout the pyramid complex, and it was the first time that the program of the wall reliefs took this direction. In Dynasties V and VI, the program was fully developed in its final form.

The subject matter dealt with in the scenes is as follows: dominating scenes, scenes of the king's identification with the gods, sed-festival scenes, and scenes of offerings. The scenes of domination portray the king victorious over disorderly elements of the universe, such as wild creatures or foreigners. The scenes associated the king with the natural world and the world of foreigners. The same idea can be seen in the hunting scenes, the scenes where offerings are brought from both inside and outside Egypt, and finally, his dedicatory titles. In all of them the king carries out his responsibilities to the gods. The scenes of the king's identification with the gods show the king as Horus. In front of him are the gods and goddesses of Egypt. He is always in their company. He makes offerings to them (a principle duty as ruler); they, in turn, reciprocate with affection.

It can be argued that the most important scenes were the sed-festival scenes. They depict the king in his palace with his officials and courtiers. He is also seated in his chapel wearing the crown of Upper and Lower Egypt. He wears his robe and carries the flail indicating his kingship and his power over Upper and Lower Egypt. Some scholars suggest that the sed-festival included the presentation of royal regalia: the scepter, and the bow and arrow (Brinks 1979, 159). Others see it as an expression of royal power

(Bonnet 1952, 159), or a guarantee of royal power (Hornung and Staehelin, 1974, 20-25). It could also be a renewal rite for the life and strength of the king as well as a guarantee of his royal power (Arnold 1977b, 11). In the Old Kingdom, the sed-festival was apparently celebrated when the king finished building his pyramid and associated temples. During the festival, the king removed his robe, put it in the palace (ʿḥ) or the ritual (satellite) pyramid. (The ritual pyramid of Khufu was found recently. It is located to the immediate southeast corner of the Great Pyramid.) The burial chamber of this satellite pyramid was the changing room for the sed-festival. (Figure 1) Khafre did not have a ritual pyramid. The pyramid located to the south of his pyramid was a queen's pyramid (See Figure 6.1). The ʿḥ palace of Khafre was used as the changing room for his sed-festival. Menkaure's subsidiary pyramid (GIII-C) has no entrance for burial. The burial chamber was not lined and there is no evidence that a sarcophagus existed there (Vyse 1840-42, 41 ff.; Reisner 1931, 133. I suggest that this pyramid represents the cult pyramid of Menkaure.) The king then performed his dance to celebrate his success, his good government, and to show that he had accomplished what the gods required of him. Finally, there are the offering scenes. They always occur in the offering room, and showed the king receiving offerings and divinity. He was accepted by all the gods and became equal to them. Because he accomplished what they required him to do on earth, he is now a god.

Common to all of these scenes is the fact that they focus primarily on the king. The scenes of the first three categories are also scenes suitable for decorating the walls of the king's palace. The only subject that would not be represented in his palace, however, is that of the gods giving offerings to the king. The king cannot be equal to the gods unless he has completed the first three accomplishments depicted on his palace and his temples. Furthermore, certain scenes are always repeated three times. The repetition emphasized the importance of the activity.

In addition, there is evidence that shows that the wall reliefs had a program that was developed early in the Old Kingdom. One might suggest that this program was continued throughout Egyptian history with some additions. For example, the scene of King Sahure smiting a Libyan chieftain on the head with a mace, while his wife and two sons are in the background, was copied exactly on the temple of Pepi II. Even the name of the wife and sons are is the same in both temples, although they are separated in time by two hundred years.

There are other scenes found in wall reliefs that have a parallel in New Kingdom scenes at Karnak. Furthermore, the development of the scenes from Sneferu to Pepi II shows the repetition of scenes with some additions in each period. Therefore, care must be given in interpreting historical events from these representative scenes, because they may have been depicted within the pyramid complex to show the ideal life that the king would like to live in the beyond. However, at the same time, some scenes, such as those involving foreigners, may have some validity.

The statuary program indicates a formula for the placement and types of statuary. It also suggests that the statues were related to the other programs. My interpretation of the triads of Menkaure implies that the pyramid complex was dedicated to the gods Re, Hathor, and Horus. The triads were the focus of the cult. The sun-god Re was the creator god who kept the world running. Hathor was the daughter and eye of Re, as well as the wife and mother of the king. She gave birth to him and was also his wife. The king was in the pyramid complex because he was Horus, and the triads were there because they were essential to the kingship. The triads of Menkaure not only suggest that the pyramid complex was dedicated to the king and his deities, but also revealed the king's relationship to the gods, as was the case in the reliefs. The statuary program also showed the power of the king as a ruler through the representation of sm3-t3wy, "the unification of the Twohands," on the base of the statues, paralleling the dominating and ruling motifs in the reliefs.

The correlation of the wall reliefs and the statuary can be seen from the reconstructed court of Khafre's upper temple. The king was seated in the court and above him were his Horus titles and the srh, "palace façade." It also suggests that the king was seated in his palace. The court with its statues, and the five niches in the upper temple, also suggest that the upper temple was built to secure the continued existence of the king in the form of an extensive statue program. In addition, the program for the objects in the magazines parallel the dual functions of the temple and the palace, attested to by the reliefs and the statuary. They also match the programs of the temple and the palace. The program of objects in the magazines in the upper and lower temple of Menkaure was as follows: (1) the southern magazines contained the objects used in the cult and (2) the northern magazines contained the palace objects that the king would use in the beyond.

The architectural program correlated with all the other programs of the wall reliefs, statuary, and cult objects. It provided the space for wall reliefs, statuary and cult objects, and this fact suggests that the temples were built mainly for the purposes of worship. The later Old Kingdom reliefs indicate that the temples were cult buildings for the king and the gods.

On the basis of the development of the programs, the plan of the architectural elements of the pyramid complex took its shape in Dynasty IV, especially in the time of Khufu, and it continued to develop throughout the Old Kingdom. Small changes or additions occurred according to the demands of each king.

The lower temple, causeway and upper temple were directed to the East to follow the worship of Re. The open court was another feature that indicated that Re was worshipped in the pyramid complex, because the sun rose and set in the open court. Khufu's upper temple was the first to contain the five niches; four were to house his four statues representing him as Re and Horus, and the last niche was for a cult statue for Hathor. The upper temple of Khafre also had five niches for three statues of Khafre representing himself as king of Upper and Lower Egypt and Horus. The other two niches were for statues of Khufu as Re and Hathor. Menkaure's upper temple had only one niche for a cult object of the sun-god.

I noted above that Khufu identified himself with Re. This statement can be justified by the fact that no wall reliefs have been found of Khufu with other gods because he attempted to identify himself as Re, who is united with Horus. Khafre accepted his father Khufu as a god and worshipped him, as Re, in his pyramid complex in the so-called "Sphinx Temple." Menkaure, however, did not follow these directions. He accepted the king as a god, but, only as a manifestation of Re, not as the god himself.

The existence of Hathor as member of the triad of deities at Giza was discussed earlier in more detail. One of the most important pieces of evidence supporting this is the existence of priests and a priestess of Hathor at Giza, at least as early as Khufu's reign. Hathor was also assisted by Neith, the daughter of Re. However, Neith did not have a main cult at Giza, as did Hathor. The three gods were worshipped throughout the pyramid complex. There is no evidence of any temple of other gods elsewhere in Dynasty IV. Also, the niches in the temples of the pyramid complex contained statues of the triad. At the same time, the pyramid complex contained a specific place for each god.

The king, as Horus, was worshipped in the lower temple as indicated by the suggested statuary program of the king in the lower temples of Khafre and Menkaure. Hathor was worshipped in the chapels of the Queen's pyramid because she was identified with the wife of the king. Re was worshipped in the upper temple. He was the universal god who accepted all that the king did in the last element of the program of the pyramid complex. He also protected the king who was buried in the "Horizon of Re," i. e., the pyramid.

The architectural program indicates that Menkaure's lower temple court was influenced by the plan of the so-called "Sphinx Temple." This type of temple did not occur later in the Old Kingdom. Finally, the Egyptian building identifications that are found in the Abu Sir Papyri, such as: *pr-wrw, wsḫt, tpḥt,* and *zḥ* can be located in the temples of Dynasties IV to VI.

Apparently, the architectural program was formulated to create a pyramid complex in which the triad could have been worshipped, and in which the myth of the kingship could have been celebrated. The triads of deities were worshipped there because of their connection with kingship. Therefore, the evidence cited above suggests that the pyramid complex was as much a palace as it was a temple.

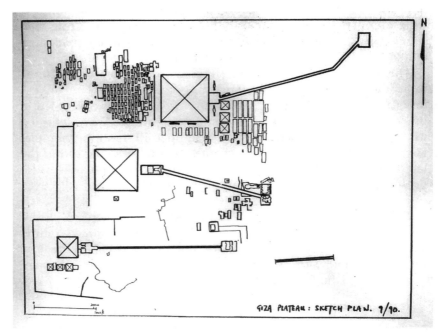

6.1. Plan of the Giza Plateau. Drawn by Michael Jones.

6.2. The pyramids at Giza. Photograph coutesy of Zahi Hawass.

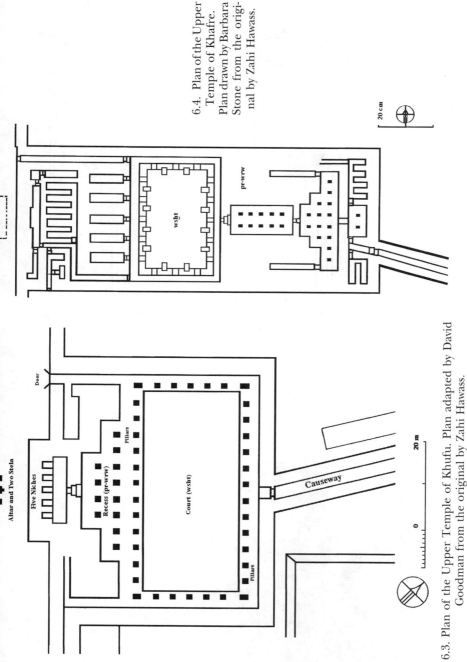

6.4. Plan of the Upper Temple of Khafre. Plan drawn by Barbara Stone from the original by Zahi Hawass.

6.3. Plan of the Upper Temple of Khufu. Plan adapted by David Goodman from the original by Zahi Hawass.

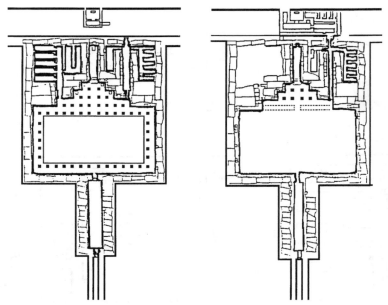

6.5. Plan of the Upper Temple of Menkaure (left) and Reconstruction of the Southern Magazines (right). Plan drawn by Barbara Stone from the original by Ricke.

6.6. Work on the modern sewage system. Photograph courtesy of Zahi Hawass.

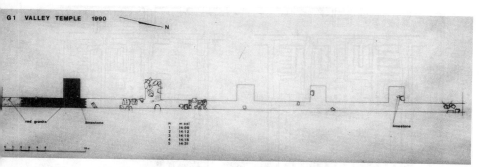

6.7. Excavation plan of the Lower Temple. Plan drawn by M. Jones.

6.8. Plan of the Lower Temple
of Khafre, the Sphinx and the
Sphinx Temple. Plan drawn
by Barbara Stone from the
original by Zahi Hawass.

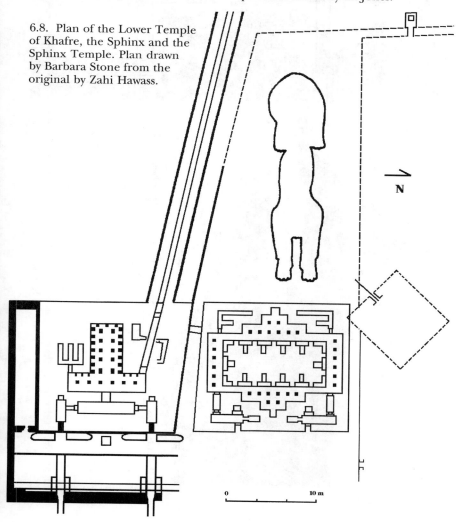

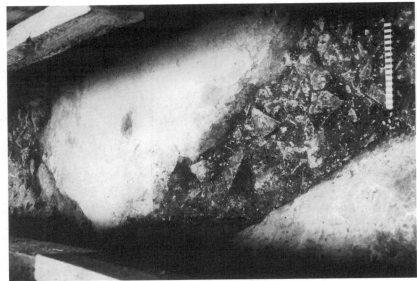

6.9. The Causeway of Khufu from Sinn el Aquz. Photograph courtesy of Zahi Hawass.

6.10. Nazlet el Samman. Excavation of Causeway Trench No. 1. Photograph by M. Jones.

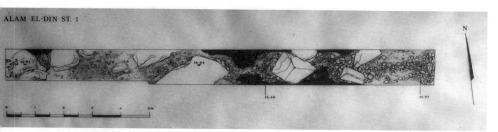

6.11. Plan of Trench 1, causeway route. Plan drawn by M. Jones.

6.12. Statue of Khufu in the Cairo Museum. Photograph courtesy of Zahi Hawass.

6.14. Triad depicting Menkaure, Hathor, and a nome deity, now in the Cairo Museum. Photograph courtesy of David P.

6.13. Statue of Khafre in the Cairo Museum. Photograph courtesy of Zahi Hawass.

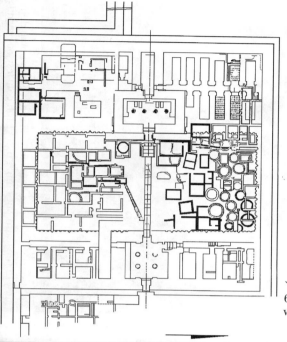

←
6.15. The pyramid city of Menkaure, located outside and inside of his lower temple. Plan courtesy of Zahi Hawass.

↓
6.16. Part of the cemetary of the workmen and the artisans. Photograph courtesy of Zahi Hawass.

6.17. The wall of Heit el Ghorab. Photograph courtesy of Zahi Hawass.

6.18. The settlement located east of the Sphinx under the village of Nazlet el Samma
Photograph courtesy of Zahi Hawass.

CHAPTER SEVEN

BELOVED OF MAAT, THE HORIZON OF RE: THE ROYAL PALACE IN NEW KINGDOM EGYPT

David B. O'Connor

1. Scenes From Royal Life

As readers of this volume will have realized, in the New Kingdom (as in other periods) the Egyptians displayed complex and multifaceted attitudes to their supreme ruler, the pharaoh. These attitudes varied greatly, depending on the frame of reference in which they were displayed, upon the greater or lesser decorum imposed by a specific situation. An Egyptian might, in a letter or private conversation, speak in a mundane and matter of fact way about pharaoh, or even poke fun at and express contempt for him. However, at a council meeting or at some other administrative encounter due deference was shown to the king, while at court ceremonies he was lauded to the skies as a divine being of immeasurable power and stunning beauty (e.g., Barucq and Daumas 1980, 481 ff.). Such varied attitudes can be gleaned from the written sources but, in reality—for reasons both of culture and archaeological survival—most of the extant texts referring to the pharaoh are idealized, hyperbolic and laudatory. The individual personality, even the simple biographical facts about a given ruler become hazy and lost in a flood of metaphor and imagery, operating at a highly generalized level.

Yet now and then a particular description or narrative becomes specific and personalized enough that, for a moment at least, we glimpse some of the realities, and sense some of the immediacy of royal life in New Kingdom Egypt. Sometimes the specific events involved, such as those describing Thutmose I formally identifying Hatshepsut as heir to the throne, may be fictitious; yet for our purposes this is irrelevant for the narrative remains based on the actual experiences of other rulers and is visualized as occurring in the appropriate and specific locale.

Whether a text is generalized and vague, or specific and immediate, the locale envisaged is in most cases a temple or a palace.
The former is a natural one for an Egyptian king who, like the
ruler in many cultures, had a pivotal role in linking Egyptians to
their gods, and Egypt to the cosmos; and, naturally, a palace is
normally where we expect to find a king in any society. Yet, for
Egypt, the nature and significance of the royal palace has hardly
been explored, although the role of the temple (and the king's
ritual activities within it) have been discussed extensively. For
example, in a standard reference work such as the *Lexikon der
Ägyptologie* some sixteen and two-thirds columns are dedicated to
the concept, architecture and other aspects of temples (*LÄ* VI,
355-365, 377-379, 407-414) but 'Palast' and its chief components
are covered by only about four columns of text (*LÄ* I, 554; II, 14;
IV, 644-646; cf. also Vandier's 1955 encyclopedic survey of the
religious and secular architecture of Egypt which devotes 307 pages to New Kingdom temples but only some 18 pages to the
palaces of the New Kingdom pharaohs). Palaces, it is true, have
rarely been excavated, for they typically lay in dense urban settings
infrequently explored by archaeologists in Egypt; and, since they
were built mainly of mud brick, even the excavated palaces are
poorly preserved while a good number of stone-built temples have
survived substantially intact. Nevertheless, the available information on palaces is surprisingly rich and my purpose here is to
discuss some major aspects of New Kingdom palaces that have not,
I believe, been treated in any depth elsewhere (a recent discussion
of Late Bronze Age palaces [Kemp 1989, 213-223] is valuable, but
is focused on issues other than those discussed here). Royal
palaces varied considerably in function, and much remains to be
said about the purposes for which individual palaces were intended. However, I believe it will also emerge that the palace was
not just a royal residence and governmental center, although these
are important functions; but that it was also—like the temple—
structured so as to be a vital link between Egypt and the cosmos. In
brief, the plan, architectural form and "decorative" scenes and
texts of the temple integrated the earthly reality of the rituals
performed in the temple with the supra-reality of the cosmic
processes of creation and the renewal of creation. This integration
ensured that ritual would have meaning, authority and effective
power. Similarly, major and recurrent attributes of the palace
(however varied in function individual palaces might be)

integrated royal private, ceremonial and administrative life with the cosmic processes; all these aspects of royal activity thus became cosmically meaningful and effective as did, by extension, the administrative and economic structure of Egypt and its empire. This conclusion is based in part on some close similarities between temples and palaces in New Kingdom Egypt, to be discussed further below. (cf. O'Connor 1993).

Before taking up these issues however, we should remind ourselves of what Egypt's rulers did in temple and palace respectively. That royal activity often occurs in a temple is a natural result of that intensely close and unique relationship between the Egyptian king and the gods, a relationship often described (e.g., in Barta 1979; cf. also Hornung 1982a, 135-142). The king was simultaneously human and divine, servant and delegate of the gods on the one hand, but himself the embodiment of divine kingship on the other. The king built and endowed the gods' temples and was the sole priest of their cults, all the priests who actually carried out the rituals being considered embodiments of the king. But, as possessor of the ka of kingship and as son of the chief god the king also had a divine nature, always present but periodically given special emphasis in a ritual setting (Bell 1985a).

Thus the female pharaoh Hatshepsut, while offering an abundance of incense from Punt or "God's Land" and gold from other southern regions to the imperial god Amun-Re in the semi-public setting of a forecourt in front of his temple (Spencer 1984, 82), appears to the onlookers to be a god herself. Like a god, her skin breathes forth sweet-smelling incense and gleams like electrum, so that she shines like the stars "in the presence of the whole land" (Urk. IV, 339.4-340.2). On another semi-public occasion, the future pharaoh Thutmose III underwent an even more exalted experience (Urk. IV, 156.17-159.17). As a young prince he participated in a festival held in the hypostyle hall of Amun-Re's temple at Karnak (Spencer 1984, 68-69). To the amazement of those spectators privileged to be present the god—having emerged from his sanctuary in the form of an image placed in a sacred boat carried by priests—forced his bearers to carry him around the hall while he clearly searched for someone. Having found Thutmose, Amun's image placed him at "the Stations of the Lord of the king" (Lacau and Chevrier 1977, 101-102, note d.), a semi-public location at which the image habitually delivered "oracles," in effect divine decisions about who should be next king, or other important matters of state (Kákosy 1982). Here it was revealed "in the sight of the people" that the gods recognized Thutmose as the future king, a decision that meant for Thutmose an ecstatic vision into the mysterious workings of the cosmos itself. The "door-leaves of the sky" and the "gateways of its horizon" were opened to him and in the form of a divine falcon he flew up into heaven and beheld the secret form of the sun-god, the splendid shapes of the god of the two horizons upon his mysterious route in the sky. To thus perceive the "true," normally hidden forms of a god (as distinct from its images on earth) was a unique privilege (Hornung 1982a, 128-135); in addition, this revelatory introduction to the arcana of the solar cult was necessary for the king to carry out his crucial role as ritual-priest of the sun-god (Assmann 1989, 57).

Sometimes pharaoh's activities bring the outside world and the sacred world of the temple together in ways that startle us. In ca. 1425 BC, the splendid boat of Amenhotep II, who had just returned from a victorious campaign in southern Syria, swept up to the quay at Thebes, the southern royal capital. Hanging upside down from its prow were the rotting bodies of seven Syrian princes, their heads smashed in by pharaoh's club, their bodies perhaps naked or dangling with the tattered remnants of once gorgeous robes. Amun-Re had granted Amenhotep victory and to show how "joyful his heart was to Amun" he had six of the corpses hung "on the face of the enclosure wall at Thebes," i.e. perhaps the high, towered enclosure wall of Karnak temple itself (Urk. IV, 1296.13-1297.12).

The other typical locale for the public and private life of Egypt's kings and queens is the palace, a locale often only implied or summarily referred to, but sometimes evoked in richer detail. Here, in the palace or its environs, the range of royal activity is wide. Councils meet under the presidency of pharaoh; officials are formally appointed to office by the king, report on their activities to him, banquet under his aegis or receive from him rich rewards for loyalty and meritorious service. Enthroned within a palace hall pharaoh might ceremonially decree a military campaign, a trading expedition, or the building and endowing of a great temple; or he might report the successful achievement of such activities, on a scale and with a success naturally far surpassing those of his predecessors. At such elaborate court ceremonies courtiers and officials were expected to respond to the king's speech, or indeed his mere presence, with laudatory hymns and eulogies; while all, to show their deep respect, bowed low or prostrated themselves, "kissing the earth" as the Egyptians put it. Envoys from foreign lands, inherently inferior to Egyptians according to the latters' world view, displayed a more humiliating obeisance, "seven times on the belly and seven times on the back" (Drower 1973, 469). The grandest royal ceremonies of all involved large numbers of participants and extensive spaces; they included the performances of royal rituals such as the *sed*-festival (Martin 1984; Bleeker 1967, 96-123) and the reception of foreign tribute from all over the empire.

Most references to activity in the palace are conventional and generalized, but some describe events more specifically. The royal family, for example, was closely linked in a personal way to the cult of Amun-Re. In the Eighteenth dynasty, and perhaps later, the "God's Wife of Amun-Re" was a special title held by a king's daughter or mother, a fact of ideological significance (Troy 1986: 97-99; cf. also Graefe 1981, II, 101ff), but also one creating a special relationship between the royal family and the wealthiest and most influential of the temple establishments. Moreover, it was believed that the king was truly the "bodily son of Amun," and thus heir to his divine father's universal dominion.

This was no mere formality, but a deeply held belief; and its fundamental reality was experienced in the palace. Thus, queen Ahmose, sleeping in "the beauty of her palace," was woken by a powerful fragrance of incense, as strong as that emanating from all of the incense-land of Punt and given off by the figure of her husband, pharaoh Thutmose I, standing by her bed in a state of sexual excitement. Ahmose realized that in fact Amun-Re himself had taken on the form of her husband, and she welcomed him to her bed; as intercourse took place, the text makes clear, the future pharaoh Hatshepsut was conceived (Urk. IV, 219. 10-221.9).

Hatshepsut herself underwent an important experience in a palace setting, an experience perhaps fictitious to some degree, but nevertheless based on a real event which occurred in a specific palace locale (Redford 1967, 82). On this occasion, the inhabitants of Thebes, no doubt forewarned, assembled in the vicinity of a great palace, probably located just north-west of the Amun temple of Karnak. The Thebans at first heard—floating over the palace's high brick walls—a dim sound, far off at the center of the palace; but the sound grew in volume as it surged like a wave through crowds assembled in the courtyards and buildings making up the palace complex. Now it could be heard as celebratory chanting and shouting and, as the sound finally passed through the buildings closest to the palace enclosure walls, it reached what was for the spectators a crescendo as the shouting was taken up by the soldiers guarding the gates and perimeter of the palace. No doubt marshaled in unusually large numbers for the occasion, the soldiers literally leaped and danced for joy, as did soon the townspeople themselves; for the message of the shouting was that Thutmose I, enthroned in state in the palace audience hall and with his courtiers and officials assembled nearby, had just formally identified his young daughter Hatshepsut as the heir to his throne. The rejoicing that spread throughout the palace and from thence to the city was of course stage-managed in honor of a major political event, but the joy was also genuine. Not only would there be much feasting at the state's expense; more importantly, the event forged yet another link in that chain of divinely born rulers which—in the Egyptian view—ran back through the millennia to the very creation of kingship itself in incredibly remote and primeval times (Urk. IV 255.4 - 260.13).

These few scenes of royal life, in temple and palace, take us into a world that seems very strange, at least in terms of the recent, western history of royalty. Within the palace, a queen couples delightedly with a god who is fragrant with incense; within the temple, one ruler feels herself mystically transformed into a god, another is literally lifted up into the realms of the sky and its wonders. And from the pure white walls of the Amun temple enclosure at Thebes the smell of death wafts out over the town as slaughtered foreigners hang rotting from them. All of this seems quite unlike the public and private life of, shall we say, Queen Victoria! Yet even Victoria's generals, in far away India, shot rebellious Indian soldiers or sepoys from cannons, literally blowing them to pieces and far exceeding normal modes of execution in order to express rage and contempt (Woodham-Smith 1972, 496); and only a few generations earlier, public hangings and the exposure of executed criminals, enemies of king and state, were not uncommon in England and Europe. As we move back into the earlier centuries of European and other kingship, with its elaborate ceremonies and sanctified status, we naturally find more parallels in attitude and action with ancient Near Eastern monarchies such as the Egyptian. Even in the realms of ideology and theory fascinating similarities may exist (Bell 1985a, 293-294).

Yet rewarding as such cross-cultural and comparative studies might be, every form of kingship has a unique shape and character, derived from the specific culture that generated it. Egyptian kingship bears the unmistakable attributes of specifically Egyptian thought and belief, Egyptian imagery and iconography, Egyptian historical experience and environment. An Egyptian temple and its god can never be mistaken for that of another culture; the distinctive costume and regalia of a pharaoh cannot be confused with those of a Persian, Assyrian, or Hittite monarch; the imagery of Egyptian royal hymns and eulogies has an irreducibly Egyptian character. Many of the culturally determined attributes of Egyptian kingship have been more or less thoroughly studied— its myths and ideology, its ceremonies and rituals, its regalia, even the royal throne itself (Kuhlmann 1977); but one attribute, as I noted earlier, has received comparatively slight attention, namely the royal palace. Palaces and their functions and symbolism will therefore be the focus of this essay.

I will deal here only with palaces of the New Kingdom. Although the palace, as an institution, can be traced back to Early Dynastic times, and sporadic archaeologically attested remains exist from Early Dynastic times onwards (Arnold 1982, Palast, *LÄ* IV, 643-646; Helck 1982, Palastverwaltung, *LÄ* IV, 647-652), only in the New Kingdom is the archaeology rich enough to lend some substantial degree of precision to the typically allusive, abbreviated or vague references to palaces found in texts.

Within the New Kingdom, I shall focus on only three sites, each a royal city, i.e. a permanent center of royal residence, ceremonial and government—Thebes, Tell el Amarna and Memphis. (Figure 7.1) The fourth royal city, Pi-Ramses in the eastern Delta, also contained palaces, one of which is currently under excavation, but its denuded remains are not germane to my purposes here (Bietak 1984; Leclant and Clère 1986, 246 and note 58). Palaces were not confined to the royal cities; for example, we hear of a royal prince practicing archery in the court-yard of the palace of Tjeny or Thinis (Urk. IV, 976.13); palatial structures have been excavated at Deir el Ballas (Eggebrecht 1975); and a "harem palace" is documented both archaeologically and textually at Mi-wer, in the mouth of the Fayyum depression (Kemp 1978). These peripheral palaces however, are not relevant to this discussion. The value of

Thebes is that it has yielded textual and, to a lesser degree, archaeological data that enable us to examine a variety of functionally different palaces within the framework of the ritual, ceremonial and administrative life of a traditional royal city. Tell el Amarna, the short-lived national and imperial capital founded by the "heretic" pharaoh Akhenaten, was undoubtedly innovative and non-traditional in important aspects; but it also followed or at least adapted in some ways the traditional model of a royal city. Equally importantly, its palaces are uniquely well-documented both archaeologically and pictorially, so that the specific functions of each can be discussed in greater detail than is possible, for the most part, elsewhere. Finally, there were apparently—as one might expect—a number of royal palaces at Memphis, the most ancient by far of the New Kingdom royal cities, at the apex of the Delta (Zivie 1982; Helck, 1958b, 98-99). One particularly famous one was built by Thutmose I and was still in use over 150 years later, during Tutankhamun's time and even beyond (Helck 1958b, 97). However, these palaces are not well-documented save for a single excavated example, a palace of pharaoh Merneptah. Exceptionally well-preserved, this palace is especially important for our understanding of the symbolic roles of palaces, and a brief discussion of it will close this essay.

Finally, it should be noted that I shall not attempt any consistent correlation between the different Egyptian words for "palace" and any of the palaces discussed below, or the different functions of each. Such an analysis for both the New Kingdom and other periods would be potentially most productive, as Goelet has recently demonstrated in his analysis of *stp-s3*, one of the five most common words for "palace" (1986); but it would go beyond the scope of this particular essay.

2. The Palaces of Thebes, The Palace of Karnak, the Place of Honor

In any given reign there were probably several palaces in use at Thebes (Figure 7.2), each differing in function from the others; but it seems generally accepted amongst scholars that there was only one principal palace, a "Regierungspalast" or governmental palace. Any formal governmental activity involving the pharaoh— such as announcing the heir to the throne, or announcing or reporting on a major initiative of war or peace, or appointing and

promoting a great official—is reasonably assumed to have occurred in this palace as did perhaps also the less formal and more
routine administrative activities involving the king. No doubt, from
time to time, perhaps even from reign to reign, the old main
palace would be replaced by a new one, but the functions of the
governmental palace would continue to be the same even if the
setting was new.

Substantial disagreement exists about the location of the
Theban governmental palace. Some argue vigorously for a *west*
bank location for both this palace and the offices, archives and
presumably residences of the bureaucracy which ran the city, the
state and the empire (e.g., Helck 1954b, 204-206; 1968b, 119-120;
Stadelmann 1985a, 467). Other scholars, while recognizing the
evidence is not fully decisive one way or the other, favor an *east*
bank location for governmental palace and bureaucratic center
(e.g., Otto 1952, 25-26, 45; Redford 1973, 88-90). Certainly the
principal Theban temple, that of Amun-Re at Karnak, was on the
east bank and so apparently was the "original and most important
settlement of Thebes" (Redford 1973, 89). More specifically, a
location near Karnak itself is suggested (Otto 1952, 25-26, 70;
Gitton 1974, 72-73) and an extended analysis of the relevant
data—an analysis not attempted before, so far as I can determine—suggests to me that this hypothesis is the most probable.
The significance of the disagreement is not merely topographical.
The two alternative locations—west bank, or east bank near
Karnak—have important and different implications for the relationship between the governmental palace and the administrative
and the ritual life of the city; and for the conceptual role of this
palace in the relationship between Egypt and the universe, the
microcosmos and the macrocosmos.

The starting point for the argument that the governmental
palace was always near Karnak temple, and specifically immediately north-west of it, is the certain fact that pharaoh Hatshepsut
had a palace in precisely this location (Gitton 1974). In her time,
the fourth pylon was the front of the temple, and probably had an
enclosed court before it; north-west of the court was a palace: "The
royal palace (ʿḥ nswt)" of Hatshepsut, called "I am not far from him
(Amun-Re)" (Lacau and Chevrier 1977, 78). It faced onto the
temple quay and the processional way running from the quay into
the temple (figure 7.3). Some have argued that, whether in
Hatshepsut's reign or others,' this palace of Karnak was used only

by the ruler when he or she was present to participate in the temple ritual (Helck 1954b, 205-206; Stadelmann 1985a, 467); but this seems unlikely, for two reasons. First, after being identified by Amun-Re as the future pharaoh, Hatshepsut is taken into this palace by the god, and there enthroned, adorned with a uraeus and assigned a titulary or set of royal names; thus "appearing in glory (*ḫ3i*)" she is adored by prostrate courtiers (Lacau and Chevrier 1977, 99-123). By their very nature, these events suggest the palace "I am not far from him" was governmental in function. Second, evidence from other reigns provides evidence for a governmental (not cultic) palace in this same location. (See Figure 7.3)

From the reigns of Thutmose III, Amenhotep II (?), Thutmose IV, and Ramses II we have extended descriptions of the "Duties of the Vizier," the *Tjaty* or chief civil official of the king (Martin-Pardey 1986; Helck 1975b; van den Boorn 1982; van den Boorn 1988). The circumstances described therein may well have persisted to the end of the New Kingdom, but this cannot be proved. One responsibility the vizier performed every day, at least while the king was resident in Thebes, was to enter the palace (*pr*), greet the king and report to him "the condition of the two lands," i.e. of Egypt (Urk, IV, 1105. 12-13). A regular feature of this event was that the vizier waited before the palace, "the great double house (*prwy ʿ3wy*)" until the chief treasurer (*imy-r3 sḏ3wtyw*) took up position by the "northern flag staff (*snt*);" this must have stood before the northern wing of the pylon of a structure so well known that it was not necessary to name it. When the treasurer was in position, the vizier entered the palace, reported and exited; as soon as the treasurer saw the vizier moving through "the door (*sb3*) of the great double gate (*rwty wrty*)" of the palace, he left his post at the northern flag staff and moved to meet with the vizier (Urk. IV, 1105. 14-17; cf. below, for an alternative interpretation).

The pylon in question cannot be that of the palace itself. Conceivably a palace might be said to have a pylon in the rare sense of a gateway (Spencer 1984, 196) although no such reference is known; but flag staffs are associated only with temples. The reference then must be to a temple oriented east-west, for only then could its' pylons or entrance towers have northern and southern wings. On the east bank, Karnak temple is the only major one having an east-west orientation; the pylon in question would be either that of its façade at that time, i.e. of the fourth pylon or conceivably of a brick built pylon fronting the courtyard assumed to lie in front of the fourth pylon. In either case, the text clearly indicates that the "great double gate" of the palace was visible from the external face of the north wing of one of these two pylons, and indeed within easy walking distance of it. In other words, this evidently governmental palace, used here for important but routine administrative activity, must have lain immediately north-west of Karnak temple, just like the palace of Hatshepsut.

It should be noted that van den Boorn, in an extraordinarily valuable study of the *Duties of the Vizier* (1988), has suggested that the royal palace at Thebes wherein pharaoh conducted administrative business (the exact location of which he does not discuss) was oriented east-west, rather than north-south, the orientation I suggest here (ibid. 63-67). However, his reasons for doing so are not compelling. First, he argues that the *palace* was the building with a northern flagpole, in front of the façade, and hence an east-west orientation (ibid. 63), and not a north-south one as I suggest here. However, the objection to this still stands; palaces are never said to have flagpoles, found only with temples (ibid. 63, and 63 n. 46), and hence my assumption the flagpole belongs to Karnak temple is preferable. Second, van den Boorn suggests that when the vizier enters the palace, through its main and hence axial entryway (the doorway with the great double door) he is said to be moving "in (or from) the east," and hence an east-west axis is indicated (ibid. 64-65). One could perhaps more plausibly argue that the vizier is *leaving*, not entering the palace, for the narrative, taken at face-value, states that the vizier receives a daily report on "the affairs of the Two Lords," i.e. all of Egypt in his "house" (either his residence; or his official quarters); *then* enters the palace to salute, and implicitly to report to the king; *then* leaves the palace, and confers with the treasurer. Van den Boorn believes the conference with the treasurer *precedes* the vizier's entry into the palace (ibid. 58-68). However, even if the vizier is leaving, rather than entering the palace he would still be, according to van den Boorn, moving from or into the east, and hence be in a building oriented east-west. But, this conclusion depends upon translating the words *[ḥ]r r mnmn t3ty m wbn* as: "the vizier shall move (in) from the east," the word *wbn(t)* being taken as a fancy denotation of "the East," a circumstance which is demonstrably true (ibid. 65). However, *wbn* is allotted a determinative here indicating that it is in this context a verb related to movement, rather than orientation (ibid., 64) and one might then reasonably translate it as simply "to appear," with no reference to orientation, also a well demonstrated usage (ibid., 64-65 and 65 n. 56). This phrase, referring originally to the rising sun, is usually applied only to gods or kings, but *can* be used of a private person (ibid., 64 n. 58); here, the implication that the vizier is "appearing in glory" may refer to the fact that, having attended the pharaoh, (hence, leaving—not entering; cf. above) and having received his instructions, the vizier is now a vessel of royal authority and hence can "appear in glory" like the pharaoh himself (on the "royal allure" generated by the arrangements in the vizier's hall, cf. ibid., 324). If this interpretation is accepted—*m wbn* referring simply to an act of appearance, not to a compass orientation—then the second, and last of van den Boorn's arguments for an east-west orientation for the palace, is refuted.

Alternatively, one could argue that the temple pylon that helps fix the orientation of the palace involved belonged not to Karnak temple, but to a west bank funerary temple, all of which have east-west orientations and therefore, north wings of pylons. The palace then would be north-east of one of these temples. Two points however, are against this suggestion. First, a dummy version of the governmental palace attached to each funerary temple (discussed further below) is always *south* of its axis, and usually south-east of the temple proper. This suggests that a true governmental palace on the west bank would be in the same location. Second, and more importantly, a palace north-east of a temple facing east (as the funerary temples do) could not be described as being *n imy wrt* in the specific sense that, I would argue, this phrase is used in connection with the main, governmental palace of Thebes.

Thutmose III is described as enthroned in state in the audience hall (*ḏ3dw*) "*n imy wrt*" when he respectively announces an ambitious building project (Gardiner 1952, Plate IV col. 1) and installs a vizier in office (Urk. IV, 1380.12). Similarly Amenhotep III orders an expedition to be sent to Sinai while he is "in the southern city (Thebes) [in his palace *n imy*] *wrt* of Thebes (Waset)" (Urk. IV, 1891.6). Earlier Thutmose I, in order to formally declare Hatshepsut heir to the throne, sat enthroned in the "audience hall *n imy wrt* of the (?) courtyard" (*s3*; cf. Breasted 1906 II, 97). This audience hall was in a palace described as a *stp-s3*—a common word for palace—and also as "the palace (*ʿḥ*) of the (?) council chamber (*ist*)" and "beloved of the (?) council chamber" (Urk. IV, 255.10 and 256.15-257.2).

The activities described show the palace in question was the governmental one, as does the use of the word *stp-s3*, which was probably a type of palace in which occurred "some manner of royal council where affairs of state were discussed" and which also involved aspects of the palace "that were ceremonial in the broadest sense of the word" (Goelet 1986, 97). But what is the locational significance of the phrase "*n imy wrt*"?

This can legitimately be translated as "on the west," explicitly or implicitly of Thebes and, when interpreted in this sense, it perhaps is the strongest argument for locating the governmental palace on the west bank (Helck 1954b, 204-206; 1968b, 120; Stadelmann 1985b, 467). But there is no compelling reason to understand the phrase in this, very specific sense. Redford has cogently pointed out that *n imy wrt* may simply mean that the palace lay west of Karnak, but still on the east bank, between Karnak and the river (1973, 89). I should like to propose, very tentatively, yet a third interpretation, namely that *n imy wrt* in the references cited above is to be translated as referring to an audience hall, and implicitly a palace "on the starboard/right hand side" (Faulkner 1964, 18; Breasted 1906 II, 97 once translated the phrase as "right hand side," but has not been followed by recent commentators). *Both* meanings—starboard side and right hand side—I would suggest, are simultaneously intended, for the reference is to a sacred boat bearing a divine image which passes in front of the palace, moving westwards and hence having the palace on its right hand, starboard side. These sacred boats were carried forth through the principal entrance of a temple on the occasion of a great public festival; indeed, the principal outer doorways of any temple, distributed along its processional axis, were solely reserved for this purpose, and the return of the boat into the temple (Assmann 1984a, 41-43). That it was the departure from the temple rather than the return that was referred to here is likely because the former event was more meaningful. By leaving the temple the god departed its sacred, protected realm and initiated a major public festival during which, typically, the divine image would make oracular announcements about the king (Kákosy 1982). The significance of ensuring the palace was on the starboard, right hand side of the boat as it left the temple was that this was the position of highest status; in Egyptian symbolic thought the right

hand side was "firm and useful.... The place of honor, of confidence is on the right hand" (Posener 1965b, 72-73). The palace
was also, one would infer, close to the temple, so it would be
indeed the first building passed by the sacred boat.

Logically, *any* Theban temple might be the one referred to (and
hence fixing the palace's location) for each one had a deity whose
image was periodically carried forth in a festival procession. The
palace then might be north-west or south-east of an east-west
oriented temple; or north-east or south-west of a temple oriented
north-south. However, it seems most probable that Karnak temple
was the source of the processional appearances indicated by the
phrase *n imy wrt.* Karnak temple was by far the most important at
Thebes and the greatest Theban festival processions—those of the
Opet festival and the Festival of the Valley (Murnane 1981; Graefe
1985)—emanated from Karnak and radiated out to other temples.
A governmental palace on the starboard, right hand side of these
processions, as they emerged from Karnak, would of course be
immediately north-west of that temple.

So far we have seen that throughout much of the Eighteenth
Dynasty, the main, governmental palace of Thebes was probably
always located immediately north-west of Karnak temple; and this
seems to remain true until the end of that dynasty. Amenhotep III,
we have seen, had a palace *n imy wrt* (i.e. at Karnak), which is
perhaps to be identified with a Theban palace of his named
"Nebmaatre (Amenhotep III) is the Shining Sun-Disc" (Redford's
translation). It is usually suggested that this palace was at Malqata
on the *west* bank (Hayes 1951, 178-179; Redford 1973, 87-88;
Stadelmann 1985b, 471). However, the Malqata palace is shown by
numerous *in situ* stamped bricks to have been called "The House
of Rejoicing" of Amenhotep III (Hayes 1951, 35-36, 177), but no
such bricks occurred there bearing the name "Nebmaatre is the
Shining Sun-Disc." The latter palace was clearly important;
members of its staff are known (Legrain 1903; Wolf 1924); and its
grandiose title suggests a governmental palace, for the king is
often identified with sun-god and sun disc in ceremonial court
hymns. Like the other governmental palaces, this one, I would
suggest (O'Connor 1980, 1175), was located just north-west of
Karnak, but farther west than earlier ones, because under
Amenhotep III Karnak temple itself was extended westward
(Golvin and Goyon 1987, 14). This suggestion is reinforced by
slight but significant archaeological evidence (Redford 1973, 87-

90) that Amenhotep's successor Akhenaten not only had a palace in this location, but that it bore a name—"(Akhenaten) Rejoices in the Horizon of the Sun-Disc," i.e. Akhenaten *is* the sun disc—very similar to the name of Amenhotep's palace.

Finally, even at the close of the Eighteenth dynasty, the governmental palace can still be plausibly located near Karnak, presumably still north-west of the temple. (Figure 7.4) This conclusion is based on a reading of pharaoh Horemheb's "Coronation Inscription" which differs from the more usual one. According to the interpretation current at the moment, the text describes Horemheb being escorted to Karnak temple at the time of the Opet Festival; he is received by Amun-Re, who takes him to Luxor temple for the coronation rites; then the god, and presumably the king, return to Karnak (Gardiner 1953, 21-28). However, an earlier text describing very similar events suggests that this interpretation be modified in a major way.

The earlier text describes the investiture with royal office of Hatshepsut (Lacau and Chevrier 1977, 92-96). The events described (ibid. 96-133) have been reconstructed as follows. The image of Amun-Re, carried out of Karnak temple, summons Hatshepsut from her nearby palace, takes her into Karnak temple and declares he is assigning the kingship to her. A procession, "out of doors" and witnessed by a crowd, follows and Amun-Re and Hatshepsut enter her palace. Here he formally enthrones her and she receives the obeisance of her courtiers. Amun-Re and Hatshepsut then leave the palace and re-enter Karnak temple (Gitton 1974, especially 65, figure 1; Lacau and Chevrier, op. cit.). This interpretation however, overlooks certain difficulties.

First, before being joined by Hatshepsut, Amun-Re embarks on his real boat, one floating in the harbor before the temple, and then sails by canal around to the west side of the palace (Lacau and Chevrier 103, note V; Gitton 1974, 66). This seems a meaningless act, if he is to shortly *disembark* and return, with Hatshepsut, to Karnak temple, from which he has only just emerged. Second, Hatshepsut joins Amun-Re via the west gate of her palace, facing onto the canal referred to above; this also seems unnecessary, for if the pair are to then go into Karnak temple, it would seem more convenient (and more dignified) if Hatshepsut had joined Amun-Re via the southern palace-gateway, which opened onto the processional way itself. Moreover, returning to Karnak via the west gate and the palace forces Amun-Re to re-enter his temple through side-entrances, a procedure which seems inappropriate for any Egyptian god.

These difficulties disappear however, if we suggest that Amun-Re embarks, and Hatshepsut leaves her palace via its "canal-gate," because both are preparing to sail south together to Luxor temple, which certainly existed at this time and was linked by canal to Karnak (Murnane 1981; Barguet 1979). This suggestion is reinforced by the fact that as soon as Amun-Re and Hatshepsut are together he takes her to the "Great Temple of *Maat* (Universal Order)." Until now, this has been thought to lie in Karnak temple (Gitton 1974, 68-69; Lacau and Chevrier 1977, 104 notes y and ac); but in fact the term is never applied explicitly to Karnak, whereas very similar names *are* applied specifically to Luxor temple, which later in the New Kingdom is called the "palace (*st*) of *Maat*" and "the august temple (*ḥwt*) of Wn-*Maat* (i.e. of "justification" or "true being, reality")" (cf. the citations in Bell 1985a, 254 and notes 5 and 6). It is therefore in *Luxor* temple that Amun-Re identifies Hatshepsut as future king after which they return, presumably by canal, to the Karnak palace and from thence go to Karnak temple.

These events involving Hatshepsut provide the basis for a reinterpretation of Horemheb's "Coronation Text." Horemheb arrives at Karnak, but is met by Amun-Re's image not inside the temple, as Gardiner inferred (1953, 24) but outside of it; this is suggested by the analogy with Hatshepsut, and because Amun-Re would emerge from Karnak temple anyway, in order to initiate the Opet Festival. Horemheb and Amun-Re proceed to Luxor temple (the event is not specifically described, but is implied by the Opet Festival setting) and there Horemheb's identity as pharaoh is presumably proclaimed. They then go together to a "royal palace" or *pr nswt*; this has been identified as Luxor temple itself (Gardiner 1953, 24-25; Bell 1985a, 273) but unlike other words for palace, such as *ʿḥ*, *pr nswt* in fact seems never applied to a temple (Gardiner 1953, 25). Therefore, the reference is to a palace, not a temple, probably the palace at Karnak, for in the *pr nswt* Horemheb undergoes essentially the same ceremonies as those held for Hatshepsut in *her* Karnak palace. Finally, just as Hatshepsut and Amun-Re leave the palace and enter Karnak, so do Horemheb and Amun-Re, thus bringing—as the text itself states—the Opet Festival to an end (compare Lacau and Chevrier 1977, 114-133 with Urk. IV, 2116.9 - 2119.9).

As to the location of the main or governmental palace in

Thebes in Ramesside times, we have no definite evidence; but there certainly was such a palace where proclamations and reports were issued and officials appointed and rewarded. In the absence of any evidence to the contrary, it is reasonable to assume this palace continued to be near Karnak, perhaps still immediately north-west of it. In this connection we should take note of an important, recent discussion by Van Dijk (1988) in which he argues that, as early as Thutmose III, "the more or less permanent residence" of the king was Memphis, "which city the king left for Thebes only on important religious occasions such as the celebration of the Opet Feast" (*ibid.* 38), a view advanced by other scholars also. Indeed, Memphis may have been a royal residence as early as the reign of Thutmose I (cf. Tutankhamun's decree, issued *from* the palace of Thutmose I at Memphis; *ibid.* 37). However, while Memphis may have become the preferred place of royal residence (at least until Ramses II moved to Pi-Ramesse) and more of a "national" capital (eventually replaced by such as Pi-Ramesse?) than Thebes, Thebes obviously continued to be the administrative capital of southern Egypt, and perhaps, to a substantial degree, oversaw Nubia as well. However limited royal visits to Thebes may have been throughout the New Kingdom, they must often or always have involved administrative as well as ritual activities, and required an administrative palace as much as any other kind.

Palace, Temple and City at Thebes

If the main or governmental palace of Thebes was always located near Karnak, then our understanding of the role of this and other palaces in the overall life of the city becomes more coherent. It seems that in any given reign more palaces other than the governmental were in use at Thebes, but their nature is hard to establish. Amenhotep III, for example, may have had a main palace at Karnak, and another at Malqata (O'Connor 1980). The latter was clearly residential in part and so large in scale it might have been the genuine, long-term "Wohnpalast" of the king while he was at Thebes; but it also includes large-scale ceremonial areas, as well as its own Amun temple, and was certainly the setting for some aspects of the *sed*-festival (Martin 1984; Kemp 1989: 213-217). However, this rite of royal renewal was performed rarely during a reign (although Amenhotep III did celebrate three close together in his last years of rule) and we cannot tell if the combination of sed-festival and (?) residential palace seen at Malqata was usual or not. Hatshepsut also had, in addition to the governmental palace at Karnak, one or more other palaces (the relevant list is incomplete; Lacau and Chevrier 1977, 76-78); but their functions are unknown. A similar pattern—of two or more contemporary Theban palaces—may reasonably be assumed for other rulers; possibly, as at Amarna (below) the residential palace was always some distance away from the governmental, but this cannot be proven.

Yet a third type of Theban palace was that attached to each royal funerary temple on the west bank from at least reign of Hatshepsut onwards (Stadelmann 1985a). Stadelmann's searching analysis has shown these palaces were not used as residence or even ceremonial palaces by the living king but were intended primarily, perhaps solely for the use of the deceased ruler (1973, especially 223-224, 235-241). Originally Stadelmann suggested that these funerary temple palaces were also used by the living ruler as a sacristy during festivals at the funerary temple, and that he even rewarded officials from it on special occasions (ibid., 227-228, 236, 241), but later he stressed even more strongly their cultic and funerary character, envisaging the throne-dais as occupied permanently by a royal statue and not intended for the use of a living ruler (Stadelmann 1979, 312 n. 68). From the viewpoint of the living pharaoh these palaces were functionless, merely simulcra or dummy palaces intended solely for deceased pharaohs.

Two aspects of the funerary temple palace need further comment. Stadelmann points out that originally it was small and schematized, and located next to the temple sanctuary (Hatshepsut); over time, it grew larger and more complex and "palatial" in plan, and was gradually moved towards the front of the temple, so as to have the necessary room. Eventually, the palace—always south of the temple axis—stabilized on the south side of the first court of the temple (Seti I onwards) (Stadelmann 1973). To explain the process, Stadelmann suggests the funerary temple palace began as a combination of temple sacristy (used by the king when performing rituals in the temple) and a "Window of Appearance" derived from the sanctuary of the sun-god's temple at Heliopolis. The concept of the latter as a heavenly palace caused the funerary temple palace to be increasingly modeled on the real "Wohnpalast" or residential palace of the king (Stadelmann 1973, 223-229, 236-242). However, one might suggest as an alternative theory that from the outset (Hatshepsut) the funerary temple palace was inspired by the governmental palace at Karnak, i.e. that just as each funerary temple was a modified version of the Amun-Re temple of Karnak, so each palace represented the governmental palace near Karnak. Since each funerary temple reversed Karnak's orientation (they face east, Karnak faces west), the location of the governmental palace moved from north-west of the temple to south-east. As time went on, this dummy governmental palace moved from a highly symbolic structure (Hatshepsut) to ones truly palatial in form; and provided the setting wherein the deceased king continued to exercise his role as ruler of the world.

Secondly, Stadelmann argues that "Windows of Appearance" were never found in true palaces, except aberrantly in the reign of Amenhotep IV/Akhenaten (1973, 224-227). However, Hatshepsut's funerary temple does have a "Window of Appearance" and, if from the beginning these palaces were modeled on the governmental palace, then that suggests the latter regularly had such a window, in any reign. Certainly, scenes depicting windows used for appointing and rewarding officials under post Amarna pharaohs suggest that post-Amarna governmental palaces had such windows.

What then may we reasonably speculate about the roles and the symbolism of palaces at Thebes? The data already discussed above indicate that the Karnak governmental palace was the primary focus for royal ceremonials and for bureaucratic life. Rulers appeared in state in its audience hall to make formal declarations of policy and the great ceremony of the annual reception of foreign tribute, requiring a large open space, may well have occurred in the area fronted on by both Karnak temple and Karnak palace. Officials were appointed, promoted and rewarded in this palace, the mixture of bureaucratic routine and awe inspiring ceremony being well evoked in the autobiography of the vizier Rekhmire. He described his bureaucratic colleagues (*snnw nb m ḫȝ*; van den Boorn 1988, 231) as being "outside" (*r rwty*: possibly in the "court" of the palace, referred to both under Thutmose I and Hatshepsut, and recalling the scenes in el Amarna tombs of officials assembled in the palace courtyard at such ceremonies) while he reaches the "doorway (*sbȝ*) of the palace portico" (*ʿrʿryt*: cf. Spencer 1984, 147-155) and then is permitted to follow the "secret path," i.e. the route leading into the audience-hall, access to which was clearly very restricted. Rekhmire receives his appointment and, on a second occasion, boasted of having seen the king (Thutmose III) in his true form as Re, lord of heaven, the solar disc showing itself i.e. referring to the king enthroned in glory in his hall (Urk. IV, 1072.16 - 1073.6, 1075.12-14). More routine administration also occurred in the palace (cf. "Duties of the Vizier," above) and the offices of the bureaucracy were surely located nearby.

Given these functions, the juxtaposition of Amun-Re's main temple and the king's principal palace is most significant, for it clearly reflects the complex relationship between these two entities in the New Kingdom. Amun-Re rules Egypt and the world through the king; but simultaneously the latter takes on the aspect of the god himself, both processes reinforcing and stabilizing the structure of New Kingdom government (cf. Grundlach and Mitarbeiter 1987; Assmann 1987). But beyond this, the governmental palace has a key role to play in the principal rituals of Thebes, those which most obviously bind Egypt and its ruler to the workings of the cosmos as a whole (on those, cf. generally Kemp, 1989, 201-213).

As I have suggested above, Karnak, the palace and Luxor form the structural triangle for key rituals and festivals, the recognition of royal status, the coronation itself and the annually celebrated Opet Festival. In each case, the ruler goes through a ritual process at Luxor that reveals, or rereveals him to be the possessor of the ka of kingship and transforms him into the embodiment of Amun-Re himself (Bell 1985a); and then, having undergone this as it were celestial, or otherworldly experience, the transformed ruler moves to the Karnak palace, where enthronement and other ceremonies make manifest his rulership of Egypt and the entire world. This done, Amun-Re and king enter Karnak temple, affirming or reaffirming the close ritual and other contacts that will bind the two together throughout the reign. The sequence of events involving the palace seems just as important as those in Luxor and Karnak temples; and periodically divine image and deified king appear from within an august structure—Luxor and the Karnak palace—amidst the jubilation of their entourage and the public as a whole. Thus the entire city is drawn in this awesome process, and becomes part of it.

Moreover, the rituals of Thebes achieved cosmological completeness by linking the worlds of gods and living men respectively, to the world of the dead . Again, the focus was as much political as religious, for the key figure was again the king, whose authority derived from the chain of his predecessors stretching back through time to the creation of the universe. Annually, the living ruler led the Festival of the Valley, co-celebrating it with his other persona as a deceased ruler already inhabiting its funerary temple. In its final, developed form the festival apparently involved the departure of Amun-Re's image from Karnak, accompanied by the pharaoh; an interlude at Luxor temple, presumably to evoke the divine aspects of the king, as possessor of the royal ka and living embodiment of Amun-Re on earth; a crossing to the west bank and the royal funerary temple where the rituals ensuring the full identification of the deceased king with Amun-Re were performed; and finally movement to the Hathor temple at Deir el Bahri, for this complex goddess—mistress of the dead, mother of the sun-god and the king, consort of Amun-Re and the king (Troy 1986: 53-72)—played a key role in these events. Then, the festival terminated and the chief participants retired to their respective venues (for the events, cf. Graefe 1985; Arnold 1978; Stadelmann 1978; some of the interpretations are my own). Throughout the ritual, just as the living flocked to witness and benefit from the miracles of the Opet Festival, and the Valley Festival itself, so were the dead imagined to pour from their tombs and gather in ghostly multitudes along the processional ways of the west bank, where their tombs lay. Thus the circle was closed, and the universe made ritually complete by the union of those upon whom its stability depended—Amun-Re as rising and setting sun and the king in both his living and deceased aspects.

Although their role is not clear, the Theban palaces necessarily played a part in the Valley Festival. The living king emerged from his Karnak palace to lead the ritual; the deceased king from his funerary palace to join it; in the funerary palace also perhaps a subsequent enthronement by Amun-Re was imagined, since the funerary palace seems to be, for the world of the dead, the counterpart of the Karnak governmental palace. And, since living king and the images of Amun-Re and deceased king were all parts of the procession, ultimately Amun-Re retired to his Karnak temple, the living king to his palace at Karnak, and Amun-Re as the deceased form of the sun-god and the deceased persona of pharaoh withdrew to, respectively, the funerary temple and its dummy palace.

3. The Palaces of Amarna: The Structure of the City

The relationship of its palaces to the over-all structure of the short-lived city of Akhetaten, founded by Amenhotep IV/Akhenaten (Redford 1984) at Amarna does not require the elaborate discussion necessary in the case of Thebes (Figure 7.5). Due to extensive if incomplete excavation the archaeology of much of the city has been planned (Kemp 1985a; and for a useful, detailed survey Hulin 1982). Moreover, Kemp has significantly advanced our understanding of several palaces in particular, and of the city's structure, its deliberately intended pattern of ceremonial and other life, in an important study of 1976; and published a significant interpretive overview (1989; 261 ff.). Yet much remains to be said about the palaces at Amarna; and the structure of the city can usefully be examined from a view point different from these taken so far.

Kemp properly emphasized the structural significance of the "Royal Road," a broad avenue ca. 30 meters wide running north-south through much of the ribbon-like city; and of royal progresses along this road from the "North City" to the "Central City," and back. However, seen from a broader perspective, it can be suggested that overall, the city of Amarna, in its broadest sense, falls into four zones, forming a pattern that seems intentional.

In the extreme north lies, with other structures, the "North Riverside Palace," convincingly identified by Kemp as the (largely unexcavated) residential palace complex. Fronted by a strong double wall with a towered or buttressed face and a monumental gateway, the complex probably included separate palaces for king, queen and queen-mother and occupied some 10 ha., being quite comparable to the southern, palatial segment—with three palaces and other buildings occupying about 8 ha.—of the Malqata palace complex of Amenhotep III (O'Connor 1980; Kemp 1989: 213-217). The "Royal Road" began at this complex, and ran south, through and under a monumental gateway (?) ("Great Ramp") marking the end of this zone; north of this line, in the eastern cliffs, were the tombs of the two queens' stewards.

The second zone might be termed the "sacred city," an area dedicated to the mystical relationship between Aten, the god, and its celestial (sun-disc) and terrestrial (the king) embodiments (cf. Assmann 1984a: 243 ff., especially 249-257; Allen 1989, esp. 92-94, 97-100); or, in another interpretation, between the god and the king as "a living divine ka" of the god (Silverman, this volume). This zone runs from the gateway just mentioned to another, equally impressive one spanning the "Royal Road" at the southern end of the "Central City." Within this zone we find the "North Palace," the "North Suburb" (possibly inhabited by the lower personnel serving both residential palace and the temple complex in the "Central City"), the "Great Aten Temple" with enormous bakeries, kitchens and magazines on its south, and much of the "Great Palace;" also belonging to this zone, in the eastern cliffs, are the tombs of the royal family and of the chief ritualists and servitors of Aten and the king, namely Merya and Panehesy, Pentu and Ahmose, whose responsibilities were exercised within the "sacred city."

The transition to the third zone, from the sacred to the mundane, was marked not only by the gateway (and an abrupt shift in the line of the "Royal Road") but more generally by the southern segment of the "Great Palace," by the "King's House" palace and by an extensive zone of bureaucratic offices and police and military installations. The northern edges of all three entities forms an almost continuous line, marking the southern end of the "sacred city." Beyond these, we are in the "secular city'," which includes the "Smaller Aten Temple"—which, unlike the "Great Temple," is surrounded by a pseudo-fortified wall (on such walls, cf. Kemp 1972, 653) to indicate it is in a mundane, potentially polluting setting—the "estates" where the foodstuffs, livestock and other impedimentia of the two temples were stored (cf. Kemp 1985b, ch. 5), and the "South Suburb/Main City" where the chief officials, soldiers and priests of the city, state and empire lived. Also falling within this zone but further east were the tombs of these same officials and the village(s) occupied by the artisans who cut and decorated the tombs, and by the serfs who met their needs.

The last zone, occupying the southern segment of the plain, was a recreational one, used by the royal family and their entourage and modeled perhaps, to some extent, on features of the Amenhotep III palace complex, and its environs, at Malqata. This fourth zone included two "Maru Atens'," garden-like settings including both cultic and palatial type structures and associated with an artificial lake, very substantial but much smaller than its probable prototype, the vast harbor of Malqata (Kemp and O'Connor 1974). Further east, out in the desert, a large if enigmatic structure at Kom el Nana appears to be an isolated, but important temple complex (Kemp 1989: 285). This intentional zoning needs also to be considered in relationship to the list of the main structures intended for Amarna given on some of the boundary stelae of the city (Urk. IV, 1973.11 - 1975. 5; Helck 1961, 341-342; Davies 1908a, 30; Murnane and Van Siclen 1993; O'Connor 1987/88). The sequence, which is continuous and without serious gaps, begins with the *Pr itn* (the "Great Temple") and the *ḥwt itn* (the "Small Temple," and also the "King's House" palace on its north: Fairman 1951, 191). Then comes a "Chapel of Re-Horakhty (*ḥwt-rᶜ ḥrȝḫty*)" built probably for the queen (her name is erased), the only one mentioned in the list of the several actually built for royal women at Amarna (Spencer 1984, 119-125). Its location is uncertain, but for reasons which cannot be gone into here, I would tentatively suggest it lay in the "North Palace," just north of its first court (cf. plan Smith 1981, 317); and that further the North Palace itself—with its "Maru"-like characteristics (Badawy 1962, 92)—is actually the "Northern Maru of the Disc ... in Akhetaten" (Redford 1973, 81 and note 10). Kemp has identified the North Palace as a "harem palace," perhaps the "main residence" of Akhenaten's eldest daughter, Meritaten (1989: 279); but it seems to me that the palace lacks the necessary residential features, and is more ceremonial in type; its east-west orientation is also unusual for a palace. The "chapel of Re-Horakhty" is followed by two similarly named, yet significantly differently located structures; one is a *Pr hᶜy* or "House of Re-joicing for the Aten," the other a "House of Rejoicing in Akhetaten for the Aten" (Murnane and van Siclen, 1993, 40). The "Great Palace" is securely identified as the *Pr hᶜy* (Fairman 1951, 139), and it clearly falls into two segments, respectively north and south of a great court. The north segment lies within the "sacred city" and is, I would suggest, the *Pr hᶜy* "of the Aten;" the latter is in, or abuts the "secular city," and is the *Pr hᶜy* specified to be "in Akhetaten." After a few generalized remarks perhaps intended to cover the city as a whole, the list moves to the "apartments" of the king and queen respectively, perhaps their palaces in the "North City," to the tombs which belonged to the "sacred city" (the royal tombs, that of the Mnevis bull, and the ritualists' tombs) and finally, to the those of the "secular city," the southern tombs of the officials.

The list then has a complex structure, ranking buildings in

hierarchical importance and therefore moving from zone to zone, but also apparently using east and west as ordering principles. The actual structure would seem to be as follows:

Zone 1 Royal Residential City	Zone 2 The Sacred City	Zone 3 The Secular City
East of the Royal Road	1. The Great Temple	
		2. The Small Temple (and administrative palace)
	3. Chapel of Re-Horakhty (in the North Palace)	
West of the Royal Road	4. The Aton's House of Rejoicing	
		5. The Aten's House of Rejoicing in Akhetaten
	6. Royal Residential Palaces	
East of the City	7. Royal Tombs Mnevis Tomb Ritualists' Tombs	
		8. Officials' Tombs

Palace and City at Amarna

With the various structural aspects of Amarna in mind we can turn to its palaces, their functions and their possible relationships to the palaces of Thebes and *their* urban setting. The "secular city" appears to be modeled closely on eastern Thebes itself; more specifically, the "Small Temple" and its "King's House" palace on the north correspond to Karnak temple and its adjacent governmental palace. Both in formal and functional terms the correspondences are close.

The architectonic form of the "Small Temple" is severely modified to meet the needs of the new cult, but is similar in its orientation, processional lay-out, proportions and size to Karnak temple; it occupied 1.38 ha, Karnak temple under Amenhotep III (excluding the Thutmose III building on its east) between 1.30 and 1.50 ha. The "Small Temple" may have functioned as a royal funerary temple (Redford 1984, 146), but was also akin in important ways to Karnak temple in that it seems to provide the cultic focus for the "secular city." The ritual celebrated here by Akhenaten linked the city to the cosmos, just as Thebes was so linked primarily through Karnak, and it was probably before the "Small Temple" that officials made a thanks-offering after an appointment or reward ceremony in the nearby "King's House" palace (Davies 1908b, plate XX, definitely the "Small Temple;" Davies 1906a, plate XVIII). Theban officials did the same in front of Karnak (cf. Davies and Gardiner 1926, 13-15 and pls. IX, XI).

The "King's House" palace approximates to the Karnak governmental palace, lying like the latter north of the temple, although not as far to the north-west (although it *is* north-west of the "Small Temple" proper). Like the Karnak palace (cf. above and Lacau and Chevrier 1977, 98 line 11), the Amarna palace has a large, columned audience-hall and a broad courtyard. Functionally, both palaces were used for appointing and rewarding officials with great ceremony (Kemp 1976; Arnold 1977b), and since the bureaucratic zone was immediately adjacent, routine governmental activity involving the king probably occurred in the "King's House," as was also the case with the Karnak palace. How similar in plan the two palaces were is unknown; we do not know if the "officials' city" stretched south of Karnak as it did with the "Small Temple."

The "secular city" at Amarna was modeled on Thebes, but what was the model for the "sacred city"? The dominant features are the two cultic structures forming the "Great Temple" within an enclosed area of 22 ha.; and—at right angles to the east-west axis of the "Great Temple" and immediately south-west of it—the "Great Palace," originally occupying some 10 ha. (for recent descriptions, Kemp 1989: 279-283). The functions and nature of the "Great Palace" have been much debated (Uphill 1970; Assmann 1972; see now also Kemp 1989: 279-281). I would suggest that while the "Great Palace" *did* incorporate true palaces in its eastern and western wings (O'Connor 1993); the main section of it was cultic, and formed in effect a giant corridor, for it has "exits" on its south, and presumably exits also on its unexcavated north. If the "Great Palace" indeed consists of northern and southern "Houses of Rejoicing," it seems possible that disc and king co-celebrated *sed*-festivals within it (Assmann 1972, 150-151) and that on the north the king emerged into the "sacred city," onto the processional way running to the "Great Temple," as coequal with the disc; but that on the south, he passed through a columned, presumably roofed hall to emerge onto the processional way leading to the "Small Aten" Temple and appeared to the "secular city" as the embodiment of the Aten on earth, or as a "living divine ka" of the Aten (cf. above) separate from the disc (note the "Great Pillared Hall" blocking the southern exits is a later addition). The prototype for the "Great Palace" surely lies east of Karnak, where Akhenaten built a court of 2.6 ha. with colossi running around its edges which is very similar to the colossi flanked "Great Palace" court of 2.9 ha.

The Karnak structure was dominated by relief scenes of the *sed*-festival, further reinforcing its' relationships to the "Great Palace" (on the Karnak structure, Redford 1984, chs. 5 and 7). Whether there was also a "Great Temple" adjacent to the Karnak structure is unknown and the "Great Temple" may be an innovation restricted to Amarna, although it may equally possibly have had a prototype at Thebes (O'Connor 1989a: 85); the "Great Temple" provided the "sacred city" with a temple appropriate to its status.

It is within this framework that we must place the king's periodic progresses documented episodically by scenes in the Amarna tombs; he rode forth from his residential palace, entered the "sacred city," performed rituals at the "Great Temple," from thence moved into the "secular city," visited the "Small Temple," inspected the estates of both, and finally made his way to the "King's House" palace. Here he rested, ate and attended to the business and ceremonies of government. Whether the "Great Palace" was regularly used as the means of entering the "secular city," or was used on special festival occasions, we do not know. Finally, the king and his entourage return, late in the day, to the residential palace in the north. The whole sequence can reasonably be seen in terms of propaganda, and a need for public acclaim (Kemp 1989: 279), but it can be argued that the sequence, and the settings—palaces, temples and the city—in which it occurs, is evidently rich in cosmological significance, which can only be touched on here. The fundamental point is the identification between king and disc as the two manifestations of a single divine power. The disc rises from his horizon in the east, the king rides in his electrum chariot, shining like the sun, from his northern palace and the inhabitants of the "sacred city" adore them both, for the universe is being revitalized and renewed by their dual appearance. The two meet at the "Central City," thus bringing the two axes—east-west, north-south—of the universe together, and celebrate their essential unity. Then they separate; the disc sails on westward through the sky, overseeing the celestial realm; the king proceeds southward into the "secular city" to carry out the divinely-ordained governance of the terrestrial realm. In effect, he descends from heaven, the sacred city, to earth, the secular city. Governance concluded, the king departs and disappears into his remote northern residence as the disc sinks into the western horizon; darkness and sleep fill the cosmos, while the "sacred city" lies enshadowed and empty; both await the return of their lords and creators (cf. O'Connor 1989a: 86).

4. The Palace as Cosmos

We have seen above that it can be reasonably argued that temples, palaces and city at Thebes and Amarna, and presumably at the other royal cities, interrelate with each other so as to establish an appropriate setting for ritual, ceremony and governance; and simultaneously create a replica of the cosmos and its workings as envisaged by the Egyptians, thus imparting effectiveness and authority to the ritual, ceremonial and governing activities involved. In these circumstances, it is not surprising to find that— however varied their specific functions might have been—New Kingdom palaces were shaped so as embody the Egyptian version of the cosmos, more specifically those aspects of the cosmos that were directly linked to the nature and activities of the Egyptian king. In this shaping, the primary influence upon the palace was the temple, the cosmological significance of the architecture and pictorial and textual embellishments of which is well understood (Assmann 1984a, 35-63; Baines 1976).

I have explored this theme in detail elsewhere (O'Connor 1993), so here a brief summary of the salient points will serve to close this essay. The key datum is the relatively well preserved palace of Merneptah at Memphis, (Figures 7.6 and 7.7) although evidence from other palaces, especially those of Amarna and Thebes, helps to supplement and enrich our understanding of the Merneptah information. Kuhlmann (1977) has already demonstrated that the royal throne, the baldachin over it and the pedestal supporting it are rich in symbolism, forming in effect a miniature cosmos; but these same fundamental concepts influence the whole palace, in ways which are more complex and varied than is possible with the throne itself, and its associated features.

Briefly, New Kingdom palaces had an architectural form strongly and deliberately recalling that of the temple, with an elevated façade (akin to a temple pylon), a court with surrounding colonnade, and large scale, high roofed columned vestibules and throne rooms which can be equated with hypostyle hall and sanctuary (containing the divine image) in the temple. The implication is clear: the king enthroned in state within his palace is to be identified with the divine image of a temple; and the royal departures from and returns to the palace—laid out in processional form like the temple—are identical to the emergences and returns of a divine image during a public festival. In such contexts, the ka of kingship animating the pharaoh is manifest, and he is virtually a god on earth.

But temple form and decoration also have direct cosmological significance, and so do those of the palace. Temple pylon and elevated palace façade represent the horizon from which the sun-god rises and into which he sets, from which the king emerges and into which he returns; in both cases the renewal, and then the temporary cessation of the cosmos is represented. Around the temple scenes of royal victory over foreigners mark the contact line, in cosmological terms, between the ideal universe, including Egypt, and the chaotic exterior world, occupied by rebellious foreigners—as Assmann notes, Egyptian belief "implies that there can be only one state in space and time" (1989, 59) and foreign states by definition are "chaotic;" simultaneously the scenes magically protect the temple from pollution and intrusion by chaotic supernatural forces. On the outer and inner brick walls of palaces similar scenes were probably painted, and are certainly reiterated on many of the stone columns and door jambs of the palace.

Finally, and most powerfully, the inner halls of the palace evoke, like those of the temple, the sacred and orderly universe itself. Temple floor and palace floor rise gradually in height, to indicate that sanctuary and throne respectively are to be equated with the primeval mound upon which the creator god initiated the process that brought the orderly universe into being. Giant columns in

plant form fill temple and palace halls, the upward thrusting
vegetation of creation that simultaneously supports the sky of the
universe, the temple and palace ceilings, both decorated with
celestial iconography. But while temple floors were plain, those of
the palace—stretching before the throne—were richly painted,
with scenes of pools teeming with fish, and fringed with vegetation
through which animals gambol and from which birds fly upward;
these are literally illustrations of a principal theme of hymns to the
sun-god, the bursting into life and adoration of the world as the
rays of the rising sun illuminate and energize it. Again, the
meaning is clear; the king on his throne is the sun-god in his horizon, and both are bringing the world to life. In the words of royal
eulogies, the palace is indeed the Horizon of Re and beloved of
Maat, the personification of universal order.

Conclusions

The preceding discussion of the royal palace in New Kingdom
Egypt, while tentative in many ways, is particularly relevant to some
of the recent discussions about the role of kingship as an
institution in the New Kingdom context. In particular Assmann
has emphasized that in the Egyptian world view of the Late Bronze
Age we have "the complete homology of the cosmic and the
political sphere." In order to avoid a descent into universal chaos,
the cosmos needs to be "constantly ruled," and the solar cycle—
the endlessly repeated departure, and revitalizing return of the
sun—is "an institution of cosmic government," and is equated with
"the political institution of pharaonic kingship" (Assmann 1989:
63-65). The state, in turn, is "the exact imitation of this cosmic
government on earth." The king, installed on earth by the sun-
god, and the latter's son, is charged with providing cult action and
recitation to accompany the cosmic process (and thus participate
in maintaining it) and with providing men with justice, and the
gods with their cults and endowments—these are the chief aims of
royal governance in Egypt (ibid., 57-66).

As the preceding discussion indicates, the Egyptians, at their
royal cities, literally enacted out in the ceremonies, and indeed in
much of the "business" of both temple and palace (which often
interacted with each other) this dominant concept of the "complete homology" of cosmic rule and earthly rule, of solar cycle and

royal cycle; and the shape of this reenactment was provided in large part by the locations; forms and embellishments; and interrelationships, of both palace and temple (although the city as a whole also had a role to play; cf. above and O'Connor 1989a).

The Egyptians' view of the relationship between king and sun-god; and between Egypt and the cosmos changed in important ways through the New Kingdom. Under Akhenaten, Assmann argues, both the cosmic and the sociopolitical order are "depoliticized," for the sun's role is now not to "rule" the cosmos, but only to keep it "alive," while the kings role is to "share" the "divine activity of creative vivification," mediating it to mankind (Assmann 1989: 66-68). Allen, expanding on Assmann's insights, points out that under Akhenaten the new, exclusive god, or "divine principle," is a comparatively abstract entity, in fact the light which animates, creates, sustains and determines the life cycle of all that is in the cosmos. This life-giving power is made effective in the world by being transmitted through the king, and the king becomes the "only image of the god" replacing the traditional ima-ges of the gods "as the medium for human contacts with the divine" (Allen 1989; and Assmann 1984a: 249 ff.). The visualization of Akhenaten as the "divine living ka" of the Aten (see Silverman, this volume), represents an important alternative concept, but one leading to the same result in the political realm.

However, despite the "depoliticization" of the cosmic and socio-political orders these theological, even philosophical (Allen 1989), developments imply, royal life necessarily remained rooted in political reality. The cognitive changes might have been them-selves due to a politically charged concern for the stability of the institution of kingship, to an anxiety that the great state-god Amun himself was eroding this institution with which he seemed so inextricably linked. Amun, as the speaking god, the divine will that can intervene in history, the god whom an individual person can directly experience and to whom an individual can directly devote himself, was taking on the traditional roles of pharaoh, as unique mediator between the gods and men, and as dispenser of justice to men (paraphrased from Assmann 1984a: 253-254). By functionally replacing Amun, by ritually becoming his equivalent, Akhenaten sought to stem this development, and found in his new theology or philosophy the rationale for this, in part, politically motivated policy (cf. also Allen 1989: 98-99 and with a different perspective, Silverman, this volume).

Moreover, Akhenaten also had to run a large state, and an

extensive empire, and on the whole seems to have done so effectively; the machinery of governance continued to be as much a
part of the life of the royal city as the rituals of the temples, and
the ritual-like ceremonies of, and emanating from, the palace.

The discussions summarized above provide a useful framework
of reference for attempts to understand the purposes of the city of
Akhetaten, the functioning of which (in terms of its temples and
palaces) has been described above. Thus, if we assume that the
god of the Amarna age is "other than the [sun]-disc" (Allen 1989:
94), which serves as its celestial "image," while the pharaoh is,
quite literally and continuously, the god's image on earth (ibid.,
99) or its "living divine ka" (Silverman, this volume), we can see
that the processional arrival of both disc and pharaoh in the city is
designed to graphically enact this dictum, and make it literally part
of the life of the city (O'Connor 1989a). It has also been noted
that Akhenaten's ceremonial (at the same time politically potent,
and at times directly administrative) activities in the city seem to be
modeled upon, and in effect replace in actuality and in meaning,
the processional activities of Amun of Thebes (Assmann 1984a:
253-257). This observation too finds material expression in the
city, in that what I have called the "secular city" seems modeled in
its essentials upon the plan of Thebes under Amun, but it is now a
city in which Amun has been replaced by the king, for the "secular
city" is precisely that zone of the city in which Akhenaten manifests
himself to men as dispenser of justice and care, on a god-like level,
and even of life itself. The "sacred city," to which the "secular city"
is appended, is a unique creation of the Amarna period (anti-
cipated at Thebes itself in Akhenaten's early years) where disc and
pharaoh interact ritually as they perform the cosmological/
terrestrial roles required of them by the unique god or divine
principle of which they are the embodiments or images.

A final observation about Akhetaten is merited. It has been
observed that religious life at Akhetaten was focused on a triad of
disc, pharaoh and queen (Assmann 1984a: 251-252)—perhaps to
be taken as the three images representing the unique god—and
that the triad can be equated with that of Atum, Shu, and Tefnut
(*ibid*: 252; on the rich range of meanings associated with Shu and
Tefnut, see Allen 1988: 14-27). Private cults dedicated to this triad
were common in the city (Assmann 1984a: 252), but perhaps its
existence was evident on a larger scale. It is noteworthy that the
"sacred city," and the transition to the "secular city," include two

large temples (the great and the small Aten temples) and a palatial-like structure that is nevertheless oriented as if it was a temple (the North Palace). These three structures are linked to the sacred landscape of the city: the North Palace lines up approximately with a large stela (V) cut in the eastern cliffs, and the Great Temple with Stela U, also set in the cliffs, and the Small Temple with the notch marking the wadi with the royal tomb, a notch that may have had peculiar significance to the city from a cosmological point of view (Aldred 1976). The North Palace is associated with the office of queen; it was ultimately dedicated to Meritaten, Akhenaten's oldest daughter who became, in some sense, his consort (Redford 1984: 187-188; Troy 1986: 108, 113). Perhaps it was originally linked to Nefertiti, although there is no proof for this. The great temple is clearly focused on the divine principle, or light, and here (and only here ?) Akhenaten performed the cult. The Small Temple is a "compressed version" of the greater temple (Kemp 1989: 283); it perhaps includes the site at which the cult was first performed to inaugurate the site, prior to the building of the city (Wells 1987: 318) and, more importantly, has a close association with Akhenaten himself, being identified as in some sense his "mortuary temple" (cf. above). One might suggest that the god of the Small Temple was in fact Akhenaten himself, although its "image" was somehow associated with the rising sun, rather than an actual royal statue, for which no emplacement appears to have existed. Given all the circumstances outlined, the three buildings may represent the triad of queen—god or disc—king, an architectonic version of the often repeated triadic iconography on stelae and other objects; the three temples lead the eye to the mysterious horizon or *akhet*, where ultimately each of the three manifestations of the divine principle has its origin, although for the terrestrial embodiment of the god the remote palace functions as the equivalent of the *akhet*.

Akhenaten failed to stem the growth of what Assmann has called a "theology of volition" (Assmann 1989b: 68), which is characterized by the "pious man who attunes and subordinates himself to the will of god," as the functional equivalent of "the poor and weak," of whom god is the protector (ibid., 72-73). In the realm of political ideology, these concepts meant the god has "absolute sovereignty" and the basis of royal legitimization changes; pharaoh, and his people, seek visible signs that the god is directly intervening on his behalf, while pharaoh, like his subjects, "has recourse to the virtues of piety" so as to merit divine support (ibid., 75-80). However, while this change in "inner attitude" on the part of the kings may have been real, government in Ramesside Egypt was both a practical necessity, and a ceremonial entity that continued to draw much of its inspiration from the models of the earlier New Kingdom. Palaces, in their forms and functions, appear to display great continuities throughout the New Kingdom (cf. above); and the point I should like to emphasize in conclusion is that they are always important links, amongst others, between Egyptians and their cosmos, despite changing perceptions of the latter, and of Egypt's place within it.

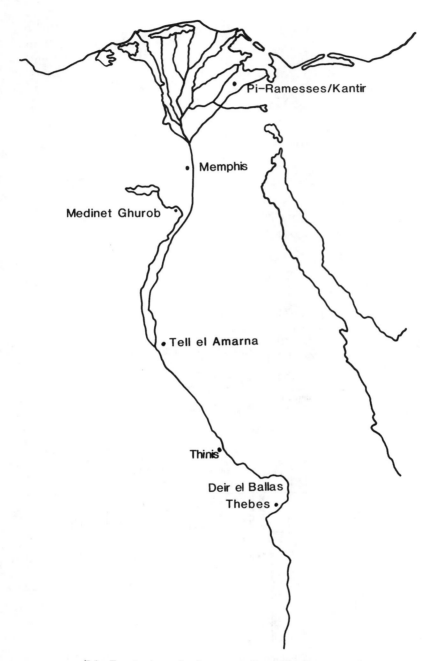

7.1. Egypt: sites of palaces mentioned in the text.

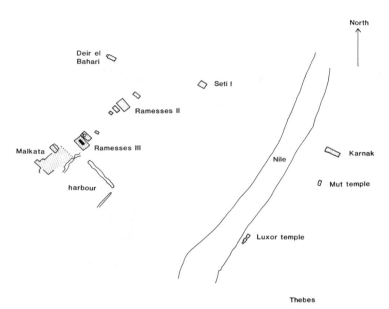

7.2. New Kingdom Thebes.

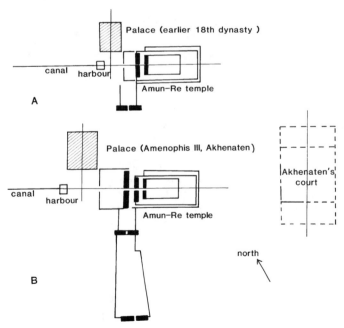

7.3. The Karnak Palace: A: in the earlier 18th Dynasty; B: Under
Amenhotep III and Akhenaten.

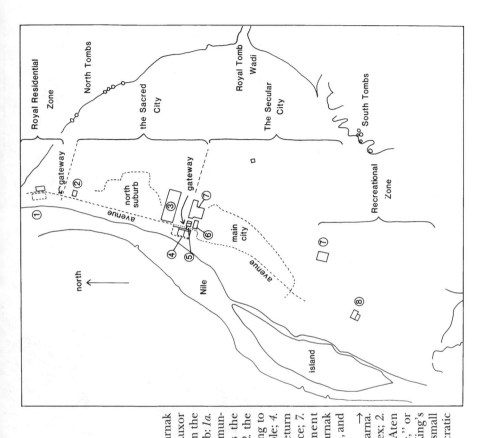

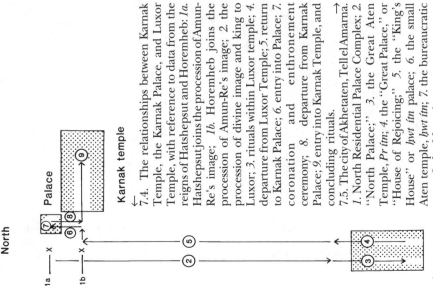

7.4. The relationships between Karnak Temple, the Karnak Palace, and Luxor Temple, with reference to data from the reigns of Hatshepsut and Horemheb: *1a.* Hatshepsut joins the procession of Amun-Re's image; *1b.* Horemheb joins the procession of Amun-Re's image; *2.* the procession of divine image and king to Luxor; *3.* rituals within Luxor temple; *4.* departure from Luxor Temple; *5.* return to Karnak Palace; *6.* entry into Palace; *7.* coronation and enthronement ceremony; *8.* departure from Karnak Palace; *9.* entry into Karnak Temple, and concluding rituals.

7.5. The city of Akhetaten, Tell el Amarna. *1.* North Residential Palace Complex; *2.* "North Palace;" *3.* the Great Aten Temple, *Pr ítn; 4.* the "Great Palace," or "House of Rejoicing;" *5.* the "King's House" or *ḥwt ítn* palace; *6.* the small Aten temple, *ḥwt ítn; 7.* the bureaucratic zone; *8.* the Maru Aten.

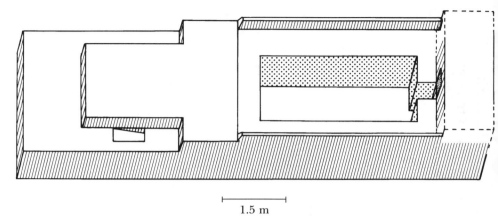

1.5 m

7.6. Schematic Restoration of the Palace of Merneptah, Memphis.

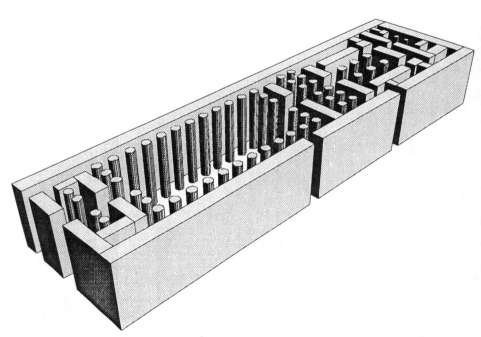

7.7. Three-dimensional elevation of lower segments of the palace of Merneptah. From left to right: antechamber, columned court, columned hall, and columned throne room. Illustration drawn by Kellee Barnard based on Clarence Fischer's plan.

BIBLIOGRAPHY

Adams, Barbara
  1974. *Ancient Hierakonpolis* and *Ancient Hierakonpolis: Supplement.* Warminster: Aris & Phillips.

Adams, Barbara, and Renée F. Friedman eds.
  1992. *The Followers of Horus: Studies dedicated to Michael Allen Hoffman.* Egyptian Studies Association Publication no. 2. Oxbow Monograph 20. Oxford: Oxbow Books.

Albright, W. F.
  1937. "The Egyptian Correspondence of Abi-milki, Prince of Tyre," *JEA* 23: 190-203.

Aldred, Cyril
  1971. "Some Royal Portraits of the Middle Kingdom in Ancient Egypt," *MMJ* 3: 27-50.
  1973. *Akhenaten and Nefertiti.* London: Thames and Hudson.
  1976. "The Horizon of the Aten," *JEA* 62: 184.
  1988. *Akhenaten, King of Egypt.* London and New York: Thames and Hudson.

Allam, Shafik
  1963. *Beiträge zum Hathorkult (bis zum Ende des Mittleren Reiches).* MÄS, vol. 4. Berlin: Bruno Hessling.

Allen, James
  1988. *Genesis in Egypt. The Philosophy of Ancient Egyptian Creation Accounts.* Yale Egyptological Studies 2. New Haven: Yale Egyptological Seminar.
  1989. "The Natural Philosophy of Akhenaton," *Religion and Philosophy in Ancient Egypt.* W. K. Simpson ed. Yale Egyptological Studies 3. New Haven: Yale Egyptological Seminar, pp. 89-101.
  1992. "Rē꜂wer's Incident," in *Studies in Philology, Religion, and Society in Honor of J. Gwyn Griffiths.* Alan Lloyd ed. Occasional Publications 8. London: EES, pp. 14-20.

Allen, T. George
  1974. *The Book of the Dead or Going Forth by Day: Ideas of the Ancient Egyptians Concerning the Hereafter as Expressed in Their Own Terms.* SAOC, vol. 37. Chicago: University of Chicago Press.

Altenmüller, Hartwig
  1971-72. "Die Bedeutung der 'Gotteshalle des Anubis' in Begrabnisritual," *JEOL* 22: 307-317.
  1972. *Die Texte zum Begräbnisritual in den Pyramiden das Alten Reiches.* Äg Ab 24, Wiesbaden: Otto Harrassowitz.
  1974. "Bemerkungen zum Hirtenlied des Alten Reiches," *CdE* 48, no. 96: 211-31.
  1980a. "Jagd," *LÄ* 3: cols. 221-24.
  1980b. "Jagdritual," *LÄ* 3: cols. 231-3.

Arnold, Dieter
    1982. "Per-nu," *LÄ* 4: cols. 932-33.
    1977a. "Rituale und pyramidentempel," *MDAIK* 33: 101-4.
    1977b. "Erscheinungsfenster," *LÄ* 2: col. 14.
    1978. "Vom Pyramidenbezirk zum 'Haus fur Millionen Jahre'," *MDAIK* 34: 1-8.

Anthes, Rudolph
    1928. *Die Felseninschriften von Hatnub.* Leipzig: J. C. Hinrich'sche.

Asselberghs, Henri
    1961. *Chaos en Beheersing: documenten uit het aeneolitisch Egypte.* Documenta et Monumenta Orientis Antiqui, vol. 8. Leiden: E. J. Brill.

Assmann, Jan
    1970. *Der König als Sonnenpriester: ein kosmographischer Begleittext zur liturgischen Sonnenhymnik.* ADAIK, vol. 7. Glückstadt: J. J. Augustin.
    1972. "Palast oder Tempel? Überlegungen zur Architektur und Topographie von Amarna," *JNES* 31: 143-155.
    1975. *Ägyptische Hymnen und Gebete.* Zurich: Artemis Verlag.
    1976. "Das Bild des Vaters im Alten Ägypten," in *Das Vaterbild in Mythos und Geschichte.* H. Tellenbach ed. Stuttgart: W. Kohlhammer, pp. 12-49.
    1977. "Die Verborgenheit des Mythos in Ägypten," *GM* 25: 7-43.
    1979. "Weisheit, Loyalismus und Frommigkeit," in *Studien zu altägyptischen Lebenslehren.* Eric Hornung and Othmar Keel eds. OBO, vol. 28. Göttingen: Vandenhoeck and Ruprecht, pp. 11-72.
    1980a. "Die 'loyalistische Lehre' Echnatons," *SAK* 8: 1-32.
    1980b. "Primat und Transzendenz: Struktur und Genese der Ägyptischen Vorstellung eines 'Höchsten Wesens'," in *Aspekte der spätägyptischen Religion.* Wolfhart Westendorf ed. GOF 4, vol. 9. Wiesbaden: Otto Harrassowitz, pp. 7-42.
    1982. "Die Zeugung des Sohnes: Bild, Spiel, Erzählung und das Problem des Ägyptischen Mythos," in Jan Assmann et al., *Funktion und Leistungen des Mythos: drei altorientalische Beispiele,* OBO, vol. 48. Göttingen: Vandenhoeck and Ruprecht, pp. 13-61.
    1983a. *Re und Amun: die Krise des polytheistischen Weltbilds im Ägypten der 18.-20. Dynastie.* OBO, vol. 51. Göttingen: Vandenhoeck and Ruprecht.
    1983b. "Krieg und Frieden im alten Ägypten: Ramses II. und die Schlacht bei Kadesch," *Mannheimer Forum* 1983-1984: 130-231.
    1983c. Sonnenhymnen in thebanischen Gräbern. Theben, vol. 1. Mainz: Philipp von Zabern.
    1984a. *Ägypten-Theologie und Frömmigkeit einer frühen Hochkultur.* Stuttgart etc.: W. Kohlhammer.
    1984b. "Politik zwischen Ritual und Dogma. Spielräume politischen Handelns im pharaonischen Ägypten," *Saeculum* 35: 97-114.
    1984c. "Vergeltung und Erinnerung," in *Studien zu Sprache und Religion Ägyptens zu Ehren von Wolfhart Westendorf,* [Friedrich Junge (ed.)]. vol. 2. Göttingen: no publ., pp. 687-701.
    1987. "Die Zeit Hatschepsuts und Thutmosis III in religionsgeschichtlicher Sicht," in: *Ägyptens Aufsteig zur Weltmacht.* Roemeur-und Pelizaues Museum, Hildesheim und Mainz: Verlag Philip von Zabern, pp. 47-55.
    1989. "State and Religion in the New Kingdom," in J. P. Allen et al., *Religion and Philosophy in Ancient Egypt.* Yale Egyptological Studies 3. New Haven: Yale Egyptological Seminar, pp. 55-88.
    1990. *Ma'at: Gerechtigkeit und Unsterblichkeit im Alten Ägypten.* Munich: C. H. Beck.

Atzler, Michael
  1974. "Einige Erwägungen zum *sr*," *Oriens* 23-24: 406-34.
  1981. *Untersuchungen zur Herausbildung von Herrschaftsformen in Ägypten.* HÄB, vol. 16. Hildesheim: Gerstenberg Verlag.

Badawy, Alexander
  1962. "The symbolism of the temples at Amarna," *ZÄS* 87: 79-95.

Baer, Klaus
  1960. *Rank and Title in the Old Kingdom: The Structure of the Egyptian Administration in the Fifth and Sixth Dynasties.* Chicago: University of Chicago Press.

Baillet, Jules.
  1912-13. *Le régime pharonique dans ses rapports avec l'évolution de la morale un Égypte.* Blois: E. Riviere.

Baines, John
  1974. "The Inundation Stela of Sebekhotpe VIII," *AcOr* 36: 39-54.
  1976. "Temple Symbolism," *Royal Anthropological Institute Newsletter* 15: 10-15.
  1983. "'Greatest god' or Category of Gods?," *GM* 67: 13-28.
  1985a. *Fecundity Figures: Egyptian Personification and the Iconology of a Genre.* Warminster, England: Aris & Phillips; Chicago: Bolchazy Carducci.
  1985b. "Egyptian Twins," *Orientalia* 54: 461-82.
  1986. "The Stela of Emhab: Innovation, Tradition, Hierarchy," *JEA* 72: 41-53.
  1987a. "Practical Religion and Piety," *JEA* 73: 79-98.
  1987b. "The Stela of Khusobek: Private and Royal Military narrative and Values," in *Form und Mass. Festschrift fur Gerhard Fecht.* Jürgen Osing and Günter Dreyer (eds.). ÄAT, vol. 12. Wiesbaden: Otto Harrassowitz, pp. 41-61.
  1987c. J. Baines, rev. of Redford *Akhenaten,* in *AHR* October 1987: 932.
  1988. "Literacy, Social Organization and the Archaeological Record: the Case of Early Egypt," in *State and Society: The Emergence and Development of Social Hierarchy and Political Centralization.* Barbara Bender et al. eds. London: Unwin Hyman, pp. 192-214.
  1989a. "Ancient Egyptian Concepts and Uses of the Past: 3rd to 2nd Millennium BC Evidence," in *Who Needs the Past? Indigenous Values and Archaeology,* Robert Layton ed. London: Allen and Unwin, pp. 131-49.
  1989b. "Communication and Display: The Integration of Early Egyptian Art and Writing," *Antiquity* 63: 47-82.
  1990a. "Trône et dieu: aspects du symbolisme royal et divin des temps archaïques," *BSFE* 118: 5-37.
  1990b. "Restricted Knowledge, Hierarchy, and Decorum: Modern Perceptions and Ancient Institutions," *JARCE* 27: 1-23.
  1991a. "On the symbolic context of the principal hieroglyph for 'god'," in *Religion und Philosophie im Alten Ägypten: Festgabe für Philippe Derchain zu seinem Geburtstag am 24. Juli 1991.* Ursula Verhoeven and Erhart Graefe eds. OLA, vol. 39. Leuven: Leuven University Press, pp. 29-46.
  1991b. "Society, Morality, and Religious Practice," in *Religion in Ancient Egypt: Gods, Myths, and Personal Practice,* Byron E. Shafer ed. Ithaca: Cornell University Press, pp. 123-200.
  1991c. "Egyptian Myth and Discourse: Myth, Gods, and the Early Written and Iconographic Record," *JNES* 51: 81-105.
  1993. "Symbolic Roles of Canine Figures on Early Monuments," *Archéo-Nil* 3: 57-74.
in press a. "Contextualizing Egyptian Representations of Society and Ethnicity," in *The Study of the Ancient Near East in the 21st Century: The William Foxwell*

Albright Centennial Conference. Jerrold S. Cooper and Glenn Schwartz eds.
   Winona Lake: Eisenbrauns.
in press b . "On the Status and Purposes of Ancient Egyptian Art," *Cambridge
   Archaeological Journal.*

Baines, John, and Jaromír Málek
   1980. *Atlas of Ancient Egypt.* New York: Facts on File.

Baines, John, and Norman Yoffee
   forthcoming. "Order, Legitimacy, and Wealth in Ancient Egypt and Mesopotamia," in *The Archaic State: A Comparative Perspective.* Gary Feinman and
   Joyce Marcus eds.

Balout, L. and C. Roubet.
   1985. *La momie de Ramsès II.* Paris.

Barbotin, C., and Jacques-J. Clère
   1991. "L'inscription de Sésostris Ier à Tôd," *BIFAO* 91: 1-32.

Bard, Kathryn A.
   1989. "The Evolution of Social Complexity in Predynastic Egypt: An Analysis of
   the Nagada Cemeteries," *Journal of Mediterranean Archaeology* 2: 223-48.
   1992. "Toward an Interpretation of the Role of Ideology in the Evolution of
   Complex Society in Egypt," *Journal of Anthropological Archaeology* 11: 1-24.

Barguet, Paul.
   1962. *Le temple d'Amon-re à Karnak.* Cairo: IFAO.
   1968. "Le pharaon Aménophis IV Akhénaton et l'exaltation du pouvoir royal,
   Cahiers d'Histoire. Grenoble: les Universités de Clermont-Lyon-Grenoble,
   pp. 27-30.
   1976. "Note sur le grand temple d'Aton à El-Amarna," *RdE* 28: 148-50.
   1979. "Luxor," *LÄ* 3: cols. 1103-1107.

Barta, Winfried
   1968. *Aufbau und Bedeutung der Altägyptischen Opferformel.* Glückstadt: J. J.
   Augustin.
   1973. *Untersuchungen zum Götterkreis der Neunheit.* MÄS, vol. 28. Berlin: Bruno
   Hessling.
   1975. *Untersuchungen zur Göttlichkeit des regierenden Königs: Ritus und Sakralkönigtum nach Zeugnissen der Frühzeit und des Alten Reiches.* MÄS, vol. 32.
   Berlin: Bruno Hessling.
   1978. "Königsbezeichnung," *LÄ* 3: cols. 478-481.
   1979. "Königsdogma," *LÄ* 3: cols. 486-494.
   1980. "Kult," *LÄ* 3: cols. 839-48.

Barucq, André and François Daumas
   1980. *Hymnes et prières de l'Égypte ancienne.* Littératures Anciennes du Proche-
   Orient. Paris: Editions du Cerf.

Baumgartel, Elise J.
   1966. "Scorpion and Rosette and the Fragment of the Large Hierakonpolis
   Mace Head," *ZÄS* 93: 9-13.

Beattie, J. H. M.
   1968. "Kingship," *International Encyclopaedia of the Social Sciences.* David L. Sills

(ed.). 8: 386-89. [New York]: Macmillan and Free Press.
n.d.. "Nature and Origins of Kingship: An Anthropological Perspective," MS.

von Beckerath, Jürgen
1965. *Untersuchungen zum politischen Geschichte der zweiten Zwischenzeit Ägyptens.* Glückstadt: J. J. Augustin.
1979. "Königslisten," *LÄ* 3: cols. 534-535.
1984. *Handbuch der ägyptischen Königsnamen.* MÄS, vol. 20. Berlin: Bruno Hessling.

Behrmann, Almuth
1989. *Das Nilpferd in der Vorstellungswelt der alten Ägypter.* Europaische Hochschukschriften, vol. 38. Frankfort am Main: Peter Lang.

Beidelman, Thomas O.
1966. "Swazi Royal Ritual," *Africa* 36: 373-405.

Bell, Lanny
1981-82. "The Epigraphic Survey," *The Oriental Institute 1981-82 Annual Report:* 4-25.
1985a. "Luxor Temple and the Cult of the Royal *Ka,*" *JNES* 44: 251-294.
1985b. "Aspects of the Cult of the Deified Tutankh-amun," in *Mélanges Gamal Eddin Mokhtar,* vol. I. Bibliotheque d'Etude, no. 97. Cairo: IFAO, pp. 31-60.
1986. "Le Cult du ka royal," *Dossiers Histoires et Archéologie* 101: 57 ff.
forthcoming. "The New Kingdom 'Divine' Temple: The Example of Luxor" in *Ancient Egyptian Temples: Rituals, Functions, and Meanings.* Byron Shafer ed.

Berg, D.
1988. *The Juridical Oracle in Ancient Egypt to the End of Dynasty 22,* PhD Dissertation, University of Toronto; 1988.

Berger, Peter L.
1973. *The Social Reality of Religion* (originally *The Sacred Canopy*). Harmondsworth: Penguin Books.

Berlev, Oleg
1981. "The Eleventh Dynasty in the Dynastic History of Egypt," in *Studies Presented to Hans Jakob Polotsky.* Dwight W. Young ed. Beacon Hill, Mass.: Pirtle & Polson, pp. 361-77.

Bettleheim, Bruno
1976. *The Uses of Enchantment: the Meaning and Importance of Fairy Tales.* New York: Alfred Knopf.

Bevan, Edwyn
1927. *A History of Egypt Under the Ptolemaic Dynasty.* London: Methuen.

Bierbrier, Morris
1977. "Hoherpriester des Amun," *LÄ* 3: cols. 1241-1249.

Bietak, Manfred
1981. *Avaris and Piramesse.* London: Oxford University Press.

1984. "Ramesstadt," *LÄ* 5: cols. 127-146.
1986a. "La naissance de la notion de ville dans l'Egypte ancienne, un acte politique?," *CRIPEL* 8: 29-35.
1986b. "Tell ed-Dabᶜa," *LÄ* 6: cols. 321-323.

von Bissing, Friedrich Wilhelm von and Hermann Kees
1922. *Untersuchungen zu den Reliefs aus dem Re-Heiligtum des Rathures II-III.* Abhandlungen der Bayerischen Akademie der Wissenschaften, philoso-phische-philologische und historische Klasse, vol. 32. Munich: Bayerischen Akademie der Wissenschaften.
1923. *Das Re-Heiligtum des Königs Ne-woser-Re (Rathures)*II. Leipzig: J. C. Hinrichs.
1928. *Das Re-Heiligtum des Königs Ne-woser-Re (Rathures)*III. Leipzig: J. C. Hinrichs

Björkman, Gun
1971. *Kings at Karnak: A Study of the Treatment of Royal Predecessors in the Early New Kingdom.* Boreas, vol. 2. Uppsala: University of Uppsala.

Blackman, Aylward M.
1918. "'The 'House of the Morning'," *JEA* 5: 148-65.
1941. "The Stela of Shoshenk, Great Chief of the Meshwesh," *JEA* 27: 83-95.

Blankenberg-van Delden, C.
1969. *The Large Commemorative Scarabs of Amenhotep III.* Documenta et Monu-menta Orientis Antiqui, vol. 15. Leiden: E. J. Brill.

Bleeker, Claas Jouco
1965. "Initiation in Ancient Egypt," in *Initiation. Studies in the History of Religions,* vol. X. Leiden: E. J. Brill, pp. 49-58.
1967. *Egyptian Festivals: Enactments of Religious Renewal. Studies in the History of Religions,* vol. 13. Leiden: E. J. Brill.
1973. *Hathor and Thoth: Two Key Figures of Ancient Egyptian Religion.* Leiden: E. J. Brill.

Bloch, Maurice
1987. "The Ritual of the Royal Bath in Madagascar: The Dissolution of Death, Birth and Fertility in Authority," in Cannadine and Price eds., 1987, pp. 271-98.

Blumenthal, Elke
1970. *Untersuchungen zum ägyptischen Königtum des Mittleren Reiches I: Die Phraseologie.* Abhandlungen der Sächsischen Akademie der Wissenschaf-ten, phil.-hist. Klasse 61: 1. Berlin (East): Akademie-Verlag.
1978. "Zur Göttlichkeit des regierenden Königs in Ägypten," *OLZ* 73: 533 ff.
1979. "Königsideologie," in *LÄ* 3: cols. 526-531.

Bodde, Derk
1986. "The State and Empire of Ch'in," in *The Cambridge History of China* 1. Denis Twitchett and Michael Loewe eds. Cambridge etc.: Cambridge University Press, pp. 20-102.

Bonhême, Marie-Ange
1979. "Hérihor fut-il effectivement roi?" *BIFAO* 79: 267-83.

Bonhême, Marie-Ange, and Annie Forgeau
1988. *Pharaon — Les secrets du pouvoir.* Paris: Armand Colin.

Bonneau, Danielle
1961. "Le souverain d'Égypte voyageait-il sur le Nil en crue?" *CdE* 36, no. 72: 377-85.
1964. *La crue du Nil, divinité égyptienne à travers mille ans d'histoire (332 av.-641 ap. J.-C.)*. Études et commentaires, vol. 52. Paris: C. Klincksieck.

Bonnet, Hans.
1952. *Reallexikon der ägyptischen Religionsgeschichte*. Berlin: Walter de Gruyter.

Borchardt, Ludwig, et al.
1913. *Das Grabdenkmal des Königs Saȝḥu-Rēʿ*, vol. 2: Die Wandbilder. Ausgrabungen der Deutschen Orient-Gesellschaft in Abusir 1902-1908, vol. 7. Leipzig: J. C. Hinrichs.

Borghouts, Joris F.
1978. *Ancient Egyptian Magical Texts*. NISABA: Religious Texts Translation Series, vol. 9. Leiden: E. J. Brill.

Bothmer, Bernard V.
1969. *Egyptian Sculpture of the Late Period, 700 B.C. to A.D. 100*. Corrected reprint. New York: Arno Press.

Bourriau, Janine
1981. *[Umm el-Gaʿab]: Pottery from the Nile Valley Before the Arab Conquest*. Exhibition catalogue, Fitzwilliam Museum, Cambridge. Cambridge etc.: Cambridge University Press.

Brack, Annelies and Artur Brack
1977. *Das Grab des Tjanuni: Theben Nr. 74*. AV, vol. 19. Mainz am Rhein: Philip von Zabern.

Breasted, James Henry
1899. "Ramesses II and the Princes in the Karnak Reliefs of Sety I," *ZÄS* 37: 130-139.
1905. *A History of Egypt*. 1967 ed. New York-Toronto-London: C. Scribner's sons.
1906. *Ancient Records of Egypt*, vol. 4: The Twentieth to the Twenty-sixth Dynasties. Chicago: University of Chicago Press.
1930. "The Predynastic Union of Egypt," *BIFAO* 30: 709-24.
1988. *Ancient Records of Egypt*, vols. 1-5. London: Histories and Mysteries of Man.

Brinks, Jürgen
1979. *Die Entwicklung der königlichen Grablagen des Alten Reiches*. Hildesheim: Gerstenberg.

Brovarski, Edward
1977. "Doors of Heaven," *Orientalia* 46/1: 107-115.
1981. "Ahanakht of Bersheh and the Hare Nome in the First Intermediate Period," in *Studies in Ancient Egypt, the Aegean, and the Sudan*. William Kelly Simpson and W. Davis eds. Boston: Museum of Fine Arts, pp. 14-30.

Brunner, Hellmut
1956. "Das Gottkönigtum der Pharaonen," *Universitas* 11: 797-806.
1964. *Die Geburt des Gottkönigs: Studien zur Überlieferung eines altägyptischen Mythos*. Äg Ab 10. Wiesbaden: Otto Harrassowitz.

1970. "Zum Verständnis der archaisierenden Tendenzen in der ägyptischen Spätzeit," *Saeculum* 21: 151-61.
1977. *Die südlichen Räume des Tempels von Luxor.* AV, vol. 18. Mainz: Philip von Zabern.
1978. "König-Gott-Verhaltnis," *LÄ* 3: cols. 461-464.
1979. "Lehren," *LÄ* 3: cols. 964-968.

Brunner-Traut, Emma
1971. "Ein Königskopf der Spätzeit mit dem 'Blauen Helm' in Tübingen," *ZÄS* 97: 18-31.
1982. "Pap. d'Orbiney," in *LÄ* 4: cols. 697-704.

de Buck, Adriaan
1938. "The Building Inscription of the Berlin Leather Roll," *Analecta Orientalia* 17: 48-57.

Buhl, Marie Louise
1947. "The Goddesses of the Egyptian Tree Cult," *JNES* 6: 80-97.

Burkard, Günter
1977. *Textkritische Untersuchungen zu ägyptischen Weisheitslehren des Alten und Mittleren Reiches.* Äg Ab, vol. 34. Wiesbaden: Otto Harrassowitz.

Butzer, Karl W.
1976. *Early Hydraulic Society in Egypt: A Study in Cultural Ecology.* Prehistoric Archaeology and Ecology Series. Chicago and London: University of Chicago Press.

Caminos, Ricardo A.
1956. *Late Egyptian Miscellanies.* London: Oxford, Griffith Institute.
1964. "The Nitocris Adoption Stela," *JEA* 50: 71-101.

Campbell, Edward F.
1964. *The Chronology of the Amarna Letters.* Baltimore: The Johns Hopkins Press.

Cannadine, David
1987. "Introduction: Divine Rites of Kings," in Cannadine and Price eds., 1987, pp. 1-19.

Cannadine, David, and Simon Price eds.
1987. *Rituals of Royalty: Power and Ceremonial in Traditional Societies.* Past and Present Publications. Cambridge: Cambridge University Press.

Carter, Howard
1923. *The Tomb of Tut-ankh-amen,* New York: George H. Doran.

Case, Humphrey, and Joan Crowfoot Payne
1962. "Tomb 100: The Decorated Tomb at Hierakonpolis," *JEA* 48: 5-8.

Cavaignac, E.
1935. "Le lettre de Ramsès II au roi de Mira," *Révue Hittite et Asianique* 18: 25-29.

Černý, Jaroslav
1929. "Papyrus Salt 124 (British Museum 1005)," *JEA* 15: 243-258.
1958. "Stela of Ramesses II from Beisan," *Eretz Israel* 5, 75*-82*.

Cialowicz, Krzysztof M.
1987. *Les têtes de massues des périodes prédynastique et archaïque dans la Vallée du Nil.* Zesyty Naukowe Uniwersytetu Jagiellonskiego 829, Prace archeologiczne, vol. 41. Cracow: Jagellonian University.
1993. *Symbolika przedstawien´ wladcy egipskiego w okresie predynsatycznym* (La symbolique de représentations du souverain égyptien à l'époque prédynastique). Rozprawy Habilitacyne Uj 258. Cracow: Jagellonian University.

Claessen, Henri J. M., and Peter Skalník eds.
1978. *The Early State.* New Babylon: Studies in the Social Sciences. The Hague, Paris, New York: Mouton.

Clarysse, Willy and G. van der Veken
1983. *The Eponymous Priests of Ptolemaic Egypt.* Papyrologica Lugduno-Batava 24. Leiden: E. J. Brill.

Clère, Jacques J.
1951. "Une statuette du fils ainé du roi Nectanabo," *RdÉ* 6: 135-56.

Cline, Eric C., and David O'Connor eds.
forthcoming. *Amenhotep III: Perspectives on His Reign.*

Cooney, John D.
1965. *Amarna Reliefs from Hermopolis in American Collections.* Brooklyn NY: The Brooklyn Museum.

Cruz-Uribe, Eugene
1978. "The Father of Ramses I: OI 11456," *JNES* 37: 237-244.

Daressy, Georges
1900. "Stèle de l'an III d'Amasis," *RT* 22: 1-9.

Daumas, François
1952. *Les moyens d'expression du grec et de l'égyptien,* Cairo: IFAO.
1977. "Hathor," *LÄ* 2: cols. 1024-33.

D'Auria, Sue
1988. *Mummies and Magic.* with P. Lacovara and C. Roehring. Boston: Museum of Fine Arts.

Davies, Norman de Garis
1905. *The Rock Tombs of El Amarna,* Part III. Archaeological Survey of Egypt 15. London: Egypt Exploration Fund.
1906. *The Rock Tombs of El Amarna,* Part IV. Archaeological Survey of Egypt 16. London: Egypt Exploration Fund.
1908a. *The Rock Tombs of El Amarna,* Part V. Archaeological Survey of Egypt 17. London: Egypt Exploration Fund.
1908b. *The Rock Tombs of El Amarna,* Part VI. Archaeological Survey of Egypt 18. London: Egypt Exploration Fund.
1920. *The Tomb of Antefoker, vizier of Sesostris I and of his wife, Senet.* London: George Allen and Unwin, Ltd.
1923. "Akhenaten at Thebes," *JEA* 9: 132-152.

Davies, Norman M. de Garis and Gardiner, Alan
1926. *The Tomb of Huy*. Theban Tomb Series, no. 4. London: Egypt Exploration Society.

Davies, Nina and Norman de Garis Davies
1933. *The Tombs of Menkheperrasonb, Amenmose, and Another*. Theban Tombs Series, No. 5. London: Egypt Exploration Society.

Decker, Wolfgang
1971. *Die physische Leistung Pharaos*: Untersuchungen zu Heldentum, Jagd und Leibes der ägyptischen Könige. Köln: Historisches Institut der Deutschen Sporthochschule.
1984. "Sport," *LÄ* 5: cols. 1161-9.

Derchain, Philippe
1962. "Le rôle du roi d'Égypte dans le maintien de l'ordre cosmique," in Luc de Heusch et al., *Le pouvoir et le sacré*. Annales du Centre d'Étude des Religions, vol. 1. Université Libre de Bruxelles: Institut de Sociologie, pp. 61-73.
1980. "Comment les Égyptiens écrivaient un traité de la royauté," *BSFE* 87-88: 14-17.
1987. "Magie et politique: À propos de l'hymne à Sésostris III," *CdÉ* 62, nos. 123-24: 21-29.

de Wit, Constant
1951. *Le rôle et le sens du lion dans l'Égypte ancienne*. Leiden: E. J. Brill.

Doret, Eric
1986. *The Narrative Verbal System of Old and Middle Egyptian*. Geneva: Cramer.

Drenkhahn, Rosemarie
1980. *Die Elephantine-Stele des Sethnacht und ihr historischer Hintergrund*. ÄgAb, vol. 36. Wiesbaden: Otto Harrassowitz.

Dreyer, Günter
1986. *Elephantine VIII. Der Tempel der Satet: Die Funde der Frühzeit und des Alten Reiches*. AV, vol. 39. Mainz am Rhein: Philip von Zabern.
1987. "Ein Siegel der frühzeitlichen Königsnekropole von Abydos," *MDAIK* 43: 33-43.
1992. "Horus Krokodil, ein Gegenkönig der Dynastie 0," in Adams and Friedman 1992, 259-62.
in press. "Die Datierung der Min-Statuen aus Koptos," in *1. Symposium zur Kunst des Alten Reiches*. SDAIK, vol. 27. Mainz am Rhein: Philip von Zabern.
n. d. Paper on excavations at Abydos delivered at the British Museum, July 1987.

Dreyer, Günter, et al.
1990. "Umm el-Qaab: Nachuntersuchungen im frühzeitlichen Königsfriedhof. 3./4. Vorbericht," *MDAIK* 46: 53-90.
1993. "Umm el-Qaab: Nachuntersuchungen im frühzeitlichen Königsfriedhof. 5./6. Vorbericht," *MDAIK* 49: 23-62.

Drioton, Étienne
1940 . "Review of B. Grdseloff, *Das Ägyptische Reinigungszelt*," *ASAE* 40: 1007-1014.
1942-3."Une Représentation de famine sur un bas-relief égyptien de la Ve dynastie," *BIE* 25: 45-54.

Drioton, Étienne and Jacques Vandier
1962. *L'Égypte.* 4th ed. rev. Paris: Presses universitaires de France.

Drower, Margaret S.
1973. "Syria c. 1550-1400 B.C.," = Edwards et al. eds. *The Cambridge Ancient History*[3]II. 1., Cambridge: Cambridge University Press.

Edel, Elmar
1945. "Untersuchungen zur Phaseologie der Ägyptischen Inschriften des Alten Reiches," *MDAIK* 13/1: 1-90.
1956. "Ein 'Vorsteher der farafra-oase' in Alten Reich," *ZÄS* 81: 67-68.
1961-1964. "Zu den Inschriften auf den Jahreszeitenreliefs der 'Weltkammer' aus dem Sonnenheiligtum des Niuserre," *Nachrichten der Akademie der Wissenschaften in Göttingen*, Phil.-hist. Klasse 1961, no. 8, 1964, nos. 4-5. Göttingen: Vandenhoeck & Ruprecht.
1978a. "Amasis und Nebukadrezar II," *GM* 29: 13-20.
1978b. "Der Brief des ägyptischen Wesirs Paßijara an den Hethiterkönig Ḫattušili III und verwandte Keilschriftbriefe," *Nachrichten der Akademie der Wissenschaften in Göttingen, I. Philologisch-historische Klasse*, Nr. 4: 117-158.
1979. "Bemerkungen zu den Sciessporttexten der Könige der 18. Dynastie," *SAK* 7: 23-39.

Edel, Elmar, and Steffen Wenig,
1974. *Die Jahreszeitenreliefs aus dem Sonnenheiligtum des Königs Ne-user-Re.* Staatliche Museen zu Berlin, Mitteilungen aus der ägyptischen Sammlung, vol. 7. Berlin (East): Akademie-Verlag.

Edgerton, William
1951. "The Strikes in Ramesses III's Twenty Ninth Year," *JNES* 10: 137-145.

Edwards, I. E. S.
1961. *The Pyramids of Egypt.* Harmondsworth: Penquin Books.
1971. "The Early Dynastic Period in Egypt," in *The Cambridge Ancient history*, vol. 1, part 2: *The Early History of the Middle East*, I. E. S. Edwards, et al. eds., 1-70. Cambridge: University Press.
1977. *Tutankhamun: His Tomb and Its Treasures.* New York: The Metropolitan Museum of Art and Alfred A. Knopf, Inc.
1982. "Egypt: From the Twenty-second Dynasty to the Twenty-fourth Dynasty," in *Cambridge Ancient History*, vol. 3, 2nd ed., part 1: *The Prehistory of the Balkans; and the Middle East and the Aegean World, Tenth to Eighth Centuries B.C.*, John Boardman et al. eds. Cambridge: Cambridge University Press, pp. 534-81.

Edzard, Dietz et al.
1970. Kamid el-Loz — Kumidi. Bonn: R. Habelt

Eggebrecht, Arne
1975. "Deir el-Ballas," *LÄ* 1: cols. 1025-1027.

Eiwanger, Josef
1987. "Die Archäologie der späten Vorgeschichte: Bestand und Perspektiven,"

in *Problems and Priorities in Egyptian Archaeology*, Jan Assmann et al. eds. London and New York: Kegan Paul International, pp. 81-103.

Emery, Walter B.
1954.   *Great Tombs of the First Dynasty* 2. Service des Antiquités de l'Égypte; Egypt Exploration Society. London: Egypt Exploration Society.
1961.   *Archaic Egypt.* Harmondsworth: Penguin Books.

Endesfelder, Erika
1991.   "Die Formierung der altägyptischen Klassengesellschaft. Probleme und Beobachtungen," in *Probleme der frühen Gesellschaftsentwicklung im alten Ägypten*, Erika Endesfelder ed. Humboldt-Universität zu Berlin, Institut für Sudanarcharchäologie und Ägyptologie. Berlin, pp. 5-61.

Epigraphic Survey, The
1940.   *Medinet Habu, Vol. IV: Festival Scenes of Ramses III.* OIP, vol. 51. Chicago: University of Chicago Press.
1957.   *Medinet Habu, Vol. V: Demotic Ostraca of Medinet Habu.* OIP, vol. 80. Chicago: University of Chicago Press.
1980.   *The Tomb of Kheruef: Theban Tomb 192.* OIP, vol. 102. Chicago: The Oriental Institute.
1986.   *Reliefs and Inscriptions at Karnak, Vol. IV. The Battle Reliefs of King Sety I.* Oriental Institute Publications, vol. 107. Chicago: The Oriental Institute.

Erichsen, Wolja
1933.   "Papyrus Harris I: hieroglyphische Transkription," BiAe, vol. 5. Brussels: Fondation Egyptologique Reine Elisabeth.

Evans-Pritchard, Edward Evan
1969 [1948] "The Divine Kingship of the Shilluk of the Nilotic Sudan," in id., *Essays in Social Anthropology*, 2nd ed. London: Faber & Faber, pp. 66-86.
1971.   *The Azande: History and Political Institutions.* Oxford: Clarendon Press.

Evers, Hans Gerhard
1929.   *Staat aus dem Stein: Denkmäler, Geschichte und Bedeutung der ägyptischen Plastik während des Mittleren Reiches.* 2 vols. Munich: F. Bruckmann.

Eyre, Christopher J.
1990.   "The Semna Stelae: Quotation, Genre, and Functions of literature," in *Studies in Egyptology presented to Miriam Lichtheim*, Sarah Israelit-Groll ed. The Hebrew University of Jerusalem, Department of Egyptology. Jerusalem: Magnes Press, pp. 134-65.

Fairman, Herbert W.
1951.   "The Inscriptions," Chapter X in J. D. S. Pendlebury. *The City of Akhenaten III.* London: Egypt Exploration Fund, pp. 143-223.
1958.   "The Kingship Rituals of Ancient Egypt," in *Myth, Ritual and Kingship*, S. H. Hooke ed. Oxford: Clarendon Press, pp. 74-104.

Fairservis, Walter A. et al.
1971-72. "Preliminary Report on the First Two Seasons at Hierakonpolis," *JARCE* 9: 7-68.
1983.   *Hierakonpolis — the Graffiti and the Origins of Egyptian Hieroglyphic Writing.* The Hierakonpolis Project: Occasional Papers in Anthropology, no. 2. Poughkeepsie NY: Vassar College.

Fakhry, Ahmed
1954. "The Excavations of Sneferu's Monuments at Dahshur, Second Preliminary Report," *ASAE* 52: 563-594.
1961. *The Monuments of Sneferu at Dahshur II: The Valley Temple,* 2 pts. Cairo: General Organization for Government Printing.
1969. *The Pyramids.* Chicago: University of Chicago Press.

Farag, Sami
1980. "Une inscription memphite de la XIIe dynastie," *RdÉ* 32: 75-82.

Faulkner, Raymond O.
1958. "The Battle of Kadesh," *MDAIK* 16: 93-111.
1969a. *The Ancient Egyptian Pyramid Texts.* Oxford: Clarendon Press.
1969b. *Ancient Egyptian Pyramid Texts, supplement.* Oxford: Clarendon Press.
1973-77. *The Ancient Egyptian Coffin Text,* vols. I-III. Warminster: Aris and Phillips.

Fecht, Gerhard
1960a. *Wortakzent und Silbenstruktur: Untersuchungen zur Geschichte der ägyptischen Sprache.* ÄF, vol. 21. Glückstadt: J. J. Augustin.
1960b. "Amarna-Probleme (1-2)," *ZÄS* 85: 82-118.
1968. "Zu den Inschriften des ersten Pfeilers im Grab des Anchtifi (Mo'alla)." in *Festschrift für Siegfried Schott zu seinem 70. Geburtstag,* Wolfgang Helck ed. Wiesbaden: Otto Harrassowitz, pp. 50-60.
1978. "Schicksalsgöttinnen und König in der 'Lehre eines Mannes an seinen Sohn'," *ZÄS* 105: 14-42.

Finkenstaedt, Elizabeth
1984. "Violence and Kingship: The Evidence of the Palettes," *ZÄS* 111: 107-10.
1985. "On the Life-span of Decorated Ware of the Gerzean Period," *ZÄS* 112: 17-19.

Finnestad, Ragnhild Bjerre
1989. "The Pharoah and the Democratization of Post-Mortem Life," in *The Religions of the Ancient Egyptians: Cognitive Structures and Popular Expressions,* G. Englund ed., Uppsala: Uppsala University, pp. 29-40.

Firth, Cecil M., and J. E. Quibell
1935. *The Step Pyramid.* 2 vols. Service des Antiquités de l'Égypte, Excavations at Saqqara. Cairo: IFAO.

Fischer, Henry George
1961. "A First Dynasty Bowl Inscribed with the Group *Ḥt,*" *CdE* 36, no. 71: 19-22.
1962. "The Cult and Nome of the Goddess Bat," *JARCE* 1: 7-23.
1963. "A Stela of the Heracleopolitan Period at Saqqara: The Osiris Iti," *ZÄS* 90: 35-41.
1968. *Dendera in the Third Millenium B.C., Down to the Theban Domination of Upper Egypt.* Locust Valley: J. J. Augustin Publisher.
1973. "An Eleventh Dynasty Couple Holding the Sign of Life," *ZÄS* 100: 16-28.
1976. "Archaeological Aspects of Epigraphy and Palaeography," in Ricardo A. Caminos and Henry G. Fischer, *Ancient Egyptian Epigraphy and Palaeography.* New York: Metropolitan Museum of Art, pp. 27-55.

Fowden, Garth
  1986. *The Egyptian Hermes: An Historical Approach to the Late Pagan Mind.*
     Cambridge etc.: Cambridge University Press.

Franke, Detlef
  1991. *Studien zum Heiligtum des Heqaib.* Habilitationsschrift, University of Heidel-
     berg.

Frankfort, Henri
  1948 [1978]. *Kingship and the Gods: A Study of Ancient Near Eastern Religion as the
     Integration of Society and Nature.* Chicago: University of Chicago Press.

Friedman, Florence
  1982. "Review of G. Englund, *Akh — Une Notion Religieuse dans L'Égypte
     Pharaonique*," *JARCE* 19: 145-147.

Friedrich, Carl J.
  1968. "Monarchy," *International Encyclopaedia of the Social Sciences*, David L. Sills
     ed., 10: 412-15. [New York]: MacMillan and Free Press.

Gaballa, G. A.
  1977. *The Memphite Tomb Chapel of Mose.* Warminster: Aris & Phillips.

Gaballa, G. A. and Kenneth A. Kitchen
  1968. "Ramesside Varia I," *CdÉ* 43: 259-270.

Gardiner, Alan H.
  1938. "The Mansion of Life and the Master of the King's Largess," *JEA* 24: 83-91.
  1944. "Horus the Behdetite," *JEA* 30: 23-60.
  1945. "Regnal Years and Civil Calendar in Pharaonic Egypt," *JEA* 31: 11-28.
  1946. "Davies' Copy of the Great Speos Artemidos Inscription," *JEA* 32: 43-56.
  1952. "Tuthmosis III returns thanks to Amun," *JEA* 38: 6-23.
  1953. "The Coronation of King Haremhab," *JEA* 39: 13-31.
  1957. *Egyptian Grammar, Being an Introduction to the Study of Hieroglyphs.* 3rd ed.
     London: Oxford University Press for Griffith Institute.
  1960. *The Kadesh Inscriptions of Ramesses II.* Oxford: University Press.
  1961. *Egypt of the Pharaohs.* Oxford: University Press.
  1966. *Egypt of the Pharaohs.* New York: Oxford University Press.

Gauthier, Henri
  1912. *Le livre des rois d'Égypte*, vol. 2. MIFAO, vol. 18. Cairo: IFAO.

Geertz, Clifford
  1980. *Negara: The Theatre State in Nineteenth-century Bali.* Princeton NJ: Princeton
     University Press.
  1983. "Centers, Kings and Charisma: Reflections on the Symbolics of Power," in
     Clifford Geertz, *Local Knowledge: Further Essays in Interpretive Anthropology.*
     New York: Basic Books, pp. 121-46.

Gestermann, Louise
  1984. "Hathor, Harsomtus, und *Mntw-htp.w* II," in *Studien zu Sprache und Religion
     Ägyptens* II. F. Junge ed. Göttingen: Hubert and Co., pp. 763-776.

Gitton, Michel
  1974. "Le palais de Karnak," *BIFAO* 74, 63-73.

1976. "La resiliation d'une fonction religieuse: Nouvelle interpretation de la stele de donation d'Ahmes Nefertary," *BIFAO* 76: 65-89 with 1 pl.

Goedicke, Hans
1960. *Die Stellung des Königs im Alten Reich*, Äg Ab Band 2. Wiesbaden: Otto Harrassowitz.
1971. *Re-Used Blocks from the Pyramid of Amenemhet I at Lisht.* Egyptian Expedition, vol. 20. New York: Metropolitan Museum of Art.
1974. "The Berlin Leather Roll (P. Berlin 3029)," in *Festschrift zum 150 Jahrigen Bestehen des Berliner ägyptischen Musuem.* Berlin, pp. 87-104.
1985. "The 'Battle of Kadesh:' A Reassessment," *Perspectives on the Battle of Kadesh*, ed. H. Goedicke. Baltimore: Halgo.
1986. "Vergottlichung," *LÄ* 6: cols. 989-992.

Goelet, Ogden
1986. "The term *stp-s3* in the Old Kingdom and its later development," *JARCE* 23: 85-98.

Gomaà, Farouk
1973. *Chaemwese, Sohn Ramses' II. und Hoherpriester von Memphis.* Äg Ab, vol. 27. Wiesbaden: Otto Harrassowitz.

Goldwasser, Orly
1990 . "The Literary Letter — A Crossroad of Dynamic Canonicity," in *Crossroads* II. Los Angeles: UCLA, pp. 55-69.

Golvin, Jean-Claude and Jean-Claude Goyon.
1987. Les bâtisseurs de Karnak. Paris: CNRS.

Goyon, Jean-Clause
1969 . "La chausée monumentale at le temple de la pyramide de Kheops," *BIFAO* 67: 49-69.
1971 . "Les navires de transport de la chausée monumentale d'Ounas," *BIFAO* 69: 11-41.
1977. *Le secret des Bâtisseurs des grandes pyramides, Khéops.* Paris: Pygmalion.

Graefe, Erhart
1966. "Some Remarks on the 400-Year Stela," *CdÉ* 41: 23-39.
1981. *Untersuchungen zur Verwaltung und Geschichte der Institution der Gottes-gemahlin des Amun vom Beginn des neuen Reiches bis zur Spätzeit.* Wiesbaden: Otto Harrassowitz.
1985. "Talfest," *LÄ* 6: cols. 187-189.
1990. "Dir gute Reputation des Königs 'Snofru'," in *Studies in Egyptology Presented to Miriam Lichtheim*, Sarah Israelit-Groll ed. Jerusalem: The Magnes Press, The Hebrew University, vol. 1, pp. 257-63.

Greven, Liselotte
1952. *Der ka in Theologie und Königskult der Ägypter der Alten Reiches.* Glückstadt: J. J. Augustin.

Grdseloff, Bernhard
1941 . *Das Ägyptische reinigngszelt.* Cairo.

Grieshammer, Reinhard
1974. "Zum 'Sitz im Leben' des negativen Sündenbekenntnisses," *ZDMG Supplement* 2: 19-25.

1975/76   "Zur Formgeschichte der Sprüche 38-41 der Sargtexte," *Orientalia Lovaniensia Periodica* 6-7: 231-35.

Griffiths, J. Gwyn
1966.   *The Origins of Osiris.* MÄS, vol. 9. Berlin: Bruno Hessling.
1981.   "Osiris," *LÄ* 4: cols. 623-633.

Grimal, Nicholas-C.
1981.   *La stèle triomphale de Pi('ankh)y au Musée du Caire, JE 48862 et 47086-47089. Études sur la propagande royal égyptienne,* vol. 1. MIFAO, vol. 105. Cairo: IFAO.

Groll, Sarah I.
1975-76.   "The Literary and Non-Literary Verbal Systems in Late Egyptian," in *Miscellanea in Honorem Josephi Vergote.* Orientalia Louvaniensia Periodica 6/7: 238-246.

Grundlach, R. and Mitarbeiter
1987.   "Die Staat des frühen Neuen Reiches: Königtum, Verwaltung und Beamtenschaft," in: *Ägyptens Aufstieg zur Weltmacht.* Roemer-und Pelizaues-Museum. Hildesheim und Mainz: Verlag Phillip von Zabern, pp. 29-40.

Habachi, Labib
1954.   "Khatana-Qantir: Importance," *ASAE* 52: 443-562.
1963.   "King Nebhepetre Mentuhotep: His Monuments, Place in History, Deification and Unusual Representation in the Form of Gods," *MDAIK* 19: 16-52.
1965.   "Varia from the Reign of King Akhenaten," *MDAIK* 20: 70-92.
1969.   *Features of the Deification of Ramesses II.* ADAIK Ägyptologische Reihe 5. Glückstadt: J. J. Augustin.
1972.   *The Second Stela of Kamose.* Glückstadt: J. J. Augustin
1973.   "Two Rock Stelae of Sethos I in the Cataract Area Speaking of Huge Statues and Obelisks," *BIFAO* 73: 119-123.
1975.   "The Four-Hundred Year Stela Originally Standing in Khatana-Qantir or Avaris-Piramesse," *Actes du 29e Congresse des Orientalistes 1, Egyptologie,* pp. 41-44.
1977a. "Gottesvater," *LÄ* 2: cols. 825-26.
1977b. "Heqaib," *LÄ* 2: cols. 1120-1122.
1978.   *The Obelisks of Egypt.* New York: Charles Scribner's Sons.
1980.   "Königssohn von Kusch," *LÄ* 3: cols. 630-640.
1985.   *Elephantine IV. The Sanctuary of Heqaib.* 2 vols. AV, vol. 33. Mainz am Rhein: Philip von Zabern.

Hari, Robert
1965.   *Horemheb et la reine Moutnedjemet.* Geneva: Éditions de Belles lettres.
1985.   *La tombe thebaine du pere divin Neferhotep (TT 50).* Geneva: Éditions de Belles lettres.

Harris, James E. and Kent R. Weeks,
1972.   *X-Raying the Pharaohs.* Harris, James E. and Edward F. Wente (eds.). New York:

Harris, James E. and Edward F. Wente
1980.   *An X-Ray Atlas of the Royal Mummies.* Chicago: University of Chicago Press.

Hassan, Selim
1932. Excavations at Giza, Season 1929-1930. Oxford: University Press.
1936. Excavations at Giza, Season 1936-1937. Oxford: University Press.
1960. Excavations at Giza, Season 1938-1939. Cairo: General Organization for Government Printing Offices.
1955. "The Causeway of Unis in Sakkara," *ZÄS* 80: 136-144.

Hawass, Zahi
1987. *The Funerary Establishments of Khufu, Khafra and Menkaura.* Ann Arbor: Michigan University Microfilm.
1990. *The Pyramids of Ancient Egypt.* Pittsburgh, PA: Carnegie Museum of Natural History.
1993. "The Great Sphinx: Date and Function," *VI Congresso Internazionale di Egittologia. Atti,* vol. 2. Turin, pp. 177-196.
1993. "History of the Sphinx Conservation," *The First International Symposium on the Great Sphinx: Book of Proceedings.* Cairo: Egyptian Antiquities Organization Press, pp. 165-214.
forthcoming "The Workmen Community at Giza."

Hawass, Zahi and Michael Jones,
forthcoming. *The Discovery of the Causeway and the Lower Temple.*
forthcoming. *The Discovery of the Settlement at Giza.*

Hayes, William C.
1938. "A Writing-palette of the Chief Steward Amenhotpe and Some Notes on Its Owner," *JEA* 24: 9-24.
1951. "Inscriptions from the palace of Amenhotep III," *JNES* 10: 35f, 82f, 156f, 231f.
1953. *The Scepter of Egypt* I. New York: Metropolitan Museum of Art.

Heerma von Voss, Matthieu
1985. "Totenbuch," *LÄ* 6: cols. 641-643.

Heinrich, Ernst
1982. *Die Tempel im alten Mesopotamien: Typologie, Morphologie und Geschichte.* 2 vols. Deutsches Archäologisches Institut, Denkmäler Antiker Architektur, vol. 14. Berlin: Walter de Gruyter.

Helck, Wolfgang
1939. *Der Einfluss der Militarführer in der 18. ägyptischen Dynastie.* Untersuchungen zur Geschichte und Altertumskunde Ägyptens 14. Leipzig: J. C. Hinrichs.
1950. "Rp^ct auf dem Thron des Gb," *Orientalia n.s.* 19: 416-34.
1951. *Zur Vorstellung von der Grenze in der ägyptischen Frühgeschichte.* Vorträge der Orientalistischen Tagung in Marburg 1950: Ägyptologie. Hildesheim: Gerstenberg.
1952. "Die Bedeutung der ägyptischen Besucherinschriften," *ZDMG* 102: 39-46.
1953. "Gab es einen König Menes?" *ZDMG* 103: 354-59.
1954a. *Untersuchungen zu den Beamtentiteln des ägyptischen Alten Reiches.* ÄF, vol. 18. Glückstadt: J. J. Augustin.
1954b. "Die Sinai-Inschrift des Amenmose," *Mitteilungen des Instituts für Orientforschung,* vol. II. Berlin: Akademie-Verlag.
1957. "Bemerkungen zu den pyramidenstäden in Alten Reich," *MDAIK* 15: 91-111.
1958a. *Urkunden der 18. Dynastie.* Berlin: Akademie-Verlag.

1958b. *Zur Verwaltung des mittleren und neuen Reichs.* Probleme der Ägyptologie 3. Leiden/Koln: E. J. Brill.

1960. "Die soziale Schichtung des ägyptischen Volkes im 3. und 2. Jahrtausend v. Chr.," *JESHO* 2: 1-36.

1961. *Übersetzung zu den Heften 17-22.* Urkunden des Ägyptischen Altertums. Berlin (East): Akademie-Verlag.

1963. "Urḫi-Tešup in Ägypten," *Journal of Cuneiform Studies* 17: 87-97.

1965. "Pyramiden," *REA* 23: cols. 2207-2208.

1966. "Nilhöhe und Jubiläumsfest," *ZÄS* 93: 74-79.

1968a. *Geschichte des Alten Ägypten.* Handbuch der Orientalistik 1:1:3. Leiden and Cologne: E. J. Brill.

1968b. "Ritualszenen in Karnak," *MDAIK* 23: 117-137.

1970. "Zwei Einzelprobleme der thinitischen Chronologie," *MDAIK* 26: 83-85.

1971. *Die Beziehungen Ägyptens zu Vorderasien im 3. und 2. Jahrtausend v. Chr.* 2nd ed. rev. Äg Ab, vol. 5. Wiesbaden: Otto Harrassowitz.

1974a. *Altägyptische Aktenkunde des 3 und 2 Jahrtausends V. chr.* Munich and Berlin: Deutscher Kunstverlag.

1974b. "Bemerkungen zum Annalenstein," *MDAIK* 30: 31-35.

1975. *Historisch-biographische Texte der 2. Zwischenzeit und neue Texte der 18. Dynastie.* Wiesbaden: Otto Harrassowitz.

1975. "Dienstanweisung fur den Wesir," *LÄ* 1: col. 1084.

1978. "Die Weihinschrift Sesostris I. am Satet-Tempel von Elephantine," *MDAIK* 34: 69-78.

1981. "Probleme der Königsfolge in der Übergangszeit von 18. zu 19. Dynastie," *MDAIK* 37: 207-215.

1987. *Untersuchungen zur Thinitenzeit.* ÄgAb, vol. 45. Wiesbaden: Otto Harrassowitz.

1988. "Der 'Geheimnisvolle' Mehy," *SAK* 15: 143-148.

Hickmann, Hans
1956. *45 siècles de musique dans l'Égypte ancienne.* Paris: Richard-Masses.

Hoffman, Michael A.
1979. *Egypt Before the Pharaohs: The Prehistoric Foundations of Egyptian Civilization.* New York: Alfred A. Knopf.

1986. An Interim Report to the National Endowment for the Humanities on Predynastic Research at Hierakonpolis.

Hoffman, Michael A., et al.
1982. *The Predynastic of Hierakonpolis — an Interim Report.* Egyptian Studies Association, Publication no. 1. Giza, Egypt: Cairo University Herbarium, Faculty of Science; Macomb, Ill.: Department of Sociology and Anthropology, Western Illinois University.

Hölscher, Uvo
1912. *Das Grabdenkmal des Königs Chephren.* Leipzig: J. C. Hinrichs.

Hornung, Erik
1957. "Zur geschichtlichen Rolle des Königs in der 18. Dynastie," *MDAIK* 15: 120-33.

1966. *Geschichte als Fest: Zwei Vorträge zum Geschichtsbild der frühen Menschheit.* Libelli, vol. 246. Darmstadt: Wissenschaftliche Buchgesellschaft.

1973. "Amenophis I," *LÄ* 1: cols. 202-203.

1982a. *Conceptions of God in Ancient Egypt: The One and the Many.* Trans. John Baines. Ithaca NY: Cornell University Press.

1982b. *Das altägyptische Buch von der Himmelskuh: eine Ätiologie des Unvollkommenen.* OBO, vol. 46. Göttingen: Vandenhoeck and Ruprecht.
1983. "Pharao Ludens," *Eranos-Jahrbuch* 51/1982: 479-516.
1985. *Conceptions of God in Ancient Egypt: The One and the Many.* translated by J. Baines. Ithaca: Cornell University Press.
1992. *The Valley of the Kings: Horizon of Eternity.* Trans. David Warburton. New York: Timken.

Hornung, Erik and Elisabeth Staehelin,
1974. *Studien zum Sedfest.* Aegyptiaca Helvetica, vol. 1. Geneva: Editions de Belles-Lettres.
1976. *Skarabäen und andere Siegelamulette aus Basler Sammlungen.* Ägyptische Denkmäler in der Schweiz, vol. 1. Mainz: Philipp von Zabern.

Hulin, Christopher
1982. "The Archaeology of the Amarna Plain," in *Papers for Discussion*, Vol. 1. Presented by the Department of Egyptology Hebrew University: Jerusalem, pp. 210-269.

Jacobsohn, Helmuth
1939. *Die dogmatische Stellung des Königs im der Theologie der alten Ägypter.* Äg Fo, vol. 8. Glückstadt: J. J. Augustin.

Jacotin, Col. Pierre
1822 . Déscription de l'Égypte ou recueil des observations at les recherches qui ont été faites en Égypte pendant l'éxpedition de l'armée Française: Antiquities.

Jacquet-Gordon, Helen K.
1962 . *Les noms domaines funéraires sous l'Ancien Empire égyptien.* BdÉ, vol. 34. Cairo: IFAO.

Jaeger, Bertrand
1982. *Essai de classification et datation des scarabées Menkhéperrê.* OBO, Series Archaeologica, vol. 2. Göttingen: Vanderhoeck and Ruprect.

Janssen Jac. J.
1960. "Nine Letters from the time of Ramses II," *Oudheidkundige Mededelingen uit het Rijksmuseum van Oudheden te Leiden* 41: 31-39.
1978. "The Early State in Egypt," in Claessen and Skalník, pp. 213-34.

Jeffreys, David G.
1985. *The Survey of Memphis* I. London: Egypt Exploration Society.

Jéquier, Gustave
1936-1940. *Le monument funéraire de Pépi II.* 3 vols. Service des Antiquités de l'Égypte, Fouilles à Saqqarah. Cairo: IFAO.

Johnson, Janet H.
1983. "The Demotic Chronicle as a Statement of a Theory of Kingship," *JSSEA* 13: 61-72.

Johnson, W. Raymond
1990. "Images of Amenhotep III at Thebes: Styles and Intentions," in *The Art of*

Amenhotep III: Art Historical Analysis. L. M. Berman, ed. Cleveland, OH: Cleveland Museum of Art, pp. 26-46.

Junge, Friedrich
1985. "Sprache," *LÄ* 5: cols. 1176-1211.

Junker, Hermann
1938. *Giza*, vol. III. Vienna and Leipzig: Höder-Pincher-Temsley.
1956. "Die Feinde auf den Sockeln der Chasechem-Statuen und die Darstellung von geopferten Tieren," in *Ägyptologische Studien, [Hermann Grapow zum 70. Geburtstag gewidmet]*, Otto Firchow ed. Deutsche Akademie der Wissenschaften, Institut für Orientforschung, Veröffentlichung 29. Berlin (East): Akademie-Verlag, pp. 162-175.

Kaiser, Werner
1956. "Zu den Sonnenheiligtümern der 5. Dynastie," *MDAIK* 14: 104-116.
1959. "Einige Bemerkungen zur ägyptischen Frühzeit I: Zu den *šmsw-Ḥr*," *ZÄS* 84: 119-32.
1961. "Einige Bemerkungen zur ägyptischen Frühzeit II: Zur Frage einer über Menes hinausreichenden Geschichtsüberlieferung," *ZÄS* 86: 39-61.
1964. "Einige Bemerkungen zur ägyptischen Frühzeit III: Die Reichseinigung," *ZÄS* 91: 86-115.
1969. "Zu den Talbezirken der 1. und 2. Dynastie in Abydos und zur Baugeschichte des Djoser-Grabmals," *MDAIK* 25: 1-21.
1983. "Zu den der älteren Bilddarstellungen und der Bedeutung von *rpw.t*," *MDAIK* 39: 261-96.
1985a. "Ein Kultbezirk des Königs Den in Sakkara," *MDAIK* 41: 47-60.
1985b. "Zur Entwicklung und Vorformen der frühzeitlichen Gräber mit reich gegliederter Oberbaufassade," in *Mélanges Gamal Eddin Mokhtar* 2: 25-38. IFAO BE, vol. 97. Cairo: IFAO.
1986. "Die dekorierte Torfassade des spätzeitlichen Palastbezirkes von Memphis," *MDAIK* 43: 123-54.
1987a. "Zum Siegel mit frühen Königsnamen von Umm el-Qaab," *MDAIK* 43: 115-19.
1987b. "Zum Friedhof der Naqadakultur von Minshat Abu Omar," *ASAE* 71: 119-25.
1990. "Zur Entstehung des gesamtägyptischen Staats," *MDAIK* 46: 287-99.

Kaiser, Werner, and Günter Dreyer
1982. "Umm el-Qaab: Nachuntersuchungen im frühzeitlichen Königsfriedhof, 2. Vorbericht," *MDAIK* 38: 211-69.

Kaiser, Werner, et al.
1984. "Stadt und Tempel von Elephantine: elfter/zwölfter Grabungsbericht," *MDAIK* 40: 169-205.

Kákosy, László.
1982. "Orakel," *LÄ* 4: cols. 600-606.

Kaplony, Peter
1958. "Zu den beiden Harpunenzeichen der Narmerpalette," *ZÄS* 83: 76-78.
1962-63. "Gottespalast und Götterfestung in der ägyptischen Frühzeit," *ZÄS* 88: 5-6.
1963. *Die Inschriften der ägyptischen Frühzeit.* 3 vols. Äg Ab 8. Wiesbaden: Otto Harrassowitz.
1965. "Eine Schminkpalette von König Skorpion aus Abu Umuri (Unter-

suchung zur ältesten Horustitulatur)," *Orientalia n.s.* 34: 132-67.
1968. "Eine neue Weisheitslehre des Alten Reiches (Die Lehre des Mt-t-j in der altägyptischen Weisheitsliteratur)," *Orientalia* 37: 1-62, 339-45.
1972. "Das papyrus archiv von Abusir," *Orientalia* 41: 56-57.
1978. "Ka," *LÄ* 3: cols. 275-282.
1979. "Königstitulatur," *LÄ* 3: cols. 641-661.
1980. "Iripat," *LÄ* 3: cols. 177-180.

Kees, Hermann
1938. *Die Königin Ahmes-Nefretere als Amonspriester* (NGWGNF no. 2), Göttingen: Vandenhoeck and Ruprecht.
1948. "Die phylen und ihre Vorsteher im die Dienst der Tempel und Totenstiftungen," *Orientalia* 71: 71-90 and 314-325.
1953. *Das Priesterum in Ägyptischen Staat vom Neuen Reich bis zur Spätzeit.* Probleme der Ägyptologie 1. Leiden: E. J. Brill.
1956. *Der Götterglaube im alten Aegypten.* Leipzig: J. C. Hinrichs.
1958. "Archaisches [t-t] = [3t-t] 'Erzieher'?," *ZÄS* 82: 58-62.
1961. *Ancient Egypt: a cultural topography.* Trans. Ian F. D. Morrow, ed. T. G. H. James. London: Faber & Faber.

Keller, C. A.
1992. "Speculations Concerning Interconnections Between Royal Policy and Reputation of Ramesses IV," in *For his Ka: Essays in Memory of Klaus Baer.* D. P. Silverman ed. SAOC, vol. 55. Chicago: Oriental Institute, pp. 145-157.

Kemp, Barry J.
1963. "Excavations at Hierakonpolis Fort: A Preliminary Note," *JEA* 49: 24-28.
1966. "Abydos and the Royal Tombs of the First Dynasty," *JEA* 52: 13-22.
1967. "The Egyptian 1st Dynasty Royal Cemetery," *Antiquity* 41: 22-32.
1972. "Temple and town in ancient Egypt," in. Ucko, P., Tringham, R. and Dimbleby, G. *Man, Settlement and Urbanism.* London: London University.
1973. "Photographs of the Decorated Tomb at Hierakonpolis," *JEA* 59: 36-43.
1976. "The window of appearance at el-Amarna, and the basic structure of this city," *JEA* 62: 82-99.
1977. "The Early Development of Towns in Egypt," *Antiquity* 51: 185-200.
1978. "The harim-palace at Medinet el-Ghurab," *ZÄS* 105: 122-133.
1983. "Old Kingdom, Middle Kingdom and Second Intermediate Period, ca. 2886-1552," in B. Trigger, et al., *Ancient Egypt: A Social History*, Cambridge: University Press, pp. 71-182.
1985a. "Tell el-Amarna," *LÄ* 6: cols. 309-319.
1985b. *Amarna Reports II.* London: Egyptian Exploration Society.
1989. *Ancient Egypt: Anatomy of a Civilization.* London and New York: Routledge.

Kemp, Barry and David B. O'Connor
1974. "An ancient Nile harbour," *International Journal of Nautical Archaeology and Underwater Exploration* 3: 101-136.

Kitchen, Kenneth A.
1964. "Some New Light on the Asiatic Wars of Ramesses II," *JEA* 50: 47-70.
1972. "Ramesses VII and the Twentieth Dynasty," *JEA* 58: 182-194.
1975. *Ramesside Inscriptions*, I. Oxford: B. H. Blackwell.
1979. *Ramesside Inscriptions*, II. Oxford: B. H. Blackwell.
1980. *Ramesside Inscriptions*, III. Oxford: B. H. Blackwell.
1982. *Pharaoh Triumphant: The Life and Times of Ramesses II.* Mississauga: Benben Publications.

1983. *Ramesside Inscriptions,* V. Oxford: B. H. Blackwell.
1986. *The Third Intermediate Period in Egypt.* 2nd ed., with Supplement. Warminster, England: Aris and Phillips.

Koenen, Ludwig
1983. "Die Adaptation ägyptischer Königsideologie am ptolemäischen Königshof," in *Egypt and the hellenistic world: proceedings of the international colloquium Leuven — 24-26 May 1982,* E. Van 't Dack et al. eds. Studia Hellenistica, vol. 27. Leuven, pp. 143-90.

Korostovtsev, Mikhail
1947. "Stèle de Ramsès IV d'Abydos," *BIFAO* 45: 155-73.

Kozloff, Arielle P. and Betsy M. Bryan
1992. *Egypt's Dazzling Sun: Amenhotep III and his World.* Exhibition catalogue, The Cleveland Museum. Bloomington: Indiana University Press.

Krauss, Rolf
1978. *Das Ende der Amarnazeit: Studien zur Geschichte des Neuen Reiches.* HÄB, vol. 7. Hildesheim: Gerstenberg Verlag.
1985. *Sothis- und Monddaten: Studien zur astronomischen und technischen Chronologie Altägyptens.* HÄB, vol. 20. Hildesheim: Gerstenberg Verlag.
1991. "Die amarnazeitliche Familienstele Berlin 14145 unter besonderer Berücksichtigung von Massordnung und Komposition," *Jahrbuch der Berliner Museen* 33: 7-36.
1992. *Astronomische Konzepte und Jenseitsvorstellungen in den Pyramidentexten.* Habilitationsschrift, University of Hamburg.

Kroeber, Burkhart
1970. *Die Neuägyptizismen vor der Amanazeit.* Tubingen: Ph. D. Diss. Eberhard-Karls University.

Kroeper, Karla and Dietrich Wildung
1985. *Minschat Abu Omar: Münchner Ostdelta-Expedition, Vorbericht, 1978-1984.* Schriften aus der ägyptischen Sammlung, vol. 3. Munich: Karl M. Lipp.

Kuhlmann, Klaus-Peter
1977. *Der Thron im alten Ägypten: Untersuchungen zu Semantik, Ikonographie und Symbolik eines Herrschaftszeichens.* ADAIK, vol. 10. Glückstadt: J. J. Augustin.

Kühne, Cord and Heinrich Otten
1971. *Der Íaušgamuwa-Vertrag.* Studien zu den Boghazköy-Texten 16. Wiesbaden: Otto Harrassowitz.

Kuschke, Arnulf
1983. "Qadesch-Schlacht," *LÄ* 5: cols. 31-37.

Lacau, Pierre and Henri Chevrier
1969. *Une chapelle de Sesostris Ier à Karnak.* Cairo: IFAO.
1977. *Une chapelle d'Hatshepsout à Karnak.* Cairo: IFAO.

Lange, Kurt and Max Hirmer
1967. *Ägypten: Architektur, Plastik, Malerei in drei Jahrtausenden.* 4th ed. Munich: Hirmer Verlag.

Largacha, Antonio Pérez
1993. *El nacimiento del estado in Egipto.* Aegyptiaca Complutensia, vol. 2. Henares: University of Alcalá de Henares.

Leahy, Anthony
1985. "The Libyan Period in Egypt: An Essay in Interpretation," *Libyan Studies* 16: 51-65.
1990a. *Libya and Egypt c 1300—750 BC.* London: SOAS Centre of Near and Middle Eastern Studies and Society for Libyan Studies.
1990b. "Abydos in the Libyan Period," In A. Leahy 1990a: 155-76.
forthcoming. *Aspects of Saite Kingship.*

Leahy, Lisa Montagno
1988. *Private Tomb Reliefs of the Late Period from Lower Egypt.* Doctoral dissertation, University of Oxford.

Leclant, Jean and Jacques Clère
1986. "Fouilles et travaux en Égypte et au Soudan, 1985-1985," *Orientalia* 55: 236-319.

Lefebvre, Gustave
1929. *Histoire des grands-prêtres d'Amon de Karnak jusqu'à la XXIe Dynastie.* Paris: P. Geuthner.

Legrain, Georges
1903. "Fragments de canopes," *ASAE* 4: 138-149.

Lehner, Mark
1983. "Some observations on the layout of the Khufu and Khafre pyramids," *JARCE* 20: 7-25.
1985. *The Pyramid Tomb of Hetep-heres and the Satellite Pyramid of Khufur.* Mainz am Rhein: Philip von Zabern.
1986. "The Devlopment of the Giza Necropolis: The Khufu project," *MDAIK* 41: 16-17.
1993. "Giza," *The Oriental Institute 1991-1992 Annual Report,* Oriental Institute: 56-67.

Lepsius, C. Richard
1972-73. *Denkmäler aus Ägypten und Äthiopien.* 12 vols. (always cited by subsuming 6 Abteilungen). Geneva: Édition de Belles-Lettres (reprint of Berlin: Nicholaische Buchhandlung, 1849-59).

Lichtheim, Miriam
1973. *Ancient Egyptian Literature: A Book of Readings,* vol. 1: *The Old and Middle Kingdoms.* Berkeley etc.: University of California Press.
1976. *Ancient Egyptian Literature: A Book of Readings,* vol. 2: *The New Kingdom.* Berkeley etc.: University of California Press.
1980. *Ancient Egyptian Literature: A Book of Readings,* vol. 3: *The Late Period.* Berkeley etc.: University of California Press.

Lincoln, Bruce
1987. "Ritual, Rebellion and Resistance: Once More the Swazi Ncwala," *Man n.s.* 22: 132-56.

Lloyd, Alan B.
1982a. "Nationalist Propaganda in Ptolemaic Egypt," *Historia* 31: 33-53.

1982b. "The Inscription of Udjahorresnet: A Collaborator's Testament," *JEA* 68: 166-80.

Lorton, David
1971. "The Supposed Expedition of Ptolemy II to Persia," *JEA* 57: 160-64.
1979. "Towards a Constitutional Approach to Ancient Egyptian Kingship," *JAOS* 99: 460ff.
1986. "Terms of Coregency in the Middle Kingdom," *Varia Aegyptiaca* 2: 113-130.

Lucas, Alfred
1962. *Ancient Egyptian Materials and Industries.* J. R. Harris ed. London: E. Arnold.

Luft, Ulrich
1976. "Seit der Zeit Gottes," *Studia Aegyptiaca* 2: 47-78.
1978. *Beiträge zur Historisierung der Götterwelt und der Mythenschreibung.* Budapest.

Macadam, M. F. Laming
1949. *The Temples of Kawa*, vol. 1: *The Inscriptions.* 2 vols. London: Geoffrey Cumberlege, Oxford University Press, for Griffith Institute.

Manniche, Lise
1977. "Some Aspects of Ancient Egyptian Sexual Life," *Acta Orientalia* 38: 21.

Maragioglio, Vito and Celeste Rinaldi
1965. *L'Architettura della Pyramidi Menfite, Partie* IV. Turin and Rapello: Tip. Artale.
1966. *L'Architettura della Pyramidi Menfite, Partie* V. Turin and Rapello: Tip. Artale.
1967. *L'Architettura della Pyramidi Menfite, Partie* VI. Turin and Rapello: Tip. Artale.

Martin, Geoffrey T.
1982. "Queen Mutnodjmet at Memphis and El-Amarna," *L'Égyptologie en 1979* II. Cahiers internationaux du C.N.R.S., No. 595: 275-278. Paris: CNRS.

Martin, Karl
1984. "Sedfest," *LÄ* 5: cols. 782-790.

Martin-Pardey, Eva
1986. "Wesir, Wesirat," *LÄ* 6: cols. 1227-1235.

McMullen, David
1987. "The Ritual Code of T'ang China," In Cannadine and Price 1987, pp. 181-236.

Meeks, Dimitri
1982. *Année lexicographique* III, Paris: D. Meeks.

Meyer, Eduard
1904. *Aegyptische Chronologie.* Berlin.

Midant-Reynes, Béatrix
1987. "Contribution à l'étude de la sociètè prédynastique: le cas du couteau 'ripple-flake'," *SAK* 14: 185-224.

1992. *Préhistoire de l'Égypte des premiers hommes aux premiers pharaons.* Paris: Armand Colin.

Millar, Fergus
1977. *The Emperor in the Roman World (31 BC-AD 337).* London: Duckworth.

Milne, J. Grafton
1924. *A History of Egypt under Roman rule.* 3rd ed. Vol. 5 of W. M. F. Petrie, *A History of Egypt.* London: Methuen.

Minas, Martina
1993. *The Eponymous Priesthoods of the Ptolemaic Period: A Study of the Demotic Evidence.* M.Phil. thesis, University of Oxford.

Moftah, Ramses
1985. *Studien zum ägyptischen Königsdogma im Neuen Reich.* SDAIK vol. 20. Mainz am Rhein: Philip von Zabern.

Monnet Saleh, Janine
1983. "Les représentations de temples sur plate-formes à pieux, de la poterie gerzéene d'Egypte," *BIFAO* 83: 263-96.
1987. "Remarques sur les représentations de la peinture d'Hierakonpolis (Tombe n° 100)," *JEA* 73: 51-58.

Montet, Pierre
1929. *Byblos et l'Égypte.* Paris: Paul Geuthner.

Moorey, P. R. S.
1987. "On Tracking Cultural Transfers in Prehistory: The Case of Egypt and Lower Mesopotamia in the Fourth Millennium B.C.," In *Centre and Periphery in the Ancient World,* Michael Rowlands, Mogens Larsen, and Kristian Kristiansen eds. *New Directions in Archaeology.* Cambridge etc.: Cambridge University Press, pp. 36-46.

Morenz, Siegfried
1973a. "Traditionen um Menes," *ZÄS* 99: 10-16.
1973b [1960] *Egyptian Religion.* Trans. Ann. E. Keep. London: Methuen.
1975 [1964] Die Heraufkunft des transzendenten Gottes in Ägypten," In *Religion und Geschichte des alten Ägypten*: gesammelte Aufsätze, Elke Blumenthal et al. eds. Weimar: Hermann Böhlaus Nachfolger, pp. 77-119.

Moret, Alexandre
1902. *Du caractère religieux de la royauté pharaonique.* Doctoral dissertation. Paris: Ernest Leroux.

Morgan, Jacques de, et al.
[1894]. *Catalogue des monuments et inscriptions de l'Égypte antique* I, 1: *De la frontière de Nubie à Kom Ombos.* [Vienna: Adolf Holzhausen.]

Müller, Hugo
1938. *Die formale Entwicklung der ägyptischen Königstitulatur.* ÄF, vol. 7. Glückstadt: J. J. Augustin.

Murnane, William J.
1975. "The Earlier Reign of Ramesses II and his Coregency with Sety I," *JNES* 34: 153-190.

1977. *Ancient Egyptian Coregencies*. SAOC, vol. 40. Chicago: The Oriental Institute.
1979. "The Bark of Amun on the Third Pylon at Karnak," *JARCE* 16: 11-27.
1980. *United with Eternity*. Chicago: Oriental Institute.
1981. "Opetfest," *LÄ* 4: cols. 574-579.
1985a. "False Doors and Religious Ritual inside Luxor Temple," in *Mélanges Gamal Eddin Mokhtar* II. BdÉ, vol. 97.2. Cairo: IFAO, pp. 135-148.
1985b. *The Road to Kadesh*. SAOC, vol. 42. Chicago: The Oriental Institute.
1987. "The Gebel Sheikh Suleiman Monument: Epigraphic Remarks," Appendix C in Williams and Logan 1987, 282-85
1990. *The Road to Kadesh*, second revised ed. SAOC, vol. 42. Chicago: The Oriental Institute.

Murnane, William and Chuck van Siclen III
1993. *The Boundary Stelae of Akhenaten*. London and New York: Kegan Paul International.

Murray, Oswyn
1970. "Hecataeus of Abdera and Pharaonic Kingship," *JEA* 56: 141ff.

Museum of Fine Arts, Boston
1988. *Mummies and Magic: The Funerary Arts of Ancient Egypt*. Boston: Museum of Fine Arts.

Mysliwiec, Karol
1978. "Le Naos de Pithom," *BIFAO* 78: 171-95.
1980. "Die Rolle des Atum in der *išd*-Baum-Szene," *MDAIK* 36: 349-356.

Needler, Winifred
1984. *Predynastic and Archaic Egypt in the Brooklyn Museum*. Wilbour Monographs, vol. 9. Brooklyn: The Brooklyn Museum.

Newberry, Percy
1893. *Beni Hasan* I. Oxford: University Press.
1894. *El Bersheh* I. ASE. London: The Egypt Exploration Society.
1928. "Akhenaten's Eldest Son-in-Law, 'Ankhkheprure," *JEA* 14: 3-9.

Nims, Charles
1965. *Thebes of the Pharaohs*. London: Elek Books Ltd.

Norden, F. L.
1757. *Travels in Egypt and Nubia* I. London.

O' Connor, David B.
1980. "Malkata," *LÄ* 3: 1173-1177.
1983. "New Kingdom and Third Intermediate Period, 1552-664 B.C.," in B. G. Trigger, et al., *Ancient Egypt: A Social History*. Cambridge: Cambridge University Press, pp. 183-278.
1987. "The Earliest Pharaohs and the University Museum, Old and New Excavations: 1900-1987," *Expedition* 29, no. 1: 27-39.
1987/88. "Demarcating the boundaries: an interpretation of a scene in the tomb of Mahu, el-Amarna," *BES* 9: 41-52.
1989a. "City and Palace in New Kingdom Egypt," *CRIPEL* 11: 73-87.
1989b. "New Funerary Enclosures (Talbezirke) of the Early Dynastic Period at Abydos," *JARCE* 26: 51-86.
1991. "Boat Graves and Pyramid Origins," *Expedition* 33, no. 3: 5-7.

1992. "The Status of Early Egyptian Temples: An Alternate Theory," In Friedman and Adams 1992, 83-97.

1993 "Mirror of the cosmos: the palace of Merenptah," in *Fragments of a shattered visage. The Proceedings of the International Seminar on Ramesses the Great.* Edward Bleiberg and Rita Freed eds. Memphis, Tennessee: Institute of Egyptian Art and Archaeology, pp. 167-198.

in press . "Social and Economic Aspects of the Egyptian Temple," In *Civilizations of the Ancient Near East,* Jack M. Sasson et al. eds. New York: Scribners.

forthcoming. *City and Cosmos in Ancient Egypt.*

n.d. "The Royal City of Dynasty 18 and the Urban Process in Egypt," ms.

Olmstead, A. T.
1948. *History of the Persian Empire.* Chicago: University of Chicago Press.

Osing, Jürgen
1976. "Achtungstexte aus dem Alten Reich (II)," *MDAIK* 32: 133-85.

Otto, Eberhard
1952. *Topographie des thebanischen Gaues.* Leipzig.
1954. *Die biographischen Inschriften der ägyptischen Spätzeit: ihre geistesgeschichtliche und literarische Bedeutung.* PÄ, vol. 2. Leiden: E. J. Brill.
1957. "Zwei Bemerkungen zum Königskult der Spätzeit," *MDAIK* 15: 193-208.
1960. "Der Gebrauch des Königstitels *bjtj*," *ZÄS* 85: 143-52.
1964. *Gott und Mensch nach den ägyptischen Tempelinschriften der griechischrömischen Zeit: Eine Untersuchung zur Phraseologie der Tempelinschriften.* AHAW. Heidelberg: C. Winter.
1968. *Egyptian Art and the Cults of Osiris and Amon.* Trans. Kate Bosse-Griffiths. London: Thames and Hudson.
1969. "Legitimation des Herrschens im pharaonischen Ägypten," *Saeculum* 20: 385-411.

Payne, Joan Crowfoot
1993. *Catalogue of the Predynastic Egyptian Collection in the Ashmolean Museum.* Oxford: Clarendon Press.

Peet, T. Eric
1923. *The City of Akhenaten.* with C. L. Woolley London: Egypt Exploration Society.
1930. *The Great Tomb Robberies of the Twentieth Dynasty* I, *Texts.* Oxford: Clarendon Press.

Pereyra de Fidanza, María Violeta
1990. "La realeza egipcia: Su origen y fundamentación temprana," *Revista de Estudios de Egiptología* 1: 53-78.

Pérez Die, Maria del Carmen
1990. "Fouilles récentes à Herakleopolis Magna," In A. Leahy 1990a: 115-29.

Perring, John E.
1839-1842. *The Pyramids of Giza* (from actual survey and measurements), 3 vols. London: J. Fraser.

Petrie, Sir W. M. Flinders
1899. *Kahun, Gurob and Hawara.* London: K. Paul, Trench, Trübner and co.
1920. *Prehistoric Egypt.* British School of Archaeology in Egypt and Egyptian Re-

search Account, twenty-third year, 1917. London: British School of Archaeology in Egypt; Bernard Quaritch.

Phillips, Alan K.
1977. "Horemheb, Founder of the Nineteenth Dynasty?," *Orientalia* 46: 116-121.

Piankoff, Alexandre
1954. *The Tomb of Ramesses VI, Texts.* New York: Pantheon Books.

Pinch, Geraldine
1993. *Votive Offerings to Hathor.* Oxford: Griffith Institute.

Porada, Edith
1980. "A Lapis Lazuli Figurine from Hierakonpolis in Egypt," *Iranica Antiqua* 15: 175-80.

Porter, Bertha, and Rosalind L. B. Moss
1939. *Topographical Bibliography of Ancient Egyptian Hieroglyphic Texts, Reliefs, and Paintings*, volume 6: *Upper Egypt: Chief Temples.* Oxford: Clarendon Press.

Posener, Georges
1956. *Littérature et politique dans l'Égypte de la XIIe dynastie.* Bibliothèque de l'École des Hautes Études, vol. 307. Paris: Librarie Ancienne Honore Champion.
1957. "Le conte de Néferkarê et du général Siséné (Recherches littéraires, VI)," *RdÉ* 11: 119-37.
1960. *De la divinité du pharaon.* Cahiers de la Société Asiatique, no. 15. Paris: Imprimerie Nationale.
1965a. "Le nom de l'enseigne appelée 'Khons' (𓊍)," *RdE* 17: 193-95.
1965b. "Sur l'orientation et l'ordre des points cardinaux chez les Égyptiens," in *Göttinger Vorträge.* NAWG, No. 2. Göttingen: Vandenhoeck & Ruprecht, pp. 69-78.
1976. *L'enseignement loyaliste, sagesse égyptienne du Moyen Empire.* Centre de Recherches d'histoire et de philologie ... École pratique des Hautes Études, 2: Hautes Études Orientales, vol. 5. Geneva: Droz.
1979a. "Lehre, loyalistiche," *LÄ* 3: cols. 981-984.
1979b. "L'enseignement d'un homme à son fils," in *Studien zu altägyptischen Lebenslehren.* Erik Hornung and Othmar Keel eds. OBO, vol. 28. Göttingen: Vandenhoeck and Ruprecht: 307-316.
1985. *Le Papyrus Vandier.* Bibliothèque Générale, vol. 7. Cairo: IFAO.
1987. *Cinq figurines d'envoûtement.* IFAO BE, vol. 101. Cairo: IFAO.

Posener-Kriéger, Paule
1976. *Les Archives du temple funéraire de Néferirkarê-kakai: les papyrus d'Abou Sir.* 2 vols. Cairo: IFAO.
1986. "Old Kingdom Papyri: External Features," in *Papyrus: Structure and Usage*, M. L. Bierbrier ed. British Museum, Occasional Paper no. 60. London: British Museum, pp. 25-41.

Préaux, Claire
1976. "L'image du roi de l'époque hellénistique," In *Images of Man in Ancient and Medieval Thought: Studia Gerardo Verbeke ab Amicis et Collegis Dicata*, F. Bossier et al. eds. Symbolae Facultatis Litterarum et Philosophiae Lovaniensis, vol. A 1. Louvain: Leuven University Press, pp. 53-75.

Price, S. R. F.
1984. *Rituals and Power: The Roman Imperial Cult in Asia Minor.* Cambridge etc.:
  Cambridge University Press.

Pritchard, James B. (ed.)
1969 [1955]. *Ancient Near Eastern Texts Relating to the Old Testament.* 3rd ed. with
  Supplement. Princeton, NJ: Princeton University Press.

Quaegebeur, Jan
1988. "Cleopatra VII and the Cults of the Ptolemaic Queens," In [Robert S.
  Bianchi,] *Cleopatra's Egypt: Age of the Ptolemies.* Exhibition catalogue.
  Brooklyn NY: The Brooklyn Museum, pp. 41-54.
1989. "The Egyptian Clergy and the Cult of the Ptolemaic Dynasty," *Ancient Society* 20: 93-116.

Quibell, J. E.
1900. *Hierakonpolis*, vol. 1. Egyptian Research Account, vol. 4. London: Bernard
  Quaritch.

Quibell, J. E., and F. W. Green
1902. *Hierakonpolis*, vol. 2. Egyptian Research Account, vol. 5. London: Bernard
  Quaritch.

Radwan, Ali
1969. *Die Darstellungen des Königs und seiner Familienangehörigen in des Privat-
  gräbern der 18. Dynastie.* Berlin: B. Hessling.
1975a. "Der Königsnamen: epigraphisches zum göttlichen Königtum im Alten
  Ägypten," *SAK* 2: 212-34.
1975b. "Zur bildlichen Gleichsetzung des ägyptischen Königs mit der Gottheit,"
  MDAIK 31: 99ff.
1985. "Einige Aspekte der Vergöttlichung des ägyptischen Königs," in *Ägypten,
  Dauer und Wandel: Symposium anlässisch des 75 jahrigen Bestehens des DAIK,
  10. und 11. Oktober 1982.* SDAIK, vol. 18. Mainz am Rhein: Philip von
  Zabern, pp. 53-69.

Raslan, Mohammed Awad
1973. "The Causeway of Ounas Pyramid," *ASAE* 61: 151-169.

Ratié, Suzanne
1979. *La reine Hatchepsout: sources et problems.* Orientalia Monspeliensia, vol 1.
  Leiden: E. J. Brill.

Redford, Donald B.
1967. *History and Chronology of the Egyptian Eighteenth Dynasty: Seven Studies.*
  Toronto: University of Toronto Press.
1970. "The Hyksos in History and Tradition," *Orientalia* 39: 1-51.
1973. "Studies on Akhenaten at Thebes I," *JARCE* 10: 77-94.
1975. "Studies on Akhenaten at Thebes, II...," *JARCE* 12: 9-14.
1976. "The Sun-disc in Akhenaten's Program: Its Worship and Antecedents,"
  JARCE 13: 47-61.
1981. "A Royal Speech from the Blocks of the 10th Pylon," *BES* 3: 87-102.
1982. "An Offering Inscription from the Second Pylon at Karnak," in *Studies in
  Philology in Honour of Ronald James Williams.* Toronto: SSEA Publications,
  pp. 125-31.
1984. *Akhenaten. The Heretic King.* Princeton, NJ: Princeton University Press.

1986a. *Pharaonic King-lists, Annals and Day-books: A Contribution to the Study of the Egyptian Sense of History.* SSEA Publication no. 4. Mississauga, Ont.: Benben Publications.

1986b. "Egypt and Western Asia in the Old Kingdom," *JARCE* 23: 125-44.

1987. " The Tod Inscription of Senwosret I and Early 12th Dynasty Involvement in Nubia and the South," *JSSEA* 17 (1/2): 36-55.

1992. *Egypt, Canaan, and Israel in Ancient Times.* Princeton, NJ: Princeton University Press.

Reeves, C. N. and John H. Taylor
1992. *Howard Carter: Before Tutankhamun.* New York: H. N. Abrams.

Reisner, George Andrew
1931. *Mycerinus: The Temples of The Third Pyramid of Giza.* Cambridge: Harvard Universtiy Press.

1936. *The Development of the Egyptian Tomb down to the Accession of Cheops.* Cambridge: Harvard University Press.

1942. *A History of the Giza Necropolis*, vol. 1. Cambridge: Harvard University Press.

1955. *A History of the Giza Necropolis*, vol. 2. Completed and revised by William Stevenson-Smith. Cambridge: Harvard University Press.

Ricke, Herbert
1944. "Bemerkungen zu ägyptischen Baukunst des Alten Reichs I," in *Beiträge zur ägyptische Bauforschung und Altertumskunde* IV. Zurich: Borchardt Institut.

1950. "Bemerkungen zu ägyptischen Baukunst des Alten Reichs II," in *Beiträge zur ägyptische Bauforschung und Altertumskunde* V. Zurich: Borchardt Institut.

Ricke, Herbert, George R. Hughes, and Edward F. Wente
1967. *The Beit el-Wali Temple of Ramesses II.* Chicago: University of Chicago Press.

Ridley, Ronald T.
1973. *The Unification of Egypt as Seen Through a Study of the Major Knife-handles, Palettes and Maceheads.* Deception Bay (Australia): Shield Press.

Rizkana, Ibrahim and Jürgen Seeher
1987-1990. *Maadi.* 4 vols. Excavations at the Predynastic Site of Maadi and Its Cemeteries Conducted by Mustapha Amer and Ibrahim Rizkana on Behalf of the Department of Geography, Faculty of Arts of Cairo University, 1930-1953. AV, vols. 64, 65, 80, 81. Mainz: Philip von Zabern.

Roccati, Alessandro
1982. *La littérature historique sous l'Ancien Empire égyptien.* Littératures anciennes du Proche-Orient. Paris: Editions du Cerf.

Roeder, Günther
1954. "Zwei hieroglyphische Inschriften aus Hermopolis (Ober-ägypten)," *ASAE* 52: 315-442.

Roemer, M.
1980. "Kronprinz," *LÄ* 3: cols. 816-818.

Romano, James F.
1979. *The Luxor Museum of Ancient Egyptian Art.* Cairo: American Research Center in Egypt.

Romer, John
1982. *Romer's Egypt: A New Light on the Civilization of Ancient Egypt.* London: Michael Joseph/Rainbird.
1984. *Ancient Lives: Daily Life in Egypt of the Pharaohs.* New York: Holt, Rinehart and Winston.

Rose, Herbert J.
1970. "Sol," *Oxford Classical Dictionary.* Oxford: 999

Rosellini, I.
1832. *I Monumenti dell'Egitto e della Nubia I, Monumenti storici.* Pisa: Presso N. Capurro.

Rössler-Köhler, Ursula
1991. *Individuelle Haltungen zum ägyptischen Königtum der Spätzeit. Private Quellen und ihre Königswertung im Spannungsfeld zwischen Erwartung and Erfahrung.* GOF 4, vol. 21. Wiesbaden: Otto Harrassowitz.

Rowton, M. B.
1959. "The Background of the Treaty between Ramesses II and Hattušilis III," *Journal of Cuneiform Studies* 13: 1-11.
1960. "Comparative Chronology at the Time of Dynasty XIX," *JNES* 19: 15-22.
1966. "The Material from Western Asia and the Chronology of the Nineteenth Dynasty," *JNES* 25: 240-258.

Runciman, Walter G.
1982. "Origins of States: The Case of Archaic Greece," *Comparative Studies in Society and History* 24: 351-77.

Rupp, Alfred
1969. "Geschichte und Seinszusammenhang," *BiOr* 26: 19-26.

Sahlins, Marshall
1985. *Islands of History.* Chicago: University of Chicago Press.

Samson, Julia
1978. *Amarna, City of Akhenaten and Nefertiti. Nefertiti as Pharaoh.* Warminster.

Sandman, Maj
1938. *Texts from the Time of Akhenaten.* BiAe, vol. 8. Bruxelles: La Fondation Égyptologique Reine Élisabeth.

Save-Soderbergh, Torgny
1953. *On Egyptian Representation of Hippopotamus Hunting as a Religious Motive.* Horae Soederblomianae, vol. 3. Uppsala: C. W. K. Gleerup.

Scamuzzi, Ernesto
1965. *Egyptian Art in the Egyptian Museum of Turin.* New York: Harry N. Abrams.

Schäfer, Heinrich
1902. *Ein Bruchstäck altägyptischer Annalen.* Abhandlungen der Preussischen Akademie der Wissenschaften, Anhang, 1902. Berlin: Georg Reimer.
1957. "Das Niederschlagen der Feinde," *WZKM* 54: 168-76.

Schäfer, Heinrich, and Walter Andrae
1942. *Die Kunst des alten Orients.* 3rd ed. Propyläen-Kunstgeschichte, vol. 2. Berlin: Propyläen-Verlag.

Schele, Linda and Mary Ellen Miller
1986. *The Blood of Kings: Dynasty and Ritual in Maya Art.* Fort Worth: Kimbell Art Museum; London: Sotheby's Publications.

Schenkel, Wolfgang
1986. "Das Wort fur 'König (von Oberägypten)'," *GM* 94: 57-73.

Schmitz, Bettina
1976. *Untersuchungen zum Titel S3-Njswt, "Königssohn."* Bonn: R. Habelt.
1980. "Königssohn," *LÄ* 3: cols. 626-630.
1986. "Weldträger," *LÄ* 6: cols. 1161-1163.

Schnepel, Burkhart
1987. "Max Weber's Theory of Charisma and Its Applicability to Anthropological Research," *Journal of the Anthropological Society of Oxford* 18: 26-48.

Schott, Siegfried
1950. *Hieroglyphen: Untersuchungen zum Ursprung der Schrift.* Akademie der Wissenschaften und der Literatur in Mainz, Abhandlungen, Geistes- und Sozialwissenschaftliche Klasse 1950, no. 24. Wiesbaden: Franz Steiner.
1950. "Bemerkungen zur ägyptischen pyramiden kult," in *Beiträge zur ägyptische Bauforschung und Altertumskunde* V. Zurich: Borchardt Institut, pp. 135-253.
1969. "Ein Kult der Götten Neith in Das Sonnenheiligtum des Userkaf," in *Beiträge zur ägyptische Bauforschung und Altertumskunde* VIII. Zurich: Borchardt Institut, pp. 123-138.
1970. "Ägyptischen quellen zum plan des Sphinxtemple," in *Beiträge zur ägyptische Bauforschung und Altertumskunde* X. Zurich: Borchardt Institut, pp. 49-79.

Schulman, Alan R.
1964. *Military Rank, Title and Organization in the Egyptian New Kingdom.* MÄS, vol. 6. Berlin: Bruno Hessling.
1965. "The Berlin 'Trauerrelief' (No. 12411) and Some Officials of Tut'ankhamun and Ay," *JARCE* 4: 55-68.
1978. "Aspects of Ramesside Diplomacy: the Treaty of Year 21," *JSSEA* 8: 112-130.
1979. "Diplomatic Marriage in the Egyptian New Kingdom," *JNES* 38: 177-193.
1982. "The Nubian War of Akhenaton," in *L'Égyptologie en 1979.* Paris: CNRS, pp. 299-316.

Schweitzer, Ursula
1956. *Das Wesen des Ka in Deisseits und Jenseits der Alten Ägypter.* Äg Fo, vol. 19. Glückstadt: J. J. Augustin.

Seipel, Wilfried
1980. *Untersuchungen zu den ägyptischen Königinnen der Frühzeit und des Alten*

Reiches: Quellen und historische Einordnung. Dissertation, University of Hamburg.

Sethe, Kurt
1896. *Die Thronwirren unter den nachfolgen Königs Thutmosis I.* Leipzig: J. C. Hinrichs.
1907. "Uber einige Kurznamen des Neuen Reiches," *ZÄS* 44: 87-92.
1929. *Amun und die Acht Urgotter von Hermopolis.* Berlin.
1930. *Urgeschichte und älteste Religion der Ägypter.* Abhandlungen zur Kunde des Morgenlandes 18, no. 4. Leipzig: Brockhaus.

Sievertsen, Uwe
1992. "Das Messer vom Gebel el-Arak," *Baghdader Mitteilungen* 23: 1-75.

Silverman, David P.
1980. *Interrogative Constructions with Jn and Jn-jw in Old and Middle Egyptian.* Malibu: Undena.
1982. "Wit and Humor," in *Egypt's Golden Age: The Art of Living in the New Kingdom 1558-1085.* Boston: Museum of Fine Arts: 277-278.
1991a. "Deities and Divinity in Ancient Egypt," in *Religion in Ancient Egypt: Gods, Myths, and Personal Practice.* Byron E. Shafer ed. Ithaca: Cornell University Press, pp. 7-87.
1991b. "Texts from the Amarna period and their position in the development of Ancient Egyptian," *Lingua Aegyptia* 1: 301-314.
in press. "Coffin Texts From Bersheh, Kom el Hisn, and Mendes," in *Coffin Texts.* Leiden: Nederlands Instituut voor het Nabije Oosten, 1995.

Simpson, William Kelly
1956. "The Single-Dated Monuments of Sesostris I: An Aspect in the Institution of Coregency in the Twelfth Dynasty," *JNES* 15: 214-219.
1972. *The Literature of Ancient Egypt.* New Haven: Yale University Press.
1982a. "Pap. Westcar," *LÄ* 4: cols. 744-746.
1982b. "Egyptian Sculpture and Two-dimensional Representation as Propaganda," *JEA* 68: 266-71.
1983. "Sarenput I," *LÄ* 5: cols. 428-430.
1984. "Sinuhe," *LÄ* 5: cols. 950-955.

Smith, George Elliot
1912. *The Royal Mummies.* Cairo: Musée des Antiquités Égyptiennes.

Smith, Harry S. and David G. Jeffereys
1986. "A Survey of Memphis, Egypt," *Antiquity* 60: 89-95.

Smith, Harry S. and A. Smith
1976. "A Reconsideration of the Kamose Texts," *ZÄS* 103: 38-76.

Smith, W. Stevenson
1941. "Old Kingdom Sculpture," *AJA* 45: 514-28.
1946. *A History of Egyptian Sculpture and Painting in the Old Kingdom.* Boston and London: Oxford University Press for the Museum of Fine Arts Boston.
1971. "The Old Kingdom in Egypt," in *The Cambridge Ancient History*, I:2: *Early History of the Middle East*, 3rd ed., I. E. S. Edwards et al. eds. Cambridge: University Press: 145-207.
1981. *The Art and Architecture of Ancient Egypt.* Revised by W. K. Simpson. Harmondsworth: Penguin Books.

Smith, Ray Winfield, and Donald B. Redford
1976. *The Akhenaten Temple Project*, vol. 1: *Initial Discoveries*. Warminster: Aris & Phillips.

Sørenson, Jørgen Podemann
1989. "Divine Access: the So-called Democratization of Egyptian Funerary Literature as A Socio-cultural Process," *Cognitive Structures and Popular Expressions*, ed. G. Englund Uppsala: Uppsala University, pp. 109-125.

Spalinger, Anthony
1978a. "The Foreign Policy of Egypt Preceding the Assyrian Conquest," *CdÉ* 53, no. 105: 22-47.
1978b. "The Concept of the Monarchy During the Saite Epoch — An Essay of Synthesis," *Orientalia* 47: 12-36.
1988. "A Hymn of Praise to Akhenaten," *Akhenaten Temple Project*, vol. II. Toronto.

Spencer, A. Jeffrey
1993. *Early Egypt: The Rise of Civilisation in the Nile Valley*. London: British Museum Press.

Spencer, Patricia
1984. *The Egyptian Temple. A Lexicographical Study*. London: Kegan Paul.

Spiegel, Joachim
1938. "Die Grundbedeutung des Stammes $ḥm$," *ZÄS* 74: 112-21.

Stadelmann, Rainer
1965. "Die 400-Jahr-Stele," *CdÉ* 40: 46-60.
1971. "Das Grab im Tempelhof. Der Typus des Königsgrabes in der Spätzeit," *MDAIK* 27: 111-23.
1973. "Templepalast und Erscheinungsfenster in den Thebanischen Totentempeln," *MDAIK* 29: 221-242.
1978. "Tempel und Tempelnamen in Theben -Ost und -West," *MDAIK* 34: 171-180.
1979. "Totentempel und Millionenjahrhaus in Theben," *MDAIK* 35: 303-322.
1981a. "La ville de Pyramide l'ancien Empire," *RdÉ* 33: 67-77.
1981b. "Die lange Regierung Ramses' II," *MDAIK* 37: 457-463.
1982. "Pyramiden," *LÄ* 4: cols. 1205-63.
1984. "Sethos I," *LÄ* 5: cols. 911-917.
1985a. "Totentempel," *LÄ* 6: cols. 694-711.
1985b. "Theben," *LÄ* 6: cols. 465-474.
1985c. *Die ägyptischen Pyramiden: vom Ziegelbau zum Weltwunder*. Darmstadt: Wissenschaftliche Buchgesellschaft.
1986. "Vierhundertjahrstele," *LÄ* 6: cols. 1039-1043.

Swan Hall, Emma
1986. *The Pharaoh Smites his Enemies: A Comparative Study*. MÄS, vol. 44. Berlin: Bruno Hessling.

Swelim, Nabil
1983. *Some Problems on the History of the Third Dynasty*. Publications of the Archaeological Society of Alexandria: Philological and Historical Studies 7. Alexandria: Archaeological Society of Alexandria.

te Velde, Herman
1977. *Seth, God of Confusion*. 2nd ed. PÄ, vol. 6. Leiden: E. J. Brill.

1990. "Some Remarks on the Concept 'Person' in the Ancient Egyptian Culture," in *Concepts of Person in Religion and Thought*, ed. H. G. Kippenberg. Berlin-New York, pp. 83-101.

Tefnin, Roland,
1979. "Image et histoire: réflexions sur l'usage documentaire de l'image égyptienne," *CdÉ* 54, no. 108: 218-44.
1992. "Les yeux et les oreilles du Roi," in *L'atelier de l'orfèvre: Mélanges offerts à Ph. Derchain*, M. Broze and P. Talon eds. Louvain: Peeters, pp. 147-56.

Terrace, Edward L.
1961. "A Fragmentary Triad of King Mycerinus," *BMFA* 59: 40-49.

Tobin, Vincent A.
1986. *The Intellectual Organization of the Amarna Period*. PhD Thesis; Hebrew University.
1989. *Theological Principles of Egyptian Religion*. New York: Peter Long.

Toynbee, Arnold J.
1962. *A Study of History*, VI. Oxford and New York: Oxford University Press.

Trigger, Bruce G., et al.
1983. *Ancient Egypt. A Social History*. Cambridge: Cambridge University Press.

Troy, Lana
1986 . *Patterns of Queenship in Ancient Egyptian Myth and History*. Boreas, vol. 14. Uppsala: University of Uppsala.

Ünal, Ahmet
1974. *Ḫattušili III*, 1.1. Texte der Hethiter 4.1. Heidelberg: C. Winter.

Uphill, E.
1970. "The Per Aten at Amarna," *JNES* 29: 151-166.

Valeri, Valerio
1985. *Kingship and Sacrifice: Ritual and Society in Ancient Hawaii*. Trans. Paula Wissing. Chicago: University of Chicago Press.

Valloggia, Michel
1986. *Le Mastabe de Medou-Nefer*. Fouilles de l'Institut Français d'Archéologie Orientale du Caire, no. 31. Cairo: IFAO.

van den Brink, Edwin C. M. (ed.)
1992. *The Nile Delta in Transition: 4th.-3rd. Millennium B.C.* Tel Aviv: published by the editor.

Van den Boorn, G. P. F.
1982. "On the Date of 'The Duties of the Vizier'," *Orientalia* 51: 369-381.
1988. *The Duties of the Vizier*. London and New York: Kegan Paul International.

Van Dijk, J.
1988. "The development of the Memphite Necropolis in the Post-Amarna Period," in A. P. Zivie ed., *Memphis et ses Nécropoles au Nouvel Empire*. Paris: CNRS, pp. 37-46.

Vandersleyen, Claude
    1967. "Une tempête sous le règne d'Amosis," *RdE* 19: 123-59.
    1968. "Deux nouveaux fragments de la stèle d'Amosis relatant une tempête," *RdÉ* 20: 127-34.

Vandier, Jacques
    1950. *Mo'alla.* IFAO BE, vol. 18. Cairo: IFAO.
    1955. *Manuel d'archéologie égyptienne* II. *Les grandes époques. L'architecture religieuses et civile.* Paris: A. et J. Picard.
    1961. *Le Papyrus Jumilhac.* [Paris]: Centre Nationale de la Recherche Scientifique.

Varille, A.
    1968. *Inscriptions concernant l'architecte Amenhotep fils de Hapou.* Bibliothèque d'Étude, vol. 44. Cairo: IFAO.

Vernus, Pascal
    1979. "La stèle du roi Sekhemsankhtowy Neferhotep Iykhernofret et la domination Hyksos," *ASAE* 68: 129-35.
    1993. "La naissance de l'écriture dans l'Égypte ancienne," *Archéo-Nil* 3: 75-108.

Vyse, Howard
    1840-1842. *Operations carried on at the pyramid of Gizeh.* 3 vols. London: J. Fraser.

von der Way, Thomas
    1984. *Die Textüberlieferung Ramses II. zur Qadeš-Schlacht: Analyse und Struktur.* HÅB, vol. 22. Hildesheim: Gerstenberg Verlag.
    1991. "Die Grabungen in Buto und die Reichseinigung," *MDAIK* 47: 419-24.
    1992. "Excavations at Tell el-Fara'in/Buto in 1987-1989," in van den Brink 1992, pp. 1-8.

von der Way, Thomas, and Klaus Schmidt
    1987. "Tell el-Fara'in — Buto: 2. Bericht," *MDAIK* 43: 241-57.

Waddell, W. G.
    1940. *Manetho.* Loeb Classical Library. Cambridge, Mass.: Harvard University Press; London: William Heinemann.

Wells, Ronald A.
    1987. "The Amarna M, X, K, Boundary Stela Date: A Modern Calendar Equivalent," *SAK* 14: 313-333.

Wenig, Steffen
    1975. "Amenophis IV," *LÄ* 1: cols. 210-19.

Wente, Edward F.
    1967. *Late Ramesside Letters.* Chicago: University of Chicago Press.
    1969. "Hathor at the Jubilee," in *Studies in Honor of John A. Wilson.* SAOC, vol. 35. Chicago: University of Chicago Press, pp. 83-91.
    1972a. "The Tale of Two Brothers," in *The Literature of Ancient Egypt,* ed. W. K. Simpson. New Haven: Yale University Press, pp. 92-102.
    1972b. "The Doomed Prince," in *The Literature of Ancient Egypt,* ed. W. K. Simpson. New Haven: Yale University Press, pp. 85-91.
    1972c. "The Contendings of Horus and Seth," in *The Literature of Ancient Egypt,*

ed. W. K. Simpson. New Haven: Yale University Press, pp. 108-126.

1982. "Funerary Beliefs of the Ancient Egyptians," *Expedition* 24: 17-26.

1984. "Some Graffiti from the Reign of Hatshepsut," *JNES* 43: 47-54.

1990. *Letters from Egypt.* Atlanta: Scholars Press.

Wente, E. F. and C. C. Van Siclen III
1976. "A Chronology of the New Kingdom," in *Studies in Honor of George R. Hughes.* SAOC, vol. 39. Chicago: The Oriental Institute, pp. 217-262.

Westendorf, Wolfhart
1966. *Altägyptische Darstellungen des Sonnenlaufs auf der abschüssigen Himmelsbahn.* MÄS, vol. 10. Berlin: Bruno Hessling.

1984. "Der Eine im Himmel, der Andere in der Erde," in *Mélanges (Adolph) Gutbub.* Montpellier: Université de Montpellier, pp. 240-44.

Whitehouse, Helen
1987. "King Den in Oxford," *Oxford Journal of Archaeology* 6: 257-67.

Wildung, Dietrich
1972. "Ramses, die grosse Sonne Ägyptens," *ZÄS* 99: 33-41.

1973a. "Göttlichkeitsstufen des Pharao," *OLZ* 59: 549-65.

1973b. "Der König Ägyptens als Herr der Welt?," *AFO* 24: 108

1977. "Höherpriester von Memphis," *LÄ* 3: cols. 1256-1263.

1979. "Königskult," *LÄ* 3: cols. 533-534.

Wilkinson, John Gardner
1878. *Manners and Customs of the Ancient Egyptians.* 3 volumes. London: J. Murray.

Wilkinson, Richard H.
1985 [1987]. "The Horus Name and the Form and Significance of the Serekh in the Royal Egyptian Titulary," *JSSEA* 15: 98-104.

Willems, Harco
1988. *Chests of Life.* Ex Oriente Lux, vol. 15. Belgium: Orientalist Leuven.

Williams, Bruce
1986. *Excavations Between Abu Simbel and the Sudan Frontier, vol. 1, The A-Group Royal Cemetery at Qustul: Cemetery L.* Oriental Institute Nubian Expedition, vol. 3. Chicago: University of Chicago Press.

1987. "Forbears of Menes in Nubia: Myth or Reality?," *JNES* 46: 15-26.

1988a. *Decorated Pottery and the Art of Naqada III.* MÄS, vol. 45. Berlin: Bruno Hessling.

1988b. "Narmer and the Coptos Colossi," *JARCE* 25: 35-59.

Williams, Bruce, and Thomas J. Logan
1987. "The Metropolitan Museum Knife Handle and Aspects of Pharaonic Imagery before Narmer," *JNES* 46: 245-85.

Wilson, John A.
1944. "Funerary Services of the Egyptian Old Kingdom," *JNES* 3: 201-218.

1947. "The Artist of the Egyptian Old Kingdom," *JNES* 6: 231-249.

1948. "The Oath in Ancient Egypt," *JNES* 7: 129-156.

1949. *Before Philosophy.* Harmondsworth: Penguin Books.

1951. *The Burden of Egypt* (=*The Culture of Ancient Egypt*). Chicago: University of Chicago Press.
1955. *Ancient Near Eastern Texts,* J. Pritchard ed., Princeton: Princeton University Press.
1955. "Buto and Hierakonpolis in the Geography of Egypt," *JNES* 14: 209-36.

Winkler, Hans A.
1938. *Rock-drawings of Southern Upper Egypt,* vol. 1. Archaeological Survey of Egypt. London: Egypt Exploration Society. Humphrey Milford, Oxford University Press.

Winter, Erich
1957. "Zur Deutung der Sonnenheiligtumer der 5. Dynastie," *WZKM* 54: 222-233.
1978. "Der Herrscherkult in den ägyptischen Ptolemäertempeln," In *Das ptolemäische Ägypten: Akten des internationalen Symposions 27.-29. September 1976 in Berlin,* Herwig Maehler and Volker Michael Strocka eds. Mainz: Philipp von Zabern, pp. 147-60.

Wolf, Walther
1924. "Vorlaufer der Reformation Echnatons," *ZÄS* 59: 109-119.

Wood, Wendy
1974 . "A Reconstruction of The Triads of King Mycerinus," *JEA* 60: 82-93.
1987. "The Archaic Stone Tombs at Helwan," *JEA* 73: 59-70.

Woodham-Smith, Cecil
1972. *Queen Victoria.* New York: Knopf.

Yoyotte, Jean
1959. "Le bassin de Djaroukhé," *Kêmi* 15: 23-33.

Zandee, Jan
1987. "Review of Jan Assmann, *Sonnenhymnen in thebanischen Gräbern.*" *BiOr* 44: 126-32.

Zivie, Alain-P.
1984. "Ramses I," *LÄ* 5: cols. 100-108.

Zivie, Christiane M.
1982. "Memphis," *LÄ* 4: cols. 24-41.

GENERAL INDEX

EGYPTIAN WORD INDEX